ONE DISH

recipes & more

Publications International, Ltd.

Favorite Brand Name Recipes at www.fbnr.com

Illustrations by Denise Hilton Campbell, Martha Collins, Jane Dippold, Julie Ecklund, Roger Gorringe, Robin Moro, Elizabeth Golz Rush, Joyce Shelton and Jody Wheeler.

Pictured on the front cover *(clockwise from top):* Easy Moroccan Casserole *(page 67),* Saucy Tropical Turkey *(page 602)* and Bistro Chicken Skillet *(page 550).*

Pictured on the back cover *(clockwise from top):* Carrie's Sweet Potato Casserole *(page 265),* Caribbean Sweet Potato & Bean Stew *(page 611)* and Cajun-Style Country Ribs *(page 600).*

ISBN: 0-7853-9817-1

Manufactured in U.S.A.

8 7 6 5 4 3 2 1

Microwave Cooking: Microwave ovens vary in wattage. Use the cooking times as guidelines and check for doneness before adding more time.

Preparation/Cooking Times: Preparation times are based on the approximate amount of time required to assemble the recipe before cooking, baking, chilling or serving. These times include preparation steps such as measuring, chopping and mixing. The fact that some preparations and cooking can be done simultaneously is taken into account. Preparation of optional ingredients and serving suggestions is not included.

Contents

Delicious
Beef
Classics

CHAPTER ONE

Beef & Artichoke Casserole

Makes 4 servings

Note:

To make dry bread crumbs, bake cubed stale bread slices on a baking sheet in a 325°F oven until very dry and lightly browned. Place in a food processor and process until fine crumbs are formed.

¾ pound extra-lean (90% lean) ground beef
½ cup sliced mushrooms
¼ cup chopped onion
1 clove garlic, minced
1 can (14 ounces) artichoke hearts, drained, chopped
½ cup dry bread crumbs
¼ cup (1 ounce) grated Parmesan cheese

2 tablespoons chopped fresh rosemary *or* 1 teaspoon dried rosemary
1½ teaspoons chopped fresh marjoram *or* ½ teaspoon dried marjoram leaves
Salt and black pepper
3 egg whites

1. Preheat oven to 400°F. Spray 1-quart casserole with nonstick cooking spray.

2. Brown ground beef in medium skillet, stirring to break up meat; drain. Add mushrooms, onion and garlic; cook until tender.

3. Combine ground beef mixture, artichokes, bread crumbs, cheese, rosemary and marjoram; mix lightly. Season with salt and pepper to taste.

4. Beat egg whites until stiff peaks form; fold into ground beef mixture. Spoon into prepared casserole. Bake 20 minutes or until lightly browned around edges.

Greek-Style Lasagna

Makes 6 to 8 servings

1 pound ground beef
1 cup chopped onion
1 clove garlic, crushed OR
    ¼ teaspoon LAWRY'S®
    Garlic Powder with Parsley
1 teaspoon LAWRY'S®
    Seasoned Salt
½ teaspoon LAWRY'S®
    Seasoned Pepper
1 package (1.5 ounces)
    LAWRY'S® Original-Style
    Spaghetti Sauce Spices &
    Seasonings

1 can (6 ounces) tomato paste
2 cups water
¼ cup flour
½ teaspoon LAWRY'S®
    Seasoned Salt
1 eggplant
¾ cup salad oil
1 cup grated Parmesan cheese

In large skillet, cook ground beef until browned and crumbly; drain fat. Add onion, garlic, 1 teaspoon Seasoned Salt, Seasoned Pepper, Original-Style Spaghetti Sauce Spices & Seasonings, tomato paste and water. Bring to a boil over medium-high heat; reduce heat to low, cover and simmer 15 minutes, stirring occasionally. Meanwhile, in small bowl, combine flour and ½ teaspoon Seasoned Salt. Peel eggplant and slice crosswise into ¼-inch-thick slices. Place small amount of salad oil in medium skillet and heat. Lightly coat eggplant slices with seasoned flour. Quickly cook eggplant slices over medium-high heat, adding oil as necessary. (Use as little oil as possible). Pour ¼ of meat sauce into a 12×8×2-inch baking dish. Cover meat sauce with ⅓ of eggplant slices. Sprinkle ¼ of Parmesan cheese over eggplant. Repeat layers 2 more times, ending with meat sauce and Parmesan cheese. Bake, uncovered, in 350°F oven 30 minutes.

Serving Suggestion: *Serve with a tossed green salad and fruit dessert.*

Chop Suey Casserole

Makes 4 servings

2 cups (12 ounces) cooked
roast beef strips
1 can (10¾ ounces) condensed
cream of mushroom soup
½ cup milk
1 package (10 ounces) frozen
French-style green beans,
thawed and drained

1 can (8 ounces) sliced water
chestnuts, drained
½ cup diagonally sliced celery
2 tablespoons soy sauce
1⅓ cups *French's*® French Fried
Onions, divided
1 medium tomato, cut into
wedges

Preheat oven to 350°F. In large bowl, combine beef, soup, milk, beans, water chestnuts, celery, soy sauce and ⅔ cup French Fried Onions. Spoon beef mixture into 1½-quart casserole. Bake, covered, at 350°F for 30 minutes or until heated through. Arrange tomato wedges around edge of casserole and top with remaining ⅔ *cup* onions. Bake, uncovered, 5 minutes or until onions are golden brown.

Microwave Directions: *Prepare beef mixture as above; spoon into 1½-quart microwave-safe casserole. Cook, covered, on HIGH 10 to 12 minutes or until heated through. Stir beef mixture halfway through cooking time. Top with tomato wedges and remaining onions as above; cook, uncovered, 1 minute. Let stand 5 minutes.*

Layered Mexicali Casserole

1 pound ground beef
1 can (16 ounces) ROSARITA®
   Refried Beans
1 can (14.5 ounces) HUNT'S®
   Diced Tomatoes with Mild
   Green Chiles
1 package (1 ounce) taco
   seasoning mix
1 teaspoon garlic salt
   PAM® No-Stick Cooking Spray
6 (8-inch) flour tortillas
1 can (14.5 ounces) HUNT'S®
   Diced Tomatoes in Juice,
   drained

¾ cup sliced green onions
1 can (4 ounces) diced green
   chiles
1 can (2¼ ounces) sliced ripe
   olives, drained
4 cups (16 ounces) shredded
   Cheddar cheese
Sour cream (optional)
Avocado slices (optional)

**Makes 8 to
10 servings**

Preheat oven to 350°F. In large skillet, brown ground beef;
drain. Stir in beans, diced tomatoes with mild green chiles, taco
seasoning and garlic salt. Bring to a boil; reduce heat and simmer
5 minutes. In 13×9×2-inch baking dish, lightly sprayed with
cooking spray, place 2 tortillas side by side on bottom of dish.
Spread ⅓ of the meat mixture over tortillas and sprinkle with
⅓ of each of the diced tomatoes, green onions, chiles, olives and
cheese. Repeat layers twice, ending with cheese.

Bake for 40 minutes. Let stand 10 minutes before serving.
Garnish each serving with sour cream and an avocado
slice, if desired.

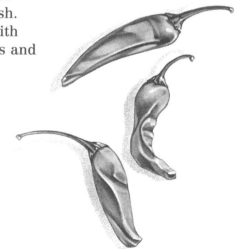

Johnnie Marzetti

Makes 8 servings

1 tablespoon CRISCO® Oil*
1 cup chopped celery
1 cup chopped onion
1 medium green bell pepper,
   chopped
1 pound ground beef round
1 can (14½ ounces) Italian-style
   stewed tomatoes,
   undrained
1 can (8 ounces) tomato sauce
1 can (6 ounces) tomato paste
1 cup water

1 bay leaf
1½ teaspoons dried basil leaves
1¼ teaspoons salt
¼ teaspoon black pepper
1 package (12 ounces) egg
   noodles, cooked and well
   drained
½ cup plain dry bread crumbs
1 cup (4 ounces) shredded
   sharp Cheddar cheese

Use your favorite Crisco Oil product.

Note:

Store dried herbs and spices in a cool, dry place in tightly covered lightproof containers. Do not place them above the range as heat and moisture will cause their flavor to deteriorate more quickly.

1. Heat oven to 375°F. Oil 12½×8½×2-inch baking dish lightly. Place cooling rack on countertop.

2. Heat oil in large skillet on medium heat. Add celery, onion and green pepper. Cook and stir until tender. Remove vegetables from skillet. Set aside. Add meat to skillet. Cook until browned, stirring occasionally. Return vegetables to skillet. Add tomatoes, tomato sauce, tomato paste, water, bay leaf, basil, salt and black pepper. Reduce heat to low. Simmer 5 minutes, stirring occasionally. Remove bay leaf.

3. Place noodles in baking dish. Spoon meat mixture over noodles. Sprinkle with bread crumbs and cheese.

4. Bake at 375°F for 15 to 20 minutes or until cheese melts. *Do not overbake.* Remove baking dish to cooling rack. Garnish, if desired.

Chili Beef Casserole

1 pound ground beef
1 medium onion, chopped
½ cup chopped celery (optional)
1 package (1.48 ounces)
    LAWRY'S® Spices &
    Seasonings for Chili
1 can (8 ounces) tomato sauce
1 can (12 ounces) whole kernel
    corn, drained (optional)

1 can (15.5 ounces) kidney OR
    pinto beans, drained
2 cans (2.25 ounces each) sliced
    ripe olives
1 cup coarsely crushed corn
    chips
1 cup (4 ounces) shredded
    cheddar cheese

In large skillet, brown ground beef with onion and celery until beef is crumbly; drain fat. Add Spices & Seasonings for Chili and tomato sauce. Bring to a boil over medium-high heat; reduce heat to low and simmer, uncovered, 10 minutes. Add corn, beans and olives; mix well. Pour into 2½-quart casserole. Cover with corn chips and top with cheese. Bake, uncovered, in 350°F oven 35 minutes.

Hint: *Can use 1 package (1.0 ounce) LAWRY'S® Taco Spices & Seasonings in place of 1 package (1.48 ounces) LAWRY'S® Spices & Seasonings for Chili.*

Main-Dish Pie

Makes 6 servings

Prep Time:
10 minutes

Cook Time:
20 to 25 minutes

1 package (8 rolls) refrigerated
  crescent rolls
1 pound lean ground beef
1 medium onion, chopped
1 can (12 ounces) beef or
  mushroom gravy

1 box (10 ounces) BIRDS EYE®
  frozen Green Peas, thawed
½ cup shredded Swiss cheese
6 slices tomato

• Preheat oven to 350°F.

• Unroll dough and separate rolls. Spread to cover bottom of ungreased 9-inch pie pan. Press together to form lower crust. Bake 10 minutes.

• Meanwhile, in large skillet, brown ground beef and onion; drain excess fat.

• Stir in gravy and peas; cook until heated through.

• Pour mixture into partially baked crust. Sprinkle with cheese.

• Bake 10 to 15 minutes or until crust is brown and cheese is melted.

• Arrange tomato slices over pie; bake 2 minutes more.

Fix-It-Fast Corned Beef & Cabbage

1 small head cabbage (about
   1½ pounds), cored and cut
   into 6 wedges
1 can (12 ounces) corned beef,
   sliced, *or* ½ pound sliced
   deli corned beef
1 can (14 ounces) sliced carrots,
   drained

1 can (16 ounces) sliced
   potatoes, drained
1⅓ cups *French's®* French Fried
   Onions, divided
1 can (10¾ ounces) condensed
   cream of celery soup
¾ cup water

Makes 4 to 6 servings

Preheat oven to 375°F. Arrange cabbage wedges and corned beef slices alternately down center of 13×9-inch baking dish. Place carrots, potatoes and ⅔ cup French Fried Onions along sides of dish. In small bowl, combine soup and water; pour over meat and vegetables. Bake, covered, at 375°F for 40 minutes or until cabbage is tender. Top with remaining ⅔ *cup* onions; bake, uncovered, 3 minutes or until onions are golden brown.

<u>Microwave Directions:</u> *Arrange cabbage wedges down center of 12×8-inch microwave-safe dish; add 2 tablespoons water. Cook, covered, on HIGH 10 to 12 minutes or until fork-tender. Rotate dish halfway through cooking time. Drain. Arrange cabbage, corned beef, carrots, potatoes and ⅔ cup onions in dish as above. Reduce water to ¼ cup. In small bowl, combine soup and water; pour over meat and vegetables. Cook, covered, 8 to 10 minutes or until vegetables are heated through. Rotate dish halfway through cooking time. Top with remaining ⅔ cup onions; cook, uncovered, 1 minute. Let stand 5 minutes.*

Note:

When buying green cabbage, look for a well-trimmed, compact head that feels heavy for its size. It should have a bright color and be free of withered leaves. Avoid cabbage with badly discolored or dry outer leaves.

Souper Quick "Lasagna"

Makes about
6 servings

1½ pounds ground beef
1 envelope LIPTON® RECIPE
    SECRETS® Onion or Onion-
    Mushroom Soup Mix
3 cans (8 ounces each) tomato
    sauce
1 cup water
½ teaspoon dried oregano
    leaves (optional)

1 package (8 ounces) broad egg
    noodles, cooked and
    drained
1 package (16 ounces)
    mozzarella cheese,
    shredded

Note:

**Oregano grows in
profusion in the
Mediterranean, spilling
down the hillsides and
filling the air with
fragrance. Literally
translated, it means
"joy of the mountain."**

Preheat oven to 375°F.

In 12-inch skillet, brown ground beef over medium-high heat; drain. Stir in onion soup mix, tomato sauce, water and oregano. Simmer covered, stirring occasionally, 15 minutes.

In 2-quart oblong baking dish, spoon enough ground beef mixture to cover bottom. Alternately layer noodles, ground beef mixture and cheese, ending with cheese. Bake 30 minutes or until bubbling.

Microwave Directions: *In 2-quart casserole, microwave ground beef, uncovered, at HIGH (Full Power) 7 minutes, stirring once; drain. Stir in onion soup mix, tomato sauce, water and oregano. Microwave at MEDIUM (50% Power) 5 minutes, stirring once. In 2-quart oblong microwavable dish, spoon enough of mixture to cover bottom. Alternately layer as above. Microwave covered at MEDIUM, turning dish occasionally, 10 minutes or until bubbling. Let stand covered 5 minutes.*

Stuffed Bell Peppers

1 cup chopped fresh tomatoes
1 teaspoon chopped fresh
   cilantro
1 jalapeño pepper,* seeded and
   chopped (optional)
½ clove garlic, finely minced
½ teaspoon dried oregano
   leaves, divided
¼ teaspoon ground cumin
6 ounces lean ground round
½ cup cooked brown rice
¼ cup cholesterol-free egg
   substitute *or* 1 egg white
2 tablespoons finely chopped
   onion

¼ teaspoon salt
⅛ teaspoon black pepper
2 large bell peppers, any color,
   seeded and cut in half
   lengthwise
4 sheets (12×12 inches) heavy-
   duty foil, lightly sprayed
   with nonstick cooking
   spray

Makes 6 servings

Jalapeño peppers can sting and irritate the skin; wear rubber gloves when handling peppers and do not touch eyes. Wash hands after handling.

1. Preheat oven to 400°F.

2. Combine tomatoes, cilantro, jalapeño pepper, garlic, ¼ teaspoon oregano and cumin in small bowl. Set aside.

3. Thoroughly combine beef, rice, egg substitute, onion, salt and black pepper in large bowl. Stir in ⅔ cup of tomato mixture. Spoon filling evenly into pepper halves.

4. Place each pepper half on foil sheet. Double fold sides and ends of foil to seal packets. Place packets on baking sheet.

5. Bake 45 minutes or until meat is browned and vegetables are tender. Remove from oven. Carefully open one end of each packet to allow steam to escape. Open packets and transfer pepper halves to serving plates. Serve with remaining tomato salsa, if desired.

Southwestern Beef and Bean Lasagna

Makes 6 servings

½ pound extra-lean ground beef
1 can (16 ounces) pinto beans, drained
1 teaspoon cumin seeds *or*
  ½ teaspoon ground cumin
1 teaspoon olive oil
1½ cups chopped onions
1 tablespoon seeded and minced jalapeño pepper*
1 clove garlic, minced
4 cups no-salt-added tomato sauce
1 can (4 ounces) diced green chilies, undrained
2 teaspoons chili powder
1 teaspoon dried oregano leaves

1 container (8 ounces) fat-free cottage cheese
1½ cups (6 ounces) shredded reduced-fat Cheddar cheese, divided
1 egg white
¼ cup chopped fresh cilantro
½ teaspoon salt
¼ teaspoon black pepper
8 ounces uncooked lasagna noodles
1 cup water

Jalapeño peppers can sting and irritate the skin; wear rubber gloves when handling peppers and do not touch eyes. Wash hands after handling.

1. Brown beef in large skillet. Drain off fat. Stir in beans; set aside. Place cumin seeds in large nonstick skillet. Cook and stir over medium heat 2 minutes or until fragrant. Remove from skillet. In same skillet, heat oil. Add onions, jalapeño and garlic; cook until onions are soft. Add tomato sauce, green chilies, chili powder, oregano and cumin seeds. Bring to a boil; reduce heat. Simmer, uncovered, 20 minutes.

2. Preheat oven to 350°F. Combine cottage cheese, ½ cup Cheddar cheese, egg white, cilantro, salt and black pepper in medium bowl. Spray 13×9-inch baking pan with cooking spray. Cover bottom with ¾ cup tomato sauce mixture. Place layer of noodles on sauce. Spread half the beef mixture over noodles, then place another layer of noodles on top. Spread cheese mixture over noodles. Spread with remaining beef mixture. Layer with noodles. Pour remaining sauce mixture over all; sprinkle with remaining 1 cup Cheddar cheese. Pour water around edges. Cover tightly with foil. Bake 1 hour and 15 minutes or until pasta is tender. Cool 10 minutes before serving.

Smoked Beef Casserole

1 jar (8 ounces) pasteurized processed cheese spread
¾ cup milk
2 packages (6 ounces each) HILLSHIRE FARM® Deli Select Smoked Beef, cut into strips
4 cups frozen hash brown potatoes, thawed

1 package (16 ounces) frozen peas
2 cups crushed potato chips, divided
½ cup (2 ounces) shredded Cheddar cheese

Makes 4 to 6 servings

Preheat oven to 375°F.

Spoon cheese spread into 12×8-inch baking dish. Bake until cheese is melted. Stir milk into melted cheese. Mix in Smoked Beef, potatoes, peas and 1 cup potato chips. Bake, covered, 30 minutes. Top with Cheddar cheese and remaining 1 cup potato chips. Bake, uncovered, 3 minutes or until Cheddar cheese is melted.

Tijuana Torte

Makes 4 to 6 servings

1 pound ground beef
1 medium onion, chopped
1 can (16 ounces) stewed
    tomatoes
1 can (8 ounces) tomato sauce
1 can (4 ounces) diced green
    chiles (optional)

1 package (1.0 ounce)
    LAWRY'S® Taco Spices &
    Seasonings
12 corn tortillas
4 cups (16 ounces) shredded
    cheddar cheese

Note:

This torte is a great make-ahead dish! After baking the torte, wrap it well and freeze it. To reheat, simply place in a preheated 350°F oven and bake for 35 to 40 minutes or until heated through. Freeze one "stack" for later use if only 2 servings are needed.

In large skillet, brown ground beef and onion until beef is crumbly; drain fat. Add tomatoes, tomato sauce, chiles and Taco Spices & Seasonings; mix well. Bring to a boil over medium-high heat; reduce heat to low and simmer, uncovered, 10 to 15 minutes. In 13×9×2-inch baking dish, place about ¼ meat mixture, spreading to cover bottom of dish. Place 2 tortillas, side by side, on meat mixture. Top each tortilla with some meat mixture and grated cheese. Repeat until each stack contains 6 tortillas layered with meat and cheese. Bake, uncovered, in 350°F oven 20 to 25 minutes.

Tip: *To serve, cut each torte (stack) into quarters with a sharp knife.*

Countdown Casserole

1 jar (8 ounces) pasteurized
   process cheese spread
¾ cup milk
2 cups (12 ounces) cubed
   cooked roast beef
1 bag (16 ounces) frozen
   vegetable combination
   (broccoli, corn, red pepper),
   thawed and drained

4 cups frozen hash brown
   potatoes, thawed
1⅓ cups *French's*® French Fried
   Onions, divided
½ teaspoon seasoned salt
¼ teaspoon freshly ground
   black pepper
½ cup (2 ounces) shredded
   Cheddar cheese

Preheat oven to 375°F. Spoon cheese spread into 12×8-inch
baking dish; place in oven just until cheese melts, about
5 minutes. Using fork, stir milk into melted cheese until well
blended. Stir in beef, vegetables, potatoes, *⅔ cup* French Fried
Onions and the seasonings. Bake, covered, at 375°F 30 minutes
or until heated through. Top with Cheddar cheese; sprinkle
remaining *⅔ cup* onions down center. Bake, uncovered,
3 minutes or until onions are golden brown.

Microwave Directions: *In 12×8-inch microwave-safe dish,
combine cheese spread and milk. Cook, covered, on HIGH
3 minutes; stir. Add ingredients as directed. Cook, covered,
14 minutes or until heated through, stirring beef mixture
halfway through cooking time. Top with Cheddar cheese and
remaining ⅔ cup onions as directed. Cook, uncovered,
1 minute or until cheese melts. Let stand 5 minutes.*

Beef Picante and Sour Cream Casserole

Makes 4 servings

Note:

Sour cream is a thick, tangy dairy product made by commercially treating cream with lactic acid, a process that thickens the cream and adds an acidic taste.

6 ounces uncooked wagon wheel pasta
8 ounces 95% lean ground beef
1½ cups reduced-sodium mild picante sauce
1 cup red kidney beans, rinsed and drained
¾ cup water
1 tablespoon chili powder

1 teaspoon ground cumin
½ cup nonfat cottage cheese
½ cup nonfat sour cream
½ cup chopped green onions, with tops
1 can (2¼ ounces) sliced black olives
¼ cup chopped fresh cilantro or fresh parsley

1. Preheat oven to 325°F. Spray 9-inch square baking pan with nonstick cooking spray; set aside. Cook pasta according to package directions, omitting salt. Drain. Place in bottom of prepared pan; set aside.

2. Brown beef in large nonstick skillet over medium-high heat 4 to 5 minutes or until no longer pink, stirring to separate meat; drain fat.

3. Add picante sauce, beans, water, chili powder and cumin; blend well. Bring to a boil over high heat. Reduce heat to low; simmer, covered, 20 minutes.

4. Combine cottage cheese, sour cream and green onions in food processor or blender; process until smooth. Spread cottage cheese mixture over pasta in prepared pan. Spoon meat mixture over cottage cheese mixture; cover with foil. Bake 20 minutes or until heated through. Remove from oven; let stand 10 minutes to allow flavors to blend. Top with olives and cilantro.

Jarlsberg Pasta Pie

3 cups cooked thin spaghetti	1 cup chopped onion
1½ cups shredded JARLSBERG Cheese, divided	1 medium clove garlic, minced
	1 teaspoon dried basil, crushed
1 egg, slightly beaten	1 can (16 ounces) stewed
1 pound ground beef	tomatoes, undrained
2 cups sliced zucchini	1 can (8 ounces) tomato sauce

Makes 6 to 8 servings

In large bowl, blend pasta, 1 cup cheese and egg. Line bottom and side of 10-inch pie plate with mixture; set aside. In large skillet, brown beef; pour off fat. Add zucchini, onion, garlic and basil; cook until vegetables are tender. Blend in tomatoes with juice and tomato sauce. Spoon into pasta mixture in pie plate. Bake at 350°F for 30 minutes. Sprinkle with remaining ½ cup cheese. Bake an additional 10 minutes.

Casserole Cookware

Casserole cookware comes in a variety of shapes, sizes and materials that fall into two general descriptions. They can be either deep, round containers with handles and tight-fitting lids, or square and rectangular baking dishes. Casserole cookware can be made out of glass, ceramic or metal. When making a casserole, it is important to bake it in the proper size dish so that the ingredients cook evenly in the time specified.

If you don't know the size of the casserole or baking dish you want to use, and it isn't marked on the bottom of the dish, it can be measured to determine the size.

Round and oval casseroles are measured by volume, not inches, and are always listed by quart capacity. To measure the casserole, fill a measuring cup with water and pour it into the empty casserole. Repeat until the casserole is filled with water, keeping track of the amount of water added. The amount of water is equivalent to the size of the dish.

Square and rectangular baking dishes are usually measured in inches. If the dimensions are not marked on the bottom of a square or rectangular baking dish, use a ruler to measure on top from the inside of one edge to the inside of the edge across.

Twisty Beef Bake

Makes 4 to 6 servings

1 pound ground beef
2 cups elbow macaroni or rotini, cooked in unsalted water and drained
1⅓ cups *French's®* French Fried Onions, divided
1 cup (4 ounces) shredded Cheddar cheese, divided
1 can (10¾ ounces) condensed cream of mushroom soup, undiluted

1 can (14½ ounces) whole tomatoes, undrained and chopped
¼ cup chopped green bell pepper
¼ teaspoon seasoned salt

Preheat oven to 375°F. In large skillet, brown ground beef; drain. Stir in hot macaroni, ⅔ *cup* French Fried Onions, ½ cup cheese, soup, tomatoes, bell pepper and seasoned salt. Mix well. Pour into 2-quart casserole. Bake, covered, for 30 minutes or until heated through. Top with remaining ½ cup cheese and ⅔ *cup* onions; bake, uncovered, 3 minutes or until onions are golden brown.

Microwave Directions: *Crumble ground beef into 2-quart microwave-safe casserole. Cook, covered, on HIGH 4 to 6 minutes or until beef is cooked. Stir beef halfway through cooking time. Drain well. Add remaining ingredients as above. Cook, covered, 10 to 14 minutes or until heated through. Stir beef mixture halfway through cooking time. Top with remaining cheese and onions; cook, uncovered, 1 minute or until cheese melts. Let stand 5 minutes.*

Beef Mole Tamale Pie

1½ pounds ground chuck
1 medium onion, chopped
1 green bell pepper, chopped
2 cloves garlic, minced
1¼ cups medium-hot salsa
1 package (10 ounces) frozen whole kernel corn, partially thawed
1 tablespoon unsweetened cocoa powder
2 teaspoons ground cumin
1 teaspoon dried oregano leaves
1½ teaspoons salt, divided
¼ teaspoon ground cinnamon
2 cups (8 ounces) shredded Monterey Jack or Cheddar cheese
⅓ cup chopped fresh cilantro
1 cup all-purpose flour
¾ cup yellow cornmeal
3 tablespoons sugar
2 teaspoons baking powder
⅔ cup milk
3 tablespoons butter, melted
1 egg, beaten
Cilantro leaves, chili pepper and sour cream for garnish

Preheat oven to 400°F. Spray 11×7-inch baking dish with nonstick cooking spray. Brown ground chuck with onion, bell pepper and garlic in large deep skillet or Dutch oven over medium heat until meat just loses its pink color. Pour off drippings. Stir in salsa, corn, cocoa, cumin, oregano, 1 teaspoon salt and cinnamon. Bring to a boil. Reduce heat to medium-low; simmer, uncovered, 8 minutes, stirring occasionally. Remove from heat; stir in cheese and cilantro. Spread in prepared dish.

Combine flour, cornmeal, sugar, baking powder and remaining ½ teaspoon salt in large bowl. Add milk, butter and egg; stir just until dry ingredients are moistened. Drop by spoonfuls evenly over meat mixture; spread batter evenly with spatula.

Bake 15 minutes. *Reduce oven temperature to 350°F.* Bake 20 minutes or until topping is light brown and filling is bubbly. Let stand 5 minutes before serving. Garnish, if desired.

Taco Bake

Makes 4 to 6 servings

Taco Meat Filling
1 pound ground beef
½ cup chopped onion
1 package taco seasoning
¾ cup water

Taco Crust
1¾ to 2 cups all-purpose flour, divided
1 package RED STAR® Active Dry Yeast or QUICK•RISE™ Yeast

1 tablespoon sugar
2 teaspoons finely chopped onion
¾ teaspoon salt
⅔ cup warm water
2 tablespoons oil
½ cup crushed corn chips

Topping
1 cup shredded Cheddar cheese
1 cup shredded lettuce
1½ cups chopped tomatoes

Brown ground beef with onion; drain. Add taco seasoning and water. Simmer for 25 minutes.

In medium mixing bowl, combine 1 cup flour, yeast, sugar, onion, and salt; mix well. Add very warm water (120° to 130°F) and oil to flour mixture. Mix by hand until almost smooth. Stir in corn chips and enough remaining flour to make a stiff batter. Spread in well-greased 10-inch pie pan, forming a rim around edge. Cover; let rise in warm place about 20 minutes (10 minutes for Quick•Rise™ Yeast). Spread meat filling over dough. Bake in preheated oven at 375°F 30 to 35 minutes until edge is crisp and light golden brown. Sprinkle cheese, lettuce, and tomatoes on top. Serve immediately.

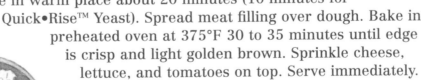

Oven-Easy Beef & Potato Dinner

4 cups frozen hash brown
    potatoes, thawed
3 tablespoons vegetable oil
⅛ teaspoon pepper
1 pound ground beef
1 cup water
1 package (about ¾ ounce)
    brown gravy mix

½ teaspoon garlic salt
1 package (10 ounces) frozen
    mixed vegetables, thawed
    and drained
1 cup (4 ounces) shredded
    Cheddar cheese, divided
1⅓ cups *French's®* French Fried
    Onions, divided

Makes 4 to 6 servings

Preheat oven to 400°F. In 12×8-inch baking dish, combine potatoes, oil and pepper. Firmly press potato mixture evenly across bottom and up sides of dish to form a shell. Bake, uncovered, at 400°F for 15 minutes. Meanwhile, in large skillet, brown ground beef; drain. Stir in water, gravy mix and garlic salt; bring to a boil. Add mixed vegetables; reduce heat to medium and cook, uncovered, 5 minutes. Remove from heat and stir in ½ cup cheese and *⅔ cup* French Fried Onions; spoon into hot potato shell. *Reduce oven temperature to 350°F.* Bake, uncovered, at 350°F for 15 minutes or until heated through. Top with remaining ½ cup cheese and *⅔ cup* onions; bake, uncovered, 5 minutes or until onions are golden brown.

Note:

Cheese should be refrigerated. Unopened packaged cheese can be left in the original wrapping, but bulk cheese should be wrapped tightly in plastic wrap or foil. With the exception of cream-style cottage cheese, cheese can be frozen for two to three months; however, texture and taste will be affected to some degree.

Baked Pasta with Beef and Beans

Makes 4 servings

Prep Time:
30 minutes

Total Time:
50 to 60 minutes

Note:

If possible, use a pepper grinder or mortar and pestle to grind pepper as you need it for cooking—the taste is far superior to that of preground pepper, which loses its flavor very quickly.

¼ cup CRISCO® Oil,* divided
½ pound mostaccioli or penne pasta
1 pound ground beef *or*
½ pound ground beef and
½ pound Italian sausage
1 small onion, peeled and chopped
2 teaspoons jarred minced garlic *or* 1 large garlic clove, peeled and minced
1 teaspoon Italian seasoning
½ teaspoon salt
¼ teaspoon freshly ground black pepper

1 can (14½ ounces) chopped tomatoes, drained
1 tablespoon tomato paste
1 can (8 ounces) kidney beans, drained and rinsed
¼ cup freshly grated Parmesan cheese
1 cup (4 ounces) shredded mozzarella or provolone cheese

*Use your favorite Crisco Oil product.

1. Heat oven to 400°F.

2. Bring large pot of salted water to a boil. Add 2 tablespoons oil and pasta. Cook pasta according to package directions until al dente. Drain.

3. While pasta is cooking, heat large skillet on medium-high heat. Add beef. Cook 3 minutes, breaking up with fork, or until no longer pink. Remove from pan. Discard drippings. Wipe out skillet.

4. Heat remaining 2 tablespoons oil in skillet on medium-high heat. Add onion and garlic. Cook 3 minutes, or until onion is translucent. Return beef to pan. Add Italian seasoning, salt, pepper, tomatoes and tomato paste. Stir well. Cook 5 minutes.

5. Combine pasta, meat mixture and beans in 13×9×2-inch baking dish. Sprinkle with cheeses. Bake at 400°F for 20 to 30 minutes, or until cheese is melted. Serve immediately.

<u>Hint:</u> *This dish can be prepared a day in advance of baking and refrigerated, tightly covered with plastic wrap. If chilled, bake at 375°F for 35 to 45 minutes.*

<u>Tip:</u> *To remove as much saturated fat from the meat as possible, drain it on paper towels or place it in a mesh sieve or colander and pour hot water over it after it has browned.*

String Pie

	Makes 6 to 8 servings
1 pound ground beef	⅓ cup grated Parmesan cheese
½ cup chopped onion	2 eggs, beaten
¼ cup chopped green pepper	2 teaspoons butter, melted
1 jar (15½ ounces) spaghetti sauce	1 cup cottage cheese
8 ounces spaghetti, cooked and drained	½ cup (2 ounces) shredded mozzarella cheese

Preheat oven to 350°F. Cook beef, onion and green pepper in large skillet over medium-high heat until meat is browned. Drain fat. Stir in spaghetti sauce. Combine spaghetti, Parmesan cheese, eggs and butter in large bowl; mix well. Place in bottom of 13×9-inch baking pan. Spread cottage cheese over top; cover with sauce mixture. Sprinkle with mozzarella cheese. Bake until mixture is thoroughly heated and cheese is melted, about 20 minutes.

Favorite recipe from **North Dakota Beef Commission**

Speedy Sirloin Steak Casserole

Makes 6 servings

Prep Time:
30 minutes

Cook Time:
10 to 12 minutes

1 (1½-pound) beef top sirloin steak, cut 1 inch thick
2 tablespoons Lucini Premium Select extra virgin olive oil, divided
1 sheet refrigerated pie dough
1 teaspoon dried dill weed
½ teaspoon salt
1 medium onion, coarsely chopped

½ pound mushrooms, cut into quarters
1 tablespoon all-purpose flour
½ cup milk
1 teaspoon ground nutmeg
1 teaspoon beef bouillon granules
8 ounces (2 cups) shredded JARLSBERG cheese
2 cups frozen peas

Cut beef into ¼-inch-thick slices. Cut each slice into 1-inch pieces. Combine with 1 tablespoon oil. Allow pie dough to stand at room temperature, as package directs.

Heat large nonstick skillet until hot. Stir-fry beef mixture (half at a time) 1 to 2 minutes. Remove from skillet. Combine beef mixture, dill and salt; set aside.

Heat remaining 1 tablespoon oil in same skillet; add onion and cook until softened, about 3 to 4 minutes. Add mushrooms; cook 5 minutes, stirring frequently. Sprinkle with flour; cook 1 minute. Add milk, nutmeg and bouillon. Bring mixture to a boil and cook, stirring constantly, until mixture thickens. Add cheese; mix lightly until cheese melts. Stir in reserved beef mixture with accumulated juices and peas.

Spoon mixture into round 2-quart casserole. Fold pie crust edges under, to fit inside circumference of casserole, and place on top of meat mixture. Crimp edges decoratively and cut slits in several places near center (to prevent "cracking"). Bake casserole in preheated 450°F oven 10 to 12 minutes or until crust is browned.

Tortilla Pie

1½ pounds ground beef
½ teaspoon LAWRY'S®
  Seasoned Salt
1 package (1.48 ounces)
  LAWRY'S® Spices &
  Seasonings for Chili
2 cans (8 ounces each) tomato
  sauce

1 cup water
8 to 10 corn tortillas
1¼ cups finely chopped onion
2 cans (2¼ ounces each) sliced
  ripe olives, drained
2½ cups (10 ounces) shredded
  cheddar cheese

In medium skillet, brown ground beef until crumbly; drain fat. In large saucepan, combine Seasoned Salt, Spices & Seasonings for Chili, tomato sauce and water; mix well. Bring to a boil over medium-high heat; reduce heat to low and simmer, uncovered, 5 minutes. Dip 4 to 5 tortillas in sauce and line bottom and sides of 2-quart casserole. Cut in half if necessary to conform to shape. On the tortillas layer ½ of each of the following; meat, onion and olives. Top with 1 cup cheese. Repeat layers, saving 2 tortillas for the top "crust." Pour all but ½ cup sauce over the last layer. Dip remaining tortillas in sauce and arrange on top. Sprinkle with remaining cheese. Bake, uncovered, in 350°F oven 30 minutes.

<u>Serving Suggestion:</u> *Serve with Mexican rice and a tossed green salad.*

<u>Hint:</u> *Substitute 1 package (1.62 ounces) LAWRY'S® Spices & Seasonings for Enchilada Sauce for LAWRY'S® Spices & Seasonings for Chili, if desired.*

Mini Meat Loaves & Vegetables

Makes 6 servings

1½ pounds lean ground beef
1 egg
1 can (8 ounces) tomato sauce, divided
1⅓ cups *French's*® French Fried Onions, divided
½ teaspoon salt
½ teaspoon Italian seasoning

6 small red potatoes, thinly sliced (about 1½ cups)
1 bag (16 ounces) frozen vegetable combination (broccoli, corn, red pepper), thawed and drained
Salt
Black pepper

Note:

To meet USDA standards, all ground beef must be at least 70 percent lean. Ground sirloin and ground round are the leanest. Ground chuck contains more fat and therefore produces juicier hamburgers and meat loaf.

Preheat oven to 375°F. In medium bowl, combine ground beef, egg, *½ can* tomato sauce, *⅔ cup* French Fried Onions, ½ teaspoon salt and Italian seasoning. Shape into 3 mini loaves and place in 13×9-inch baking dish. Arrange potatoes around loaves. Bake, covered, at 375°F for 35 minutes. Spoon vegetables around meat loaves; stir to combine with potatoes. Lightly season vegetables with salt and pepper, if desired. Top meat loaves with remaining tomato sauce. Bake, uncovered, 15 minutes or until meat loaves are done. Top loaves with remaining *⅔ cup* onions; bake, uncovered, 3 minutes or until onions are golden brown.

Microwave Directions: *Prepare meat loaves as above. Arrange potatoes on bottom of 12×8-inch microwave-safe dish; place meat loaves on potatoes. Cook, covered, on HIGH 13 minutes. Rotate dish halfway through cooking time. Add vegetables and season as above. Top meat loaves with remaining tomato sauce. Cook, covered, 7 minutes or until meat loaves are done. Rotate dish halfway through cooking time. Top loaves with remaining ⅔ cup onions; cook, uncovered, 1 minute. Let stand 5 minutes.*

Reuben Casserole

1 cup FRANK'S® or
    SNOWFLOSS® Kraut,
    drained
½ cup chopped onion
2 tablespoons butter
1 apple, peeled and chopped
½ teaspoon caraway seeds
1 cup cubed corned beef

¼ cup Thousand Island dressing
1 cup cubed Swiss cheese
2 slices rye bread, toasted and
    cubed
2 tablespoons melted butter
1 small jar red pimiento
1 green bell pepper, sliced

Makes 4 servings

Prep Time:
15 minutes

Bake Time:
20 minutes

1. Preheat oven to 400°F. Sauté the onion in 2 tablespoons butter until soft.

2. Add apple and sauté until soft.

3. Add caraway seeds, kraut and corned beef; sauté 1 minute to blend flavors. Place mixture in medium casserole dish.

4. Drizzle kraut mixture with Thousand Island dressing, top with Swiss cheese and toasted bread cubes.

5. Pour remaining 2 tablespoons melted butter over top, dot with pimiento and decorate with bell pepper.

6. Bake at 400°F for 20 minutes.

Zucchini Lasagne

Prep Time:
20 minutes

Cook Time:
70 minutes

3 cans (8 ounces each)
CONTADINA® Tomato
Sauce
1 can (14.5 ounces)
CONTADINA Stewed
Tomatoes, undrained
1 teaspoon granulated sugar
1 teaspoon Italian herb
seasoning
1 teaspoon ground black
pepper

1 pound lean ground beef
3 teaspoons seasoned salt
6 medium zucchini squash,
sliced ⅛ inch thick
2 cups (8 ounces) shredded
mozzarella cheese
2 cups (15 ounces) ricotta
cheese
3 tablespoons grated Parmesan
cheese

1. Combine tomato sauce, undrained stewed tomatoes, sugar, Italian seasoning and pepper in medium saucepan.

2. Simmer, uncovered, for 25 minutes, stirring occasionally. In medium skillet, brown beef; drain. Stir in seasoned salt and tomato sauce mixture.

3. Butter bottom of 13×9-inch baking dish. Layer half of zucchini slices on bottom of baking dish; sprinkle lightly with salt. Spread half of ground beef mixture over zucchini. Sprinkle with mozzarella cheese; spread ricotta cheese evenly over mozzarella. Top with remaining zucchini slices; sprinkle lightly with salt. Spread with remaining beef mixture. Sprinkle Parmesan cheese on top.

4. Bake in preheated 350°F oven for 45 minutes.

Biscuit-Topped Hearty Steak Pie

1½ pounds top round steak, cooked and cut into 1-inch cubes
1 package (9 ounces) frozen baby carrots
1 package (9 ounces) frozen peas and pearl onions
1 large baking potato, cooked and cut into ½-inch pieces

1 jar (18 ounces) home-style brown gravy
½ teaspoon dried thyme leaves
½ teaspoon black pepper
1 can (10 ounces) flaky buttermilk biscuits

Makes 6 servings

Preheat oven to 375°F. Spray 2-quart casserole with nonstick cooking spray.

Combine steak, frozen vegetables and potato in prepared dish. Stir in gravy, thyme and pepper.

Bake, uncovered, 40 minutes. Remove from oven. *Increase oven temperature to 400°F.* Top with biscuits and bake 8 to 10 minutes or until biscuits are golden brown.

<u>Hint:</u> *This casserole can be prepared with leftovers of almost any kind. Other steaks, roast beef, stew meat, pork, lamb or chicken can be substituted for round steak; adjust gravy flavor to complement meat. Red potatoes can be used in place of baking potato. Choose your favorite vegetable combination, such as broccoli, cauliflower and carrots, or broccoli, corn and red peppers, as a substitute for the peas and carrots.*

Moussaka

Makes 6 to 8 servings

1 large eggplant
2½ teaspoons salt, divided
2 large zucchini
2 large russet potatoes, peeled
½ cup olive oil, divided
1½ pounds ground beef or lamb
1 large onion, chopped
2 cloves garlic, minced
1 cup chopped tomatoes
½ cup dry red or white wine

¼ cup chopped fresh parsley
¼ teaspoon ground cinnamon
⅛ teaspoon black pepper
1 cup grated Parmesan cheese, divided
4 tablespoons butter or margarine
⅓ cup all-purpose flour
¼ teaspoon ground nutmeg
2 cups milk

Cut eggplant lengthwise into ½-inch-thick slices. Place in large colander; sprinkle with 1 teaspoon salt. Drain 30 minutes. Cut zucchini lengthwise into ⅜-inch-thick slices. Cut potatoes lengthwise into ¼-inch-thick slices.

Heat ¼ cup oil in large skillet over medium heat until hot. Add potatoes in single layer. Cook 5 minutes per side or until tender and lightly browned. Remove potatoes from skillet; drain on paper towels. Add more oil to skillet, if needed. Cook zucchini 2 minutes per side or until tender. Drain on paper towels. Add more oil to skillet. Cook eggplant 5 minutes per side or until tender. Drain on paper towels. Drain oil from skillet; discard.

Heat skillet over medium-high heat just until hot. Add beef, onion and garlic; cook and stir 5 minutes or until meat is no longer pink. Pour off drippings. Stir in tomatoes, wine, parsley, 1 teaspoon salt, cinnamon and pepper. Bring to a boil over high heat. Reduce heat to low. Simmer 10 minutes or until liquid is evaporated.

Preheat oven to 325°F. Grease 13×9-inch baking dish. Arrange potatoes in bottom; sprinkle with ¼ cup cheese. Top with zucchini and ¼ cup cheese, then eggplant and ¼ cup cheese. Spoon meat mixture over top.

To prepare sauce, melt butter in medium saucepan over low heat. Blend in flour, remaining ½ teaspoon salt and nutmeg with wire whisk. Cook 1 minute, whisking constantly. Gradually whisk in milk. Cook over medium heat, until mixture boils and thickens, whisking constantly. Pour sauce evenly over meat mixture in dish; sprinkle with remaining ¼ cup cheese. Bake 30 to 40 minutes or until hot and bubbly. Garnish as desired.

Note:

One of the best known of all Greek dishes, moussaka is a layered casserole that usually includes eggplant, ground lamb or beef, and a white sauce to which eggs and cheese have been added.

Chili Cornbread Casserole

1 pound ground beef
1 medium onion, chopped
1 jar (1 pound) RAGÚ® Cheese Creations!® Double Cheddar Sauce
1 can (19 ounces) red kidney beans, rinsed and drained
1 can (8¾ ounces) whole kernel corn, drained
2 to 3 teaspoons chili powder
1 package (12 ounces) cornbread mix

Makes 6 servings

Prep Time: *10 minutes*

Cook Time: *20 minutes*

Preheat oven to 400°F. In 12-inch skillet, brown ground beef and onion over medium-high heat; drain. Stir in Ragú Cheese Creations! Sauce, beans, corn and chili powder.

Meanwhile, prepare cornbread mix according to package directions. Do not bake.

In ungreased 2-quart baking dish, spread ground beef mixture. Top with cornbread mixture. Bake uncovered 20 minutes or until toothpick inserted in center of cornbread comes out clean and top is golden.

Easy Baked Ravioli

Makes 4 servings

Prep Time:
5 minutes

Cook Time:
27 minutes

½ pound ground beef, cooked, drained
1 package (15 ounces) DI GIORNO® Marinara Sauce
1 package (9 ounces) DI GIORNO® Four Cheese Ravioli, cooked, drained

1 cup KRAFT® Shredded Low-Moisture Part-Skim Mozzarella Cheese, divided
¼ cup DI GIORNO® 100% Grated Parmesan Cheese

MIX cooked meat and sauce together. Gently stir in pasta and ½ cup Mozzarella cheese.

POUR into a 2-quart casserole. Top with remaining Mozzarella and Parmesan cheese.

BAKE at 375°F, uncovered, for 20 minutes.

Serving Suggestion: *Try serving with a simple tossed salad with your favorite KRAFT® dressing and bakery-fresh garlic bread for a complete meal.*

Variation: *For a tasty change, try substituting 1 package (15 ounces) DI GIORNO® Mushroom Marinara for the Marinara Sauce.*

Beef Stroganoff Casserole

1 pound lean ground beef
¼ teaspoon salt
⅛ teaspoon black pepper
1 teaspoon vegetable oil
8 ounces sliced mushrooms
1 large onion, chopped
3 cloves garlic, minced
¼ cup dry white wine

1 can (10¾ ounces) condensed
   cream of mushroom soup
½ cup sour cream
1 tablespoon Dijon mustard
4 cups cooked egg noodles
   Chopped fresh parsley
   (optional)

Makes 6 servings

1. Preheat oven to 350°F. Spray 13×9-inch baking dish with nonstick cooking spray.

2. Place beef in large skillet; season with salt and pepper. Brown beef over medium-high heat until no longer pink, stirring to separate meat. Drain fat from skillet; set aside.

3. Heat oil in same skillet over medium-high heat until hot. Add mushrooms, onion and garlic; cook and stir 2 minutes or until onion is tender. Add wine. Reduce heat to medium-low and simmer 3 minutes. Remove from heat; stir in soup, sour cream and mustard until well combined. Return beef to skillet.

4. Place noodles in prepared dish. Pour beef mixture over noodles; stir until noodles are well coated. Bake, uncovered, 30 minutes or until heated through. Sprinkle with parsley, if desired.

Note:

Casserole refers both to a specific baking utensil and the food it contains. A casserole dish is a deep round or oval ovenproof container often with two short handles. It is usually made of glass, earthenware or porcelain.

Pasta "Pizza"

Makes 8 servings

Prep Time:
50 minutes

3 eggs, slightly beaten
½ cup milk
2 cups corkscrew macaroni,
　　cooked and drained
½ cup (2 ounces) shredded
　　Wisconsin Cheddar cheese
¼ cup finely chopped onion
1 pound lean ground beef
1 can (15 ounces) tomato sauce

1 teaspoon dried basil leaves
1 teaspoon dried oregano
　　leaves
½ teaspoon garlic salt
1 medium tomato, thinly sliced
1 green pepper, sliced into rings
1½ cups (6 ounces) shredded
　　Wisconsin Mozzarella
　　cheese

Combine eggs and milk in small bowl. Add to hot macaroni; mix lightly to coat. Stir in Cheddar cheese and onion; mix well. Spread macaroni mixture onto bottom of well-buttered 14-inch pizza pan. Bake at 350°F, 25 minutes. Meanwhile, in large skillet over medium-high heat, brown meat, stirring occasionally to separate meat; drain. Stir in tomato sauce, basil, oregano and garlic salt. Spoon over macaroni crust. Arrange tomato slices and pepper rings on top. Sprinkle with Mozzarella cheese. Continue baking 15 minutes or until cheese is bubbly.

Favorite recipe from **Wisconsin Milk Marketing Board**

Mexican Stuffed Shells

Makes 6 servings

1 pound ground beef
1 jar (12 ounces) mild or
    medium picante sauce
½ cup water
1 can (8 ounces) tomato sauce
1 can (4 ounces) chopped green
    chilies, drained
1 cup (4 ounces) shredded
    Monterey Jack cheese,
    divided

1⅓ cups *French's®* French Fried
    Onions
12 pasta stuffing shells, cooked
    in unsalted water and
    drained

Preheat oven to 350°F. In large skillet, brown ground beef; drain. In small bowl, combine picante sauce, water and tomato sauce. Stir ½ cup sauce mixture into beef along with chilies, ½ cup cheese and *⅔ cup* French Fried Onions; mix well. Spread half the remaining sauce mixture in bottom of 10-inch round baking dish. Stuff cooked shells with beef mixture. Arrange shells in baking dish; top with remaining sauce. Bake, covered, at 350°F for 30 minutes or until heated through. Top with remaining *⅔ cup* onions and cheese; bake, uncovered, 5 minutes or until cheese is melted.

<u>Microwave Directions:</u> *Crumble ground beef into medium microwave-safe bowl. Cook, covered, on HIGH (100%) 4 to 6 minutes or until beef is cooked. Stir beef halfway through cooking time. Drain well. Prepare sauce mixture as above; spread ½ cup in 12×8-inch microwave-safe dish. Prepare beef mixture as above. Stuff cooked shells with beef mixture. Arrange shells in dish; top with remaining sauce. Cook, covered, 10 to 12 minutes or until heated through. Rotate dish halfway through cooking time. Top with remaining onions and cheese; cook, uncovered, 1 minute or until cheese is melted. Let stand 5 minutes.*

Spetzque

Makes 6 servings

9 lasagna noodles
2 pounds ground beef
1 can (4½ ounces) chopped ripe
    olives, drained
1 can (4 ounces) mushroom
    stems and pieces, drained
1 small onion, finely chopped
1 jar (16 ounces) spaghetti
    sauce

Dash black pepper
Dash dried oregano leaves
   Dash dried Italian seasoning
1¼ cups frozen corn, thawed
1¼ cups frozen peas, thawed
2 cups (8 ounces) shredded
    mozzarella cheese

1. Cook lasagna noodles according to package directions; drain.

2. Cook beef in large skillet over medium-high heat until meat is brown, stirring to separate meat; drain drippings.

3. Add olives, mushrooms and onion. Cook, stirring occasionally, until vegetables are tender. Add spaghetti sauce, pepper, oregano and Italian seasoning. Heat through, stirring occasionally; set aside.

4. Preheat oven to 350°F.

5. Place 3 noodles in bottom of 13×9-inch baking pan. Spread half the beef mixture over noodles, then half the corn and peas. Repeat layers ending with noodles.

6. Bake lasagna 25 minutes. Sprinkle with cheese; bake 5 minutes more or until bubbly. Let stand 10 minutes before cutting. Garnish as desired.

Red Cloud Beef and Onions

2¼ cups nonfat milk
1½ cups water
1½ cups yellow cornmeal
½ cup grated Parmesan cheese
1 tablespoon butter or
   margarine
4 medium yellow onions, sliced
   (1 pound 6 ounces)
2 teaspoons vegetable oil
1 pound lean ground beef or
   pork

2 to 3 teaspoons chili powder
   (or to taste)
½ cup canned whole pimientos
   or roasted red bell peppers,
   cut into ½-inch strips
2 cans (4 ounces each) whole
   green chilies, cut into
   ½-inch strips

Makes 6 servings

For cornmeal base, combine milk, water and cornmeal in saucepan. Place over medium heat and cook, stirring, until mixture bubbles. Continue cooking 30 to 60 seconds or until mixture is consistency of soft mashed potatoes. Remove from heat; stir in cheese and butter. Spoon into 2½-quart casserole. Sauté onions in oil in large skillet until soft. Spoon into casserole in ring around edge. In same skillet, sauté beef or pork until browned; stir in chili powder. Spoon meat mixture into center of casserole. Arrange pimientos and chilies in latticework pattern over top. Cover and bake at 400°F for 25 to 30 minutes or until hot in center. Serve with dollops of sour cream, if desired.

Favorite recipe from **National Onion Association**

Note:

Globe onions (also called yellow onions) are the most common of the dry onions. They are round and small or medium in size with yellowish-gold skins and a strong flavor.

Mexican Delight Casserole

Makes 8 servings

1 pound ground beef
1 medium onion, chopped
1 package (1.5 ounces)
    LAWRY'S® Burrito Spices &
    Seasonings
1 can (1 pound 12 ounces)
    whole tomatoes, cut up
1 can (30 ounces) hominy,
    drained and rinsed

1 can (4 ounces) diced green
    chiles
4 cups tortilla chips
1½ cups (6 ounces) shredded
    cheddar cheese
1 can (8 ounces) tomato sauce

In large skillet, cook ground beef and onion until beef is browned; drain fat. Add Burrito Spices & Seasonings and tomatoes; mix well. Bring to a boil over medium-high heat; reduce heat to low and simmer, uncovered, 10 minutes. Combine hominy and green chiles. In 2-quart oblong casserole dish, layer half of meat mixture, tortilla chips and hominy mixture; add ½ cup cheese. Repeat layers, ending with ½ cup cheese. Top with tomato sauce and remaining ½ cup cheese. Bake, uncovered, in 350°F oven 35 minutes or until thoroughly heated.

<u>Hint:</u> *Use purchased or homemade tortilla chips. To make chips, cut fresh corn tortillas into ½-inch strips. Fry in ½-inch salad oil until slightly crisp, about 30 seconds. Drain well on paper towels.*

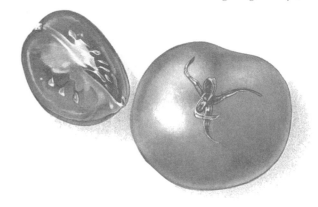

Spinach-Potato Bake

1 pound extra-lean (90% lean)
  ground beef
½ cup sliced fresh mushrooms
1 small onion, chopped
2 cloves garlic, minced
1 package (10 ounces) frozen
  chopped spinach, thawed,
  well drained

½ teaspoon ground nutmeg
1 pound russet potatoes,
  peeled, cooked and mashed
¼ cup light sour cream
¼ cup fat-free (skim) milk
  Salt and black pepper
½ cup (2 ounces) shredded
  Cheddar cheese

Makes 6 servings

1. Preheat oven to 400°F. Spray deep 9-inch casserole dish with nonstick cooking spray.

2. Brown ground beef in large skillet, stirring to break up meat; drain. Add mushrooms, onion and garlic; cook until tender. Stir in spinach and nutmeg; cover. Heat thoroughly, stirring occasionally.

3. Combine potatoes, sour cream and milk. Add to ground beef mixture; season with salt and pepper to taste. Spoon into prepared casserole dish; sprinkle with cheese.

4. Bake 15 to 20 minutes or until slightly puffed and cheese is melted.

Four-Cheese Lasagna

Makes 6 servings

Prep Time:
1½ hours

½ pound ground beef
½ cup chopped onion
⅓ cup chopped celery
1 clove garlic, minced
1½ teaspoons dried basil leaves
¼ teaspoon dried oregano
    leaves
¼ teaspoon salt
⅛ teaspoon ground black
    pepper
1 package (3 ounces) cream
    cheese, cubed

⅓ cup light cream or milk
½ cup dry white wine
½ cup (2 ounces) shredded
    Wisconsin Cheddar or
    Gouda cheese
1 egg, slightly beaten
1 cup cream-style cottage
    cheese
6 ounces lasagna noodles,
    cooked and drained
6 ounces sliced Wisconsin
    Mozzarella cheese

In large skillet, brown meat with onion, celery and garlic; drain. Stir in basil, oregano, salt and pepper. Reduce heat to low. Add cream cheese and cream. Cook, stirring frequently, until cream cheese is melted. Stir in wine. Gradually add Cheddar cheese, stirring until Cheddar cheese is almost melted. Remove from heat. In small bowl, combine egg and cottage cheese.

Into greased 10×6-inch baking dish, layer ½ each of the noodles, meat sauce, cottage cheese mixture and Mozzarella cheese; repeat layers. Bake, uncovered, at 375°F, 30 to 35 minutes or until hot and bubbly. Let stand 10 minutes before cutting to serve.

Favorite recipe from **Wisconsin Milk Marketing Board**

Chili & Potato Casserole

1 pound HILLSHIRE FARM®
  Yard-O-Beef, cut into small
  cubes
1 cup chopped yellow onion
1 egg, lightly beaten
¼ cup bread crumbs
1 tablespoon chili powder
  Salt to taste

3 cups prepared mashed
  potatoes
1 can (11 ounces) succotash,
  drained
¼ cup thinly sliced green onions
1 cup (4 ounces) shredded taco-
  flavored cheese

Makes 4 to 6 servings

Preheat oven to 375°F.

Combine Yard-O-Beef, yellow onion, egg, bread crumbs, chili powder and salt in large bowl; mix thoroughly. Pour beef mixture into medium baking dish, pressing mixture firmly onto bottom of dish. Bake 20 minutes. Pour off any juices.

Mix potatoes, succotash and green onions in medium bowl. Spread potato mixture over beef mixture; sprinkle top with cheese. Broil 3 to 4 inches from heat source 3 to 5 minutes or until top is lightly browned.

Note:

Succotash, a Southern favorite, is a cooked dish made up of a combination of corn, lima beans and sometimes green or red bell pepper.

Old-Fashioned Beef Pot Pie

Makes 4 to 6 servings

1 pound ground beef
1 can (11 ounces) condensed
    beef with vegetables and
    barley soup
½ cup water
1 package (10 ounces) frozen
    peas and carrots, thawed
    and drained
½ teaspoon seasoned salt

⅛ teaspoon garlic powder
⅛ teaspoon ground black
    pepper
1 cup (4 ounces) shredded
    Cheddar cheese, divided
1⅓ cups *French's®* French Fried
    Onions, divided
1 package (7.5 ounces)
    refrigerated biscuits

Note:

Pot pies, American in origin, are among the glories of country cooking. The term pot pie first appeared in American print as early as 1792.

Preheat oven to 350°F. In large skillet, brown ground beef in large chunks; drain. Stir in soup, water, vegetables and seasonings; bring to a boil. Reduce heat and simmer, uncovered, 5 minutes. Remove from heat; stir in ½ cup cheese and ⅔ *cup* French Fried Onions.

Pour mixture into 12×8-inch baking dish. Cut each biscuit in half; place, cut side down, around edge of casserole. Bake, uncovered, 15 to 20 minutes or until biscuits are done. Top with remaining cheese and ⅔ *cup* onions; bake, uncovered, 5 minutes or until onions are golden brown.

Baked Beef and Rice Marinara

Makes 4 servings

1 pound lean ground beef
¾ cup sliced fresh mushrooms
½ cup chopped onions
½ cup chopped celery
½ cup diced green pepper
2 cups cooked rice

1 can (15 ounces) tomato sauce
¾ teaspoon ground oregano
½ teaspoon salt
½ teaspoon dried basil leaves
½ teaspoon garlic powder
3 slices American cheese

Microwave Directions

Combine crumbled beef and vegetables in plastic colander; place colander over 2-quart microwave-safe baking dish. Cook, uncovered, on HIGH (100% power) 4 minutes; stir after 2 minutes. Drain beef mixture; return mixture to baking dish. Stir in remaining ingredients except cheese. Cook on HIGH 2 minutes. Arrange cheese slices on top; cook on HIGH 2 minutes. Let stand 5 minutes.

Conventional Directions: *Cook beef and vegetables over medium-high heat in large skillet until meat is no longer pink and vegetables are crisp-tender, stirring frequently; drain. Combine meat mixture with remaining ingredients except cheese in buttered 2-quart baking dish; arrange cheese slices on top. Bake at 350°F 20 to 25 minutes.*

Favorite recipe from **USA Rice Federation**

Zucchini Pasta Bake

Makes 4 servings

Prep and Cook Time:
33 minutes

1½ cups uncooked pasta tubes
½ pound ground beef
½ cup chopped onion
1 clove garlic, minced
Salt and pepper
1 can (14½ ounces)
   DEL MONTE® Zucchini with
   Italian-Style Tomato Sauce

1 teaspoon dried basil, crushed
1 cup (4 ounces) shredded
   Monterey Jack cheese

1. Cook pasta according to package directions; drain.

2. Cook beef with onion and garlic in large skillet; drain. Season with salt and pepper.

3. Stir in zucchini with tomato sauce and basil. Place pasta in 8-inch square baking dish. Top with meat mixture.

4. Bake at 350°F for 15 minutes. Top with cheese. Bake 3 minutes or until cheese is melted.

California Tamale Pie

1 pound ground beef
1 cup yellow corn meal
2 cups milk
2 eggs, beaten
1 package (1.48 ounces) LAWRY'S® Spices & Seasonings for Chili
2 teaspoons LAWRY'S® Seasoned Salt

1 can (17 ounces) whole kernel corn, drained
1 can (14½ ounces) whole tomatoes, cut up
1 can (2¼ ounces) sliced ripe olives, drained
1 cup (4 ounces) shredded cheddar cheese

Makes 6 to 8 servings

In medium skillet, cook ground beef until browned and crumbly; drain fat. In 2½-quart casserole dish, combine corn meal, milk and eggs; mix well. Add ground beef and remaining ingredients except cheese; stir to mix. Bake, uncovered, in 350°F oven 1 hour and 15 minutes. Add cheese and continue baking until cheese melts. Let stand 10 minutes before serving.

Microwave Directions: *In 2½-quart glass casserole, microwave ground beef on HIGH 5 to 6 minutes; drain fat and crumble beef. Mix in corn meal, milk and eggs; blend well. Add remaining ingredients except cheese. Cover with plastic wrap, venting one corner. Microwave on HIGH 15 minutes, stirring after 8 minutes. Sprinkle cheese over top and microwave on HIGH 2 minutes. Let stand 10 minutes before serving.*

Note:

Black olives are often referred to as ripe olives. They have a mellow, smooth taste and are sold pitted, unpitted, sliced and chopped.

Contadina® Classic Lasagne

Prep Time:
35 minutes

Cook Time:
30 minutes

Stand Time:
10 minutes

1 pound dry lasagne noodles, cooked
1 tablespoon olive or vegetable oil
1 cup chopped onion
½ cup chopped green bell pepper
2 cloves garlic, minced
1½ pounds lean ground beef
2 cans (14.5 ounces each) CONTADINA® Recipe Ready Diced Tomatoes, undrained
1 can (8 ounces) CONTADINA Tomato Sauce
1 can (6 ounces) CONTADINA Tomato Paste

½ cup dry red wine or beef broth
1½ teaspoons salt
1 teaspoon dried oregano leaves, crushed
1 teaspoon dried basil leaves, crushed
½ teaspoon ground black pepper
1 egg
1 cup (8 ounces) ricotta cheese
2 cups (8 ounces) shredded mozzarella cheese, divided

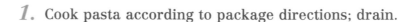

1. Cook pasta according to package directions; drain.

2. Meanwhile, heat oil in large skillet. Add onion, bell pepper and garlic; sauté for 3 minutes or until vegetables are tender.

3. Add beef; cook for 5 to 6 minutes or until evenly browned.

4. Add undrained tomatoes, tomato sauce, tomato paste, wine, salt, oregano, basil and black pepper; bring to a boil. Reduce heat to low; simmer, uncovered, for 20 minutes, stirring occasionally.

5. Beat egg slightly in medium bowl. Stir in ricotta cheese and 1 cup mozzarella cheese.

6. Layer one third of noodles, half of meat sauce, one third of noodles, all of ricotta cheese mixture, remaining noodles and remaining meat sauce in ungreased 13×9-inch baking dish. Sprinkle with remaining mozzarella cheese.

7. Bake in preheated 350°F oven for 25 to 30 minutes or until heated through. Let stand for 10 minutes before cutting to serve.

Zesty Italian Stuffed Peppers

3 bell peppers (green, red or yellow)	2 tablespoons *Frank's® RedHot®* Cayenne Pepper Sauce
1 pound ground beef	½ cup uncooked instant rice
1 jar (14 ounces) spaghetti sauce	¼ cup sliced ripe olives
1⅓ cups *French's®* French Fried Onions, divided	1 cup (4 ounces) shredded mozzarella cheese

Makes 6 servings

Prep Time:
10 minutes

Cook Time:
36 minutes

Preheat oven to 400°F. Cut bell peppers in half lengthwise through stems; discard seeds. Place pepper halves, cut side up, in shallow 2-quart baking dish; set aside.

Place beef in large microwavable bowl. Microwave on HIGH 5 minutes or until meat is browned, stirring once. Drain. Stir in spaghetti sauce, *⅔ cup* French Fried Onions, *Frank's RedHot* Sauce, rice and olives. Spoon evenly into bell pepper halves.

Cover; bake 35 minutes or until bell peppers are tender. Uncover; sprinkle with cheese and remaining *⅔ cup* onions. Bake 1 minute or until onions are golden.

Fiesta Beef Enchiladas

Makes 4 servings

Prep Time:
15 minutes

Cook Time:
35 minutes

8 ounces 93% lean ground beef
½ cup sliced green onions
2 teaspoons fresh minced or
    bottled garlic
1 cup cold cooked white or
    brown rice
1½ cups chopped tomato,
    divided
¾ cup frozen corn, thawed

1 cup (4 ounces) shredded
    Mexican cheese blend or
    Cheddar cheese, divided
½ cup salsa or picante sauce
12 (6- to 7-inch) corn tortillas
1 can (10 ounces) mild or hot
    enchilada sauce
1 cup sliced romaine lettuce
    leaves

1. Preheat oven to 375°F. Spray 13×9-inch baking dish with nonstick cooking spray. Set aside. Cook ground beef in medium nonstick skillet over medium heat until no longer pink; drain. Add green onions and garlic; cook and stir 2 minutes.

2. Combine meat mixture, rice, 1 cup tomato, corn, ½ cup cheese and salsa; mix well. Spoon mixture down center of tortillas. Roll up; place seam side down in prepared dish. Spoon enchilada sauce evenly over enchiladas.

3. Cover with foil; bake for 20 minutes or until hot. Sprinkle with remaining ½ cup cheese; bake 5 minutes or until cheese melts. Top with lettuce and remaining ½ cup tomato.

Shepherd's Pie

1 pound ground beef
1 cup chopped onion
1 teaspoon LAWRY'S®
    Seasoned Salt
1 package (10 ounces) frozen
    peas and carrots, cooked
    and drained

1 package (0.88 ounce)
    LAWRY'S® Brown Gravy
    Mix
1 cup water
1 egg, beaten
3 cups mashed potatoes
    Paprika

In large skillet, cook ground beef and onion over medium-high heat until beef is browned; drain fat. Add Seasoned Salt and peas and carrots; mix well. Prepare Brown Gravy Mix with 1 cup water according to package directions. Add some gravy to beaten egg; gradually add egg-gravy mixture to gravy, stirring constantly. Combine gravy with meat. In shallow, 2-quart casserole, place meat; arrange potatoes in mounds over meat. Sprinkle top with paprika. Bake, uncovered, in 400°F oven 15 minutes or until heated through.

Note:

When onions are cut, they release sulfur compounds that bring tears to the eyes. Believe it or not, chewing a piece of bread while peeling and chopping may help to minimize the tears.

Velveeta® Mexican Lasagna

Makes 8 servings

Prep Time:
10 minutes

Bake Time:
25 minutes

1 pound ground beef or
   1 pound boneless skinless
   chicken breasts, chopped
2 jars (16 ounces each) TACO
   BELL® HOME ORIGINALS®*
   Thick 'N Chunky Salsa
1 can (15 ounces) corn, drained
12 corn tortillas (6 inch)

1 package (8 ounces)
   VELVEETA® Mexican
   Shredded Pasteurized
   Process Cheese Food

*TACO BELL and HOME ORIGINALS are
registered trademarks owned and licensed by
Taco Bell Corp.*

1. Brown meat in large skillet; drain. Stir in salsa and corn.

2. Spoon 1 cup of the meat mixture into 12×8-inch baking dish.
Top with ½ each of the tortillas, remaining meat mixture and
VELVEETA; repeat layers. Cover with foil.

3. Bake at 375°F for 20 minutes. Uncover. Bake an additional
5 minutes or until bubbly and VELVEETA is melted. Top with
BREAKSTONE'S® or KNUDSEN® Sour Cream, if desired.

Ranch Lentil Casserole

Makes 8 servings

2 cups lentils, rinsed
4 cups water
1 pound lean ground beef
1 cup water

1 cup ketchup
1 envelope dry onion soup mix
1 teaspoon prepared mustard
1 teaspoon vinegar

Cook lentils in 4 cups water for 30 minutes. Drain. Brown ground
beef. Combine lentils, beef, 1 cup water and remaining
ingredients in baking dish. Bake at 400°F for 30 minutes.

Favorite recipe from **USA Dry Pea & Lentil Council**

Crescent Moon Meat Surprise

1½ pounds ground beef
1 package (1.25 ounces) dry onion soup mix
½ cup parboiled white rice
2 eggs
½ teaspoon pepper
1 jar (6 ounces) jalapeño peppers, halved

2 cans (10.5 ounces each) condensed cream of mushroom soup
1½ cups milk
1 bag (24 ounces) potato wedges
1 bunch green onions and stems, chopped

Mix together beef, onion soup mix, rice, eggs and pepper. Shape into 15 meatballs around jalapeño halves. Place meatballs in a single layer in center of 13×9-inch pan. Mix mushroom soup and milk together and pour over meatballs. Arrange potato wedges around outside edge of meatballs so they stick out of the soup mixture. Bake at 375°F for 1 hour. Remove from oven and sprinkle with chopped onions and decoratively arrange remaining peppers.

Favorite recipe from **North Dakota Beef Commission**

Tamale Pie

**Makes about
6 servings**

1 tablespoon BERTOLLI® Olive
   Oil
1 small onion, chopped
1 pound ground beef
1 envelope LIPTON® RECIPE
   SECRETS® Onion Soup
   Mix*
1 can (14½ ounces) stewed
   tomatoes, undrained
½ cup water

1 can (15 to 19 ounces) red
   kidney beans, rinsed and
   drained
1 package (8½ ounces) corn
   muffin mix

*Also terrific with LIPTON® RECIPE SECRETS®
Fiesta Herb with Red Pepper, Onion-
Mushroom, Beefy Onion or Beefy Mushroom
Soup Mix.

• Preheat oven to 400°F.

• In 12-inch skillet, heat oil over medium heat and cook onion,
stirring occasionally, 3 minutes or until tender. Stir in ground beef
and cook until browned.

• Stir in onion soup mix blended with tomatoes and water. Bring
to a boil over high heat, stirring with spoon to crush tomatoes.
Reduce heat to low and stir in beans. Simmer uncovered, stirring
occasionally, 10 minutes. Turn into 2-quart casserole.

• Prepare corn muffin mix according to package directions. Spoon
evenly over casserole.

• Bake uncovered 15 minutes or until corn topping is golden and
filling is hot.

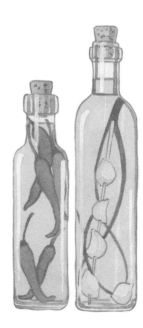

Perfect
Pork &
More

CHAPTER TWO

Italian-Glazed Pork Chops

Makes 8 servings

Prep Time:
10 minutes

Cook Time:
25 minutes

1 tablespoon BERTOLLI® Olive Oil
8 bone-in pork chops
1 medium zucchini, thinly sliced
1 medium red bell pepper, chopped
1 medium onion, thinly sliced

3 cloves garlic, finely chopped
¼ cup dry red wine or beef broth
1 jar (1 pound 10 ounces) RAGÚ® Chunky Gardenstyle Pasta Sauce

1. In 12-inch skillet, heat oil over medium-high heat and brown chops. Remove chops and set aside.

2. In same skillet, cook zucchini, red bell pepper, onion and garlic, stirring occasionally, 4 minutes. Stir in wine and Ragú Pasta Sauce.

3. Return chops to skillet, turning to coat with sauce. Simmer covered 15 minutes or until chops are tender and barely pink in the center. Serve, if desired, over hot cooked couscous or rice.

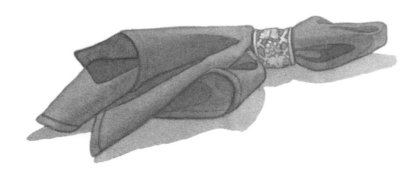

Rotini & Ham Bake

1 can (10¾ ounces) condensed
    cream of celery soup,
    undiluted
1 cup milk
1 cup (4 ounces) shredded
    Cheddar cheese, divided
¼ teaspoon salt
¼ teaspoon onion powder

¼ teaspoon garlic powder
¼ teaspoon black pepper
2 cups cooked rotini pasta
1½ cups cubed HILLSHIRE FARM®
    Ham
1 head broccoli, divided into
    spears and cooked

Preheat oven to 350°F.

Combine soup, milk, ½ cup cheese, salt, onion powder, garlic powder and pepper in medium bowl; set aside. Combine pasta and Ham in medium baking dish. Arrange broccoli spears around top of dish, pushing spears into pasta mixture. Pour soup mixture evenly over top of pasta mixture. Bake, covered, 35 minutes. Top with remaining ½ cup cheese. Bake, uncovered, 5 minutes or until cheese has melted.

Tip: *Create individual dinners with your favorite Hillshire Farm recipe. Store leftovers in individual serving size portions wrapped tightly in heavy-duty aluminum foil and frozen seam side up. To reheat, bake on the center rack of a 450°F oven until hot.*

Note:

Pepper is the dried berry of the *Piper nigum* plant family. Black peppercorn is the strongest and spiciest type; it is made from unripe berries fermented for several days before drying.

Tomato Pesto Lasagna

Makes 6 servings

Prep Time:
20 minutes

Cook Time:
30 minutes

Microwave Cook Time:
10 minutes

8 ounces lasagna noodles
(2 inches wide)
1 pound crumbled sausage
1 can (14½ ounces)
DEL MONTE® Diced
Tomatoes with Garlic &
Onion
1 can (6 ounces) DEL MONTE
Tomato Paste

8 ounces ricotta cheese
1 package (4 ounces) pesto
sauce*
2 cups (8 ounces) shredded
mozzarella cheese

Pesto sauce is available frozen or refrigerated at the supermarket.

1. Cook noodles according to package directions; rinse, drain and separate noodles.

2. Meanwhile, brown meat in large skillet; drain. Stir in undrained tomatoes, tomato paste and ¾ cup water.

3. Layer ⅓ meat sauce, then half each of noodles, ricotta cheese, pesto and mozzarella cheese in 2-quart casserole or 9-inch square baking dish; repeat layers. Top with remaining sauce. Sprinkle with grated Parmesan cheese, if desired.

4. Bake at 350°F, 30 minutes or until heated through.

Microwave Directions: *Assemble lasagna in 9-inch square microwavable dish as directed. Cover with vented plastic wrap; microwave on HIGH 10 minutes, rotating dish after 5 minutes.*

Country Sausage Macaroni and Cheese

1 pound BOB EVANS® Special
   Seasonings Roll Sausage
1½ cups milk
12 ounces pasteurized processed
   Cheddar cheese, cut into
   cubes
½ cup Dijon mustard
1 cup diced fresh or drained
   canned tomatoes
1 cup sliced mushrooms
⅓ cup sliced green onions
⅛ teaspoon cayenne pepper
12 ounces uncooked elbow
   macaroni
2 tablespoons grated
   Parmesan cheese

Preheat oven to 350°F. Crumble and cook sausage in medium skillet until browned. Drain on paper towels. Combine milk, processed cheese and mustard in medium saucepan; cook and stir over low heat until cheese melts and mixture is smooth. Stir in sausage, tomatoes, mushrooms, green onions and cayenne pepper. Remove from heat.

Cook macaroni according to package directions; drain. Combine hot macaroni and cheese mixture in large bowl; toss until well coated. Spoon into greased shallow 2-quart casserole dish. Cover and bake 15 to 20 minutes. Stir; sprinkle with Parmesan cheese. Bake, uncovered, 5 minutes more. Let stand 10 minutes before serving. Refrigerate leftovers.

Note:

Mustard is one of the most frequently eaten condiments in the world and is available in many varieties. Dijon mustard is smooth and piquant with a slight hot undertone and is made in Dijon, France. Dijon-style mustard is its American counterpart.

Hunter's Pie

Makes 6 servings

2 tablespoons salad oil
6 loin-cut lamb chops, cut into
    bite-size pieces
LAWRY'S® Seasoned Salt to
    taste
LAWRY'S® Seasoned Pepper
    to taste

4 cups mashed potatoes
¼ cup butter, melted
¼ teaspoon white pepper
1 package (0.88 ounce)
    LAWRY'S® Brown Gravy
    Mix
1 cup water

In large skillet, heat oil. Add lamb, Seasoned Salt and Seasoned Pepper and cook over medium-high heat until browned; drain fat. In medium bowl, combine potatoes, butter and white pepper; mix well. Butter shallow casserole dish and line with half of potato mixture. Top with lamb. Spread remaining potatoes over top. Bake, uncovered, in 350°F oven 45 minutes. Meanwhile, in medium saucepan, prepare Brown Gravy with water according to package directions. Cut a hole in top of potato crust; pour about half of gravy into pie.

<u>Serving Suggestion:</u> *Pass remaining gravy at the table.*

<u>Hint:</u> *Use 1½ pounds cubed lamb or ground lamb, formed into meatballs, in place of loin chops.*

Pork-Stuffed Peppers

1 pound ground pork
3 large green peppers
¼ cup raisins
½ cup chopped onion
½ cup chopped carrot
½ cup chopped celery

¼ teaspoon salt
1 cup cooked brown rice
2 tablespoons sunflower
   kernels
½ cup plain yogurt

Makes 6 servings

Prep Time:
20 minutes

Cook Time:
30 minutes

Remove tops, seeds and membranes from peppers. Cut in half lengthwise. Cook in boiling salted water 5 minutes; drain.

Soak raisins in water 10 to 15 minutes; drain and set aside. Combine pork, onion, carrot, celery and salt in medium skillet. Cook over low heat until pork is done and vegetables are tender, stirring occasionally. Drain thoroughly. Add rice, sunflower kernels, yogurt and raisins; mix well. Spoon mixture into peppers. Place in 12×8×2-inch baking dish. Bake at 350°F 30 to 35 minutes or until heated through.

Favorite recipe from **National Pork Board**

Apple, Bean and Ham Casserole

Makes 6 servings

1 pound boneless ham
3 cans (15 ounces each) Great
   Northern beans, drained
   and rinsed
1 small onion, diced
1 medium Granny Smith apple,
   diced
3 tablespoons dark molasses

3 tablespoons packed brown
   sugar
1 tablespoon Dijon mustard
1 teaspoon ground allspice
¼ cup thinly sliced green onions
   or 1 tablespoon chopped
   fresh parsley

Note:

Crisp, tart, juicy
Granny Smith apples
are not only delicious
eaten raw, but are also
excellent for cooking
and baking because
they keep their texture.
And unlike other
apples, you can enjoy
them year-round.

1. Preheat oven to 350°F. Cut ham into 1-inch cubes. Combine ham, beans, onion, apple, molasses, brown sugar, mustard and allspice in 3-quart casserole; mix well. Cover; bake 45 minutes or until most liquid is absorbed. Cool casserole completely. Cover and refrigerate up to 2 days.

2. To complete recipe, stir ⅓ cup water into casserole. Microwave at HIGH 10 minutes or until hot and bubbly. Or, heat in preheated 350°F oven 40 minutes or until hot and bubbly. Sprinkle with green onions before serving.

Sausage-Chicken Creole

1 can (14½ ounces) whole
 tomatoes, undrained and
 cut up
½ cup uncooked regular rice
½ cup hot water
2 teaspoons *Frank's® RedHot®*
 Cayenne Pepper Sauce
¼ teaspoon garlic powder
¼ teaspoon dried oregano,
 crumbled

1 bag (16 ounces) frozen
 vegetable combination
 (broccoli, corn, red pepper),
 thawed and drained
1⅓ cups *French's®* French Fried
 Onions, divided
4 chicken thighs, skinned
½ pound link Italian sausage,
 quartered and cooked*
1 can (8 ounces) tomato sauce

Preheat oven to 375°F. In 12×8-inch baking dish, combine
tomatoes, uncooked rice, hot water, *Frank's RedHot* Sauce
and seasonings. Bake, covered, at 375°F for 10 minutes. Stir
vegetables and ⅔ *cup* French Fried Onions into rice mixture;
top with chicken and cooked sausage.* Pour tomato sauce over
chicken and sausage. Bake, covered, at 375°F for 40 minutes or
until chicken is done. Top chicken with remaining ⅔ *cup* onions;
bake, uncovered, 3 minutes or until onions are golden brown.

*To cook sausage, simmer in water to cover until done. Or, place in microwave-safe dish and
cook, covered, on HIGH 3 minutes or until done.

Sausage & Feta Strata

Makes 8 servings

Prep Time:
11 minutes

Cook Time:
55 minutes

8 ounces dry medium pasta shells
1 pound Italian sausage
2 tablespoons vegetable oil
1 cup sliced green onions with tops
3 cloves garlic, minced
1 cup water
1 can (6 ounces) CONTADINA® Tomato Paste
⅔ cup dry red wine
¾ teaspoon fennel seed
½ teaspoon dried rosemary, crushed
2 cups (8 ounces) crumbled feta cheese or ricotta cheese
2 cups sliced zucchini

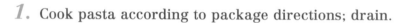

1. Cook pasta according to package directions; drain.

2. Meanwhile, brown sausage in oil in 10-inch skillet over medium heat; drain on paper towels, reserving drippings in skillet.

3. Add onions and garlic to reserved drippings. Cook and stir 3 minutes.

4. Stir in water, tomato paste, wine, fennel and rosemary. Bring to a boil. Reduce heat to low; simmer 6 minutes, stirring occasionally.

5. Spoon ½ of pasta into greased 2-quart baking dish; top with layers of ½ each of sauce and cheese. Place zucchini over cheese. Repeat layers of pasta, sauce and cheese. Arrange sausage on top to resemble pinwheel.

6. Bake at 350°F, 35 to 40 minutes or until hot and bubbly.

Easy Moroccan Casserole

2 tablespoons vegetable oil
1 pound pork stew meat, cut
    into 1-inch cubes
½ cup chopped onion
3 tablespoons all-purpose flour
1 can (about 14 ounces) diced
    tomatoes, undrained
¼ cup water
1 teaspoon ground ginger
1 teaspoon ground cumin
1 teaspoon ground cinnamon
½ teaspoon sugar
½ teaspoon salt

½ teaspoon black pepper
2 medium red potatoes,
    unpeeled and cut into
    ½-inch pieces
1 large sweet potato, unpeeled
    and cut into ½-inch pieces
1 cup frozen lima beans,
    thawed and drained
1 cup frozen cut green beans,
    thawed and drained
¾ cup sliced carrots
    Pita bread

1. Preheat oven to 325°F.

2. Heat oil in large skillet over medium-high heat. Add pork and onion; cook, stirring occasionally, until pork is browned on all sides.

3. Sprinkle flour over meat mixture in skillet. Stir until flour has absorbed pan juices. Cook 2 minutes more.

4. Stir in tomatoes with juice, water, ginger, cumin, cinnamon, sugar, salt and pepper. Transfer mixture to 2-quart casserole. Bake 30 minutes.

5. Stir in potatoes, sweet potato, lima beans, green beans and carrots. Cover and bake 1 hour or until potatoes are tender. Serve with pita bread.

Sausage & Noodle Casserole

Makes 6 servings

1 pound BOB EVANS® Original
  Recipe Roll Sausage
1 cup chopped onion
¼ cup chopped green bell
  pepper
1 (10-ounce) package frozen
  peas
1 (10¾-ounce) can condensed
  cream of chicken soup

1 (8-ounce) package egg
  noodles, cooked according
  to package directions and
  drained
Salt and black pepper to taste
1 (2.8-ounce) can French fried
  onions, crushed

Note:

**Most pastas are
prepared with wheat
flours or other cereal
grains and water. If an
egg is added to this
mix, the product is
then called a noodle.**

Preheat oven to 350°F. Crumble sausage into large skillet. Add onion and green pepper. Cook over medium heat until meat is browned and vegetables are tender, stirring occasionally. Drain off any drippings. Cook peas according to package directions. Drain, reserving liquid in 2-cup glass measuring cup; set aside. Add enough water to pea liquid to obtain 1⅓ cups liquid. Combine liquid and soup in large bowl; stir in sausage mixture, noodles, reserved peas, salt and black pepper. Mix well. Spoon mixture into greased 2½-quart baking dish. Sprinkle with onions. Bake 30 minutes or until bubbly. Serve hot. Refrigerate leftovers.

Lamb Enchilada Casserole

12 ounces lean ground American lamb
1 can (11 ounces) corn with peppers, drained
1 carton (8 ounces) low-fat sour cream, divided
2 teaspoons chili powder
½ teaspoon dried cilantro leaves *or* 2 teaspoons fresh snipped cilantro

Nonstick cooking spray
8 (6-inch) corn tortillas
1 can (10 ounces) enchilada sauce
¾ (3 ounces) cup shredded Cheddar cheese

Makes 4 servings

Prep Time:
30 to 40 minutes

Cook Time:
20 minutes

In large skillet, cook and stir lamb until browned; drain. Stir in corn, ½ cup sour cream, chili powder and cilantro; mix well.

Spray 10×6-inch or 8×8-inch baking dish with cooking spray. Arrange 4 tortillas in dish. Spoon about ⅔ of lamb mixture over tortillas. Top with remaining 4 tortillas and lamb mixture. Pour enchilada sauce over top.

Bake in 375°F oven 15 minutes. Sprinkle cheese on top and bake 5 minutes. Serve with dollops of remaining sour cream.

Favorite recipe from **American Lamb Council**

Caribbean Black Bean Casserole with Spicy Mango Salsa

Makes 6 servings

2 cups chicken broth
1 cup uncooked basmati rice
2 tablespoons olive oil, divided
½ pound chorizo sausage
2 cloves garlic, minced
1 cup chopped red bell pepper
3 cups canned black beans, rinsed and drained
½ cup chopped fresh cilantro

2 small mangoes
1 cup chopped red onion
2 tablespoons honey
2 tablespoons white wine vinegar
1 teaspoon curry powder
½ teaspoon salt
½ teaspoon ground red pepper

1. Place chicken broth in medium saucepan. Bring to a boil over high heat; stir in rice. Reduce heat to low; simmer, covered, 20 minutes or until liquid is absorbed and rice is tender.

2. Heat 1 tablespoon oil in heavy, large skillet over medium heat. Add sausage; cook, turning occasionally, 8 to 10 minutes until browned and no longer pink in center. Remove from skillet to cutting surface. Cut into ½-inch slices; set aside. Drain fat from skillet.

3. Preheat oven to 350°F. Grease 1½-quart casserole; set aside. Add remaining tablespoon oil to skillet; heat over medium-high heat. Add garlic; cook and stir 1 minute. Add bell pepper; cook and stir 5 minutes. Remove from heat. Stir in beans, sausage, rice and cilantro.

4. Spoon sausage mixture into prepared casserole; cover with foil. Bake 30 minutes or until heated through.

5. Peel mangoes; remove seeds. Chop enough flesh to measure 3 cups. Combine mango and remaining ingredients in large bowl.

6. Spoon sausage mixture onto serving plates. Serve with mango salsa. Garnish, if desired.

Sunny Day Casserole

Makes 6 servings

1 jar (8 ounces) pasteurized processed cheese spread, melted
¾ cup milk
4 cups diced potatoes, partially cooked
2 cups diced HILLSHIRE FARM® Ham

1 package (16 ounces) frozen mixed vegetables, thawed
½ cup chopped onion
1 cup (4 ounces) shredded Swiss, Cheddar or Monterey Jack cheese
1 cup cracker crumbs

Preheat oven to 350°F.

Combine cheese spread and milk in large bowl. Stir in potatoes, Ham, mixed vegetables and onion. Pour into medium casserole. Bake, covered, 45 minutes, stirring occasionally. Sprinkle Swiss cheese and cracker crumbs over top. Bake, uncovered, until Swiss cheese is melted.

Pork Chop & Wild Rice Bake

Makes 4 servings

Prep Time:
5 minutes

Cook Time:
35 minutes

1 package (6 ounces) seasoned long grain & wild rice mix
1⅓ cups *French's®* French Fried Onions, divided
1 package (10 ounces) frozen cut green beans, thawed and drained

¼ cup orange juice
1 teaspoon grated orange peel
4 boneless pork chops (1 inch thick)

1. Preheat oven to 375°F. Combine rice mix and seasoning packet, *2 cups water, ⅔ cup* French Fried Onions, green beans, orange juice and orange peel in 2-quart shallow baking dish. Arrange pork chops on top.

2. Bake, uncovered, 30 minutes or until pork chops are no longer pink near center. Sprinkle chops with remaining *⅔ cup* onions. Bake 5 minutes or until onions are golden.

Smokehouse Red Bean and Sausage Casserole

3 bacon slices, chopped
3 cups chopped onion
1 medium-sized green bell
  pepper, chopped
1 cup chopped fresh parsley
1 pound smoked sausage, cut
  into ¼-inch slices
2 cans (15¼ ounces each)
  kidney beans, undrained
1 can (8 ounces) tomato sauce

1 tablespoon Worcestershire
  sauce
1 tablespoon LAWRY'S®
  Seasoned Salt
¾ teaspoon hot pepper sauce
½ teaspoon LAWRY'S® Garlic
  Powder with Parsley
3 cups hot cooked white rice

Makes 8 servings

In Dutch oven or large saucepan, cook bacon and onion over medium-high heat until bacon is just crisp and onion is transparent; drain fat. Add remaining ingredients except rice; mix well. Bring to a boil over medium-high heat; reduce heat to low and simmer, uncovered, 20 minutes, stirring occasionally.

<u>Serving Suggestion:</u> *Serve over rice; this is perfect with a green salad and crusty bread.*

<u>Hint:</u> *Use 1 bag (12 ounces) frozen chopped onion instead of fresh onion.*

Note:

Pepper sauce, or hot pepper sauce, is a thin, spicy liquid, usually red in color, made from chili peppers (such as cayenne, jalapeño and serrano), vinegar and seasonings. It is used both as an ingredient and table condiment.

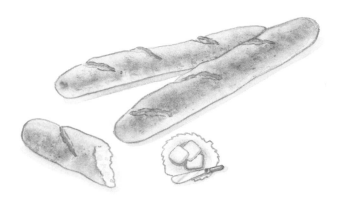

SPAM® and Rice Casserole

Makes 4 to 6 servings

1 (12-ounce) can SPAM® Classic,
   cubed
2 cups cooked white rice
½ cup chopped water chestnuts
½ cup sliced celery
¼ cup sliced green onions

¼ teaspoon black pepper
1 (10¾-ounce) can condensed
   cream of mushroom soup
⅓ cup mayonnaise or salad
   dressing

Heat oven to 350°F. In medium bowl, combine SPAM®, rice, water chestnuts, celery, green onions and pepper. In small bowl, combine soup and mayonnaise; mix with SPAM® mixture. Spoon into 1½-quart casserole. Bake 35 to 40 minutes or until thoroughly heated.

Cheesy Ham Casserole

Makes 4 to 6 servings

Prep Time:
15 minutes

Cook Time:
30 minutes

2 cups fresh or frozen broccoli
   flowerets, thawed
1½ cups KRAFT® Shredded Sharp
   Cheddar Cheese, divided
1½ cups coarsely chopped ham
1½ cups (4 ounces) corkscrew
   pasta, cooked, drained

½ cup MIRACLE WHIP® or
   MIRACLE WHIP LIGHT®
   Dressing
½ green or red bell pepper,
   chopped
¼ cup milk
   Seasoned croutons (optional)

• Heat oven to 350°F.

• Mix all ingredients except ½ cup cheese and croutons.

• Spoon into 1½-quart casserole. Sprinkle with remaining ½ cup cheese.

• Bake 30 minutes or until thoroughly heated. Sprinkle with croutons, if desired.

Hungarian Goulash Casserole

1 pound ground pork
¼ teaspoon salt
¼ teaspoon pepper
¼ teaspoon ground nutmeg
1 tablespoon vegetable oil
1 cup reduced-fat sour cream, divided
1 tablespoon cornstarch
1 can (10¾ ounces) cream of celery soup

1 cup milk
1 teaspoon sweet Hungarian paprika
1 package (12 ounces) egg noodles, cooked and drained
2 teaspoons minced fresh dill (optional)

Make 4 to 6 servings

1. Preheat oven to 325°F. Spray 13×9-inch casserole dish with nonstick cooking spray.

2. Combine pork, salt, pepper and nutmeg in bowl. Shape into 1-inch meatballs. Heat oil in large skillet over medium-high heat. Add meatballs. Cook 10 minutes or until browned on all sides and no longer pink in center. Remove meatballs from skillet; discard drippings.

3. Stir together ¼ cup sour cream and cornstarch in small bowl. Spoon into same skillet. Add remaining ¾ cup sour cream, soup, milk and paprika. Stir until smooth.

4. Spoon cooked noodles into prepared dish. Arrange meatballs over noodles and cover with sauce. Bake 20 minutes or until hot. Sprinkle with dill if desired.

Ham and Potato au Gratin

Makes 8 servings

3 tablespoons butter or
    margarine
3 tablespoons all-purpose flour
2 cups milk
1½ cups (6 ounces) shredded
    Cheddar cheese
1 tablespoon Dijon mustard
2 cups HILLSHIRE FARM® Lean
    & Hearty Ham cut into thin
    strips

1 package (24 ounces) frozen
    shredded hash brown
    potatoes, thawed
1 package (10 ounces) frozen
    chopped spinach, thawed
    and drained

Note:

**For the best results
when draining thawed
frozen spinach, press
the spinach between
two nested pie plates,
tilting the plates over
the sink to drain well.**

Preheat oven to 350°F.

Melt butter in large saucepan over medium heat; stir in flour. Add milk. Cook and stir until bubbly; cook 1 minute more. Remove from heat. Stir in cheese and mustard; set aside.

Place ½ of Ham in ungreased medium casserole. Top ham with ½ of potatoes and ½ of milk mixture. Spoon spinach over top. Repeat layers with remaining ham, potatoes and milk mixture.

Bake, uncovered, 30 minutes or until heated through.

Pork-Stuffed Eggplant

½ pound lean ground pork
1 medium eggplant
1 small green pepper, coarsely
   chopped
¼ cup chopped onion
1 clove garlic, minced
¼ cup water

⅛ teaspoon dried oregano
   leaves, crushed
⅛ teaspoon ground black
   pepper
1 medium tomato, coarsely
   chopped

Makes 2 servings

Prep Time:
25 minutes

Cook Time:
25 minutes

Wash eggplant and cut in half lengthwise. Remove pulp, leaving eggplant shell about ¼ inch thick. Cut pulp into ½-inch cubes. Set shells and pulp aside.

In large skillet cook ground pork, green pepper, onion and garlic until pork is browned; drain excess drippings. Add eggplant pulp, water, oregano and black pepper; cover and cook over low heat 10 minutes, stirring occasionally. Remove from heat and stir in tomato. Spoon mixture into eggplant shells. Place in 12×8×2-inch baking dish. Bake in 350°F oven 20 to 25 minutes or until heated through.

Favorite recipe from **National Pork Board**

Italian Sausage Lasagna

Makes 8 servings

1½ pounds BOB EVANS® Italian
   Roll Sausage
2 tablespoons olive oil
2 green bell peppers, thinly
   sliced
1 large yellow onion, thinly
   sliced
4 cloves garlic, minced and
   divided
1 (28-ounce) can whole
   tomatoes, undrained
1 (8-ounce) can tomato sauce
2 teaspoons fennel seeds
   Salt and black pepper to taste

1 tablespoon butter or
   margarine
1 large yellow onion, chopped
2 (10-ounce) packages chopped
   frozen spinach, thawed and
   squeezed dry
1 cup grated Parmesan cheese,
   divided
3 cups (24 ounces) low fat
   ricotta cheese
1 pound shredded mozzarella
   or provolone cheese
9 uncooked lasagna noodles

Crumble sausage in large heavy skillet. Cook over medium heat until well browned, stirring occasionally. Remove sausage to paper towels; set aside. Drain off drippings and wipe skillet clean with paper towels. Heat oil in same skillet over medium-high heat until hot. Add green peppers, sliced onion and half the garlic. Cook, covered, over medium heat about 10 minutes or until vegetables are wilted, stirring occasionally. Stir in tomatoes with juice, tomato sauce and fennel seeds, stirring well to break up tomatoes. Bring to a boil. Reduce heat to low; simmer, uncovered, 20 to 30 minutes to blend flavors. Stir in reserved sausage. Season sauce mixture with salt and black pepper; set aside.

Melt butter in small saucepan over medium-high heat; add chopped onion and remaining garlic. Cook and stir about 10 minutes or until onion is tender. Stir in spinach and ¼ cup Parmesan; set aside. Combine ricotta, mozzarella and ½ cup Parmesan in medium bowl. Season with salt and black pepper. Cook noodles according to package directions; drain.

Preheat oven to 350°F. Pour ⅓ of reserved sauce mixture into greased 13×9-inch baking dish; spread evenly. Arrange 3 noodles over sauce mixture; spread half the spinach mixture over noodles. Spread half the cheese mixture evenly over spinach. Repeat layers once. Top with remaining 3 noodles and sauce mixture. Sprinkle with remaining ¼ cup Parmesan. Bake about 1 hour or until sauce is bubbly and cheese is browned on top. Let stand 10 to 15 minutes before slicing. Serve hot. Refrigerate leftovers.

Pantry Provisions

Here's a basic list of pantry staples that should be part of every casserole cook's kitchen. As with casseroles themselves, it should be adjusted to suit you and your family's individual tastes.

Grains and Pasta: pasta, including long spaghetti types, shorter macaroni types, egg noodles and lasagna noodles; rice (white, brown and/or wild, flavored rice mixes, arborio rice for risotto)

Canned Goods: beans (black, kidney, white); broth and bouillon; chicken, ham or corned beef; condensed soup; olives; spaghetti sauce; tomato sauce and tomato paste; tomatoes (whole, stewed and diced with flavorings); tuna

Condiments: hot sauce; ketchup and barbecue sauce; mayonnaise; mustard; olive and vegetable oil; sour cream or yogurt; soy sauce; vinegar (white, balsamic, wine or cider); Worcestershire sauce

Dry Goods: biscuit baking mix; bread crumbs; cornmeal; cereal; all-purpose flour; nuts; stuffing mix

Vegetables and Fruit: frozen vegetables; garlic; lemons and limes; onions; potatoes (fresh and frozen)

Pork with Savory Apple Stuffing

Makes 4 servings

Prep Time:
10 minutes

Cook Time:
45 minutes

1 package (6 ounces) corn bread stuffing mix
1 can (14½ ounces) chicken broth
1 small apple, peeled, cored and chopped
¼ cup chopped celery
1⅓ cups *French's®* French Fried Onions, divided

4 boneless pork chops, ¾ inch thick (about 1 pound)
½ cup peach-apricot sweet & sour sauce
1 tablespoon *French's®* Napa Valley style Dijon Mustard

Note:

Apples will keep in a cool, dry place for a week or two. For longer storage, place apples in a plastic bag and store in the refrigerator. Apples in good condition can last up to six weeks in the refrigerator. Check them occasionally and discard any that have begun to spoil as one rotten apple can ruin the whole lot.

1. Preheat oven to 375°F. Combine stuffing mix, broth, apple, celery and ⅔ *cup* French Fried Onions in large bowl. Spoon into bottom of greased shallow 2-quart baking dish. Arrange chops on top of stuffing.

2. Combine sweet & sour sauce with mustard in small bowl. Pour over pork. Bake 40 minutes or until pork is no longer pink in center.

3. Sprinkle with remaining ⅔ *cup* onions. Bake 5 minutes or until onions are golden.

Paella

¼ cup FILIPPO BERIO® Olive Oil
1 pound boneless skinless chicken breasts, cut into 1-inch strips
½ pound Italian sausage, cut into 1-inch slices
1 onion, chopped
3 cloves garlic, minced
2 (14½-ounce) cans chicken broth
2 cups uncooked long grain white rice
1 (8-ounce) bottle clam juice
1 (2-ounce) jar chopped pimientos, drained

2 bay leaves
1 teaspoon salt
¼ teaspoon saffron threads, crumbled (optional)
1 pound raw shrimp, shelled and deveined
1 (16-ounce) can whole tomatoes, drained
1 (10-ounce) package frozen peas, thawed
12 littleneck clams, scrubbed
¼ cup water
Fresh herb sprig (optional)

Preheat oven to 350°F. In large skillet, heat olive oil over medium heat until hot. Add chicken; cook and stir 8 to 10 minutes or until brown on all sides. Remove with slotted spoon; set aside. Add sausage to skillet; cook and stir 8 to 10 minutes or until brown. Remove with slotted spoon; set aside. Add onion and garlic to skillet; cook and stir 5 to 7 minutes or until onion is tender. Transfer chicken, sausage, onion and garlic mixture to large casserole.

Add chicken broth, rice, clam juice, pimientos, bay leaves, salt and saffron, if desired, to chicken mixture. Cover; bake for 30 minutes. Add shrimp, tomatoes and peas; stir well. Cover; bake an additional 15 minutes or until rice is tender, liquid is absorbed and shrimp are opaque. Remove bay leaves.

Meanwhile, combine clams and water in stockpot or large saucepan. Cover; cook over medium heat 5 to 10 minutes or until clams open; remove clams immediately as they open. Discard any clams with unopened shells. Place clams on top of paella. Garnish with herb sprig, if desired.

Savory Lentil Casserole

Makes 4 servings

1¼ cups uncooked dried brown or green lentils, rinsed and sorted
2 tablespoons olive oil
1 large onion, chopped
3 cloves garlic, minced
8 ounces fresh shiitake or button mushrooms, sliced
2 tablespoons all-purpose flour
1½ cups beef broth

1 tablespoon Worcestershire sauce
1 tablespoon balsamic vinegar
4 ounces Canadian bacon, minced
½ teaspoon salt
½ teaspoon black pepper
½ cup grated Parmesan cheese
2 to 3 plum tomatoes, seeded and chopped

1. Preheat oven to 400°F. Place lentils in medium saucepan; cover with 1 inch water. Bring to a boil over high heat. Reduce heat to low. Simmer, covered, 20 to 25 minutes until lentils are barely tender; drain.

2. Meanwhile, heat oil in large skillet over medium heat. Add onion and garlic; cook and stir 10 minutes. Add mushrooms; cook and stir 10 minutes or until liquid is evaporated and mushrooms are tender. Sprinkle flour over mushroom mixture; stir well. Cook and stir 1 minute. Stir in beef broth, Worcestershire, vinegar, bacon, salt and pepper. Cook and stir until mixture is thick and bubbly.

3. Grease 1½-quart casserole. Stir lentils into mushroom mixture. Spread evenly in prepared casserole. Sprinkle with cheese. Bake 20 minutes.

4. Sprinkle tomatoes over casserole just before serving. Garnish with thyme and Italian parsley, if desired.

Polska Bean Casserole

¼ pound HILLSHIRE FARM®
   Bacon, diced
2 cups chopped onions
5 carrots, cut into ½-inch slices
1 can (about 14 ounces) chicken
   broth
3 cloves garlic, minced
2 teaspoons hot pepper sauce
   (optional)
½ teaspoon dried thyme leaves
½ teaspoon dried oregano
   leaves
½ teaspoon dried sage leaves
1 bay leaf

Salt and black pepper to taste
1 can (15 ounces) red kidney
   beans, rinsed and drained*
1 can (15 ounces) white kidney
   beans, rinsed and drained*
1 pound HILLSHIRE FARM®
   Polska Kielbasa, cut into
   1-inch slices
1 can (16 ounces) crushed
   tomatoes

*Or use any combination of your favorite beans.

Makes 6 to 8 servings

Preheat oven to 350°F.

Brown Bacon in Dutch oven over medium heat. Add onions, carrots, chicken broth, garlic, pepper sauce, if desired, thyme, oregano, sage, bay leaf, salt and black pepper. Stir in beans and 1 cup water. Simmer, uncovered, 20 minutes. Stir in Polska Kielbasa and tomatoes. Bake, covered, 1 hour or until almost all liquid is absorbed.

Note:

Polish sausage is also called kielbasa. It is garlic flavored and consists mainly of seasoned pork, although beef and veal are often added. It is commonly sold in long links that are smoked and precooked, ready to heat and serve.

Jambalaya

Makes 8 servings

1 teaspoon vegetable oil
½ pound smoked deli ham, cubed
½ pound smoked sausage, cut into ¼-inch-thick slices
1 large onion, chopped
1 large green bell pepper, chopped (about 1½ cups)
3 ribs celery, chopped (about 1 cup)
3 cloves garlic, minced
1 can (28 ounces) diced tomatoes, undrained

1 can (10½ ounces) chicken broth
1 cup uncooked rice
1 tablespoon Worcestershire sauce
1 teaspoon salt
1 teaspoon dried thyme leaves
½ teaspoon black pepper
¼ teaspoon ground red pepper
1 package (12 ounces) frozen ready-to-cook shrimp, thawed
Fresh chives (optional)

Preheat oven to 350°F. Spray 13×9-inch baking dish with nonstick cooking spray.

Heat oil in large skillet over medium-high heat until hot. Add ham and sausage. Cook and stir 5 minutes or until sausage is lightly browned on both sides. Remove from skillet and place in prepared dish. Place onion, bell pepper, celery and garlic in same skillet; cook and stir 3 minutes. Add to sausage mixture.

Combine tomatoes with juice, broth, rice, Worcestershire, salt, thyme, black and red peppers in same skillet; bring to a boil over high heat. Reduce heat to low and simmer 3 minutes. Pour over sausage mixture and stir until combined.

Cover tightly with foil and bake 45 minutes or until rice is almost tender. Remove from oven; place shrimp on top of rice mixture. Bake, uncovered, 10 minutes or until shrimp are pink and opaque. Garnish with chives, if desired.

French Fry SPAM™ Casserole

1 (20-ounce) bag frozen French-
  fried potatoes, thawed
2 cups (8 ounces) shredded
  Cheddar cheese
2 cups sour cream
1 (10¾-ounce) can condensed
  cream of chicken soup

1 (12-ounce) can SPAM® Classic,
  cubed
½ cup chopped red bell pepper
½ cup chopped green onions
½ cup finely crushed corn
  flakes

Makes 6 to 8 servings

Heat oven to 350°F. In large bowl, combine potatoes, cheese, sour cream and soup. Stir in SPAM®, bell pepper and green onions. Spoon into 13×9-inch baking dish. Sprinkle with corn flakes. Bake 30 to 40 minutes or until thoroughly heated.

Prize Potluck Casserole

1 cup lentils, rinsed and drained
2 cups water
1 can (16 ounces) tomatoes
¼ cup minced onion
¼ cup chopped green pepper
1 teaspoon salt
½ teaspoon dry mustard

¼ teaspoon pepper
¼ teaspoon Worcestershire
  sauce
⅛ teaspoon dried thyme leaves
1 pound Polish sausage, cut
  into 1½-inch-thick slices

Makes 6 servings

Cook lentils in water until tender, about 30 minutes; drain if necessary. Combine lentils with tomatoes, onion, green pepper and seasonings; spoon into 13×9-inch casserole. Top with sausage. Cover casserole and bake 45 minutes at 350°F. Remove cover and bake 15 minutes longer.

Favorite recipe from **USA Dry Pea & Lentil Council**

Ham & Macaroni Twists

Makes 4 to 6 servings

2 cups elbow macaroni or
rotini, cooked in unsalted
water and drained
1½ cups (8 ounces) cubed cooked
ham
1⅓ cups *French's®* French Fried
Onions, divided
1 package (10 ounces) frozen
broccoli spears,* thawed
and drained
1 cup milk

1 can (10¾ ounces) condensed
cream of celery soup
1 cup (4 ounces) shredded
Cheddar cheese, divided
¼ teaspoon garlic powder
¼ teaspoon pepper

*1 small head fresh broccoli (about ½ pound)
may be substituted for frozen spears. Divide
into spears and cook 3 to 4 minutes before
using.*

Preheat oven to 350°F. In 12×8-inch baking dish, combine hot macaroni, ham and ⅔ *cup* French Fried Onions. Divide broccoli spears into 6 small bunches. Arrange bunches of spears down center of dish, alternating direction of flowerets. In small bowl, combine milk, soup, ½ cup cheese and seasonings; pour over casserole. Bake, covered, at 350°F for 30 minutes or until heated through. Top with remaining ½ cup cheese and sprinkle remaining ⅔ *cup* onions down center; bake, uncovered, 5 minutes or until onions are golden brown.

Microwave Directions: *In 12×8-inch microwave-safe dish, prepare macaroni mixture and arrange broccoli spears as above. Prepare soup mixture as above; pour over casserole. Cook, covered, on HIGH 8 minutes or until broccoli is done. Rotate dish halfway through cooking time. Top with remaining cheese and onions as above; cook, uncovered, 1 minute or until cheese melts. Let stand 5 minutes.*

Cornmeal and Sausage Layered Dinner

1½ pounds BOB EVANS® Italian
   Roll Sausage
1 cup chopped onion
1 clove garlic, minced
1 (16-ounce) can diced
   tomatoes, undrained
1 (8-ounce) can tomato sauce
1 tablespoon chopped fresh
   basil *or* 1 teaspoon dried
   basil leaves

½ teaspoon ground black
   pepper
1½ cups yellow cornmeal
¾ teaspoon salt
3 cups water
1 cup grated Romano cheese

Makes 6 servings

Note:

The easiest and fastest

way to peel garlic

cloves is to trim off

the ends and crush the

cloves with the bottom

of a heavy saucepan or

the flat side of a large

knife. The peels can

then be easily

removed.

Crumble and cook sausage in large skillet until browned. Remove sausage from skillet and reserve. Pour off all but 1 tablespoon drippings. Add onion and garlic to skillet; cook until tender. Stir in tomatoes, tomato sauce, basil, pepper and sausage. Bring to a boil; reduce heat to low and simmer, uncovered, 25 minutes. Preheat oven to 375°F.

While sausage mixture is cooking, combine cornmeal, salt and water in medium saucepan. Bring to a boil, stirring constantly; cook and stir until thickened. Remove from heat; let cool slightly. Pour half of cornmeal mixture into greased 2½-quart casserole dish. Top with half of sausage mixture and sprinkle with half of cheese. Repeat with remaining cornmeal mixture, sausage mixture and cheese. Bake, uncovered, 30 minutes. Refrigerate leftovers.

Easy Lamb and Potato Bake

Makes 4 servings

Prep Time:
20 minutes

Cook Time:
35 minutes

Note:

Cornmeal, not to be confused with cornstarch, is a meal ground from dried corn kernels. There are two grades: fine, ground from white, yellow or blue corn and used in quick breads, as a coating and occasionally as a thickener; and coarse, used for polenta and for cornmeal mush.

Nonstick cooking spray
4 lamb shoulder blade chops or
   leg steaks, ¾ inch thick
   (1½ pounds), trimmed
2 tablespoons cornmeal

4 teaspoons water
1 tablespoon prepared mustard
1 package (about 5 ounces)
   scalloped potato mix
1 teaspoon caraway seeds

Spray large skillet with nonstick spray. Brown lamb over medium-high heat about 5 minutes on each side. In small bowl, combine cornmeal, water and mustard; mix well. In 8×8×2-inch baking dish, prepare scalloped potato mix according to package directions, omitting margarine and adding caraway seeds. Spread mustard mixture on surface of browned chops; place mustard-side up on top of potato mixture. Bake, uncovered, in 400°F oven about 35 minutes or until lightly browned. Remove from oven; let stand 5 minutes. Serve with steamed green vegetables or crisp green salad.

Favorite recipe from **American Lamb Council**

Sausage and Polenta Casserole

1 tablespoon olive oil
1 cup chopped mushrooms
1 small red bell pepper, cored,
   seeded and diced
1 small onion, diced

1 pound hot or mild Italian
   sausage, casings removed
1 jar (28 to 30 ounces) meatless
   pasta sauce
1 roll (16 to 18 ounces) polenta

Makes 4 servings

1. Preheat oven to 350°F.

2. Heat oil in large skillet. Add mushrooms, bell pepper and onion; cook and stir over medium heat 5 minutes or until tender. Add sausage; cook and stir until sausage is brown, breaking into small pieces with spoon. Drain. Stir in pasta sauce and simmer 5 minutes.

3. Cut polenta roll into 9 slices and arrange in greased 9-inch square casserole. Top with sausage mixture.

4. Bake for 15 minutes or until heated through.

Family-Style Frankfurters with Rice and Red Beans

Makes 6 servings

1 tablespoon vegetable oil
1 medium onion, chopped
½ medium green bell pepper, chopped
2 cloves garlic, minced
1 can (14 ounces) red kidney beans, rinsed and drained
1 can (14 ounces) Great Northern beans, rinsed and drained

½ pound beef frankfurters, cut into ¼-inch-thick pieces
1 cup uncooked instant brown rice
1 cup vegetable broth
¼ cup packed brown sugar
¼ cup ketchup
3 tablespoons dark molasses
1 tablespoon Dijon mustard

Preheat oven to 350°F. Spray 13×9-inch baking dish with nonstick cooking spray.

Heat oil in Dutch oven over medium-high heat until hot. Add onion, pepper and garlic; cook and stir 2 minutes or until onion is tender.

Add beans, frankfurters, rice, broth, sugar, ketchup, molasses and mustard to vegetables; stir to combine. Pour into prepared dish.

Cover tightly with foil and bake 30 minutes or until rice is tender.

Baked Rigatoni

1 pound dry rigatoni
4 ounces mild Italian sausage,
    casings removed, sliced
1 cup chopped onion
2 cloves garlic, minced
1 can (14.5 ounces)
    CONTADINA® Recipe Ready
    Diced Tomatoes, undrained
1 can (6 ounces) CONTADINA
    Tomato Paste

1 cup chicken broth
1 teaspoon salt
1 cup (4 ounces) shredded
    mozzarella cheese, divided
½ cup (2 ounces) shredded
    Parmesan cheese (optional)
2 tablespoons chopped fresh
    basil or 2 teaspoons dried
    basil leaves, crushed

Makes 8 servings

Prep Time:
10 minutes

Cook Time:
33 minutes

1. Cook pasta according to package directions. Drain and keep warm.

2. Meanwhile, cook sausage in large skillet for 4 to 6 minutes or until no longer pink. Remove sausage from skillet, reserving any drippings in skillet.

3. Add onion and garlic to skillet; sauté for 2 minutes. Stir in undrained tomatoes, tomato paste, broth and salt.

4. Bring to a boil. Reduce heat to low; simmer, uncovered, for 10 minutes, stirring occasionally.

5. Combine pasta, tomato mixture, sausage, ½ cup mozzarella cheese, Parmesan cheese and basil in large bowl; spoon into ungreased 13×9-inch baking dish. Sprinkle with remaining mozzarella cheese.

6. Bake in preheated 375°F oven for 10 to 15 minutes or until cheese is melted.

Zippy Pork Bake

Makes 6 (1½-cup) servings

8 ounces fusille pasta or other small pasta
1 tablespoon butter
1 teaspoon minced garlic
1 pound ground pork
2 medium zucchini, thinly sliced
1 cup fresh sliced mushrooms
2 tablespoons sliced green onion
1½ teaspoons chili powder

1 teaspoon salt
1 (4-ounce) can chopped green chilies
½ cup sour cream
1 cup shredded Mozzarella cheese, divided
Browned bread crumbs, optional
Chopped parsley for garnish

Cook pasta according to package directions; drain.

In large skillet over medium-high heat, melt butter; add garlic and sauté until slightly brown. Add pork and cook until no longer pink; about 6 minutes. Add zucchini, mushrooms and onion; cook and stir until tender. Drain.

Stir in chili powder and salt. Add chilies, sour cream, pasta and ½ cup cheese. Pour into 2½-quart baking dish coated with nonstick spray. Top with remaining cheese and bread crumbs, if desired. Bake, uncovered, in preheated 350°F oven for 20 minutes or until cheese is melted. Garnish with parsley.

Favorite recipe from **North Dakota Wheat Commission**

Reuben Casserole

1 can (10¾ ounces) condensed cream of mushroom soup, undiluted
¾ cup milk
¼ cup chopped onion
1½ teaspoons prepared mustard
1 can (16 ounces) sauerkraut, rinsed and drained
1 package (8 ounces) uncooked noodles

1 pound HILLSHIRE FARM® Polska Kielbasa, cut into ½-inch pieces
1 cup (4 ounces) shredded Swiss cheese
½ cup bread crumbs
2 tablespoons butter, melted

Preheat oven to 350°F.

Grease 13×9-inch baking dish. Combine soup, milk, onion and mustard in medium bowl. Spread sauerkraut onto bottom of prepared dish, pressing firmly. Add noodles. Spoon soup mixture evenly over noodles; cover with Polska Kielbasa. Top with cheese. Combine bread crumbs and butter in small bowl; sprinkle over cheese. Cover tightly. Bake 1 hour or until noodles are tender.

Note:

Sauerkraut, a popular German food, is chopped or shredded cabbage that is salted and fermented in its own juice. The brine preserves the cabbage and gives the sauerkraut its distinct sour flavor. It is available fresh in bags in the refrigerated section of the supermarket or in cans.

Lamb Tetrazzini

Makes 8 servings

4 tablespoons margarine or
   butter, softened, divided
1 small onion, diced (about
   ¼ cup)
¼ cup all-purpose flour
2¾ cups low-fat (1%) milk
1 (4-ounce) can sliced
   mushrooms, undrained
½ teaspoon salt

¼ teaspoon black pepper
¼ cup grated Parmesan cheese
4 slices bread
2 cups cooked cubed leg or
   shoulder fresh American
   lamb
1 (8-ounce) package linguini,
   cooked

Note:

Soften butter for easier
spreading or for use in
batters and doughs.
Place 1 stick of butter
on a microwavable
plate and heat at
LOW (30% power)
about 30 seconds or
just until softened.

Melt 2 tablespoons margarine in medium skillet; add onion and cook until tender, but not brown. Sprinkle flour over onion and stir. Add milk gradually, stirring constantly. Add mushrooms with liquid, salt and pepper. Cook over medium heat until slightly thickened; stir in cheese. Remove from heat.

Meanwhile, spread remaining 2 tablespoons margarine over bread; process briefly in food processor. Combine lamb, linguini and onion mixture. Spoon into greased 12×8-inch casserole. Top with bread crumbs. Bake in 350°F oven 25 to 30 minutes or until bubbling and slightly browned on top.

Favorite recipe from **American Lamb Council**

Rice & Sausage Casserole

1 cup uncooked rice
1 pound BOB EVANS® Zesty
    Hot or Special Seasonings
    Roll Sausage
2 tablespoons butter or
    margarine
1 cup chopped celery
1 large onion, chopped

¼ cup *each* chopped red and
    green bell peppers
1 (10½-ounce) can condensed
    cream of mushroom soup
1 cup milk
    Salt and black pepper to taste
½ cup (2 ounces) shredded
    longhorn or colby cheese

Cook rice according to package directions; transfer to large bowl. Preheat oven to 350°F. Crumble sausage into medium skillet. Cook over medium heat until lightly browned, stirring occasionally. Remove sausage to paper towels; set aside. Drain off any drippings and wipe skillet clean with paper towels. Stir sausage into cooked rice. Melt butter in same skillet over medium-high heat until hot. Add celery, onion and bell peppers; cook and stir until tender. Stir into rice and sausage mixture. Stir in soup, milk, salt and black pepper; mix well. Spoon mixture into lightly greased 2-quart baking dish. Sprinkle with cheese. Bake, uncovered, 40 minutes or until heated through. Serve hot. Refrigerate leftovers.

Lamb & Stuffing Dinner Casserole

Makes 6 servings

2 tablespoons margarine
1 cup chopped onion
1 clove garlic, minced
1 can (14 ounces) reduced-sodium chicken broth, divided
1 cup coarsely shredded carrots
¼ cup fresh parsley, minced *or* 1 tablespoon dried parsley flakes

12 ounces cooked fresh American lamb, cut into cubes *or* 1 pound ground American lamb, cooked and drained
1 (6-ounce) box herb-flavored stuffing mix
1 (8-ounce) can whole tomatoes, drained and chopped

Melt margarine over medium heat; sauté onion and garlic 1 minute. Add ¼ cup broth, carrots and parsley. Cover and cook until carrots are crisp-tender, about 5 minutes. In large bowl, lightly combine lamb and stuffing mix. Add vegetable mixture, remaining broth and tomatoes. Toss lightly until well mixed.

Spoon lamb mixture into greased 8×8×2-inch baking dish. Cover and bake at 375°F for 20 minutes or until heated through.

Favorite recipe from **American Lamb Council**

Hot Dogs with Potatoes and Kraut

¼ cup butter
2 large apples, cored and cut
   into ¼-inch rings
3½ cups undrained sauerkraut
2 cups dairy sour cream
⅓ cup grated Parmesan cheese
⅓ cup fine dry bread crumbs

1 teaspoon salt
3 medium potatoes, cooked
   and cut into ⅓-inch slices
1 pound HILLSHIRE FARM® Hot
   Dogs, halved lengthwise
   and crosswise

Melt butter in large skillet. Arrange apple rings in skillet and cook over medium heat about 8 minutes, turning apple rings once. Remove apple rings. Add sauerkraut to butter in skillet; mix well. Combine sour cream, cheese, crumbs, and salt; mix well. Make a layer of half each of the potatoes, sauerkraut, apple rings, Hot Dogs and sour cream mixture in buttered 2½-quart casserole. Repeat layer of potatoes, sauerkraut, apple rings and Hot Dogs. Dot top of casserole with remaining sour cream mixture. Bake in 325°F oven for 30 minutes or until sour cream mixture is lightly browned.

Creamy SPAM™ Broccoli Casserole

Makes 8 servings

Nonstick cooking spray
1 (7-ounce) package elbow
  macaroni
2 cups frozen cut broccoli,
  thawed and drained
1 (12-ounce) can SPAM® Lite,
  cubed
½ cup chopped red bell pepper

2 cups skim milk
2 tablespoons cornstarch
¼ teaspoon black pepper
1 cup (4 ounces) shredded
  fat-free Cheddar cheese
¾ cup soft bread crumbs
2 teaspoons margarine, melted

Note:

Red sweet bell peppers are simply green peppers that have matured and changed color. Fresh red peppers are high in vitamin C and are also a fair source of vitamin A and potassium.

Heat oven to 350°F. Spray 2-quart casserole with nonstick cooking spray. Cook macaroni according to package directions; drain. In prepared casserole, combine macaroni, broccoli, SPAM® and bell pepper. In small saucepan, stir together milk, cornstarch and black pepper until cornstarch is dissolved. Bring to a boil, stirring constantly, until thickened. Reduce heat to low. Add cheese; stir until melted. Stir sauce into SPAM™ mixture. Combine bread crumbs and margarine; sprinkle on top of casserole. Bake 40 minutes or until thoroughly heated.

Chile Relleno Casserole

12 ounces pork sausage
1 small onion, chopped
⅔ cup chunky salsa
¾ cup milk
4 eggs
¼ cup all-purpose flour
½ teaspoon LAWRY'S®
    Seasoned Pepper
¼ teaspoon LAWRY'S® Garlic
    Powder with Parsley
2 cups (8 ounces) shredded
    Monterey Jack cheese
2 cans (7 ounces each) whole
    green chiles, seeded

In medium skillet, brown pork until crumbly and well done. Add onion and cook over medium-high heat until tender; drain fat. Add salsa; reduce heat to low and cook, uncovered, until mixture thickens. In separate bowl, beat together milk, eggs, flour, Seasoned Pepper and Garlic Powder with Parsley; add cheese. In lightly greased 8×8×2-inch baking dish, layer half chiles, half pork mixture and half cheese-egg mixture; repeat layers. Bake, uncovered, in 350°F oven 35 minutes. Let stand 10 minutes before serving.

Serving Suggestion: *Serve with stuffed green bell peppers and chilled gazpacho soup.*

Cheesy Pork Chops 'n' Potatoes

Makes 4 to 6 servings

1 jar (8 ounces) pasteurized
   processed cheese spread
1 tablespoon vegetable oil
6 thin pork chops, ¼ to ½ inch
   thick
  Seasoned salt
½ cup milk
4 cups frozen cottage fries
1⅓ cups *French's®* French Fried
   Onions, divided

1 package (10 ounces) frozen
   broccoli spears,* thawed
   and drained

*1 small head fresh broccoli (about ½ pound) may be substituted for frozen spears. Divide into spears and cook 3 to 4 minutes before using.

Preheat oven to 350°F. Spoon cheese spread into 8×12-inch baking dish; place in oven just until cheese melts, about 5 minutes. Meanwhile, in large skillet, heat oil. Brown pork chops on both sides; drain. Sprinkle chops with seasoned salt; set aside. Using fork, stir milk into melted cheese until well blended. Stir cottage fries and ⅔ *cup* French Fried Onions into cheese mixture. Divide broccoli spears into 6 small bunches. Arrange bunches of spears over potato mixture with flowerets around edges of dish. Arrange chops over broccoli *stalks*. Bake, covered, at 350°F for 35 to 40 minutes or until pork chops are no longer pink. Top chops with remaining ⅔ cup onions; bake, uncovered, 5 minutes or until onions are golden brown.

Penne, Sausage & Ham Casserole

1 pound HILLSHIRE FARM®
   Smoked Sausage, cut into
   ½-inch slices
4 ounces HILLSHIRE FARM®
   Ham, cubed
2 cups milk
2 tablespoons all-purpose flour
8 ounces uncooked penne
   pasta, cooked and drained

2½ cups (10 ounces) shredded
   mozzarella cheese
⅓ cup grated Parmesan cheese
1 jar (16 ounces) prepared
   pasta sauce
⅓ cup bread crumbs

Makes 4 servings

Preheat oven to 350°F.

Lightly brown Smoked Sausage and Ham in large skillet over medium heat. Stir in milk and flour; bring to a boil, stirring constantly. Stir in pasta and cheeses. Pour sausage mixture into small casserole; pour pasta sauce over top. Bake, covered, 25 minutes. Uncover and sprinkle with bread crumbs; place under broiler to brown topping.

Note:

Mozzarella is a soft white cheese that melts easily. In southern Italy, where it originated, it is made from the milk of buffaloes. In other parts of Italy and in North America, it is made from cow's milk.

Pizza Pasta

Makes 6 servings

1 tablespoon vegetable oil
1 medium green bell pepper, chopped
1 medium onion, chopped
1 cup sliced mushrooms
½ teaspoon LAWRY'S® Garlic Powder with Parsley OR Garlic Salt
¼ cup sliced ripe olives
1 package (1.5 ounces) LAWRY'S® Original-Style Spaghetti Sauce Spices & Seasonings

1¾ cups water
1 can (6 ounces) tomato paste
10 ounces mostaccioli, cooked and drained
3 ounces thinly sliced pepperoni
¾ cup shredded mozzarella cheese

Note:

Pasta should be cooked at a fast boil. This method circulates the pasta during cooking so that the cooking results will be more consistent.

In large skillet, heat oil. Add bell pepper, onion, mushrooms and Garlic Powder with Parsley and cook over medium-high heat. Stir in olives, Spaghetti Sauce Spices & Seasonings, water and tomato paste; mix well. Bring sauce to a boil over medium-high heat; reduce heat to low and simmer, uncovered, 10 minutes. Add cooked mostaccioli and sliced pepperoni; mix well. Pour in 12×8×2-inch baking dish; top with cheese. Bake at 350°F 15 minutes until cheese is melted.

Serving Suggestion: *Serve with warm rolls or bread since this pizza doesn't have any crust.*

Mexi-Tortilla Casserole

1 tablespoon vegetable oil
1 small onion, chopped
1 pound ground pork*
1 can (14½ ounces) diced
    tomatoes, undrained
1 teaspoon dried oregano,
    crushed
¼ teaspoon ground cumin
¼ teaspoon salt
¼ teaspoon black pepper
1½ cups (6 ounces) shredded
    Pepper-Jack or taco-
    flavored cheese

2 cups tortilla chips
½ cup reduced-fat sour cream
1 can (4 ounces) diced chilies,
    drained
2 tablespoons minced cilantro

*For a vegetarian casserole, substitute
1 pound tofu crumbles for the pork.

1. Preheat oven to 350°F.

2. Heat oil in large skillet. Add onion and cook 5 minutes or until tender. Add pork and brown, stirring to separate meat. Pour off fat. Stir in tomatoes with juice, oregano, cumin, salt and pepper. Spoon into 11×7-inch casserole. Sprinkle cheese over casserole; arrange tortilla chips over cheese. Bake casserole 10 to 15 minutes or until cheese melts.

3. Combine sour cream and chilies; mix until well blended. Drop by tablespoonfuls over baked casserole. Sprinkle with cilantro.

Oven Jambalaya

Makes 8 servings

1 pound sweet Italian sausages
2 stalks celery, sliced
1 green bell pepper, diced
1 medium onion, diced
2 cloves garlic, minced
1 (28-ounce) can crushed
    tomatoes

2 cups chicken broth
1 cup long-grain rice
2 teaspoons TABASCO® brand
    Pepper Sauce
1 teaspoon salt
1 pound large shrimp, peeled
    and deveined

Note:

Jambalaya is a Creole dish that combines rice with ham, sausage, shrimp or chicken in a tomato based sauce containing onion, green pepper and seasonings. The name is thought to have come from the French word for ham, "jambon." Because jambalaya makes good use of leftovers, the ingredients vary widely from cook to cook.

Preheat oven to 400°F. Cook sausages in 12-inch skillet over medium-high heat until well browned on all sides, turning frequently. Remove sausages to plate; reserve drippings in skillet. When cool enough to handle, cut sausages into ½-inch slices. Add celery, green bell pepper, onion and garlic to same skillet; cook 3 minutes over medium heat, stirring occasionally.

Combine tomatoes, chicken broth, rice, TABASCO® Sauce, salt, sausages and vegetable mixture in 3-quart casserole. Bake 40 minutes. Stir in shrimp; cook 5 minutes or until rice is tender and shrimp are cooked.

Smoked Sausage and Sauerkraut Casserole

6 fully-cooked smoked sausage
   links, such as German or
   Polish sausage (about
   1½ pounds)
⅓ cup water
¼ cup packed brown sugar
2 tablespoons country-style
   Dijon mustard, Dijon
   mustard or German-style
   mustard

1 teaspoon caraway seed
½ teaspoon dill weed
1 jar (32 ounces) sauerkraut,
   drained
1 small green bell pepper,
   stemmed, seeded and diced
½ cup (2 ounces) shredded
   Swiss cheese

Makes 6 servings

Prep and Cook Time:
20 minutes

1. Place sausage in large skillet with water. Cover; bring to a boil over medium heat. Reduce heat to low; simmer, covered, 10 minutes. Uncover and simmer until water evaporates and sausage browns lightly.

2. While sausage is cooking, combine sugar, mustard, caraway and dill in medium saucepan; stir until blended. Add sauerkraut and bell pepper; stir until well mixed. Cook, covered, over medium heat 10 minutes or until very hot.

3. Spoon sauerkraut into microwavable 2- to 3-quart casserole; sprinkle with cheese. Place sausage on sauerkraut; cover. Microwave at HIGH 30 seconds or until cheese melts.

Spaghetti Bake

Makes 4 servings

1 pound BOB EVANS® Dinner
   Link Sausage (regular or
   Italian)
1 (8-ounce) can tomato sauce
1 (6-ounce) can tomato paste
1 (4-ounce) can sliced
   mushrooms, drained
½ teaspoon salt
½ teaspoon dried basil leaves
½ teaspoon dried oregano
   leaves

6 ounces spaghetti, cooked
   according to package
   directions and drained
⅓ cup shredded mozzarella
   cheese
2 tablespoons grated Parmesan
   cheese
   Fresh basil leaves and tomato
   slices (optional)

Note:

Basil, also called sweet
basil, is a member of
the mint family. Over
150 different varieties
of basil are grown,
including less common
varieties like purple
ruffle, lemon basil and
cinnamon basil.

Preheat oven to 375°F. Cut sausage links into bite-size pieces.
Cook in medium skillet over medium heat until browned, stirring
occasionally. Drain off any drippings; set aside. Combine tomato
sauce, tomato paste, mushrooms, salt, dried basil and oregano in
large bowl. Add spaghetti and reserved sausage; mix well. Spoon
into lightly greased 1½-quart casserole dish; sprinkle with
cheeses. Bake 20 to 30 minutes or until heated through. Garnish
with fresh basil and tomato slices, if desired. Serve hot.
Refrigerate leftovers.

Finger Lickin' Chicken

CHAPTER THREE

Classic Family Lasagna

Makes 12 servings

Prep Time:
35 minutes

Cook Time:
1 hour

Note:

To chop an onion, first peel the skin. Then cut the onion in half through the root end and place one half, cut side down, on a cutting board. Cut the onion into slices perpendicular to the root end, holding the onion with your fingers to keep it together. Turn the onion half and cut it crosswise. Repeat with the remaining half.

1 package (1 pound) TYSON® Fresh Ground Chicken
1 medium onion, chopped
½ cup chopped green bell pepper (optional)
2 cloves garlic, minced
1 jar (30 ounces) spaghetti sauce
1 container (15 ounces) ricotta cheese
¾ cup grated Parmesan cheese, divided
1 egg, beaten
¼ teaspoon black pepper
9 lasagna noodles, cooked according to package directions
3½ cups (14 ounces) shredded mozzarella cheese

PREP: Preheat oven to 375°F. CLEAN: Wash hands. In large skillet, cook and stir chicken, onion, bell pepper and garlic over medium-high heat until chicken is no longer pink. Stir in sauce; heat through and set aside. In medium bowl, combine ricotta cheese, ½ cup Parmesan cheese, egg and black pepper; mix well. Spray 13×9-inch baking dish with nonstick cooking spray. Spread ⅓ cup sauce on bottom of dish. Top with 3 noodles, one-third of sauce, one-third of ricotta mixture and 1 cup mozzarella cheese. Repeat layers twice, except do not top with remaining 1½ cups mozzarella cheese. Cover tightly with foil sprayed lightly with nonstick cooking spray.

COOK: Bake 40 minutes. Remove foil. Top with remaining cheese. Bake 15 minutes or until bubbly and cheese is melted.

SERVE: Serve with a green salad and garlic bread, if desired.

CHILL: Refrigerate leftovers immediately.

Chicken and Rice Enchiladas

Makes 4 servings

1 tablespoon vegetable oil
½ cup sliced celery
½ cup sliced fresh mushrooms
¼ cup sliced green onions
¼ cup chopped red bell pepper
1 can (15 ounces) tomato sauce
½ cup water
1 teaspoon chili powder
½ teaspoon garlic powder
½ teaspoon hot pepper sauce
2 cups cooked rice
2 cups cooked chicken breast
  cubes
  Vegetable oil (optional)
12 corn tortillas
2 cups (8 ounces) shredded
  Monterey Jack cheese
½ cup sliced black olives

Heat 1 tablespoon oil in large skillet over medium-high heat until hot. Add celery, mushrooms, onions and pepper; cook and stir until tender. Stir in tomato sauce, water, chili powder, garlic powder and pepper sauce; remove from heat. Combine rice, chicken and half of sauce mixture in large bowl; set aside. Heat ¼ inch oil in medium skillet until hot. Dip tortillas, one at a time, into oil a few seconds or until softened. Drain on paper towels. Spoon heaping ¼ cup rice mixture in center of each tortilla; roll up and place, seam sides down, in greased shallow 3-quart glass baking dish. Pour remaining sauce over tortillas; sprinkle with cheese and olives. Bake, uncovered, at 350°F 25 to 30 minutes or until thoroughly heated. Garnish as desired. Serve immediately.

Favorite recipe from **USA Rice Federation**

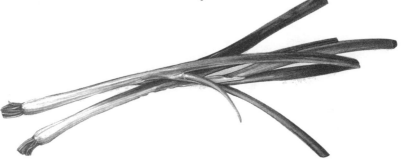

Chicken-Spinach Manicotti

Makes 4 to 8 servings

1 package (1.5 ounces)
  LAWRY'S® Original-Style
  Spaghetti Sauce Spices &
  Seasonings
1 can (1 pound 12 ounces)
  tomatoes, cut up
1 can (8 ounces) tomato sauce
¼ cup chopped green onion
8 manicotti shells
1 cup ricotta cheese

2 tablespoons milk
2 cups chopped fresh spinach
2 cups cooked, finely chopped
  chicken OR turkey
1 teaspoon LAWRY'S®
  Seasoned Pepper
¾ teaspoon LAWRY'S® Garlic
  Powder with Parsley
⅓ cup Parmesan cheese
  Chopped parsley (garnish)

In medium saucepan, combine first four ingredients. Bring to a boil over medium-high heat; reduce heat to low, cover and simmer 20 minutes, stirring occasionally. Meanwhile, cook manicotti shells according to package directions (about 7 minutes); drain. In medium bowl, combine ricotta cheese, milk, spinach, chicken, Seasoned Pepper and Garlic Powder with Parsley; mix well. Spoon mixture into shells. Pour ½ of sauce in bottom of 13×9×2-inch baking dish. Place stuffed shells over sauce; pour remaining sauce over shells. Sprinkle with Parmesan cheese. Bake, covered, in 375°F oven 30 minutes or until heated through. Garnish with chopped parsley.

Serving Suggestion: *Serve with a marinated bean salad and crusty bread.*

Substitution: *1 package (10 ounces) frozen chopped spinach, thawed and drained, can replace fresh spinach.*

Chicken Dijon & Pasta

1 (3- to 4-pound) chicken, cut
up and skinned, if desired
⅓ cup *French's®* Napa Valley
Style Dijon Mustard
⅓ cup Italian salad dressing
1 can (10¾ ounces) condensed
cream of chicken soup
4 cups hot cooked rotini pasta
(8 ounces uncooked)

1⅓ cups *French's®* French Fried
Onions, divided
1 cup diced tomatoes
1 cup diced zucchini
2 tablespoons minced parsley
or basil leaves (optional)

Makes 6 servings

Prep Time:
15 minutes

Cook Time:
about 1 hour

1. Preheat oven to 400°F. Place chicken in shallow roasting pan.
Mix mustard and dressing. Spoon half of mixture over chicken.
Bake, uncovered, 40 minutes.

2. Combine soup, *½ cup water* and remaining mustard mixture.
Toss pasta with sauce, *⅔ cup* French Fried Onions, tomatoes,
zucchini and parsley. Spoon mixture around chicken.

3. Bake, uncovered, 15 minutes or until chicken is no longer
pink in center. Sprinkle with remaining *⅔ cup* onions. Bake
1 minute or until onions are golden.

Campbell's® Chicken Asparagus Gratin

Makes 4 servings

Prep Time:
20 minutes

Cook Time:
30 minutes

1 can (10¾ ounces)
   CAMPBELL'S® Condensed
   Cream of Asparagus Soup
½ cup milk
¼ teaspoon onion powder
⅛ teaspoon pepper
3 cups hot cooked corkscrew
   macaroni (about 2½ cups
   uncooked)

1½ cups cubed cooked chicken *or*
   turkey
1½ cups cooked cut asparagus
1 cup shredded Cheddar *or*
   Swiss cheese (4 ounces)

1. In 2-quart casserole mix soup, milk, onion powder and pepper. Stir in macaroni, chicken, asparagus and ½ **cup** cheese.

2. Bake at 400°F. for 25 minutes or until hot.

3. Stir. Sprinkle remaining cheese over chicken mixture. Bake 5 minutes more or until cheese is melted.

Tip: *For 1½ cups cooked cut asparagus, cook ¾ pound fresh asparagus, trimmed and cut into 1-inch pieces or 1 package (about 9 ounces) frozen asparagus cuts.*

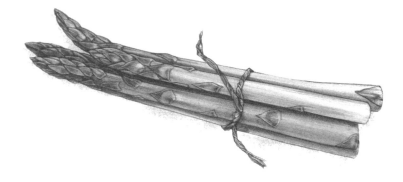

Mom's Best Chicken Tetrazzini

Makes 6 servings

8 ounces uncooked thin
  noodles or vermicelli
2 tablespoons butter
8 ounces fresh mushrooms,
  sliced
¼ cup chopped green onions
1 can (about 14 ounces) chicken
  broth
1 cup half-and-half, divided
2 tablespoons dry sherry

¼ cup all-purpose flour
½ teaspoon salt
¼ teaspoon ground nutmeg
⅛ teaspoon white pepper
1 jar (2 ounces) chopped
  pimiento, drained
½ cup (4 ounces) grated
  Parmesan cheese, divided
½ cup sour cream
2 cups cubed cooked chicken

Note:

White peppercorn is milder than black peppercorn. It is made from fully ripe pepper berries from which the outer hull has been removed. It is often used to add pepper flavor while avoiding the appearance of little black specks in light-colored dishes.

1. Preheat oven to 350°F. Cook noodles according to package directions. Drain; set aside.

2. Melt butter in large nonstick skillet over medium-high heat. Add mushrooms and onions; cook and stir until onions are tender. Add chicken broth, ½ cup half-and-half and sherry to onion mixture. Pour remaining ½ cup half-and-half into small jar with tight-fitting lid; add flour, salt, nutmeg and pepper. Shake well. Slowly stir flour mixture into skillet. Bring to a boil; cook 1 minute. Reduce heat; stir in pimiento and ¼ cup Parmesan cheese. Stir in sour cream; blend well. Add chicken and noodles; mix well.

3. Spray 1½-quart casserole with nonstick cooking spray. Spread mixture evenly into prepared casserole. Sprinkle with remaining ¼ cup Parmesan cheese. Bake 30 to 35 minutes or until hot.

Chicken and Zucchini Casserole

Makes 6 servings	

Prep Time:
10 minutes

Cook Time:
20 minutes

3 cups STOVE TOP® Chicken
   Flavor or Cornbread
   Stuffing Mix in the Canister
1¼ cups hot water
3 tablespoons margarine or
   butter, divided
¾ pound boneless skinless
   chicken breasts, cubed
2 medium zucchini, cut into
   ½-inch pieces

1½ cups (6 ounces) shredded
   Cheddar cheese
1 can (8 ounces) water
   chestnuts, drained, halved
   (optional)
½ teaspoon dried basil leaves
¼ teaspoon pepper

Microwave Directions

MIX stuffing mix, water and 2 tablespoons margarine in large bowl just until margarine is melted and Stuffing Mix Pouch is moistened.

PLACE chicken, zucchini and remaining 1 tablespoon margarine in 3-quart microwavable casserole. Cover loosely with wax paper.

MICROWAVE on HIGH 4 minutes, stirring halfway through cooking time. Stir in prepared stuffing, cheese, water chestnuts, basil and pepper until well mixed. Cover.

MICROWAVE 10 minutes, stirring halfway through cooking time. Let stand 5 minutes.

Artichoke-Olive Chicken Bake

1½ cups uncooked rotini
1 tablespoon olive oil
1 medium onion, chopped
½ green bell pepper, chopped
2 cups shredded cooked
    chicken
1 can (14½ ounces) diced
    tomatoes with Italian-style
    herbs, undrained

1 can (14 ounces) artichoke
    hearts, drained and
    quartered
1 can (6 ounces) sliced black
    olives, drained
1 teaspoon dried Italian
    seasoning
2 cups (8 ounces) shredded
    mozzarella cheese

Makes 8 servings

Preheat oven to 350°F. Spray 2-quart casserole with nonstick cooking spray.

Cook pasta according to package directions until al dente. Drain and set aside.

Meanwhile, heat oil in large deep skillet over medium heat until hot. Add onion and pepper; cook and stir 1 minute. Add chicken, tomatoes with juice, pasta, artichokes, olives and Italian seasoning; mix until combined.

Place half of chicken mixture in prepared dish; sprinkle with half of cheese. Top with remaining chicken mixture and cheese.

Bake, covered, 35 minutes or until hot and bubbly.

Note:

The literal translation of the Italian phrase *al dente* is "to the tooth." It indicates a degree of doneness when cooking pasta. Al dente pasta is slightly firm and chewy, rather than soft.

Tarragon Lemon Chicken

Makes 4 servings

¼ cup all-purpose flour
  Salt and freshly ground black
  pepper
4 boneless skinless chicken
  breast halves
4 tablespoons FILIPPO BERIO®
  Olive Oil, divided
1 large onion, chopped
1 red bell pepper, seeded and
  cut into strips
2 ribs celery, thinly sliced

1 cup chicken broth
1 cup dry white wine
1 tablespoon chopped fresh
  tarragon *or* 1 teaspoon
  dried tarragon leaves
3 cloves garlic, crushed
  Finely grated peel and juice of
  1 lemon
  Lemon slices and fresh
  tarragon sprigs (optional)

Preheat oven to 375°F. In small shallow bowl, combine flour with salt and black pepper to taste. Coat each chicken piece in flour mixture; reserve any remaining flour mixture. In large skillet, heat 2 tablespoons olive oil over medium heat until hot. Add onion, bell pepper and celery; cook and stir 5 minutes or until onion is soft. Remove onion mixture from skillet with slotted spoon; set aside.

Add remaining 2 tablespoons olive oil to skillet; heat over medium heat until hot. Add chicken; cook 5 minutes or until brown, turning occasionally. Add reserved flour mixture to skillet; mix well. Add chicken broth, wine, tarragon, garlic, lemon peel and lemon juice; bring to a boil. Return onion mixture to skillet; mix well. Transfer mixture to large casserole. Cover with foil. Bake 40 minutes or until chicken is no longer pink in center and juices run clear. Garnish with lemon slices and tarragon, if desired.

Apple Curry Chicken

2 whole chicken breasts, split,
    skinned and boned
1 cup apple juice, divided
¼ teaspoon salt
    Dash black pepper
1½ cups plain croutons
1 medium apple, chopped
1 medium onion, chopped
¼ cup raisins
2 teaspoons brown sugar
1 teaspoon curry powder
¾ teaspoon poultry seasoning
⅛ teaspoon garlic powder
2 slices apple and fresh thyme
    sprigs for garnish

Makes 4 servings

1. Preheat oven to 350°F. Lightly grease 1-quart round baking dish.

2. Arrange chicken breasts in single layer in prepared dish.

3. Combine ¼ cup apple juice, salt and pepper in small bowl. Brush juice mixture over chicken.

4. Combine croutons, apple, onion, raisins, brown sugar, curry powder, poultry seasoning and garlic powder in large bowl. Toss with remaining ¾ cup apple juice.

5. Spread crouton mixture over chicken. Cover with foil; bake 45 minutes or until chicken is tender. Garnish, if desired.

Note:

Curry powder is formed by blending together a number of spices, including turmeric, cardamom, cumin, pepper, cloves, cinnamon, nutmeg and sometimes ginger. Chilies give it heat and ground dried garlic provides a depth of taste.

Barbecue Chicken with Cornbread Topper

Makes 8 servings

1½ pounds boneless skinless
  chicken breasts and thighs
1 can (15 ounces) red beans,
  drained and rinsed
1 can (8 ounces) tomato sauce
1 cup chopped green bell
  pepper

½ cup barbecue sauce
1 package (6.5 ounces)
  cornbread mix
Ingredients to prepare
  cornbread mix

Note:

Store unwashed sweet bell peppers in the refrigerator. Green peppers begin to lose their crispness after three to four days, red peppers are even more perishable.

1. Cut chicken into ¾-inch cubes. Heat nonstick skillet over medium heat. Add chicken; cook and stir 5 minutes or until cooked through.

2. Combine chicken, beans, tomato sauce, bell pepper and barbecue sauce in 8-inch microwavable ovenproof dish.

3. Preheat oven to 375°F. Loosely cover chicken mixture with plastic wrap or waxed paper. Microwave at MEDIUM-HIGH (70% power) 8 minutes or until heated through, stirring after 4 minutes.

4. While chicken mixture is heating, prepare cornbread mix according to package directions. Spoon batter over chicken mixture. Bake 15 to 18 minutes or until toothpick inserted in center of cornbread layer comes out clean.

Rocky Mountain Hash with Smoked Chicken

1½ pounds Colorado russet
    variety potatoes, unpeeled
2 tablespoons olive oil, divided
1 teaspoon salt, divided
¼ teaspoon black pepper
    Nonstick cooking spray
2 cups chopped red or yellow
    onions
2 tablespoons bottled minced
    garlic

2 cups diced red bell pepper
⅛ to ¼ teaspoon cayenne
    pepper
2 cups shredded smoked
    chicken or turkey
1 can (11 ounces) whole kernel
    corn

Makes 6 to 8 servings

Cut potatoes into ½- to ¾-inch chunks. Toss with 1 tablespoon olive oil, ½ teaspoon salt and black pepper. Spray 15×10×1-inch baking pan with nonstick cooking spray. Arrange potato chunks in single layer; roast at 450°F for 20 to 30 minutes or until tender, stirring and tossing occasionally. In large skillet heat remaining 1 tablespoon oil. Sauté onions and garlic until tender. Add red bell pepper, remaining ½ teaspoon salt and cayenne pepper. Cook and stir until peppers are crisp-tender. Stir in chicken, corn and potatoes. Cook and stir until heated through.

Favorite recipe from **Colorado Potato Administrative Committee**

Note:

Red (cayenne) pepper, chili pepper, bell pepper and paprika are all fruits from the capsicum family and are not related to black and white pepper.

Chicken Mexicana Casserole

Makes 10 to 12 servings

10 boneless, skinless chicken breast halves (about 2½ pounds), cut into 1-inch cubes

2 packages (1.0 ounce each) LAWRY'S® Taco Spices & Seasonings

2 cans (14½ ounces each) whole tomatoes, undrained, cut up

3 cups (12 ounces) shredded sharp cheddar cheese, divided

1 can (7 ounces) diced green chiles, undrained

1 can (12 ounces) whole kernel corn, drained

1 package (8¼ ounces) corn muffin mix

2 eggs

¼ cup sour cream

In large bowl, toss chicken cubes with Taco Spices & Seasonings and tomatoes; mix well. Add 1 cup cheese. Spread mixture evenly into 13×9×2-inch baking dish. Spoon chiles over chicken mixture; sprinkle with remaining cheese. Set aside. In medium bowl, combine remaining ingredients; mix well. Drop by rounded spoonfuls on top of casserole, spacing evenly. Bake in 350°F oven 50 to 60 minutes or until top is lightly browned and sauce is bubbly. Remove from oven and let stand about 20 minutes before serving.

Serving Suggestion: *Serve with black beans and sliced tomatoes.*

Chicken in French Onion Sauce

Makes 4 servings

1 package (10 ounces) frozen
    baby carrots, thawed and
    drained or 4 medium
    carrots, cut into strips
    (about 2 cups)
2 cups sliced mushrooms
½ cup thinly sliced celery
1⅓ cups *French's®* French Fried
    Onions, divided

4 chicken breast halves,
    skinned and boned
½ cup white wine
¾ cup prepared chicken
    bouillon
½ teaspoon garlic salt
½ teaspoon pepper
    Paprika

Preheat oven to 375°F. In 12×8-inch baking dish, combine vegetables and ⅔ *cup* French Fried Onions. Arrange chicken breasts on vegetables. In small bowl, combine wine, bouillon, garlic salt and pepper; pour over chicken and vegetables. Sprinkle chicken with paprika. Bake, covered, at 375°F for 35 minutes or until chicken is done. Baste chicken with wine sauce and top with remaining ⅔ *cup* onions; bake, uncovered, 3 minutes or until onions are golden brown.

<u>Microwave Directions:</u> *In 12×8-inch microwave-safe dish, combine vegetables and ⅔ cup onions. Arrange chicken breasts, skinned side down, along sides of dish. Prepare wine mixture as above, except reduce bouillon to ⅓ cup; pour over chicken and vegetables. Cook, covered, on HIGH 6 minutes. Turn chicken breasts over and sprinkle with paprika. Stir vegetables and rotate dish. Cook, covered, 7 to 9 minutes or until chicken is done. Baste chicken with wine sauce and top with remaining ⅔ cup onions; cook, uncovered, 1 minute. Let stand 5 minutes.*

Chicken 'n' Rice Filled Cabbage Rolls

Makes 4 to 6 servings

12 large green whole cabbage
  leaves
¾ medium onion, chopped
1 clove garlic, minced
1 tablespoon vegetable oil
1 can (15 ounces) tomato sauce
½ cup water
3 tablespoons packed light
  brown sugar

3 tablespoons fresh lemon juice
⅛ teaspoon ground allspice
3 cups finely chopped cooked
  chicken
1 cup cooked white rice
1 egg
¾ teaspoon salt
⅛ teaspoon black pepper

Note:

Brown sugar is a mixture of granulated sugar and molasses. Light brown sugar has a milder flavor and lighter color than the dark variety. Dark brown sugar has more molasses added and will actually give foods a darker color.

1. Bring 6 cups water to a boil in Dutch oven over high heat. Add cabbage leaves and reduce heat to low. Simmer, covered, 10 to 12 minutes or until cabbage leaves are tender. Drain; rinse under cold running water.

2. Cook and stir onion and garlic in oil in large skillet over medium heat 6 to 8 minutes or until tender. Remove ½ cup onion mixture. Add tomato sauce, water, brown sugar, lemon juice and allspice to onion mixture in skillet. Cook, uncovered, 10 minutes, stirring occasionally.

3. Combine reserved onion mixture, chicken, rice, egg, salt and black pepper; mix well. Place about ⅓ cup mixture in center of each cabbage leaf. Fold sides over filling; roll up.

4. Preheat oven to 350°F. Spread ½ cup tomato sauce over bottom of 13×9-inch baking dish. Arrange cabbage rolls, seam side down, over sauce. Spoon remaining sauce evenly over cabbage rolls; cover. Bake 1 hour and 15 minutes or until very tender.

Sonoma® Pot Pie

2 cans (10½ ounces each)
    chicken gravy
3 cups cooked chicken or
    turkey chunks
1 package (10 ounces) frozen
    mixed vegetables
⅔ cup SONOMA® Dried Tomato
    Bits
1 can (3 ounces drained weight)
    sliced mushrooms

¼ cup water
1½ teaspoons dried thyme
    leaves, divided
2¼ cups reduced-fat buttermilk
    baking mix
¾ cup plus 2 tablespoons lowfat
    milk

Makes 4 to 6 servings

Preheat oven to 450°F. In 3-quart saucepan combine gravy,
chicken, vegetables, tomato bits, mushrooms, water and
½ teaspoon thyme. Stir occasionally over medium-low heat until
mixture comes to a boil. Meanwhile, in large bowl combine
baking mix, milk and remaining 1 teaspoon thyme; mix just to
blend thoroughly. Pour chicken mixture into shallow 2-quart
casserole or 9-inch square baking dish. Top with large spoonfuls
baking mix mixture, making equal-sized mounds. Place casserole
on baking sheet and bake about 20 minutes or until chicken
mixture is bubbly and topping is golden brown.

Cheesy Chicken Roll-Ups

Makes 6 servings

¼ cup butter
1 medium onion, finely chopped
4 ounces fresh mushrooms, sliced
3 chicken breast halves, skinned, boned, cut into bite-size pieces
¾ cup dry white wine
½ teaspoon dried tarragon leaves
½ teaspoon salt
½ teaspoon black pepper
6 lasagna noodles, cooked, drained, each cut lengthwise into halves

1 package (8 ounces) cream cheese, cubed, softened
½ cup heavy cream
½ cup dairy sour cream
1½ cups (6 ounces) shredded Swiss cheese, divided
1 cup (4 ounces) shredded Muenster cheese, divided
3 tablespoons toasted sliced almonds
Chopped fresh parsley, optional

Preheat oven to 325°F. Melt butter in large skillet over medium-high heat. Add onion and mushrooms; cook and stir until tender. Add chicken, wine, tarragon, salt and pepper; bring to a boil. Reduce heat to low; simmer 10 minutes, stirring occasionally.

Form each lasagna noodle half into circle; place in 13×9-inch baking dish. Using slotted spoon, fill center of lasagna rings with chicken mixture. To chicken mixture remaining in skillet, add cream cheese, heavy cream, sour cream, ¾ cup Swiss cheese and ½ cup Muenster cheese. Heat until cheeses melt, stirring frequently. (Do not boil.) Pour over lasagna rings. Sprinkle with remaining cheeses and almonds. Bake 35 minutes or until hot and bubbly; sprinkle with parsley. Garnish as desired.

Favorite recipe from **Southeast United Dairy Industry Association, Inc.**

Chicken Normandy Style

2 tablespoons butter, divided
3 cups peeled, thinly sliced
  sweet apples, such as Fuji
  or Braeburn (about
  3 apples)
1 pound ground chicken
¼ cup apple brandy or apple
  juice
2 teaspoons fresh minced sage
  or ½ teaspoon dried sage

¼ cup finely chopped green
  onion, green part only
1 can (10¾ ounces) cream of
  chicken soup
¼ teaspoon black pepper
1 package (12 ounces) egg
  noodles, cooked and
  drained

Makes 4 servings

Note:

**When purchasing fresh
herbs, look for brightly
colored, fresh-looking
leaves without any
brown spots or signs
of wilting.**

1. Preheat oven to 350°F.

2. Melt 1 tablespoon butter in 12-inch nonstick skillet. Add apple slices; cook and stir over medium heat 7 to 10 minutes or until tender. Remove apple slices from skillet.

3. Add ground chicken to same skillet; cook and stir over medium heat until brown, breaking up with spoon. Stir in apple brandy and cook 2 minutes. Stir in sage, green onion, soup, pepper and apple slices. Simmer 5 minutes.

4. Toss noodles with remaining 1 tablespoon butter. Spoon into well-greased 9-inch square pan. Top with chicken mixture. Bake for 15 minutes or until hot.

Tip: *Substitute ground turkey, tofu crumbles or ground pork for chicken if desired.*

Campbell's® Country Chicken Casserole

Makes 5 servings

Prep Time:
20 minutes

Cook Time:
25 minutes

1 can (10¾ ounces)
    CAMPBELL'S® Condensed
    Cream of Celery Soup *or*
    98% Fat Free Cream of
    Celery Soup
1 can (10¾ ounces)
    CAMPBELL'S® Condensed
    Cream of Potato Soup
1 cup milk
¼ teaspoon dried thyme leaves,
    crushed

⅛ teaspoon pepper
4 cups cooked cut-up
    vegetables*
2 cups cubed cooked chicken *or*
    turkey
4 cups prepared PEPPERIDGE
    FARM® Herb Seasoned
    Stuffing

* Use a combination of green beans cut into 1-inch pieces and sliced carrots.

1. In 3-quart shallow baking dish mix soups, milk, thyme, pepper, vegetables and chicken. Spoon stuffing over chicken mixture.

2. Bake at 400°F. for 25 minutes or until hot.

Tip: *For prepared stuffing, heat 1¼ cups water and 4 tablespoons margarine **or** butter to a boil. Remove from heat and add 4 cups PEPPERIDGE FARM® Herb Seasoned Stuffing. Mix lightly.*

Indian-Spiced Chicken with Wild Rice

Makes 4 servings

½ teaspoon salt
½ teaspoon ground cumin
½ teaspoon black pepper
¼ teaspoon ground cinnamon
¼ teaspoon ground turmeric
4 boneless skinless chicken
    breast halves (about
    1 pound)
2 tablespoons olive oil
2 carrots, sliced

1 red bell pepper, chopped
1 rib celery, chopped
2 cloves garlic, minced
1 package (6 ounces) long grain
    and wild rice mix
2 cups reduced-sodium chicken
    broth
1 cup raisins
¼ cup sliced almonds

Combine salt, cumin, black pepper, cinnamon and turmeric in small bowl. Rub spice mixture on both sides of chicken. Place chicken on plate; cover and refrigerate 30 minutes.

Preheat oven to 350°F. Spray 13×9-inch baking dish with nonstick cooking spray.

Heat oil in large skillet over medium-high heat until hot. Add chicken; cook 2 minutes per side or until browned. Remove chicken; set aside.

Place carrots, bell pepper, celery and garlic in same skillet. Cook and stir 2 minutes. Add rice; cook 5 minutes, stirring frequently. Add seasoning packet from rice mix and broth; bring to a boil over high heat. Remove from heat; stir in raisins. Pour into prepared dish. Place chicken on rice mixture; sprinkle with almonds.

Cover tightly with foil and bake 35 minutes or until chicken is no longer pink in center and rice is tender.

Hearty Chicken Bake

Makes 4 to 6 servings

3 cups hot mashed potatoes
1 cup (4 ounces) shredded
    Cheddar cheese, divided
1⅓ cups *French's®* French Fried
    Onions, divided
1½ cups (7 ounces) cubed cooked
    chicken
1 package (10 ounces) frozen
    mixed vegetables, thawed
    and drained

1 can (10¾ ounces) condensed
    cream of chicken soup
¼ cup milk
½ teaspoon ground mustard
¼ teaspoon garlic powder
¼ teaspoon pepper

Note:

To mash is to crush a food into a soft, smooth mixture, as in mashed potatoes or bananas. For best results, make sure that potatoes are fully cooked so they are soft enough to become completely smooth.

Preheat oven to 375°F. In medium bowl, combine mashed potatoes, ½ cup cheese and ⅔ *cup* French Fried Onions; mix thoroughly. Spoon potato mixture into greased 1½-quart casserole. Using back of spoon, spread potatoes across bottom and up sides of dish to form a shell. In large bowl, combine chicken, mixed vegetables, soup, milk and seasonings; pour into potato shell. Bake, uncovered, at 375°F for 30 minutes or until heated through. Top with remaining ½ cup cheese and ⅔ *cup* onions; bake, uncovered, 3 minutes or until onions are golden brown. Let stand 5 minutes before serving.

Creamy Chicken and Pasta with Spinach

6 ounces uncooked egg
    noodles
1 tablespoon olive oil
¼ cup chopped onion
¼ cup chopped red bell pepper
1 package (10 ounces) frozen
    spinach, thawed and
    drained
2 boneless skinless chicken
    breasts (¾ pound), cooked
    and cut into 1-inch pieces

1 can (4 ounces) sliced
    mushrooms, drained
2 cups (8 ounces) shredded
    Swiss cheese
1 container (8 ounces) sour
    cream
¾ cup half-and-half
2 eggs, lightly beaten
½ teaspoon salt
    Red onion and fresh spinach
    for garnish

1. Preheat oven to 350°F. Prepare noodles according to package directions; set aside. Spray 13×9-inch baking dish with nonstick cooking spray; set aside.

2. Heat oil in large skillet over medium-high heat. Add onion and bell pepper; cook and stir 2 minutes or until onion is tender. Add spinach, chicken, mushrooms and cooked noodles; stir to combine.

3. Combine cheese, sour cream, half-and-half, eggs and salt in medium bowl; blend well.

4. Add cheese mixture to chicken mixture; stir to combine. Pour into prepared baking dish. Bake, covered, 30 to 35 minutes or until heated through. Garnish with red onion and fresh spinach, if desired.

Chicken and Veggie Lasagna

Makes 12 servings

Tomato-Herb Sauce (recipe
follows)
Nonstick olive oil cooking
spray
1½ cups thinly sliced zucchini
1 cup thinly sliced carrots
3 cups torn fresh spinach
leaves
½ teaspoon salt

1 package (15 ounces) fat-free
ricotta cheese
½ cup grated Parmesan cheese
9 lasagna noodles, cooked and
drained
2 cups (8 ounces) reduced-fat
shredded mozzarella
cheese

Note:

When pasta will be added to a casserole, it's very important not to overcook it in the first place. Don't necessarily trust the cooking times printed on the package. They sometimes produce limp, soggy noodles. The best way to test pasta is to remove a piece and taste it. It should still be a bit firm, but not chalky or hard in the middle.

1. Prepare Tomato-Herb Sauce.

2. Preheat oven to 350°F. Spray large nonstick skillet with cooking spray; heat over medium heat until hot. Add zucchini and carrots; cook and stir about 5 minutes or until almost tender. Remove from heat; stir in spinach and salt.

3. Combine ricotta and Parmesan cheese in small bowl. Spread 1⅔ cups Tomato-Herb Sauce on bottom of 13×9-inch baking pan. Top with 3 noodles. Spoon half of ricotta cheese mixture over noodles; spread lightly with spatula. Spoon half of zucchini mixture over ricotta cheese mixture; sprinkle with 1 cup mozzarella cheese. Repeat layers; place remaining 3 noodles on top.

4. Spread remaining Tomato-Herb Sauce over noodles. Cover with aluminum foil; bake 1 hour or until sauce is bubbly. Let stand 5 to 10 minutes; cut into rectangles. Garnish as desired.

Tomato-Herb Sauce

Nonstick olive oil cooking
  spray
1½ cups chopped onions (about
  2 medium)
4 cloves garlic, minced
1 tablespoon dried basil leaves
1 teaspoon dried oregano
  leaves
½ teaspoon dried tarragon
  leaves
¼ teaspoon dried thyme leaves

2½ pounds ripe tomatoes, peeled
  and cut into wedges
1 pound ground chicken,
  cooked, crumbled and
  drained
¾ cup water
¼ cup no-salt-added tomato
  paste
½ teaspoon salt
½ teaspoon black pepper

1. Spray large nonstick skillet with cooking spray; heat over medium heat until hot. Add onions, garlic, basil, oregano, tarragon and thyme; cook and stir about 5 minutes or until onions are tender.

2. Add tomatoes, chicken, water and tomato paste; heat to a boil. Reduce heat to low and simmer, uncovered, about 20 minutes or until sauce is reduced to 5 cups. Stir in salt and pepper.

Makes 5 cups

Chicken Fajita Casserole

Makes 4 servings

Prep Time:
10 minutes

Cook Time:
50 minutes

8 TYSON® Fresh Chicken Breast Tenders or Individually Fresh Frozen® Boneless, Skinless Chicken Tenderloins
1 box UNCLE BEN'S CHEF'S RECIPE® Traditional Red Beans & Rice
1 can (4 ounces) sliced black olives, drained

1 can (4 ounces) diced green chilies, drained
2 cups boiling water
1 can (15 ounces) diced tomatoes
1 cup (4 ounces) shredded Monterey Jack cheese
1 cup crushed tortilla chips

PREP: Preheat oven to 350°F. CLEAN: Wash hands. Remove protective ice glaze from frozen chicken by holding under cool running water 1 to 2 minutes. Place red beans and rice (do not include seasoning packet) in 13×9-inch baking dish; top with olives and chilies. Place chicken in baking dish. CLEAN: Wash hands. In medium bowl, combine boiling water, tomatoes and contents of rice seasoning packet. Pour over chicken mixture.

COOK: Cover and bake 45 minutes. Remove cover; sprinkle with cheese and tortilla chips. Bake 5 minutes or until rice is cooked and internal juices of chicken run clear. (Or insert instant-read meat thermometer in thickest part of chicken. Temperature should read 170°F.)

SERVE: Serve with a tossed salad and lemon sherbet, if desired.

CHILL: Refrigerate leftovers immediately.

Herbed Chicken and Potatoes

2 medium all-purpose potatoes, thinly sliced (about 1 pound)
4 bone-in chicken breast halves (about 2 pounds)*
1 envelope LIPTON® RECIPE SECRETS® Savory Herb with Garlic Soup Mix

⅓ cup water
1 tablespoon BERTOLLI® Olive Oil

*Substitution: Use 1 (2½- to 3-pound) chicken, cut into serving pieces.

Makes 4 servings

1. Preheat oven to 425°F. In 13×9-inch baking or roasting pan, add potatoes; arrange chicken over potatoes.

2. Pour soup mix blended with water and oil over chicken and potatoes.

3. Bake uncovered 40 minutes or until chicken is thoroughly cooked and potatoes are tender.

Poultry Pointers

Fresh, raw chicken can be stored in its original wrap for up to two days in the refrigerator. If you are not using it within two days, freeze it immediately. You can freeze chicken in the original packaging for up to two months. If you plan to freeze it longer, double-wrap or rewrap with freezer paper, foil or plastic wrap. You can freeze well-wrapped chicken for up to nine months. When freezing whole chickens, first remove and rinse giblets (if any) and then pat the chicken dry with paper towels. Trim away any excess fat. Tightly wrap, label, date and freeze both chicken and giblets in separate heavy-duty plastic, paper or foil wraps.

Always thaw chicken in the refrigerator or microwave. A general guideline is to allow 24 hours thawing time for a 5-pound whole chicken or about 5 hours per pound of chicken pieces. Never thaw chicken at room temperature because this practice promotes bacterial growth.

Once cooked, you can refrigerate leftover chicken for up to three days.

Chicken Tetrazzini

Makes 6 servings

Prep Time:
20 minutes

Bake Time:
30 minutes

½ cup chopped onion
½ cup chopped celery
¼ cup (½ stick) butter or
  margarine
1 can (13¾ ounces) chicken
  broth
1 package (8 ounces)
  PHILADELPHIA® Cream
  Cheese, cubed

¾ cup KRAFT® 100% Grated
  Parmesan Cheese, divided
1 package (7 ounces) spaghetti,
  cooked, drained
1 jar (6 ounces) whole
  mushrooms, drained
1 cup chopped cooked chicken
  or turkey

Note:

Broth is a thin, clear liquid made from cooking meat, poultry or vegetables in water. Canned chicken, beef and vegetable broths are an acceptable substitute for homemade. They tend to be salty, so do not add salt to recipes using them until the cooking is complete.

COOK and stir onion and celery in butter in large skillet on medium heat until tender. Add broth, cream cheese and ½ cup of the Parmesan cheese; cook on low heat until cream cheese is melted, stirring occasionally.

ADD all remaining ingredients except remaining Parmesan cheese; mix lightly. Spoon into 12×8-inch baking dish; sprinkle with remaining ¼ cup Parmesan cheese.

BAKE at 350°F for 30 minutes.

Chicken-Asparagus Casserole

Makes 12 servings

2 teaspoons vegetable oil
1 cup seeded and chopped
    green and/or red bell
    peppers
1 medium onion, chopped
2 cloves garlic, minced
1 can (10¾ ounces) condensed
    cream of asparagus soup
1 container (8 ounces) ricotta
    cheese
2 cups (8 ounces) shredded
    Cheddar cheese, divided

2 eggs
1½ cups chopped cooked chicken
1 package (10 ounces) frozen
    chopped asparagus,*
    thawed and drained
8 ounces egg noodles, cooked
    Black pepper (optional)

*Or, substitute ½ pound fresh asparagus cut into ½-inch pieces. Bring 6 cups water to a boil over high heat in large saucepan. Add fresh asparagus. Reduce heat to medium. Cover and cook 5 to 8 minutes or until crisp-tender. Drain.

1. Preheat oven to 350°F. Grease 13×9-inch casserole; set aside.

2. Heat oil in small skillet over medium heat. Add bell peppers, onion and garlic; cook and stir until vegetables are crisp-tender.

3. Mix soup, ricotta cheese, 1 cup Cheddar cheese and eggs in large bowl until well blended. Add onion mixture, chicken, asparagus and noodles; mix well. Season with pepper, if desired.

4. Spread mixture evenly in prepared casserole. Top with remaining 1 cup Cheddar cheese.

5. Bake 30 minutes or until center is set and cheese is bubbly. Let stand 5 minutes before serving. Garnish as desired.

Moroccan Chicken, Apricot & Almond Casserole

Makes 4 to 6 servings

1 pound ground chicken*
¾ teaspoon salt, divided
¼ teaspoon ground cinnamon
¼ teaspoon black pepper
1 tablespoon olive oil
1 small onion, peeled and
    chopped
1 cup sliced dried apricots
½ teaspoon red pepper flakes
½ teaspoon ground ginger
1 can (28 ounces) diced
    tomatoes, undrained

1 can (10¾ ounces) chicken
    broth
½ cup water
1 cup large-pearl couscous**
¼ cup sliced almonds, toasted

*Substitute ground turkey or lamb if desired.

**Large-pearl couscous, which is the size of barley, is available in many supermarkets. If it is not available, substitute regular small-grain couscous.

Note:

Couscous, or semolina, is coarsely ground durum wheat. It is a staple in North African cuisines. Similar in texture and flavor to rice, it has the shape of very tiny beads. Most of the couscous found in the United States is very fast cooking as it is precooked or instant.

1. Preheat oven to 325°F.

2. Combine ground chicken, ½ teaspoon salt, cinnamon and pepper in medium bowl. Shape into 1-inch balls. Heat oil in large skillet. Add chicken meatballs and brown on all sides. Remove to a plate. Add onion and apricots to skillet. Cook 5 minutes over medium heat. Stir in remaining ¼ teaspoon salt, red pepper flakes, ginger and tomatoes with juice. Simmer 5 minutes.

3. Meanwhile, bring chicken broth and water to a boil in small saucepan. Stir in pearl couscous.*** Reduce heat; cover and simmer 10 minutes or until couscous is tender and almost all liquid has been absorbed. Drain if necessary.

4. Spoon couscous into greased 11×7-inch casserole dish. Top with chicken meatballs; spoon tomato mixture over meatballs. Bake 20 minutes or until chicken meatballs are no longer pink in centers. Sprinkle with almonds.

***To cook small-grain couscous follow package directions using 1 cup chicken broth in place of water. Remove from heat and let stand 5 minutes or until all liquid is absorbed. Fluff with a fork.

"Wildly" Delicious Casserole

Makes 6 to 8 servings

1 package (14 ounces) ground chicken
1 package (14 ounces) frozen broccoli with red peppers
2 cups cooked wild rice
1 can (10¾ ounces) condensed cream of chicken soup
½ cup mayonnaise
½ cup plain yogurt
1 teaspoon lemon juice
½ teaspoon curry powder
¼ cup dry bread crumbs
3 to 4 slices process American cheese, cut in half diagonally

Preheat oven to 375°F. Grease 8-inch square casserole; set aside. In large skillet, cook chicken until no longer pink. Drain; set aside. Cook broccoli and peppers according to package directions; set aside. In large bowl, combine rice, soup, mayonnaise, yogurt, lemon juice and curry. Stir in chicken and broccoli and peppers. Pour into prepared casserole; sprinkle with bread crumbs. Bake 45 to 55 minutes. During last 5 minutes of baking, arrange cheese slices on top of casserole. Remove from oven; let stand 5 minutes.

Favorite recipe from **Minnesota Cultivated Wild Rice Council**

Campbell's® Asian Chicken & Rice Bake

Makes 4 servings

Prep Time:
5 minutes

Cook Time:
45 minutes

¾ cup *uncooked* regular white rice
4 skinless, boneless chicken breast halves (about 1 pound)
1 can (10¾ ounces) CAMPBELL'S® Condensed Golden Mushroom Soup

¾ cup water
2 tablespoons soy sauce
2 tablespoons cider vinegar
2 tablespoons honey
1 teaspoon garlic powder
Paprika

1. Spread rice in 2-quart shallow baking dish. Place chicken on rice.

2. Mix soup, water, soy sauce, vinegar, honey and garlic powder. Pour over chicken. Sprinkle with paprika. **Cover.**

3. Bake at 375°F. for 45 minutes or until chicken is no longer pink and rice is done.

Exotic Apple-Chicken Bake

Makes 4 to 6 servings

1 cup butter, divided
2 Washington Winesap apples,
   cored and diced
1 large onion, diced
½ cup raisins
1 cup walnuts or almonds,
   coarsely chopped
1 can (16 ounces) apricot halves
1 cup bread crumbs
1 teaspoon salt

½ teaspoon *each* ground
   nutmeg, coriander, cloves
   and cinnamon
2 to 3 whole chicken breasts,
   split
Flour
Salt and pepper
Washington Winesap apple
   wedges (optional)

Melt ½ cup butter in skillet. Add diced apples and onion; cook until onion is transparent. Mix in raisins and nuts. Drain apricots, reserving syrup. Add apricots to apple mixture with bread crumbs and seasonings; blend well. Melt remaining ½ cup butter in second skillet. Roll chicken breasts in flour then brown in butter. Spread apple mixture in baking dish; place chicken breasts, skin side up, on top. Salt and pepper lightly and cover with foil. Bake at 350°F. 20 minutes; remove foil. Bake at 250°F. 15 to 20 minutes longer. Garnish with apple wedges.

Favorite recipe from **Washington Apple Commission**

Snappy Pea and Chicken Pot Pie

Makes 4 servings

2½ cups chicken broth
1 medium-size baking potato, peeled and cut into ½-inch chunks
1½ cups sliced carrots (½-inch slices)
1 cup frozen pearl onions
½ teaspoon dried rosemary
½ teaspoon TABASCO® brand Pepper Sauce
¼ teaspoon salt
1 medium red bell pepper, coarsely diced

4 ounces (about 1 cup) sugar-snap peas, trimmed and halved lengthwise
3 tablespoons butter or margarine
¼ cup flour
8 ounces cooked chicken-breast meat, cut in 3×1-inch strips
1 sheet frozen puff pastry, thawed
1 egg, beaten with 1 teaspoon water

In large heavy saucepan bring chicken broth to a boil over high heat. Add potato, carrots, pearl onions, rosemary, TABASCO® Sauce and salt. Reduce heat to medium; cover and simmer 8 to 10 minutes, until vegetables are tender. Add bell pepper and sugar-snap peas; boil 30 seconds, just until peas turn bright green. Drain vegetables, reserving chicken broth; set aside.

Melt butter in saucepan over low heat. Stir in flour and cook 3 to 4 minutes, stirring constantly. Pour in 2 cups of the reserved chicken broth and whisk until smooth. Bring to a boil over medium heat, stirring constantly. Reduce heat to low and simmer 5 minutes, stirring frequently, until thickened and bubbly.

Put chicken strips in bottoms of four lightly buttered ramekins or soufflé dishes. Top chicken with vegetables and sauce.

Heat oven to 475°F.

Unfold puff pastry on floured surface according to package directions. Cut pastry into four rectangles. Brush outside rims of ramekins with some of the beaten egg mixture. Place pastry rectangle over each ramekin and press firmly around edges to seal. Trim dough and flute edges. Brush tops with remaining beaten egg mixture.

Place ramekins on baking sheet and bake 10 to 12 minutes, until pastry is puffed and well browned. Serve at once.

Spicy Chicken & Rice Bake

Makes 4 servings

- 4 boneless, skinless chicken breast halves (about 1 pound)
- 1 jar (1 pound 10 ounces) RAGÚ® Robusto! Pasta Sauce
- 2 cups water
- ⅔ cup uncooked white rice
- ½ cup sliced pitted ripe olives
- 1 tablespoon capers, drained and chopped
- 1 teaspoon salt
- ½ teaspoon ground black pepper
- ¼ teaspoon dried oregano leaves, crushed
- ⅛ teaspoon crushed red pepper flakes

Preheat oven to 375°F. In 13×9-inch casserole, combine all ingredients. Bake uncovered 40 minutes or until rice is tender and chicken is thoroughly cooked.

Mustard Chicken & Vegetables

Makes 4 to 6 servings

Note:

Thoroughly wash cutting surfaces, utensils and your hands with hot soapy water after coming in contact with uncooked chicken. This eliminates the risk of contaminating other foods with the salmonella bacteria that is often present in raw chicken. Salmonella is killed during cooking.

¼ cup *French's®* Napa Valley Style Dijon Mustard or Classic Yellow® Mustard
¼ cup vegetable oil
1 tablespoon red wine vinegar
½ teaspoon dried oregano, crumbled
¼ teaspoon pepper
¼ teaspoon salt
2 pounds chicken pieces, fat trimmed
2 cups (8 ounces) fusilli or rotini, cooked in unsalted water and drained

1 can (10¾ ounces) condensed cream of chicken soup
1 cup yellow squash, cut into 1-inch chunks
1 cup zucchini, cut into 1-inch chunks
½ cup milk
1⅓ cups *French's®* French Fried Onions, divided
1 medium tomato, cut into wedges

Preheat oven to 375°F. In large bowl, mix mustard, oil, vinegar and seasonings; mix well. Toss chicken in mustard sauce until coated. Reserve remaining mustard sauce. Arrange chicken in 13×9-inch baking dish. Bake, uncovered, at 375°F for 30 minutes. Stir hot pasta, soup, squash, milk and ⅔ *cup* French Fried Onions into remaining mustard sauce. Spoon pasta mixture into baking dish, placing it under and around chicken. Bake, uncovered, 15 to 20 minutes or until chicken is done. Top pasta mixture with tomato wedges and top chicken with remaining ⅔ *cup* onions; bake, uncovered, 3 minutes or until onions are golden brown.

Microwave Directions: *Prepare mustard sauce as above; add chicken and toss until coated. Reserve remaining mustard sauce. In 12×8-inch microwave-safe dish, arrange chicken with meatiest parts toward edges of dish. Cook, uncovered, on HIGH 10 minutes. Rearrange chicken. Prepare pasta mixture and add to chicken as above. Cook, uncovered, 15 to 17 minutes or until chicken and vegetables are done. Stir vegetables and pasta and rotate dish halfway through cooking time. Top with tomato and remaining onions as above; cook, uncovered, 1 minute. Let stand 5 minutes.*

Mexican Chicken Casserole

8 ounces elbow or small shell
   pasta
2 teaspoons olive oil
1 large carrot, grated
1 medium green bell pepper,
   finely chopped
1 tablespoon minced garlic
¾ pound chicken tenders, cut in
   ¾-inch pieces
2 teaspoons cumin

1½ teaspoons dried oregano
   leaves
½ teaspoon salt
¼ teaspoon ground red pepper
8 ounces (2 cups) shredded
   Monterey Jack cheese,
   divided
1 jar (16 ounces) tomato salsa,
   divided

Makes 4 to 6 servings

Prep and Cook Time:
20 minutes

Microwave Directions

1. Cook pasta according to package directions. While pasta is cooking, heat oil in large nonstick skillet over medium heat. Add carrot, bell pepper and garlic; cook and stir 3 minutes until vegetables are tender. Add chicken, increase heat to medium-high; cook and stir 3 to 4 minutes or until chicken is no longer pink in center. Add cumin, oregano, salt and ground red pepper; cook and stir 1 minute. Remove from heat; set aside.

2. Grease 13×9-inch microwavable dish. Drain and rinse pasta under cold running water; place in large bowl. Add chicken mixture, 1 cup cheese and 1 cup salsa. Mix well; pour into prepared dish. Top with remaining 1 cup salsa and 1 cup cheese. Cover with plastic wrap; microwave at HIGH 4 to 6 minutes, turning dish halfway through cooking time. Serve immediately.

Savory Chicken and Biscuits

Makes 4 to 6 servings

Note:

Mushrooms are like little sponges. They readily absorb liquid and become soggy if you soak them. To clean them, wipe with a damp paper towel. If mushrooms are unusually dirty and wiping isn't enough, rinse quickly under cold running water and blot dry with paper towels.

1 pound boneless, skinless chicken thighs or breasts, cut into 1-inch pieces
1 medium potato, cut into 1-inch pieces
1 medium yellow onion, cut into 1-inch pieces
8 ounces fresh mushrooms, quartered
1 cup fresh baby carrots
1 cup chopped celery
1 (14½-ounce) can chicken broth

3 cloves garlic, minced
1 teaspoon dried rosemary leaves
1 teaspoon salt
1 teaspoon black pepper
3 tablespoons cornstarch blended with ½ cup cold water
1 cup frozen peas, thawed
1 (4-ounce) jar sliced pimentos, drained
1 package BOB EVANS® Frozen Buttermilk Biscuit Dough

Preheat oven to 375°F. Combine chicken, potato, onion, mushrooms, carrots, celery, broth, garlic, rosemary, salt and pepper in large saucepan. Bring to a boil over high heat. Reduce heat to low and simmer, uncovered, 5 minutes. Stir in cornstarch mixture; cook 2 minutes. Stir in peas and pimentos; return to a boil. Transfer chicken mixture to 2-quart casserole dish; arrange frozen biscuits on top. Bake 30 to 35 minutes or until biscuits are golden brown. Refrigerate leftovers.

Sweet & Sour Chicken and Rice

1 pound chicken tenders
1 can (8 ounces) pineapple chunks, drained and juice reserved
1 cup uncooked rice
2 carrots, thinly sliced
1 green bell pepper, cut into 1-inch pieces
1 large onion, chopped
3 cloves garlic, minced
1 can (14½ ounces) reduced-sodium chicken broth

⅓ cup soy sauce
3 tablespoons sugar
3 tablespoons apple cider vinegar
1 tablespoon sesame oil
1½ teaspoons ground ginger
¼ cup chopped peanuts (optional)
Chopped fresh cilantro (optional)

Makes 6 servings

Preheat oven to 350°F. Spray 13×9-inch baking dish with nonstick cooking spray.

Combine chicken, pineapple, rice, carrots, pepper, onion and garlic in prepared dish.

Place broth, reserved pineapple juice, soy sauce, sugar, vinegar, sesame oil and ginger in small saucepan; bring to a boil over high heat. Remove from heat and pour over chicken mixture.

Cover tightly with foil and bake 40 to 50 minutes or until chicken is no longer pink in centers and rice is tender. Sprinkle with peanuts and cilantro, if desired.

Chicken Caesar Tetrazzini

Makes 4 servings

8 ounces uncooked spaghetti
2 cups shredded or cubed
cooked chicken
1 cup chicken broth
1 cup HIDDEN VALLEY® Caesar
Dressing

1 jar (4½ ounces) sliced
mushrooms, drained
½ cup grated Parmesan cheese
2 tablespoons dry bread
crumbs

Cook spaghetti according to package directions. Drain and combine with chicken, broth, dressing and mushrooms in a large mixing bowl. Place mixture in a 2-quart casserole. Mix together cheese and bread crumbs; sprinkle over spaghetti mixture. Bake at 350°F. for 25 minutes or until casserole is hot and bubbly.

Chilaquiles

Makes 6 servings

1 can (10¾ ounces) condensed
cream of chicken soup
½ cup mild green chili salsa
1 can (4 ounces) diced green
chilies, undrained
8 cups taco chips
2 to 3 cups shredded cooked
chicken or turkey

2 cups (8 ounces) shredded
Cheddar cheese
Sliced pitted black olives for
garnish
Cilantro sprigs for garnish

Preheat oven to 350°F. Combine soup and salsa in medium bowl; stir in green chilies. Place ⅓ of chips in 2- to 2½-quart casserole; top with ⅓ of chicken. Spread ⅓ of soup mixture over chicken; sprinkle with ⅓ of cheese. Repeat layers. Bake, uncovered, 15 minutes or until casserole is heated through and cheese is melted. Garnish with olives and cilantro.

Pizza Chicken Bake

Makes 4 servings

3½ cups uncooked bow tie pasta
1 tablespoon vegetable oil
1 cup sliced mushrooms
1 jar (26 ounces) herb-flavored spaghetti sauce
1 teaspoon pizza seasoning blend
3 boneless skinless chicken breast halves (about ¾ pound), quartered
1 cup (4 ounces) shredded mozzarella cheese

Preheat oven to 350°F. Spray 2-quart round casserole with nonstick cooking spray.

Cook pasta according to package directions until al dente. Drain and place in prepared dish.

Meanwhile, heat oil in large skillet over medium-high heat until hot. Add mushrooms; cook and stir 2 minutes. Remove from heat. Stir in spaghetti sauce and pizza seasoning.

Pour half of spaghetti sauce mixture into casserole; stir until pasta is well coated. Arrange chicken on top of pasta. Pour remaining spaghetti sauce mixture evenly over chicken.

Bake, covered, 50 minutes or until chicken is no longer pink in center. Remove from oven; sprinkle with cheese. Cover and let stand 5 minutes before serving.

Tip: *Serve this casserole with grated Parmesan cheese and crushed red pepper flakes so that everyone can add their own "pizza" seasonings.*

Chicken Pot Pie with Cornmeal Crust

Makes 6 servings

1 cup diagonally sliced carrots
½ cup diagonally sliced celery
2 cups sliced fresh mushrooms
1 can (14½ ounces) fat-free reduced-sodium chicken broth, divided
⅓ cup low-fat (1%) milk
1⅓ cups unbleached flour, divided
½ teaspoon dried thyme leaves
¼ teaspoon salt

⅛ teaspoon white pepper
⅓ cup yellow cornmeal
1 teaspoon baking powder
⅛ teaspoon salt
3 tablespoons canola and vegetable oil blend
4 to 5 tablespoons cold water
2 cups diced cooked chicken breasts
1 cup frozen peas and pearl onions, thawed

1. Bring 2 tablespoons water to a boil in small saucepan over medium-high heat. Add carrots and celery. Reduce heat; cover and simmer 10 minutes or until vegetables are crisp-tender.

2. Heat large nonstick skillet over high heat. Spray with nonstick cooking spray. Add mushrooms and 2 tablespoons water. Reduce heat to medium-high; cook and stir until water evaporates and mushrooms are lightly browned. Add all but ⅓ cup chicken broth to skillet. Pour milk and remaining ⅓ cup chicken broth into small jar with tight-fitting lid. Add ⅓ cup flour, thyme, salt and pepper. Shake well. Slowly stir flour mixture into chicken broth and mushrooms. Bring to a boil. Continue to cook and stir 1 minute. Cover and set aside.

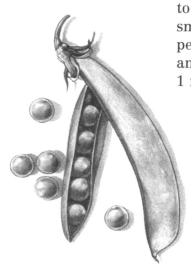

3. Preheat oven to 375°F. Combine remaining 1 cup flour, cornmeal, baking powder and salt in large bowl; form well in center. Combine oil and 4 tablespoons cold water. Pour into well; toss with fork until mixture holds together, sprinkling with additional water, if needed. Press together to form ball. Place between 2 pieces of waxed paper. Roll dough into 10-inch circle, ⅛ inch thick. Remove top piece of waxed paper. Cut air vent into crust with knife.

4. Combine chicken broth mixture, chicken, cooked vegetables, and peas and onions in large saucepan; heat thoroughly. Spray 9-inch pie plate with nonstick cooking spray. Pour hot mixture into pie plate. Carefully place top crust over filling; remove waxed paper. Flute edge of crust; brush with additional milk, if desired. Bake 30 to 35 minutes or until golden brown.

Herb Savvy

Herbs have great value in the kitchen because of their natural aromatic oils which enhance the flavor of foods. Learning how to use herbs correctly can make the difference between a bland dish and a dynamite dinner.

Basil: Available fresh and dried, this is an essential herb in Italian dishes and the basis for the popular Italian pesto sauce.

Bay Leaf: The dried whole leaves of this herb add tang to stews and meat dishes, but the leaves must be removed before serving.

Marjoram: This relative of oregano is mild in flavor and is best used in bean, poultry and seafood dishes.

Oregano: A strongly flavored herb that is best used in tomato and vegetable dishes.

Parsley: Parsley adds a refreshing peppery flavor to many different kinds of savory dishes. Of the two varieties, flat-leaf has a stronger flavor than the curly-leaf.

Rosemary: The distinctive pine flavor of rosemary does not combine well with other herbs, but it is a good choice for meats, poultry and grilled food.

Sage: Fresh or dried sage works well with game, poultry and stuffings.

Tarragon: This herb has a slightly sweet, anise-like flavor. It is most often used to flavor salads, vegetables, fish and poultry.

Thyme: Thyme is widely used to add flavor to vegetables, meat, poultry, fish dishes, soups and cream sauces.

Campbell's® One-Dish Chicken & Stuffing Bake

Makes 4 to 6 servings

Prep Time:
10 minutes

Cook Time:
30 minutes

1¼ cups boiling water
4 tablespoons margarine *or*
   butter, melted
4 cups PEPPERIDGE FARM®
   Herb Seasoned Stuffing
4 to 6 skinless, boneless
   chicken breast halves
   (about 1 to 1½ pounds)
Paprika

1 can (10¾ ounces)
   CAMPBELL'S® Condensed
   Cream of Mushroom Soup
   or 98% Fat Free Cream of
   Mushroom Soup
⅓ cup milk
1 tablespoon chopped fresh
   parsley *or* 1 teaspoon dried
   parsley flakes

Note:

To chop fresh parsley
the no-mess way, place
parsley sprigs in a
1-cup measuring cup;
snip with kitchen
scissors until finely
chopped.

1. Mix water and margarine. Add stuffing. Mix lightly.

2. Spoon stuffing across center of 3-quart shallow baking dish, leaving space on both sides for chicken. Arrange chicken on each side of stuffing. Sprinkle paprika over chicken.

3. Mix soup, milk and parsley. Pour over chicken.

4. **Cover.** Bake at 400°F. for 30 minutes or until chicken is no longer pink.

Velveeta® Spicy Chicken Spaghetti

12 ounces spaghetti, uncooked
4 boneless skinless chicken
    breast halves (about
    1¼ pounds), cut into strips
1 pound (16 ounces)
    VELVEETA® Pasteurized
    Prepared Cheese Product,
    cut up
1 can (10¾ ounces) condensed
    cream of chicken soup

1 can (10 ounces) diced
    tomatoes and green chilies,
    undrained
1 can (4½ ounces) sliced
    mushrooms, drained
⅓ cup milk

Makes 6 to 8 servings

Prep Time:
5 minutes

Bake Time:
40 minutes

1. Cook pasta as directed on package; drain. Return to same pan.

2. Spray skillet with no stick cooking spray. Add chicken; cook and stir on medium-high heat 4 to 5 minutes or until cooked through. Add VELVEETA, soup, tomatoes and green chilies, mushrooms and milk; stir on low heat until VELVEETA is melted. Add chicken mixture to pasta; toss to coat. Spoon into greased 13×9-inch baking dish.

3. Bake at 350°F for 35 to 40 minutes or until hot.

Lattice-Top Chicken

Makes 4 to 6 servings

1 can (10¾ ounces) condensed
　　cream of potato soup
1¼ cups milk
½ teaspoon seasoned salt
1½ cups (7 ounces) cubed cooked
　　chicken
1 bag (16 ounces) frozen
　　vegetable combination
　　(broccoli, carrots,
　　cauliflower), thawed and
　　drained
1 cup (4 ounces) shredded
　　Cheddar cheese, divided

1⅓ cups *French's*® French Fried
　　Onions, divided
1 cup biscuit baking mix*
¼ cup milk
1 egg, slightly beaten

* 1 package (4 ounces) refrigerated crescent rolls may be substituted for baking mix, ¼ cup milk and egg. Separate dough into 2 rectangles; press together perforated cuts. Cut each rectangle lengthwise into 3 strips. Arrange strips on hot chicken mixture to form lattice. Top as directed. Bake, uncovered, at 375°F for 15 to 20 minutes or until lattice is golden brown.

Preheat oven to 375°F. In large bowl, combine soup, 1¼ cups milk, seasoned salt, chicken, vegetables, ½ cup cheese and ⅔ *cup* French Fried Onions. Pour into 12×8-inch baking dish. Bake, covered, at 375°F for 15 minutes. Meanwhile, in small bowl, combine baking mix, ¼ cup milk and egg to form soft dough. Stir casserole and spoon dough over hot chicken mixture to form lattice design. Bake, uncovered, 20 to 25 minutes or until lattice is golden brown. Top lattice with remaining ½ cup cheese and ⅔ *cup* onions; bake, uncovered, 3 minutes or until onions are golden brown.

<u>Microwave Directions:</u> *Prepare chicken mixture as above; pour into 12×8-inch microwave-safe dish. Cook, covered, on HIGH 10 minutes or until heated through. Stir chicken mixture halfway through cooking time. Prepare biscuit dough and spoon over casserole as above. Cook, uncovered, 7 to 9 minutes or until lattice is done. Rotate dish halfway through cooking time. Top lattice with remaining cheese and onions; cook, uncovered, 1 minute or until cheese melts. Let stand 5 minutes.*

Brown Rice Chicken Bake

Vegetable cooking spray
3 cups cooked brown rice
1 package (10 ounces) frozen
   green peas
2 cups chopped cooked chicken
   breasts
½ cup cholesterol free, reduced
   calorie mayonnaise

⅓ cup slivered almonds, toasted
   (optional)
2 teaspoons soy sauce
¼ teaspoon ground black
   pepper
¼ teaspoon garlic powder
¼ teaspoon dried tarragon
   leaves

Spray 3-quart baking casserole with vegetable cooking spray.
Combine rice, peas, chicken, mayonnaise, almonds, soy sauce,
and seasonings in large bowl; mix well. Spoon into prepared
casserole; cover. Bake at 350°F for 15 to 20 minutes or until
heated through.

Favorite recipe from **USA Rice Federation**

Note:

**Brown rice grains are
unpolished with only
the inedible husk
removed. Since it
contains the bran and
the germ, it is more
nutritious than white
rice. It also takes
longer to cook. Light
tan in color, it has a
chewy texture and
nutty flavor. Quick
brown rice (cooks in
15 minutes) and
instant brown rice
(cooks in 10 minutes)
are also available.**

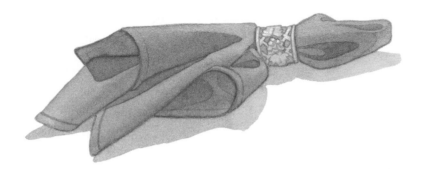

Spicy Chicken Tortilla Casserole

Makes 8 servings

1 tablespoon vegetable oil
1 cup chopped green bell pepper
1 small onion, chopped
2 cloves garlic, finely chopped
1 pound (about 4) boneless, skinless chicken breast halves, cut into bite-size pieces

1 jar (16 ounces) ORTEGA® SALSA (any flavor)
1 can (2¼ ounces) sliced ripe olives
6 corn tortillas, cut into halves
2 cups (8 ounces) shredded Monterey Jack or Cheddar cheese
Sour cream (optional)

PREHEAT oven to 350°F.

HEAT oil in large skillet over medium-high heat. Add bell pepper, onion and garlic; cook for 2 to 3 minutes or until vegetables are tender.

ADD chicken; cook, stirring frequently, for 3 to 5 minutes or until chicken is no longer pink in center. Stir in salsa and olives; remove from heat.

PLACE 6 tortilla halves onto bottom of ungreased 8-inch square baking pan. Top with half of chicken mixture and 1 cup cheese; repeat.

BAKE for 15 to 20 minutes or until bubbly. Serve with sour cream.

Quick Chicken Pot Pie

Makes 4 servings

1 pound boneless skinless
    chicken thighs, cut into
    1-inch cubes
1 can (about 14 ounces) chicken
    broth
3 tablespoons all-purpose flour
2 tablespoons butter, softened
1 package (10 ounces) frozen
    mixed vegetables, thawed

1 can (about 4 ounces) button
    mushrooms, drained
¼ teaspoon dried basil leaves
¼ teaspoon dried oregano
    leaves
¼ teaspoon dried thyme leaves
1 cup biscuit baking mix
6 tablespoons milk

1. Preheat oven to 450°F. Place chicken and broth in large skillet; cover and bring to a boil over high heat. Reduce heat to medium; simmer, uncovered, 5 minutes or until chicken is tender.

2. While chicken is cooking, mix flour and butter; set aside. Combine mixed vegetables, mushrooms, basil, oregano and thyme in greased 2-quart casserole.

3. Add flour mixture to chicken and broth in skillet; stir with wire whisk until smooth. Cook and stir until thickened. Add to vegetable mixture; mix well.

4. Blend biscuit mix and milk in medium bowl until smooth. Drop 4 scoops batter onto chicken mixture.

5. Bake 18 to 20 minutes or until biscuits are browned and casserole is hot and bubbly.

Dairyland Confetti Chicken

Makes 6 to 8 servings

1 cup diced carrots
¾ cup chopped onion
½ cup diced celery
¼ cup chicken broth
3 cups cubed cooked chicken
1 can (10½ ounces) cream of
    chicken soup
1 cup dairy sour cream
½ cup (4 ounces) sliced
    mushrooms

1 teaspoon Worcestershire
    sauce
1 teaspoon salt
⅛ teaspoon pepper
    Confetti Topping (recipe
    follows)
¼ cup (1 ounce) shredded
    Wisconsin Cheddar cheese

For casserole, in saucepan, combine carrots, onion, celery and chicken broth. Simmer 20 minutes. In 3-quart casserole, mix cubed chicken, soup, sour cream, mushrooms, Worcestershire sauce, salt and pepper. Add simmered vegetables and liquid; mix well. Prepare Confetti Topping. Drop tablespoons of Confetti Topping onto casserole. Bake in 350°F oven for 40 to 45 minutes or until golden brown. Sprinkle with cheese and return to oven until melted. Garnish as desired.

Confetti Topping

1 cup sifted all-purpose flour
2 teaspoons baking powder
½ teaspoon salt
2 eggs, slightly beaten
½ cup milk

1 tablespoon chopped green
    bell pepper
1 tablespoon chopped pimiento
1 cup (4 ounces) shredded
    Wisconsin Cheddar cheese

In mixing bowl, combine flour, baking powder and salt. Add eggs, milk, green pepper, pimiento and cheese. Mix just until well blended.

Favorite recipe from **Wisconsin Milk Marketing Board**

Chicken Enchiladas

- 2 cups chopped cooked chicken
- 2 cups shredded Wisconsin Cheddar cheese, divided
- 2 cups shredded Wisconsin Monterey Jack cheese, divided
- 1 cup Wisconsin dairy sour cream
- 1 teaspoon chili powder
- ¼ teaspoon salt
- ⅛ teaspoon ground red pepper
- 10 (6-inch) flour tortillas
- 1½ cups enchilada sauce
- ½ cup sliced black olives
- ¼ cup minced green onion

Combine chicken, 1 cup Cheddar cheese, 1 cup Monterey Jack cheese, sour cream and seasonings; mix well. Spread ¼ cup chicken mixture on each tortilla; roll up tightly. Pour ½ cup sauce on bottom of 12×8-inch baking dish. Place tortillas in baking dish, seam side down; top with remaining sauce. Sprinkle with remaining 1 cup Cheddar cheese and 1 cup Monterey Jack cheese. Bake at 350°F, 20 minutes or until thoroughly heated. Top with olives and green onion.

Favorite recipe from **Wisconsin Milk Marketing Board**

Note:

Generally, a whole 3- to 4-pound chicken will yield about 4 cups cooked, boneless meat. If you wish to use boneless, skinless chicken breasts, you'll need about ¾ pound of raw chicken to yield 2 cups of cooked meat.

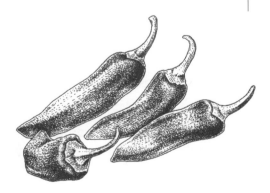

Roasted Chicken and Vegetables over Wild Rice

Makes 4 to 6 servings

Note:

Wild rice was called rice by early explorers because they found it growing in water, but it is not really rice. It is actually the seed of a marsh grass and it has a chewy texture and a nutty, earthy flavor. It is the only cereal grain native to North America.

3½ pounds chicken pieces
¾ cup olive oil vinaigrette dressing, divided
1 tablespoon margarine or butter, melted
1 package (6 ounces) long-grain and wild rice mix
1 can (about 14 ounces) reduced-sodium chicken broth
1 small eggplant, cut into 1-inch pieces
2 medium red potatoes, cut into 1-inch pieces

1 medium yellow summer squash, cut into 1-inch pieces
1 medium zucchini, cut into 1-inch pieces
1 medium red onion, cut into wedges
1 package (4 ounces) crumbled feta cheese with basil
Chopped fresh cilantro (optional)
Fresh thyme sprig (optional)

Remove skin from chicken; discard. Combine chicken and ½ cup dressing in large resealable plastic food storage bag. Seal bag and turn to coat. Refrigerate 30 minutes or overnight.

Preheat oven to 375°F. Brush bottom of 13×9-inch baking dish with melted margarine.

Add rice and seasoning packet to prepared dish; stir in broth. Combine eggplant, potatoes, squash, zucchini and onion in large bowl. Place on top of rice mixture.

Remove chicken from bag and place on top of vegetables; discard marinade. Pour remaining ¼ cup dressing over chicken.

Bake, uncovered, 45 minutes. Remove from oven and sprinkle with cheese. Bake 5 to 10 minutes or until chicken is no longer pink in center, juices run clear and cheese is melted. Sprinkle with cilantro and garnish with thyme, if desired.

Let's Talk
Turkey

CHAPTER FOUR

Turkey Manicotti

Makes 8 servings

1 pound ground turkey
½ cup finely chopped onion
1 teaspoon garlic powder
½ teaspoon Italian seasoning
½ teaspoon salt
¼ teaspoon black pepper
1½ cups reduced-fat cottage cheese
1 package (10 ounces) frozen chopped spinach, thawed and squeeze dried

½ cup Parmesan cheese, grated
½ cup plain yogurt
1 egg
1 tablespoon dried parsley
12 uncooked manicotti shells
4 cups prepared spaghetti sauce
½ cup mozzarella cheese, grated

Microwave Directions

1. In 1-quart microwave-safe dish combine turkey, onion, garlic powder, Italian seasoning, salt and pepper. Cook in microwave at HIGH (100% power) 4 to 5 minutes or until meat is no longer pink, breaking up ground turkey halfway through cooking time.

2. In large bowl combine cottage cheese, spinach, Parmesan cheese, yogurt, egg, parsley and turkey mixture.

3. Stuff shells with turkey mixture. In bottom of 13×9-inch microwave-safe baking dish spoon 2 cups spaghetti sauce. Layer shells over sauce. Top shells with remaining turkey mixture and spaghetti sauce.

4. Cover baking dish with vented plastic wrap. Cook in microwave at HIGH (100% power) 10 minutes, turning dish halfway through microwave time. Cook in microwave at MEDIUM-HIGH (70% power) 17 minutes, turning dish halfway through microwave time. Uncover dish and sprinkle mozzarella cheese over manicotti last 3 minutes of microwave time. Let stand 15 minutes before serving.

Favorite recipe from **National Turkey Federation**

Turkey Cottage Pie

¼ cup butter or margarine
¼ cup all-purpose flour
1 envelope LIPTON® RECIPE
    SECRETS® Golden Onion
    Soup Mix
2 cups water
2 cups cut-up cooked turkey or
    chicken

1 package (10 ounces) frozen
    mixed vegetables, thawed
1¼ cups shredded Swiss cheese
    (about 5 ounces), divided
⅛ teaspoon pepper
5 cups hot mashed potatoes

**Makes about
8 servings**

Preheat oven to 375°F.

In large saucepan, melt butter and add flour; cook, stirring constantly, 5 minutes or until golden. Stir in golden onion soup mix thoroughly blended with water. Bring to a boil, then simmer 15 minutes or until thickened. Stir in turkey, vegetables, 1 cup cheese and pepper. Turn into lightly greased 2-quart casserole; top with hot potatoes, then remaining ¼ cup cheese. Bake 30 minutes or until bubbling.

<u>Microwave Directions:</u> *In 2-quart casserole, heat butter at HIGH (100% power) 1 minute. Stir in flour and heat uncovered, stirring frequently, 2 minutes. Stir in golden onion soup mix thoroughly blended with water. Heat uncovered, stirring occasionally, 4 minutes or until thickened. Stir in turkey, vegetables, 1 cup cheese and pepper. Top with hot potatoes, then remaining ¼ cup cheese. Heat uncovered, turning casserole occasionally, 5 minutes or until bubbling. Let stand uncovered 5 minutes. For additional color, sprinkle, if desired, with paprika.*

Note:

A four-sided box-shaped grater is a versatile and inexpensive tool that has several different size openings for grating vegetables and cheese.

Green Bean & Turkey Bake

Makes 6 servings

Prep Time:
10 minutes

Cook Time:
50 minutes

1 can (10¾ ounces) condensed
    cream of mushroom soup
¾ cup milk
⅛ teaspoon pepper
2 packages (9 ounces *each*)
    frozen cut green beans,
    thawed

2 cups (12 ounces) cubed
    cooked turkey or chicken
1⅓ cups *French's®* French Fried
    Onions, divided
1½ cups (6 ounces) shredded
    Cheddar cheese, divided
3 cups hot mashed potatoes

1. Preheat oven to 375°F. In 3-quart casserole, combine soup, milk and pepper; mix well. Stir in beans, turkey, ⅔ *cup* French Fried Onions and *1 cup* cheese. Spoon mashed potatoes on top.

2. Bake, uncovered, 45 minutes or until hot. Sprinkle with remaining ½ *cup* cheese and ⅔ *cup* onions. Bake 3 minutes or until onions are golden.

Microwave Directions: *Prepare mixture as above except do not top with potatoes. Cover casserole with vented plastic wrap. Microwave on HIGH 15 minutes or until heated through, stirring halfway through cooking time. Uncover. Top with mashed potatoes, remaining cheese and onions. Microwave on HIGH 2 to 4 minutes. Let stand 5 minutes.*

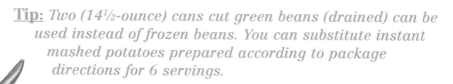

Tip: *Two (14½-ounce) cans cut green beans (drained) can be used instead of frozen beans. You can substitute instant mashed potatoes prepared according to package directions for 6 servings.*

Turkey Stuffed Chiles Rellenos

1 package (1½ pounds) BUTTERBALL® 99% Fat Free Fresh Ground Turkey Breast
1 envelope (1¼ ounces) taco seasoning mix
⅓ cup water

6 large poblano chiles, stems on, slit lengthwise and seeded
1 cup (4 ounces) shredded reduced fat Cheddar cheese
1½ cups tomato salsa

Makes 6 servings

Prep Time:
30 minutes

Spray large nonstick skillet with nonstick cooking spray; heat over medium heat until hot. Brown turkey in skillet over medium-high heat 6 to 8 minutes or until no longer pink, stirring to separate meat. Add taco seasoning and water. Bring to a boil. Reduce heat to low; simmer 5 minutes, stirring occasionally. In separate pan, cook chiles in boiling water 5 minutes; remove and drain. Combine turkey mixture and Cheddar cheese. Fill chiles with mixture. Pour salsa into 11×7-inch baking dish. Place stuffed chiles slit side up in baking dish. Bake, uncovered, in preheated 400°F oven 15 minutes. Serve hot with additional salsa and sour cream, if desired.

Note:

Poblano peppers are very dark green, large triangular-shaped chiles with pointed ends. Poblanos are usually 3½ to 5 inches long. Their flavor ranges from mild to quite hot. For a milder flavor, Anaheims can be substituted.

Pizza Rice Casserole

Makes 4 servings

1 bag SUCCESS® Rice
1 pound ground turkey or lean ground beef
½ cup chopped green bell pepper
½ cup chopped onion
1 jar (15½ ounces) pizza sauce
1 cup water

1 can (4 ounces) mushroom pieces, drained
¼ cup flour
½ cup chopped turkey ham
½ teaspoon garlic salt
1 cup (4 ounces) shredded Mozzarella cheese

Prepare rice according to package directions.

Brown ground turkey with green pepper and onion in large skillet or saucepan, stirring occasionally to separate turkey. Add rice, pizza sauce, water, mushrooms, flour, ham and garlic salt; heat thoroughly, stirring occasionally. Sprinkle with cheese.

Turkey Broccoli Bake

Makes 6 servings

1 bag (16 ounces) frozen broccoli cuts, thawed, drained
2 cups cubed cooked turkey or chicken
2 cups soft bread cubes
8 ounces sliced American cheese, divided

1 jar (12 ounces) HEINZ® HomeStyle Turkey or Chicken Gravy
½ cup undiluted evaporated milk
Dash pepper

In buttered 9-inch square baking dish, layer broccoli, turkey, bread cubes and cheese. Combine gravy, milk and pepper; pour over cheese. Bake in 375°F oven, 40 minutes. Let stand 5 minutes.

Easy Tex-Mex Bake

Makes 6 servings

8 ounces uncooked thin
    mostaccioli
Nonstick cooking spray
1 pound ground turkey breast
⅔ cup bottled medium or mild
    salsa
1 package (10 ounces) frozen
    corn, thawed and drained
1 container (16 ounces) low-fat
    cottage cheese

1 egg
1 tablespoon minced fresh
    cilantro
½ teaspoon white pepper
¼ teaspoon ground cumin
½ cup (2 ounces) shredded
    Monterey Jack cheese

1. Cook pasta according to package directions, omitting salt. Drain and rinse well; set aside.

2. Spray large nonstick skillet with cooking spray. Add turkey; cook until no longer pink, about 5 minutes. Stir in salsa and corn. Remove from heat.

3. Preheat oven to 350°F. Combine cottage cheese, egg, cilantro, white pepper and cumin in small bowl.

4. Spoon half of turkey mixture on bottom of 11×7-inch or 2-quart baking dish. Top with pasta. Spoon cottage cheese mixture over pasta. Top with remaining turkey mixture. Sprinkle Monterey Jack cheese over casserole.

5. Bake 25 to 30 minutes or until heated through.

Turkey and Biscuits

Makes 6 servings

2 cans (10¾ ounces each)
    condensed cream of
    chicken soup
¼ cup dry white wine
¼ teaspoon poultry seasoning
2 packages (8 ounces each)
    frozen cut asparagus,
    thawed

3 cups cubed cooked turkey or
    chicken
Paprika (optional)
1 can (11 ounces) refrigerated
    flaky biscuits

Note:

Commercial poultry seasonings vary widely in flavor depending on the company that produces them. Many are blends of three or more herbs, including parsley, thyme, sage, rosemary and marjoram.

1. Preheat oven to 350°F. Spray 13×9-inch baking dish with nonstick cooking spray.

2. Combine soup, wine and poultry seasoning in medium bowl.

3. Arrange asparagus in single layer in prepared dish. Place turkey evenly over asparagus. Spread soup mixture over turkey. Sprinkle lightly with paprika, if desired.

4. Cover tightly with foil and bake 20 minutes. Remove from oven. *Increase oven temperature to 425°F.* Top with biscuits and bake, uncovered, 8 to 10 minutes or until biscuits are golden brown.

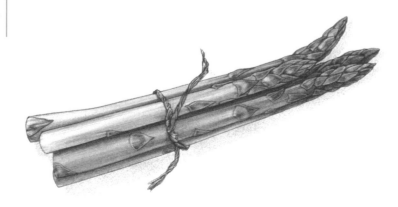

Turkey Tamale Pie with Cornbread

2 tablespoons vegetable oil
1 small onion, chopped
1 small green bell pepper, chopped
1¼ pounds turkey cutlets, chopped
1 can (15¼ ounces) whole kernel corn, drained
1 can (15 ounces) kidney beans, drained
1 can (14½ ounces) stewed tomatoes

1 can (6 ounces) tomato paste
½ cup water
1 package (1.0 ounce) LAWRY'S® Taco Spices & Seasonings
1 can (4 ounces) chopped green chiles, drained
1 package (16 ounces) cornbread mix

Makes 8 to 10 servings

In large skillet, heat oil. Add onion and bell pepper and cook 5 minutes. Add turkey and cook over medium-high heat 7 to 10 minutes or until no longer pink in center, stirring occasionally; reduce heat to low. Stir in corn, beans, stewed tomatoes, tomato paste, water, Taco Spices & Seasonings and green chiles. Cook over low heat 10 minutes, stirring occasionally. Pour mixture into lightly greased 13×9-inch baking pan. In medium bowl, prepare cornbread batter according to package directions. Spoon dollops of batter over turkey mixture. Spoon remaining batter into lightly greased muffin tins. Bake in 375°F oven 25 minutes for casserole (15 to 20 minutes for muffins) or until toothpick inserted into cornbread comes out clean.

<u>Hint:</u> *Cool muffins completely. Wrap tightly and freeze for later use, if desired.*

Spicy Lasagna Roll-Ups

Makes 4 servings

1 pound ground turkey breast
  or extra-lean ground beef
½ cup chopped onion
2 cloves garlic, minced
1 teaspoon dried Italian
  seasoning
¼ teaspoon red pepper flakes
1 can (10¾ ounces) reduced-fat
  condensed tomato soup

1 cup chopped zucchini
¾ cup water
1 (15-ounce) container fat-free
  ricotta cheese
½ cup shredded part-skim
  mozzarella cheese
1 egg
4 cooked lasagna noodles

Note:

Fresh ground turkey can be used in place of ground beef in many recipes. It has soared in popularity due to a lower fat content. Read the label carefully; if skin or fat is ground along with the meat, the amount of fat and cholesterol will increase.

1. Preheat oven to 350°F. Spray large nonstick skillet with nonstick cooking spray; heat over medium heat until hot. Add turkey, onion, garlic, Italian seasoning and red pepper flakes; cook and stir until turkey is no longer pink and onion is tender. Add soup, zucchini and water; simmer 5 minutes. Pour soup mixture into shallow 2-quart baking dish.

2. Combine ricotta, mozzarella and egg in medium bowl; mix well. Place lasagna noodles on flat surface; spread ½ cup cheese mixture on each noodle. Roll up noodles, enclosing filling; place rolls, seam sides down, over soup mixture.

3. Cover and bake 30 minutes; uncover and continue baking an additional 10 minutes or until sauce is bubbly. Place lasagna rolls on serving dish; spoon remaining sauce over rolls.

Turkey and Rice Quiche

3 cups cooked rice, cooled to
   room temperature
1½ cups chopped cooked turkey
1 medium tomato, seeded and
   finely diced
¼ cup sliced green onions
¼ cup finely diced green bell
   pepper
1 tablespoon chopped fresh
   basil *or* 1 teaspoon dried
   basil leaves

½ teaspoon seasoned salt
⅛ to ¼ teaspoon ground red
   pepper
½ cup skim milk
3 eggs, beaten
   Vegetable cooking spray
½ cup (2 ounces) shredded
   Cheddar cheese
½ cup (2 ounces) shredded
   mozzarella cheese

**Makes 8 servings
(2 triangles each)**

Combine rice, turkey, tomato, onions, bell pepper, basil, salt, red
pepper, milk and eggs in 13×9×2-inch pan coated with cooking
spray. Top with cheeses. Bake at 375°F for 20 minutes or until
knife inserted near center comes out clean. To serve, cut quiche
into 8 squares; cut each square diagonally into 2 triangles.

Favorite recipe from **USA Rice Federation**

Note:

A quiche is a savory

tart or pie with an egg

custard filling flavored

with cheese and

sometimes meat,

seafood or vegetables.

Quiches are served as

an appetizer or entrée.

Turkey Breast Provençal with Vegetables

Makes 12 servings

1 cup turkey or chicken bouillon
¼ cup dry white wine
¼ cup lemon juice
1 head garlic, cloves separated, unpeeled
1 bag (10 ounces) frozen onions
2 teaspoons dried rosemary, crushed
1 teaspoon dried thyme leaves
½ teaspoon salt
¼ teaspoon fennel seeds

¼ teaspoon black pepper
6 plum tomatoes, quartered
1 package (9 ounces) frozen artichoke hearts, slightly thawed
1 package (10 ounces) frozen asparagus spears, slightly thawed
1 can (3¼ ounces) pitted ripe olives, drained
1 bone-in (4½-pound) turkey breast

1. Preheat oven to 325°F. In 13×9-inch baking pan combine bouillon, wine, lemon juice, garlic, onions, rosemary, thyme, salt, fennel seeds and black pepper. Cover pan with foil; bake 20 minutes.

2. Remove pan from oven. Add tomatoes, artichoke hearts, asparagus and olives. Place turkey breast on top of vegetables. Loosely tent with foil and bake 1 hour. Remove foil and bake 1 hour or until meat thermometer inserted in thickest part of breast registers 170°F. Baste turkey and vegetables frequently with pan juices.

3. Remove turkey and vegetables to serving platter. Reserve 6 cloves of garlic and pan juices.

4. Remove skin from reserved garlic. Combine garlic with pan juices in food processor; process 30 to 60 seconds until mixture is smooth.

5. Serve sauce with turkey and vegetables.

Favorite recipe from **National Turkey Federation**

Tuscan Noodle Bake

½ pound Italian sausage,
   casings removed and
   sausage crumbled
½ pound BUTTERBALL® Ground
   Turkey
1 cup chopped onion
1 teaspoon fresh minced garlic
1 can (15 ounces) HUNT'S®
   Tomato Sauce
1 can (14.5 ounces) HUNT'S®
   Whole Tomatoes, undrained
   and crushed
1 can (6 ounces) sliced
   mushrooms, drained

1 can (2¼ ounces) sliced black
   olives, drained
¼ cup chopped fresh parsley
1 teaspoon dried basil leaves
1 teaspoon dried oregano
   leaves
¼ teaspoon pepper
¼ cup TREASURE CAVE®
   Shredded Parmesan Cheese
½ package (12 ounces) wide egg
   noodles, cooked and
   drained
1 cup shredded mozzarella
   cheese

Makes 6 to 8 servings

Note:

To remove a sausage
casing, use a paring
knife to slit the casing
at one end. Be careful
not to cut through the
sausage. Grasp the cut
edge and gently pull
the casing away from
the sausage.

In large Dutch oven, brown sausage and turkey with onion and
garlic until meat is no longer pink; drain. Add remaining
ingredients except Parmesan cheese, noodles and mozzarella
cheese; simmer 5 minutes. Stir in Parmesan cheese and noodles;
blend well. Pour noodle mixture into greased 13×9×2-inch
baking dish. Bake, covered, at 350°F for 20 minutes. Sprinkle
mozzarella cheese over noodle mixture and bake, uncovered, for
an additional 5 to 7 minutes.

Turkey Cazuela

Makes 4 to 6 servings

Prep Time:
20 minutes

Cook Time:
45 minutes

8 ounces uncooked linguini,
   broken in half*
1⅓ cups *French's®* French Fried
   Onions, divided
2 cups (10 ounces) cubed
   cooked turkey
1 can (10¾ ounces) condensed
   cream of chicken soup

1 jar (8 ounces) picante sauce
½ cup sour cream
1 cup (4 ounces) shredded
   Cheddar cheese

*Or, substitute 4 cups cooked pasta for
uncooked linguini.

Note:

Pasta is an excellent

source of complex

carbohydrates. It also

contains 6 essential

amino acids,

3 B-complex

vitamins and iron.

Preheat oven to 350°F. Grease 2-quart shallow baking dish. Cook linguini according to package directions, using shortest cooking time. Layer linguini, ⅔ *cup* French Fried Onions and turkey in prepared baking dish.

Combine soup, picante sauce and sour cream in large bowl. Pour over turkey.

Cover; bake 40 minutes or until hot and bubbling. Stir gently. Sprinkle with cheese and remaining ⅔ *cup* onions. Bake 5 minutes or until onions are golden.

Arizona Stew

3 tablespoons olive oil
5 medium carrots, cut into thick slices
1 large onion, wedged
1 pound sliced turkey breast, cut into 1-inch strips
1 teaspoon LAWRY'S® Garlic Powder with Parsley
3 tablespoons all-purpose flour
8 small red potatoes, cut into ½-inch cubes

1 package (1.48 ounces) LAWRY'S® Spices & Seasonings for Chili
1 package (10 ounces) frozen peas, thawed
8 ounces sliced fresh mushrooms
1 cup beef broth
1 can (8 ounces) tomato sauce

Makes 8 to 10 servings

In large skillet, heat oil. Add carrots and onion and cook over medium-high heat until tender. Stir in turkey strips and Garlic Powder with Parsley; cook 3 minutes until turkey is just browned. Stir in flour. Pour mixture into 3-quart casserole dish. Stir in remaining ingredients. Cover and bake in 450°F oven 45 to 50 minutes. Let stand 5 minutes before serving.

Stove Top Directions: *Prepare as above in Dutch oven. Bring mixture to a boil over medium-high heat; reduce heat to low, cover and simmer, 40 to 45 minutes until potatoes are tender. Let stand 5 minutes.*

Hint: *Dollop top of casserole with prepared dumpling mix during the last 15 minutes of baking.*

Turkey Parmesan

Makes 4 servings

⅔ cup milk
2 tablespoons margarine or
   butter
2 cups zucchini slices, halved
1 package (5.1 ounces) PASTA
   RONI® Angel Hair Pasta
   with Parmesan Cheese

2 cups cooked turkey strips
1 jar (2 ounces) chopped
   pimentos, drained
2 tablespoons grated Parmesan
   cheese

Note:

For microwave cooking, glass baking dishes are a good choice, but ceramic dishes containing metallic powders should not be used. Ceramic dishes suitable for use in a microwave oven are labeled "for microwave use" or "microwave-safe."

Microwave Directions

1. In round 3-quart microwavable glass casserole, combine 1½ cups water, milk, margarine and zucchini. Microwave, uncovered, on HIGH 6 minutes.

2. Stir in pasta, Special Seasonings and turkey. Separate pasta with fork, if needed.

3. Microwave, uncovered, on HIGH 7 to 8 minutes, stirring after 2 minutes. Separate pasta with fork, if needed.

4. Sauce will be very thin, but will thicken upon standing. Stir in pimentos and cheese.

5. Let stand 3 to 4 minutes or until desired consistency. Stir before serving.

Cheesy Turkey Veg•All® Bake

1 package (5½ ounces) au
    gratin potato mix
2⅔ cups boiling water
1 can (15 ounces) VEG·ALL®
    Original Mixed Vegetables,
    drained

1 cup cubed cooked turkey
2 tablespoons butter

Makes 6 servings

Prep Time:
7 minutes

Cook Time:
20 minutes

Preheat oven to 350°F. Place au gratin potato mix and sauce packet into large mixing bowl. Add water, Veg•All, turkey, and butter; mix well. Pour into ungreased 2-quart casserole. Bake for 20 minutes or until top is golden brown. Cool for 5 minutes before serving.

Casserole Dish Substitutions

If you don't have the recommended size of casserole, substitute any ovenproof baking dish in a size that is as large or slightly larger than the recommended one. (A larger dish may require a shorter baking time, so check it sooner than recommended in the recipe.)

If you don't have a:	Use a:
1-quart casserole	8×6-inch baking dish
1½-quart casserole	8×8-inch baking dish
2-quart casserole	8×8-inch or 11×7-inch baking dish
2½-quart casserole	9×9-inch baking dish
3- to 4-quart casserole	13×9-inch baking dish or Dutch oven
5-quart casserole	large Dutch oven or roasting pan

Turkey Meatball & Olive Casserole

Makes 6 to 8 servings

2 cups uncooked rotini
½ pound ground turkey
¼ cup dry bread crumbs
1 egg, lightly beaten
2 teaspoons dried minced onion
2 teaspoons white wine Worcestershire sauce
½ teaspoon dried Italian seasoning
½ teaspoon salt
⅛ teaspoon black pepper

1 tablespoon vegetable oil
1 can (10¾ ounces) condensed cream of celery soup, undiluted
½ cup low-fat plain yogurt
¾ cup pimiento-stuffed green olives, sliced
3 tablespoons Italian-style bread crumbs
1 tablespoon margarine or butter, melted
Paprika (optional)

Preheat oven to 350°F. Spray 2-quart round casserole with nonstick cooking spray.

Cook pasta according to package directions until al dente. Drain and set aside.

Meanwhile, combine turkey, dry bread crumbs, egg, onion, Worcestershire, Italian seasoning, salt and pepper in medium bowl. Shape mixture into ½-inch meatballs.

Heat oil in medium skillet over high heat until hot. Add meatballs in single layer; cook until lightly browned on all sides and still pink in centers, turning frequently. Do not overcook. Remove from skillet; drain on paper towels.

Mix soup and yogurt in bowl. Add pasta, meatballs and olives; stir gently to combine. Transfer to prepared dish.

Combine Italian-style bread crumbs and margarine in small bowl; sprinkle evenly over casserole. Sprinkle lightly with paprika, if desired.

Bake, covered, 30 minutes. Uncover and bake 12 minutes or until meatballs are no longer pink in centers and casserole is hot and bubbly.

Mexican Rice and Turkey Bake

Makes 6 servings

1 bag SUCCESS® Rice
   Vegetable cooking spray
3 cups chopped cooked turkey
1 can (10 ounces) tomatoes
   with chilies, undrained*
1 can (12 ounces) Mexican-style
   corn with sweet peppers,
   drained

1 cup fat-free sour cream
½ cup (2 ounces) shredded low-
   fat Cheddar cheese

*Or, use 1 can (14½ ounces) stewed tomatoes.
Add 1 can (4 ounces) drained chopped mild
green chilies.

Microwave Directions
Prepare rice according to package directions.

Spray 1½-quart microwave-safe casserole with cooking spray; set aside. Combine rice, turkey, tomatoes and corn in large bowl; mix well. Spoon into prepared casserole. Microwave on HIGH until hot and bubbly, 8 to 10 minutes, stirring after 5 minutes. Top with sour cream and cheese.

Conventional Oven: *Assemble casserole as directed. Spoon into ovenproof 1½-quart casserole sprayed with vegetable cooking spray. Bake at 350°F until thoroughly heated, 15 to 20 minutes.*

Spaghetti Pie

Makes 6 servings

4 ounces uncooked thin
  spaghetti
1 egg
¼ cup grated Parmesan cheese
1 teaspoon dried Italian
  seasoning
⅔ cup reduced-fat ricotta cheese
½ pound 93% lean ground
  turkey
1 teaspoon chili powder
¼ teaspoon crushed fennel
  seeds

¼ teaspoon black pepper
⅛ teaspoon ground coriander
1 can (14½ ounces) diced
  tomatoes, undrained
1½ cups sliced fresh mushrooms
1 cup chopped onion
1 can (8 ounces) tomato sauce
¼ cup tomato paste
1 clove garlic, minced
2 teaspoons dried basil leaves
1 cup (4 ounces) shredded part-
  skim mozzarella cheese

1. Cook spaghetti according to package directions, omitting salt. Drain and rinse well under cold water until pasta is cool; drain well.

2. Beat egg, Parmesan cheese and Italian seasoning lightly in medium bowl. Add spaghetti; blend well. Spray deep 9-inch pie plate with nonstick cooking spray. Place spaghetti mixture in pie plate. Press onto bottom and up side of pie plate. Spread ricotta cheese on spaghetti layer.

3. Preheat oven to 350°F. Combine turkey, chili powder, fennel seeds, pepper and coriander in medium bowl. Spray large nonstick skillet with nonstick cooking spray; heat over medium heat until hot. Brown turkey mixture until turkey is no longer pink, stirring to break up meat. Add remaining ingredients except mozzarella cheese. Cook and stir until mixture boils. Spoon mixture over ricotta cheese in pie plate.

4. Cover pie plate with foil. Bake 20 minutes. Remove foil. Sprinkle with mozzarella cheese; bake 5 minutes or until cheese is melted. Let stand before cutting and serving.

Tasty Turkey Pot Pie

½ cup MIRACLE WHIP® or
MIRACLE WHIP LIGHT®
Dressing
2 tablespoons flour
1 teaspoon instant chicken
bouillon
⅛ teaspoon black pepper
¾ cup milk

1½ cups chopped LOUIS RICH®
Oven Roasted Breast of
Turkey
1 package (10 ounces) frozen
mixed vegetables, thawed,
drained
1 can (4 ounces) refrigerated
crescent dinner rolls

Makes 4 to 6 servings

Prep Time:
15 minutes

Bake Time:
20 minutes

MIX dressing, flour, bouillon and pepper in medium saucepan; gradually add milk. Cook, stirring frequently, on medium-low heat until thickened. Add turkey and vegetables; cook until thoroughly heated, stirring occasionally. Spoon into 8-inch square baking dish.

UNROLL dough into two rectangles. Press perforations together to seal. Place rectangles, side-by-side, to form square; press edges together to form seam. Cover turkey mixture with dough. Decorate dough with cut-outs made from additional dough, if desired.

BAKE at 375°F 15 to 20 minutes or until browned.

Hint: *Substitute 2 cups chopped or sliced fresh vegetables (such as carrots, green beans or broccoli), cooked, drained, for frozen mixed vegetables.*

Terrific Tamale Pie

Makes 6 to 8 servings

1 tablespoon vegetable oil
½ cup chopped onion
⅓ cup chopped red bell pepper
1 clove garlic, minced
¾ pound ground turkey
¾ teaspoon chili powder
½ teaspoon dried oregano
    leaves
1 can (14½ ounces) Mexican-
    style stewed tomatoes,
    undrained

1 can (15 ounces) chili beans in
    mild chili sauce, undrained
1 cup corn
¼ teaspoon black pepper
1 package (8½ ounces) corn
    muffin mix plus ingredients
    to prepare mix
2 cups taco-flavored shredded
    cheese, divided

1. Heat oil in large skillet over medium heat. Add onion and bell pepper; cook until crisp-tender. Stir in garlic. Add turkey; cook until turkey is no longer pink, stirring occasionally. Stir in chili powder and oregano. Add tomatoes with juice; cook and stir 2 minutes, breaking up tomatoes with spoon. Stir in beans with sauce, corn and pepper; simmer 10 minutes or until liquid is reduced by about half.

2. Preheat oven to 375°F. Lightly grease 1½- to 2-quart casserole. Prepare corn muffin mix according to package directions; stir in ½ cup cheese. Spread half of turkey mixture in prepared casserole; sprinkle with ¾ cup cheese. Top with remaining turkey mixture and ¾ cup cheese. Top with corn muffin batter. Bake 20 to 22 minutes or until light golden brown.

Low Fat Turkey Bacon Frittata

1 package (12 ounces) BUTTERBALL® Turkey Bacon, heated and chopped
6 ounces uncooked angel hair pasta, broken
2 teaspoons olive oil
1 small onion, sliced
1 red bell pepper, cut into thin strips
4 containers (4 ounces each) egg substitute

1 container (5 ounces) fat free ricotta cheese
1 cup (4 ounces) shredded fat free mozzarella cheese
1 cup (4 ounces) shredded reduced fat Swiss cheese
½ teaspoon salt
½ teaspoon black pepper
1 package (10 ounces) frozen spinach, thawed and squeezed dry

Makes 8 servings

Prep Time:
15 minutes plus baking time

Cook and drain pasta. Heat oil in large skillet over medium heat until hot. Cook and stir onion and bell pepper until tender. Combine egg substitute, cheeses, salt, black pepper and cooked pasta in large bowl. Add vegetables, spinach and turkey bacon. Spray 10-inch quiche dish with nonstick cooking spray; pour mixture into dish. Bake in preheated 350°F oven 30 minutes. Cut into wedges. Serve with spicy salsa, if desired.

Note:

Ricotta resembles cottage cheese but is smoother, richer and creamier. It is prepared from whey left over from making mozzarella cheese. Like so many ingredients used in Italian cooking, it is inexpensive and readily available.

Turnip Shepherd's Pie

Makes 4 main-dish servings

1 pound small turnips, peeled and cut into ½-inch cubes
1 pound lean ground turkey
⅓ cup dry bread crumbs
¼ cup chopped onion
¼ cup ketchup
1 egg
½ teaspoon *each* salt, pepper and Beau Monde seasoning*

⅓ cup half-and-half
1 tablespoon butter or margarine
Salt and black pepper
1 tablespoon chopped fresh parsley
¼ cup shredded sharp Cheddar cheese

*A seasoning salt available in most supermarkets. Celery salt can be substituted.

Preheat oven to 400°F. Place turnips in large saucepan; cover with water. Cover and bring to a boil; reduce heat to medium-low. Simmer 20 minutes or until fork-tender.

Mix turkey, bread crumbs, onion, ketchup, egg, salt, pepper and seasoning. Pat on bottom and side of 9-inch pie pan. Bake 20 to 30 minutes until turkey is no longer pink. Blot with paper towel to remove any drippings.

Drain cooked turnips. Mash turnips with electric mixer until smooth, blending in half-and-half and butter. Season with salt and pepper to taste. Fill meat shell with turnip mixture; sprinkle with parsley, then cheese. Return to oven until cheese melts. Garnish as desired.

Turkey Baked with Beans and Pasta

Makes 4 servings

1 pound ½-inch slices deli-cut Honey Roasted Turkey Breast, cut into ½-inch cubes
1 (15½-ounce) can butter beans, drained
1 (15-ounce) can black beans, drained
1 (14½-ounce) can diced tomatoes, undrained
1 cup orzo, cooked according to package directions (for only 7 minutes)

1 cup chopped onion
¼ cup chopped black olives
1 teaspoon dried oregano leaves
Nonstick vegetable cooking spray
4 ounces crumbled feta cheese with basil and tomato or plain

Note:

The word orzo actually means barley, even though the shape of this pasta looks more like rice. It is available in the pasta sections of large supermarkets.

1. Preheat oven to 350°F. In large mixing bowl, combine turkey cubes, beans, tomatoes, cooked orzo, onion, olives and oregano.

2. Spray 2-quart casserole with cooking spray. Pour turkey mixture into prepared casserole. Sprinkle with cheese; cover with foil.

3. Bake 20 minutes; remove foil and continue baking until cheese is lightly browned. Serve hot.

Favorite recipe from **California Poultry Federation**

Homespun Turkey 'n' Vegetables

Makes 4 servings

1 package (9 ounces) frozen cut green beans, thawed and drained

1 can (14 ounces) sliced carrots, drained

1⅓ cups *French's®* French Fried Onions, divided

1 can (16 ounces) whole potatoes, drained

1 can (10¾ ounces) condensed cream of celery soup

¼ cup milk

1 tablespoon *French's®* Classic Yellow® Mustard

¼ teaspoon garlic powder

1 pound uncooked turkey breast slices

Preheat oven to 375°F. In 12×8-inch baking dish, combine green beans, carrots and *⅔ cup* French Fried Onions. Slice potatoes into halves; arrange as many halves as will fit, cut side down, around edges of baking dish. Combine any remaining potatoes with vegetables in dish. In medium bowl, combine soup, milk, mustard and garlic powder; pour half the soup mixture over vegetables. Overlap turkey slices on vegetables. Pour remaining soup mixture over turkey and potatoes. Bake, covered, at 375°F for 40 minutes or until turkey is done. Top turkey with remaining *⅔ cup* onions; bake, uncovered, 3 minutes or until onions are golden brown.

Turkey Green Bean Casserole

1 package (6 ounces) STOVE TOP® Traditional Sage Stuffing Mix
1 can (10¾ ounces) condensed cream of mushroom soup

¾ cup milk
3 cups cubed cooked turkey
1 package (10 ounces) frozen French-cut green beans, cooked, drained

PREPARE Stuffing Mix Pouch as directed on package.

MIX soup and milk in 12×8-inch baking dish until smooth. Stir in turkey and green beans. Spoon stuffing evenly over top.

BAKE at 375°F for 30 minutes or until thoroughly heated.

One-Dish Meal

2 bags SUCCESS® Rice
Vegetable cooking spray
1 cup cubed cooked turkey-ham*

1 cup (4 ounces) shredded low-fat Cheddar cheese
1 cup peas

*Or, use cooked turkey, ham or turkey franks.

Microwave Directions
Prepare rice according to package directions. Spray 1-quart microwave-safe dish with cooking spray; set aside. Place rice in medium bowl. Add ham, cheese and peas; mix lightly. Spoon into prepared dish; smooth into even layer with spoon. Microwave on HIGH 1 minute; stir. Microwave 30 seconds or until thoroughly heated.

Conventional Oven Directions: *Assemble casserole as directed. Spoon into ovenproof 1-quart baking dish sprayed with vegetable cooking spray. Bake at 350°F until thoroughly heated, about 15 to 20 minutes.*

Turkey Vegetable Cobbler

Makes 10 to 12 servings

Note:

This is a great after-holiday recipe! Remember, any turkey remaining after the holiday meal should be stored within 2 hours of serving. Bacteria grow very rapidly at room temperature, and refrigeration won't kill microorganisms that have already grown. Wrap the meat in plastic or foil, then seal it inside plastic bags. Cooked turkey can be stored 3 to 4 days in the refrigerator and up to 4 months in the freezer.

Filling
6 tablespoons Butter Flavor CRISCO® Stick or
6 tablespoons Butter Flavor CRISCO® all-vegetable shortening plus additional for greasing
7 tablespoons all-purpose flour
2 cups turkey or chicken stock or broth
1 cup half-and-half
¼ teaspoon salt
⅛ teaspoon white pepper, or to taste
5 cups large chunks cooked turkey (about 1½ pounds)
3 medium carrots, peeled, cubed and cooked (about 1¼ cups)
2 cups fresh or 1 package (10 ounces frozen) small white onions, cooked
1 cup (half of 10-ounce package) frozen peas
2 tablespoons finely chopped fresh parsley
2 tablespoons finely chopped fresh chives
½ teaspoon poultry seasoning

Cobbler Topping
1¾ cups all-purpose flour
1 tablespoon baking powder
½ teaspoon salt
4 tablespoons Parmesan cheese, divided
6 tablespoons Butter Flavor CRISCO® Stick or
6 tablespoons Butter Flavor CRISCO® all-vegetable shortening
½ cup whipping cream
1 egg, beaten

1. Heat oven to 400°F. Grease 13×9-inch glass baking dish.

2. For filling, melt shortening in large saucepan on medium heat. Sprinkle in flour. Cook and stir about 3 minutes, but do not brown. Add stock, half-and-half, salt and pepper. Whisk or stir sauce until thick and smooth. Add turkey, carrots, onions, peas, parsley, chives and poultry seasoning. Mix well. Pour into baking dish.

3. For cobbler topping, combine flour, baking powder, salt and 3 tablespoons Parmesan cheese in medium bowl. Cut in shortening using pastry blender (or 2 knives) until all flour is blended in to form pea-size chunks. Add cream. Toss lightly until crumbly.

4. Sprinkle crumb mixture over filling. Drizzle with egg. Sprinkle with remaining 1 tablespoon Parmesan cheese. (Or press crumbs into ball. Roll large enough to fit over filling and to edges of baking dish. Brush with beaten egg. Sprinkle with remaining 1 tablespoon cheese.) Place dish on large baking sheet.

5. Bake at 400°F for 35 to 40 minutes or until topping is browned. Serve immediately.

Cheesy Casserole

1½ cups skim milk	¼ cup grated fresh Parmesan cheese
1 can (10¾ ounces) condensed cream of chicken soup	½ teaspoon LAWRY'S® Garlic Powder with Parsley
1 package (16 ounces) frozen mixed vegetables (thawed and drained)	½ teaspoon LAWRY'S® Seasoned Pepper
2 cups finely diced cooked turkey, chicken or ham	1 tablespoon crushed potato chips or crumbled corn flakes
1 cup uncooked instant rice	
¾ cup (3 ounces) shredded cheddar cheese	

Makes 4 servings

Lightly grease 9-inch square baking dish. Add milk and soup to dish; mix well with wire whisk. Stir in vegetables, turkey, rice, ½ cup cheddar cheese, 2 tablespoons Parmesan cheese, Garlic Powder with Parsley, and Seasoned Pepper; cover. Bake in 350°F oven 30 minutes. Combine remaining ¼ cup cheddar cheese, 2 tablespoons Parmesan cheese and potato chips; sprinkle over top of casserole. Bake, uncovered, 15 minutes longer.

Campbell's® Turkey Stuffing Divan

Makes 6 servings

Prep Time:
15 minutes

Cook Time:
30 minutes

1¼ cups boiling water
4 tablespoons margarine or
   butter, melted
4 cups PEPPERIDGE FARM®
   Herb Seasoned Stuffing
2 cups cooked broccoli cuts
2 cups cubed cooked turkey

1 can (10¾ ounces)
   CAMPBELL'S® Condensed
   Cream of Celery Soup *or*
   98% Fat Free Cream of
   Celery Soup
½ cup milk
1 cup shredded Cheddar cheese
   (4 ounces)

1. Mix water and margarine. Add stuffing. Mix lightly.

2. Spoon into 2-quart shallow baking dish. Arrange broccoli and turkey over stuffing. In small bowl mix soup, milk and ½ *cup* cheese. Pour over broccoli and turkey. Sprinkle remaining cheese over soup mixture.

3. Bake at 350°F. for 30 minutes or until hot.

<u>Variation:</u> *Substitute 1 can (10¾ ounces) CAMPBELL'S® Condensed Cream of Chicken Soup **or** 98% Fat Free Cream of Chicken Soup for Cream of Celery Soup. Substitute 2 cups cubed cooked chicken for turkey.*

<u>Tip:</u> *For 2 cups cooked broccoli cuts use about 1 pound fresh broccoli, trimmed, cut into 1-inch pieces (about 2 cups) or 1 package (10 ounces) frozen broccoli cuts (2 cups).*

Italian Rotini Bake

8 ounces dry rotini pasta
1 tablespoon olive or vegetable oil
1½ cups chopped onions
2 small zucchini, quartered, sliced
3 cloves garlic, minced
1 pound ground turkey
2 cans (14.5 ounces each) CONTADINA® Recipe Ready Diced Tomatoes, undrained

1 can (6 ounces) CONTADINA Tomato Paste
1 cup water
1 tablespoon Italian herb seasoning
1 teaspoon salt
1 egg
1 container (15 ounces) ricotta cheese
3 cups (12 ounces) shredded mozzarella cheese, divided

Makes 8 to 10 servings

Prep Time:
25 minutes

Cook Time:
20 minutes

1. Cook pasta according to package directions; drain.

2. Meanwhile, heat oil over medium-high heat in large skillet. Add onions, zucchini and garlic; sauté for 2 to 3 minutes or until vegetables are tender.

3. Add turkey; cook for 4 to 5 minutes or until turkey is no longer pink. Drain. Add undrained tomatoes, tomato paste, water, Italian seasoning and salt.

4. Bring to a boil. Reduce heat to low; simmer, uncovered, for 5 minutes.

5. Beat egg lightly in small bowl. Add ricotta cheese and 1 cup mozzarella cheese.

6. Layer half of pasta and half of tomato mixture in ungreased 13×9-inch baking dish. Cover with ricotta cheese mixture and 1 cup mozzarella cheese. Top with remaining pasta, tomato mixture and mozzarella cheese.

7. Bake in preheated 350°F oven for 15 to 20 minutes or until heated through.

Lighter Stuffed Peppers

Makes 4 servings

1 can (10¾ ounces) reduced-fat condensed tomato soup, divided
¼ cup water
8 ounces extra-lean ground turkey
1 cup cooked rice
¾ cup frozen corn, thawed
¼ cup sliced celery
¼ cup chopped red bell pepper
1 teaspoon dried Italian seasoning
½ teaspoon hot pepper sauce
2 green, yellow or red bell peppers, cut in half lengthwise, seeds removed

Note:

Adding 1 to 2 teaspoons of butter or oil to rice while it cooks will prevent it from boiling over.

1. Blend ¼ cup soup and water in small bowl. Pour into 8×8-inch baking dish; set aside. Brown turkey in large skillet over medium-high heat; drain well. Combine remaining soup with cooked turkey, rice, corn, celery, chopped bell pepper, Italian seasoning and hot pepper sauce in large bowl; mix well.

2. Fill pepper halves equally with turkey mixture. Place stuffed peppers on top of soup mixture in baking dish. Cover and bake at 350°F 35 to 40 minutes. To serve, place peppers on serving dish and spoon remaining sauce from baking dish over peppers.

Turkey Pot Pie

1 (1-pound) package frozen vegetables for stew, cooked according to package directions

1 cup frozen peas, cooked according to package directions

2 cups COOKED TURKEY from a TURKEY ROAST, cut into ½-inch cubes (cook roast according to package directions)*

1 (12-ounce) jar non-fat turkey gravy

1 tablespoon dried parsley

1 teaspoon dried thyme

1 teaspoon dried rosemary

½ teaspoon salt

¼ teaspoon pepper

1 refrigerated pie crust dough (brought to room temperature)

*Leftover cooked turkey may be substituted for the pre-packaged turkey roast.

1. Drain any cooking liquid from stew vegetables and peas.

2. Add turkey cubes, gravy, parsley, thyme, rosemary, salt and pepper to vegetables in oven-safe, 2-quart cooking dish.

3. Unfold pie crust dough and place on top of dish, trimming edges to approximately 1 inch larger than dish; secure dough edges to dish. Make several 1-inch slits on crust to allow steam to escape.

4. Bake in preheated 400°F oven for 25 to 30 minutes or until crust is brown and mixture is hot and bubbly.

Favorite recipe from **National Turkey Federation**

Turkey Lasagna

Makes 8 servings

1 pound Italian turkey sausage
1 jar (25.5 ounces) light
    vegetable spaghetti sauce
2 cups no-fat cottage cheese
1 cup grated low-fat mozzarella
    cheese

¼ cup plus 2 tablespoons grated
    Parmesan cheese, divided
Vegetable cooking spray
8 uncooked lasagna noodles

1. In large nonstick skillet, over medium-high heat, crumble sausage and sauté 9 minutes or until no longer pink. Drain. Stir in sauce.

2. In medium bowl combine cottage cheese, mozzarella and ¼ cup Parmesan cheese.

3. In 13×9×2-inch baking pan sprayed with vegetable cooking spray, spread 1 cup meat sauce over bottom of pan. Place 4 uncooked noodles over sauce, breaking to fit if necessary. Spread ½ of cheese mixture over noodles. Layer with ½ of remaining sauce, 4 noodles and remaining cheese. Top with remaining sauce, covering all noodles. Sprinkle 2 tablespoons Parmesan cheese over top. Cover tightly with aluminum foil. Bake at 350°F 45 minutes or until noodles are tender. Let stand 10 to 15 minutes before cutting.

Favorite recipe from **National Turkey Federation**

Chipotle Tamale Pie

¾ pound ground turkey breast
    or lean ground beef
1 cup chopped onion
¾ cup diced green bell pepper
¾ cup diced red bell pepper
4 cloves garlic, minced
2 teaspoons ground cumin
1 can (15 ounces) pinto or red
    beans, rinsed and drained
1 can (8 ounces) no-salt-added
    stewed tomatoes,
    undrained
2 canned chipotle chilies in
    adobo sauce, minced
    (about 1 tablespoon)

1 to 2 teaspoons adobo sauce
    from canned chilies
    (optional)
1 cup (4 ounces) low-sodium
    reduced-fat shredded
    Cheddar cheese
½ cup chopped fresh cilantro
1 package (8½ ounces) corn
    bread mix
⅓ cup low-fat (1%) milk
1 egg white

1. Preheat oven to 400°F.

2. Cook turkey, onion, bell peppers and garlic in large nonstick skillet over medium-high heat 8 minutes or until turkey is no longer pink, stirring occasionally. Drain fat; sprinkle mixture with cumin.

3. Add beans, tomatoes with juice, chilies and adobo sauce; bring to a boil over high heat. Reduce heat to medium; simmer, uncovered, 5 minutes. Remove from heat; stir in cheese and cilantro.

4. Spray 8-inch square baking dish with nonstick cooking spray. Spoon turkey mixture evenly into prepared dish, pressing down to compact mixture. Combine corn bread mix, milk and egg white in medium bowl; mix just until dry ingredients are moistened. Spoon batter evenly over turkey mixture to cover completely.

5. Bake 20 to 22 minutes or until corn bread is golden brown. Let stand 5 minutes before serving.

Turkey Tetrazzini

Makes 6 servings

Prep Time:
30 minutes

Bake Time:
30 minutes

Microwave Time:
21 minutes

⅔ cup MIRACLE WHIP® Salad
 Dressing
⅓ cup flour
½ teaspoon celery salt
 Dash of pepper
2 cups milk
7 ounces spaghetti, broken into
 thirds, cooked and drained
2 cups chopped cooked LOUIS
 RICH® Oven Roasted
 Boneless Turkey Breast

¾ cup KRAFT® 100% Grated
 Parmesan Cheese, divided
1 can (4 ounces) mushrooms,
 drained
2 tablespoons chopped
 pimiento (optional)
2 cups fresh bread cubes
3 tablespoons butter or
 margarine, melted

MIX salad dressing, flour and seasonings in 3-quart saucepan until well blended.

GRADUALLY add milk; cook, stirring constantly, on low heat until thickened. Add spaghetti, turkey, ½ cup of the cheese, mushrooms and pimiento; mix lightly. Spoon into 2-quart casserole. Top with bread cubes tossed with butter and remaining ¼ cup cheese.

BAKE at 350°F for 30 minutes or until lightly browned.

<u>Microwave Directions:</u> *Reduce butter to 2 tablespoons. Microwave butter in 2-quart microwavable casserole on HIGH 30 seconds or until melted. Add bread cubes; toss. Microwave on HIGH 3½ to 4½ minutes or until crisp, stirring after 2 minutes. Remove from casserole; set aside. Mix salad dressing, flour and seasonings in same casserole; gradually add milk. Microwave on HIGH 5 to 6 minutes or until thickened, stirring after each minute. Stir in spaghetti, turkey, ½ cup of the cheese, mushrooms and pimiento; mix lightly. Cover. Microwave on HIGH 8 to*

10 minutes or until thoroughly heated, stirring after 5 minutes. Stir; top with bread cubes. Sprinkle with remaining ¼ cup cheese. Let stand 5 minutes.

<u>Make Ahead:</u> *Prepare as directed except for topping with bread cubes and baking. Cover. Refrigerate. When ready to bake, toss bread cubes with melted butter and remaining ¼ cup cheese. Top casserole; cover with foil. Bake at 350°F for 25 minutes. Uncover; bake an additional 30 minutes or until lightly browned.*

Turkey Olé

Makes 6 servings

½ cup diced onion
2 tablespoons butter or margarine
1 tablespoon all-purpose flour
1½ cups cubed cooked turkey
1½ cups prepared **HIDDEN VALLEY®** The Original **Ranch®** Dressing
3 ounces rotini (spiral macaroni), plain or spinach, cooked
½ (10-ounce) package frozen peas, thawed

⅓ cup canned diced green chiles, drained
1 teaspoon dried oregano, crushed
⅛ to ¼ teaspoon black pepper (optional)
3 tablespoons dry bread crumbs
1 tablespoon butter or margarine, melted
Tomato wedges

Preheat oven to 350°F. In skillet, sauté onion in 2 tablespoons butter until tender. Stir in flour and cook until smooth and bubbly; remove from heat. In 1½-quart casserole, combine turkey, salad dressing, rotini, peas, chiles, oregano and pepper; stir in onion. In small bowl, combine bread crumbs with melted butter; sprinkle over casserole. Bake until heated through and bread crumbs are browned, 15 to 20 minutes. Garnish with tomato wedges.

Turkey Zucchini Casserole

Makes 6 servings

3 tablespoons butter
2 medium zucchini, sliced
3 tablespoons all-purpose flour
1 cup small-curd cottage
    cheese
2 eggs
1 teaspoon LAWRY'S®
    Seasoned Salt

½ teaspoon LAWRY'S® Garlic
    Powder with Parsley
¼ cup long grain rice
3 cups cooked, cubed turkey
1 cup (4 ounces) shredded
    cheddar cheese

Note:

When purchasing zucchini, choose those that are heavy for their size, firm and well shaped. They should have a bright color and be free of cuts and any soft spots. Small zucchini are more tender because they have been harvested when they were young.

In large skillet, heat butter. Add zucchini and cook over medium-high heat until browned. Stir in flour and continue to cook, stirring constantly, until tender. In large bowl, combine cottage cheese, eggs, seasonings, rice and turkey. Add vegetable mixture; mix well. In 2½-quart baking dish, place turkey mixture and top with cheese. Bake, uncovered, in 350°F oven 30 to 40 minutes.

Turkey Vegetable Crescent Pie

Makes 8 servings

2 cans (about 14 ounces) fat-free reduced-sodium chicken broth
1 medium onion, diced
1¼ pounds turkey tenderloins, cut into ¾-inch pieces
3 cups diced red potatoes
1 teaspoon chopped fresh rosemary *or* ½ teaspoon dried rosemary
¼ teaspoon salt
⅛ teaspoon black pepper
1 bag (16 ounces) frozen mixed vegetables
1 bag (10 ounces) frozen mixed vegetables
⅓ cup fat-free (skim) milk plus additional if necessary
3 tablespoons cornstarch
1 package (8 ounces) refrigerated reduced-fat crescent rolls

1. Bring broth to a boil in large saucepan. Add onion; reduce heat and simmer 3 minutes. Add turkey; return to a boil. Reduce heat, cover and simmer 7 to 9 minutes or until turkey is no longer pink. Remove turkey from saucepan with slotted spoon; place in 13×9-inch baking dish.

2. Return broth to a boil. Add potatoes, rosemary, salt and pepper; simmer 2 minutes. Return to a boil and stir in mixed vegetables. Simmer, covered, 7 to 8 minutes or until potatoes are tender. Remove vegetables with slotted spoon. Drain in colander set over bowl; reserve broth. Transfer vegetables to baking dish with turkey.

3. Preheat oven to 375°F. Blend ⅓ cup milk with cornstarch in small bowl until smooth. Add enough milk to reserved broth to equal 3 cups. Heat in large saucepan over medium-high heat; whisk in cornstarch mixture, stirring constantly until mixture comes to a boil. Boil 1 minute; remove from heat. Pour over turkey-vegetable mixture in baking dish.

4. Roll out crescent roll dough and separate at perforations; arrange dough pieces decoratively over top of turkey-vegetable mixture. Bake 13 to 15 minutes or until crust is golden brown.

Turkey Florentine Spaghetti Pie

Makes 6 servings

8 ounces spaghetti
1 tablespoon low-fat margarine
½ cup plus 2 tablespoons grated
  Parmesan or Romano
  cheese, divided
1 egg, beaten slightly
  Vegetable cooking spray
1 cup fat-free ricotta cheese
1½ teaspoons dried basil leaves
  Dash of pepper
1 teaspoon dried parsley flakes
1 (10-ounce) package frozen
  chopped spinach, cooked
  and well drained

1 pound ground turkey
1 tablespoon olive oil
½ cup chopped onion
1 clove garlic, chopped
1 (29-ounce) can tomatoes,
  undrained, coarsely
  chopped
1 (6-ounce) can tomato paste
1 tablespoon dried Italian
  seasoning
¾ cup (3 ounces) shredded low-
  fat mozzarella cheese
1 large or 2 medium fresh
  tomatoes

Break spaghetti in half; cook according to package directions. Drain well. Stir in margarine, ½ cup Parmesan cheese and egg. Cool about 5 minutes. Place spaghetti mixture in deep-dish 10-inch pie pan which has been coated with cooking spray; form into crust.

Mix ricotta cheese, basil, pepper and parsley flakes in bowl; spoon over spaghetti crust. Layer spinach over ricotta cheese mixture.

Brown turkey in olive oil with onion and garlic, stirring to break meat into small pieces. Add canned tomatoes, tomato paste and Italian seasoning; bring to simmer and cook about 5 minutes, stirring well. Spoon over spinach layer. Sprinkle mozzarella cheese on top.

Slice fresh tomatoes into ½-inch slices and arrange on top of turkey mixture. Sprinkle with remaining 2 tablespoons Parmesan cheese. Bake, uncovered, in a preheated 350°F oven about 25 minutes.

Favorite recipe from **North Dakota Wheat Commission**

Pepperidge Farm® Turkey & Stuffing Bake

1 can (14 ounces) SWANSON®
   Chicken Broth (1¾ cups)
Generous dash pepper
1 stalk celery, chopped (about
   ½ cup)
1 small onion, coarsely
   chopped (about ¼ cup)

4 cups PEPPERIDGE FARM®
   Herb Seasoned Stuffing
4 servings sliced roasted *or* deli
   turkey (about 12 ounces)
1 jar (12 ounces) FRANCO-
   AMERICAN® Slow Roast™
   Turkey Gravy

Makes 4 servings

Prep Time:
15 minutes

Cook Time:
30 minutes

1. In medium saucepan mix broth, pepper, celery and onion. Over high heat, heat to a boil. Reduce heat to low. Cover and cook 5 minutes or until vegetables are tender. Add stuffing. Mix lightly.

2. Spoon into 2-quart shallow baking dish. Arrange turkey over stuffing. Pour gravy over turkey.

3. Bake at 350°F. for 30 minutes or until hot.

Tip: *For a variation, add ½ cup chopped nuts with the stuffing.*

Note:

Although several varieties of celery ranging from light to dark green are grown in the United States, Pascal celery is the most common. Celery root, or celeriac, comes from a variety of celery that is cultivated specifically for its root. It should not be confused with celery.

Spicy Turkey Casserole

Makes 6 (1-cup) servings

1 tablespoon olive oil
1 pound turkey breast cutlets, cut into ½-inch pieces
2 (3-ounce) spicy chicken or turkey sausages, sliced ½ inch thick
1 cup diced green bell pepper
½ cup sliced mushrooms
½ cup diced onion
1 jalapeño pepper,* seeded and minced (optional)
½ cup fat-free reduced-sodium chicken broth or water
1 can (14 ounces) reduced-sodium diced tomatoes, undrained

1 teaspoon Italian seasoning
¼ teaspoon black pepper
½ teaspoon paprika
1 cup cooked egg yolk-free egg noodles
6 tablespoons grated Parmesan cheese
2 tablespoons coarse bread crumbs

Jalapeño peppers can sting and irritate the skin; wear rubber gloves when handling peppers and do not touch eyes. Wash hands after handling.

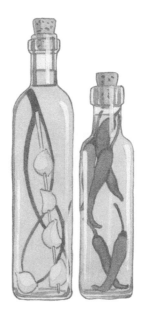

1. Preheat oven to 350°F. Heat oil in large nonstick skillet. Add turkey and sausages; cook and stir over medium heat 2 minutes. Add bell pepper, mushrooms, onion and jalapeño pepper, if desired. Cook and stir 5 minutes. Add chicken broth; cook 1 minute, scraping any browned bits off bottom of skillet. Add tomatoes with juice, seasonings and noodles.

2. Spoon turkey mixture into shallow 10-inch round casserole. Sprinkle with cheese and bread crumbs. Bake 15 to 20 minutes or until mixture is hot and bread crumbs are brown.

Gone
Fishin'

CHAPTER FIVE

Sole Almondine

Makes 4 servings

1 package (6.5 ounces) RICE-A-RONI® Broccoli Au Gratin
1 medium zucchini
4 sole, scrod or orange roughy fillets
1 tablespoon lemon juice

¼ cup grated Parmesan cheese, divided
Salt and pepper (optional)
¼ cup sliced almonds
2 tablespoons margarine or butter, melted

Note:

Sole, also known as Dover Sole or English Sole, is a saltwater flat fish. It is further classified as a lean fish. Lean fish are low in fat, have white flesh and a mild, delicate flavor.

1. Prepare Rice-A-Roni® Mix as package directs.

2. While Rice-A-Roni® is simmering, cut zucchini lengthwise into 12 thin strips. Heat oven to 350°F.

3. In 11×7-inch glass baking dish, spread prepared rice evenly. Set aside. Sprinkle fish with lemon juice, 2 tablespoons cheese, salt and pepper, if desired. Place zucchini strips over fish; roll up. Place fish seam-side down on rice.

4. Combine almonds and margarine; sprinkle evenly over fish. Top with remaining 2 tablespoons cheese. Bake 20 to 25 minutes or until fish flakes easily with fork.

Creamy Scalloped Potatoes and Tuna

2 cups milk
2 cups whipping cream
2 cloves garlic, minced
2½ pounds (about 6 medium)
    white or russet potatoes
¾ teaspoon salt
½ teaspoon white pepper

1 tablespoon butter or
    margarine
1 (7-ounce) pouch of STARKIST®
    Premium Albacore or
    Chunk Light Tuna
1½ cups shredded mozzarella
    cheese

Makes 6 to 8 servings

Prep Time:
70 minutes

In 3-quart saucepan over medium heat, heat milk, cream and garlic. Meanwhile, peel potatoes; slice about ⅛ to ¼ inch thick. Add potatoes, salt and white pepper to milk mixture; heat to simmering.

Grease 11×7-inch casserole with butter; spoon potato-milk mixture into dish. Bake in 350°F oven 25 minutes; remove from oven. Add tuna, stirring gently; top with cheese. Bake 35 more minutes or until potatoes are cooked through and top is golden brown. Let stand, covered, about 15 minutes to thicken.

Festive Baked Stuffed Fish

Makes 8 servings

4 tablespoons butter or
  margarine
2 teaspoons dill
1 clove garlic, minced
½ cup chopped celery
½ cup chopped red bell pepper
¼ cup chopped shallots
¼ pound shiitake mushrooms,
  sliced

6 slices crispbread, crumbled
1 cup diced JARLSBERG LITE™
  Cheese
1 tablespoon chopped parsley
8 flounder fillets (about
  1 pound)
8 salmon fillets (about 1 pound)
  Salt and black pepper to taste
  Additional chopped parsley

Melt butter in medium skillet. Add dill and garlic. Add celery, bell
pepper, shallots and mushrooms; cook 8 to 10 minutes or until
tender but not browned. Stir in crispbread crumbs, cheese and
1 tablespoon parsley. Spoon into 11×8×1½-inch ovenproof
shallow baking dish.

Preheat oven to 350°F. Season fillets with salt and black pepper.
Fold fillets in half or thirds and arrange over cheese stuffing in
baking dish, alternating for braid effect. Cover loosely with foil.
Bake 20 to 25 minutes or until fish flakes easily when tested with
fork and cheese is melted. Sprinkle with additional parsley.

Foolproof Clam Fettuccine

1 package (6 ounces) fettuccine-
    style noodles with creamy
    cheese sauce mix
¾ cup milk
1 can (6½ ounces) chopped
    clams, undrained
¼ cup (1 ounce) grated
    Parmesan cheese

1 teaspoon parsley flakes
1 can (4 ounces) mushroom
    stems and pieces, drained
2 tablespoons diced pimiento
1⅓ cups *French's®* French Fried
    Onions, divided

Preheat oven to 375°F. In large saucepan, cook noodles according to package directions; drain. Return hot noodles to saucepan; stir in sauce mix, milk, undrained clams, Parmesan cheese, parsley flakes, mushrooms, pimiento and *⅔ cup* French Fried Onions. Heat and stir 3 minutes or until bubbly. Pour into 10×6-inch baking dish. Bake, covered, at 375°F for 30 minutes or until thickened. Place remaining *⅔ cup* onions around edges of casserole; bake, uncovered, 3 minutes or until onions are golden brown.

Microwave Directions: *Prepare noodle mixture as above; pour into 10×6-inch microwave-safe dish. Cook, covered, on HIGH 4 to 6 minutes or until heated through. Stir noodle mixture halfway through cooking time. Top with remaining onions as above; cook, uncovered, 1 minute. Let stand 5 minutes.*

Note:

Clams are found along both the Atlantic and Pacific coasts of the United States. They may have a hard or a soft shell.

Crustless Salmon & Broccoli Quiche

Makes 2 servings

¾ cup cholesterol-free egg
   substitute
¼ cup plain nonfat yogurt
¼ cup chopped green onions
   with tops
2 teaspoons all-purpose flour
1 teaspoon dried basil leaves
⅛ teaspoon salt
⅛ teaspoon black pepper
¾ cup frozen broccoli florets,
   thawed and drained

⅓ cup (3 ounces) drained and
   flaked water-packed
   boneless, skinless canned
   salmon
2 tablespoons grated Parmesan
   cheese
1 plum tomato, thinly sliced
¼ cup fresh bread crumbs

Note:

Although salmon has a higher fat content than most fish, it is still very nutritious. Salmon's fat content is made up primarily of omega-3 fatty acids. There is a wealth of research available today that links consumption of omega-3 fatty acids with the reduced risk of heart attack and heart disease.

1. Preheat oven to 375°F. Spray 6-cup rectangular casserole or 9-inch pie plate with nonstick cooking spray.

2. Combine egg substitute, nonfat yogurt, green onions, flour, basil, salt and pepper in medium bowl until well blended. Stir in broccoli, salmon and Parmesan cheese. Spread evenly in prepared casserole. Top with tomato slices. Sprinkle bread crumbs over top.

3. Bake 20 to 25 minutes or until knife inserted into center comes out clean. Let stand 5 minutes before serving.

Company Crab

Makes 6 servings

1 pound Florida blue crabmeat, fresh, frozen or pasteurized
1 can (15 ounces) artichoke hearts, drained
1 can (4 ounces) sliced mushrooms, drained
2 tablespoons butter or margarine
2½ tablespoons all-purpose flour
½ teaspoon salt
⅛ teaspoon ground red pepper
1 cup half-and-half
2 tablespoons dry sherry
2 tablespoons crushed corn flakes
1 tablespoon grated Parmesan cheese
Paprika

Preheat oven to 450°F. Thaw crabmeat if frozen. Remove any pieces of shell or cartilage. Cut artichoke hearts in half; place artichokes in well-greased, shallow 1½-quart casserole. Add crabmeat and mushrooms; cover and set aside.

Melt butter in small saucepan over medium heat. Stir in flour, salt and ground red pepper. Gradually stir in half-and-half. Continue cooking until sauce thickens, stirring constantly. Stir in sherry. Pour sauce over crabmeat. Combine corn flakes and cheese in small bowl; sprinkle over casserole. Sprinkle with paprika. Bake 12 to 15 minutes or until bubbly.

Favorite recipe from **Florida Department of Agriculture and Consumer Services, Bureau of Seafood and Aquaculture**

Baked Fish Galician Style

Makes 4 servings

½ cup plus 4 teaspoons FILIPPO
BERIO® Olive Oil, divided
1 large onion, chopped
2 tablespoons minced fresh
parsley, divided
2 cloves garlic, crushed
2 teaspoons paprika
1½ pounds new potatoes, peeled
and cut into ⅛-inch-thick
slices

1 tablespoon all-purpose flour
3 small bay leaves
½ teaspoon dried thyme leaves
Dash ground cloves
4 orange roughy or scrod fillets,
1 inch thick (about
2 pounds)
Salt and freshly ground black
pepper
Lemon wedges (optional)

Preheat oven to 350°F. In large skillet, heat ½ cup olive oil over
medium heat until hot. Add onion; cook and stir 5 to 7 minutes or
until softened. Stir in 1 tablespoon parsley, garlic and paprika.
Add potatoes; stir until lightly coated with mixture. Sprinkle with
flour. Add enough water to cover potatoes; stir gently to blend.
Add bay leaves, thyme and cloves. Bring to a boil. Cover; reduce
heat to low and simmer 20 to 25 minutes or until potatoes are
just tender. *(Do not overcook potatoes.)*

Spoon potato mixture into 1 large or 2 small casseroles. Place fish
fillets on top of potato mixture. Drizzle 1 teaspoon of remaining
olive oil over each fillet. Spoon sauce from bottom of casserole
over each fillet.

Bake 15 to 20 minutes or until fish flakes easily when tested with
fork. Sprinkle fillets with remaining 1 tablespoon parsley. Season
to taste with salt and pepper. Remove bay leaves before serving.
Serve with lemon wedges, if desired.

Shrimp Enchiladas

1 jar (1 pound 10 ounces)
RAGÚ® Old World Style®
Pasta Sauce
1 can (4 ounces) chopped green
chilies, drained
1½ tablespoons chili powder
1 pound cooked shrimp,
coarsely chopped

2 cups shredded Monterey Jack
cheese (about 8 ounces)
1 container (8 ounces) sour
cream
1 package (8 ounces) corn
tortillas (12 tortillas),
softened

Makes 6 servings

Prep Time:
10 minutes

Cook Time:
40 minutes

1. Preheat oven to 400°F. In medium bowl, combine Ragú Pasta
Sauce, chilies and chili powder. Evenly spread 1 cup sauce
mixture in 13×9-inch baking dish; set aside.

2. In another medium bowl, combine shrimp, 1 cup cheese and
sour cream. Evenly spread mixture onto tortillas; roll up. Arrange
seam side down in prepared dish and top with remaining sauce
mixture. Cover with aluminum foil and bake 20 minutes.

3. Remove foil and sprinkle with remaining 1 cup cheese. Bake
an additional 5 minutes or until cheese is melted.

Tip: *To soften tortillas, arrange on a microwave-safe plate, cover
with a dampened paper towel and microwave at HIGH (Full
Power) 30 seconds.*

Crunchy Tuna Squares

Makes 6 servings

Prep Time:
20 minutes

1 (7-ounce) pouch of STARKIST® Premium Albacore Tuna
1 cup chopped celery
1 cup chopped roasted cashews
½ cup drained sliced water chestnuts
½ cup chopped green onions, including tops
⅓ cup chopped drained roasted red peppers

1½ cups shredded Cheddar cheese, divided
½ cup mayonnaise or light mayonnaise
½ cup sour cream or light sour cream
2 tablespoons lemon juice
¾ teaspoon seasoned salt
1 cup cheese crackers, crushed into coarse crumbs

Note:

Water chestnuts are the edible fruit of an aquatic plant native to Southeast Asia. They are encased in a black skin that must be peeled away.

In medium bowl, place tuna, celery, cashews, water chestnuts, onions, peppers and 1 cup cheese; mix lightly with fork. In small bowl, whisk together mayonnaise, sour cream, lemon juice and seasoned salt. Add to tuna mixture; mix gently.

Spoon into greased 11×7-inch baking pan. Sprinkle with crushed cracker crumbs; top with remaining ½ cup cheese. Bake in 450°F oven 12 to 15 minutes or until mixture bubbles and begins to brown. Let stand several minutes before cutting into 6 squares.

Citrus Baked Flounder

1⅓ cups *French's®* French Fried
   Onions, divided
1 teaspoon grated lemon peel
2 cups cooked white rice
2 tablespoons butter or
   margarine, melted

2 tablespoons lemon juice
4 flounder fillets, about 1 pound
   Salt and pepper to taste
   Garnish: chopped parsley,
    optional

Makes 4 servings

Prep Time:
10 minutes

Cook Time:
25 minutes

1. Preheat oven to 350°F. Stir ⅔ *cup* French Fried Onions and lemon peel into cooked rice. Mix butter and lemon juice, set aside.

2. Spoon rice mixture into lightly greased 9-inch square baking dish. Arrange fish on top of rice, folding fillets to fit if necessary. Season with salt and pepper to taste. Drizzle with butter mixture.

3. Bake 20 minutes. Sprinkle with remaining ⅔ *cup* onions. Bake 5 minutes or until fish is opaque and onions are golden. Garnish with parsley, if desired.

Egg Noodle-Crab Casserole

Makes 6 servings

12 ounces wide egg noodles, uncooked
1 can (10¾ ounces) Cheddar cheese soup
1 cup milk
1 tablespoon minced dried onions

¼ teaspoon paprika
¼ teaspoon dried marjoram
1 pound crabmeat
1 cup SONOMA® Dried Tomato Halves, snipped into strips, parboiled and drained

Cook noodles according to package directions until al dente. Set aside and keep warm.

In medium mixing bowl, combine soup and milk. Add onions, paprika and marjoram; stir. Place noodles in 2½- to 3-quart casserole. Break up crabmeat into bite-size pieces; sprinkle crabmeat and tomatoes over noodles. Pour soup mixture over crab mixture; blend well.

Cover and bake in 350°F oven for 30 minutes or until hot and bubbly.

Creamy Shrimp & Vegetable Casserole

1 can (10¾ ounces) reduced-fat
   cream of celery soup
1 pound fresh or thawed frozen
   shrimp, shelled and
   deveined
½ cup sliced fresh or thawed
   frozen asparagus (1-inch
   pieces)

½ cup sliced mushrooms
¼ cup sliced green onions
¼ cup diced red bell pepper
1 clove garlic, minced
¾ teaspoon dried thyme leaves
¼ teaspoon black pepper
   Hot cooked rice or orzo

Makes 4 servings

1. Preheat oven to 375°F. Coat 2-quart baking dish with nonstick cooking spray.

2. Combine soup, shrimp, asparagus, mushrooms, green onions, bell pepper, garlic, thyme and black pepper in large bowl; mix well. Place in prepared baking dish.

3. Cover and bake 30 minutes. Serve over rice, if desired.

Note:

To devein shrimp, make a small cut along the back and lift out the dark vein with the tip of a knife. You may find the task easier if it is done under cold running water. There are also special gadgets available that make peeling and deveining shrimp a one-step process.

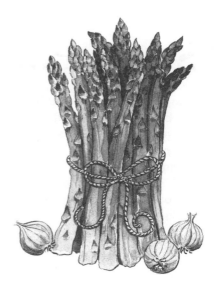

Surfer's Seafood Casserole

Makes 6 servings

½ pound Florida blue crab meat
½ pound cooked peeled
    deveined Florida shrimp
1⅓ cups chopped Florida celery
1 cup mayonnaise
½ cup chopped Florida onion
½ cup chopped Florida green
    bell pepper

1 teaspoon Worcestershire
    sauce
½ teaspoon salt
1 cup crushed potato chips
    Paprika

Preheat oven to 350°F. Grease 1½-quart casserole; set aside.

Mix crab, shrimp, celery, mayonnaise, onion, bell pepper,
Worcestershire and salt in large bowl. Pour crab mixture into
prepared casserole. Top with crushed chips and paprika. Bake
30 to 40 minutes or until knife inserted in center comes out clean.

Favorite recipe from **Florida Department of Agriculture and Consumer Services, Bureau
of Seafood and Aquaculture**

Starkist® Swiss Potato Pie

Makes 6 servings

Prep and Cook Time:
90 minutes

4 cups frozen shredded hash
    brown potatoes, thawed
2 cups shredded Swiss cheese
1 cup milk
4 eggs, beaten
½ to 1 cup chopped green
    onions, including tops

½ cup chopped green bell
    pepper (optional)
½ cup sour cream
1 (3-ounce) pouch of STARKIST®
    Premium Albacore Tuna
½ teaspoon garlic powder

In large bowl, mix all ingredients. Pour into lightly greased deep
10-inch pie plate. Bake in 350°F oven 1 hour and 20 minutes or
until golden and crusty. Let stand a few minutes before slicing
into serving portions.

Baja Fish and Rice Bake

3 tablespoons vegetable oil
¾ cup chopped onion
½ cup chopped celery
1 clove garlic, minced
½ cup uncooked white rice
2 cans (14.5 ounces each)
  CONTADINA® Stewed
  Tomatoes, cut up,
  undrained

1 teaspoon lemon pepper
  seasoning
½ teaspoon salt
⅛ teaspoon cayenne pepper
1 pound fish fillets (any firm
  white fish)
¼ cup finely chopped fresh
  parsley
Lemon slices (optional)

Makes 6 servings

Prep Time:
8 minutes

Cook Time:
58 minutes

Stand Time:
5 minutes

1. Heat oil in large skillet over medium heat; sauté onion, celery and garlic.

2. Stir in rice; sauté about 5 minutes, or until rice browns slightly. Add undrained tomatoes, lemon pepper, salt and cayenne pepper.

3. Place fish fillets in bottom of 12×7½×2-inch baking dish. Spoon rice mixture over fish.

4. Cover with foil; bake in preheated 400°F oven for 45 to 50 minutes or until rice is tender. Allow to stand 5 minutes before serving. Sprinkle with parsley. Garnish with lemon slices, if desired.

Microwave Directions: *1. Combine onion, celery and garlic in microwave-safe bowl. Microwave on HIGH (100%) for 3 minutes. 2. Stir in rice, tomatoes and juice, lemon pepper, salt and cayenne pepper. Microwave on HIGH power for an additional 5 minutes. 3. Place fish fillets in 12×7½×2-inch microwave-safe baking dish. Spoon tomato mixture over fish. 4. Cover tightly with plastic wrap, turning up corner to vent. Microwave on HIGH for 20 to 25 minutes or until rice is tender. Allow to stand 5 minutes before serving. Serve as above.*

Baked Fish with Potatoes and Onions

Makes 4 servings

1 pound baking potatoes, very thinly sliced
1 large onion, very thinly sliced
1 small red or green bell pepper, thinly sliced
Salt
Black pepper
½ teaspoon dried oregano leaves, divided

1 pound lean fish fillets, cut 1 inch thick
¼ cup butter or margarine
¼ cup all-purpose flour
2 cups milk
¾ cup (3 ounces) shredded Cheddar cheese

Note:

Fresh fish are generally separated into two categories, lean and fatty. Lean fish contain from 1 to 5 percent fat. Fatty fish contain from 5 to 35 percent fat, which makes their flesh darker, richer and stronger tasting than lean fish. The type of fish is an important factor when preparing and cooking fish.

Preheat oven to 375°F.

Arrange half of potatoes in buttered 3-quart casserole. Top with half of onion and half of bell pepper. Season with salt and black pepper. Sprinkle with ¼ teaspoon oregano. Arrange fish in one layer over vegetables. Arrange remaining potatoes, onion and bell pepper over fish. Season with salt, black pepper and remaining ¼ teaspoon oregano.

Melt butter in medium saucepan over medium heat. Stir in flour; cook until bubbly, stirring constantly. Gradually stir in milk. Cook until thickened, stirring constantly. Pour white sauce over casserole. Cover and bake at 375°F 40 minutes or until potatoes are tender. Sprinkle with cheese. Bake, uncovered, about 5 minutes or until cheese is melted.

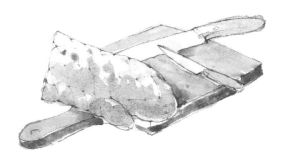

Creamy Alfredo Seafood Lasagna

1 jar (1 pound) RAGÚ® Cheese Creations!® Classic Alfredo Sauce

1 container (15 ounces) ricotta cheese

1 pound imitation crabmeat, separated into bite-sized pieces

1 green onion, chopped (optional)

¼ teaspoon ground white pepper

⅛ teaspoon ground nutmeg (optional)

9 lasagna noodles, cooked and drained

2 cups shredded mozzarella cheese (about 8 ounces)

2 tablespoons grated Parmesan cheese

Makes 8 servings

Prep Time:
20 minutes

Cook Time:
50 minutes

1. Preheat oven to 350°F. In medium bowl, combine ½ cup Ragú Cheese Creations! Sauce, ricotta cheese, crabmeat, green onion, pepper and nutmeg; set aside.

2. In 13×9-inch baking dish, spread ½ cup Ragú Cheese Creations! Sauce. Arrange 3 lasagna noodles lengthwise over sauce. Spread ½ of the ricotta mixture over noodles; evenly top with ¾ cup mozzarella cheese. Repeat layers, ending with noodles. Top with remaining ½ cup sauce, then sprinkle with remaining ½ cup mozzarella cheese and Parmesan cheese.

3. Cover with aluminum foil and bake 40 minutes. Remove foil and continue baking 10 minutes or until cheese is melted and lightly golden. Let stand 10 minutes before serving. Garnish, if desired, with additional chopped green onions.

Spicy Snapper & Black Beans

Makes 4 servings

1½ pounds fresh red snapper fillets, cut into 4 portions (6 ounces each)
Juice of 1 lime
½ teaspoon coarsely ground black pepper
Nonstick cooking spray
1 cup GUILTLESS GOURMET® Spicy Black Bean Dip

½ cup water
½ cup (about 35) crushed GUILTLESS GOURMET® Baked Tortilla Chips (yellow or white corn)
1 cup GUILTLESS GOURMET® Roasted Red Pepper Salsa

Wash fish thoroughly; pat dry with paper towels. Place fish in 13×9-inch glass baking dish. Pour juice over top; sprinkle with pepper. Cover and refrigerate 1 hour.

Preheat oven to 350°F. Coat 11×7-inch glass baking dish with cooking spray. Combine bean dip and water in small bowl; spread 1 cup bean mixture in bottom of prepared baking dish. Place fish over bean mixture, discarding juice. Spread remaining bean mixture over top of fish; sprinkle with crushed chips.

Bake about 20 minutes or until chips are lightly browned and fish turns opaque and flakes easily when tested with fork. To serve, divide fish among 4 serving plates; spoon ¼ cup salsa over top of each serving.

Hint: This recipe can be made with 4 boneless skinless chicken breast halves in place of red snapper fillets. Prepare as directed and bake about 40 minutes or until chicken is no longer pink in center. Serve as directed.

Homestyle Tuna Pot Pie

1 package (15 ounces)
    refrigerated pie crust dough
1 can (10¾ ounces) condensed
    cream of potato or cream of
    mushroom soup
1 package (10 ounces) frozen
    peas and carrots, thawed
    and drained

1 (7-ounce) pouch of STARKIST®
    Premium Albacore or
    Chunk Light Tuna
½ cup chopped onion
⅓ cup milk
½ teaspoon poultry seasoning
    or dried thyme leaves
Salt and pepper to taste

Makes 6 servings

Prep and Cook Time:
55 to 60 minutes

Line 9-inch pie pan with 1 pie crust dough round; set aside.
Reserve second dough round. In medium bowl, combine remaining
ingredients; mix well. Pour tuna mixture into pie shell; top with
second crust. Crimp edges to seal. Cut slits in top crust to vent.
Bake in 375°F oven 45 to 50 minutes or until golden brown.

Fishing for Freshness

Fish is versatile, delicious and nutritious.
It also cooks quickly. Fish come in various
forms, including whole, dressed, pan-dressed,
fillets and steaks. Fillets and steaks are a
good choice for inexperienced cooks.

It is important to know what to look for
when purchasing fresh fish. One can find
fresh fish at most large supermarkets or at
retail fish markets. An independent retail fish
market usually buys its fish on a daily basis,
whereas chain stores order in large quantities
and often do not receive daily shipments.

When buying whole fish, look for bright,
clear and protruding eyes rather than dull,
hazy sunken ones. The skin should be moist
and shiny, the gills red or pink and the flesh
firm and elastic. A fresh fish should have a
mild, slightly oceanlike odor rather than a
fishy or sour smell.

Fish fillets and steaks should have moist
flesh that is free from discoloration and skin
that is shiny and resilient. Again, if the fillet
or steak has a strong odor, it is not fresh.

Frozen fish should have its original shape
with the wrapper intact. There should be no
ice crystals, visible blood or discoloration on
the skin and flesh. Do not allow frozen fish
to thaw on the way home from the store.

Chesapeake Crab Strata

Makes 6 to 8 servings

4 tablespoons butter or
    margarine
4 cups unseasoned croutons
2 cups shredded Cheddar
    cheese
2 cups milk

8 eggs, beaten
½ teaspoon dry mustard
½ teaspoon seafood seasoning
    Salt and black pepper to taste
1 pound crabmeat, picked over
    to remove any shells

Note:

Canned crabmeat is usually taken from snow crabs, although sometimes it is taken from Alaska king or Dungeness crabs. Crabmeat will keep in the refrigerator for a few days after opening.

1. Preheat oven to 325°F. Place butter in 11×7-inch baking dish. Heat in oven until melted, tilting to coat dish. Remove dish from oven; spread croutons over melted butter. Top with cheese; set aside.

2. Combine milk, eggs, dry mustard, seafood seasoning, salt and black pepper; mix well. Pour egg mixture over cheese in dish; sprinkle with crabmeat. Bake 50 minutes or until mixture is set. Remove from oven and let stand about 10 minutes. Garnish, if desired.

Salmon Linguini Supper

Makes 4 servings

8 ounces linguini, cooked in
    unsalted water and drained
1 package (10 ounces) frozen
    peas
1 cup milk
1 can (10¾ ounces) condensed
    cream of celery soup
¼ cup (1 ounce) grated
    Parmesan cheese

⅛ teaspoon dried tarragon,
    crumbled (optional)
1 can (15½ ounces) salmon,
    drained and flaked
1 egg, slightly beaten
¼ teaspoon salt
¼ teaspoon pepper
1⅓ cups *French's®* French Fried
    Onions, divided

Preheat oven to 375°F. Return hot pasta to saucepan; stir in peas, milk, soup, cheese and tarragon; spoon into 12×8-inch baking dish. In medium bowl, using fork, combine salmon, egg, salt, pepper and ⅔ *cup* French Fried Onions. Shape salmon mixture into 4 oval patties. Place patties on pasta mixture. Bake, covered, at 375°F for 40 minutes or until patties are done. Top patties with remaining ⅔ *cup* onions; bake, uncovered, 3 minutes or until onions are golden brown.

Microwave Directions: *Prepare pasta mixture as above, except increase milk to 1¼ cups; spoon into 12×8-inch microwave-safe dish. Cook, covered, on HIGH 3 minutes; stir. Prepare salmon patties as above using 2 eggs. Place patties on pasta mixture. Cook, covered, 10 to 12 minutes or until patties are done. Rotate dish halfway through cooking time. Top patties with remaining onions; cook, uncovered, 1 minute. Let stand 5 minutes.*

Seafood Lasagna with Spaghetti Squash and Broccoli

Makes 10 to 12 servings

2 tablespoons Lucini Premium Select extra virgin olive oil
1 cup minced shallots
16 small mushrooms, cut in half
1 tablespoon minced garlic (2 to 4 cloves)
1 teaspoon dried thyme leaves
3 tablespoons all-purpose flour
2 cups dry white wine or chicken broth
1 cup bottled clam juice
¼ teaspoon freshly ground nutmeg
Ground pepper to taste

1½ pounds cooked seafood mixture of firm-textured fish (such as salmon) and scallops, cut into bite-sized pieces, divided
6 lasagna noodles, cooked and drained
4 ounces (1½ to 2 cups) stuffing mix
1 (10-ounce) package frozen chopped broccoli, thawed
1 pound JARLSBERG LITE™ Cheese, shredded
3 cups cooked spaghetti squash

Heat oil in large skillet over medium-high heat. Sauté shallots, mushrooms, garlic and thyme in oil 4 minutes or until shallots begin to brown. Add flour; cook, stirring constantly, 2 to 3 minutes. Add wine, clam juice, nutmeg and pepper. Boil 3 minutes to thicken and reduce liquid. Add fish pieces and simmer 3 minutes. Add scallops; remove skillet from heat and set aside.

Arrange 3 lasagna noodles on bottom of 3½-quart, rectangular baking dish. Evenly sprinkle with stuffing mix. Reserve 1 cup sauce mixture; spoon remaining sauce mixture over stuffing mix.

Cover evenly with broccoli, ⅔ of cheese and 2 cups spaghetti squash. Cover with remaining lasagna noodles, cheese, reserved sauce mixture and remaining spaghetti squash. Press down firmly.* Cover tightly with tented foil and bake at 350°F, 45 to 50 minutes or until heated through.

*Recipe can be made ahead up to this point and refrigerated. Bring to room temperature before baking.

Tip: *To cook spaghetti squash, pierce in several places and place on baking sheet in 350°F oven for 1 hour or until tender when pierced with knife. When squash is cool, cut in half, scoop out seeds and remove strands with two forks. Squash may be prepared ahead and refrigerated until needed.*

Campbell's® Cod Vera Cruz

1 pound fresh *or* thawed frozen cod *or* haddock fillets
1 can (10¾ ounces) CAMPBELL'S® Condensed Tomato Soup
1 can (10½ ounces) CAMPBELL'S® Condensed Chicken Broth
⅓ cup PACE® Chunky Salsa *or* Picante Sauce

1 tablespoon lime juice
2 teaspoons chopped fresh cilantro
1 teaspoon dried oregano leaves, crushed
⅛ teaspoon garlic powder *or* 1 clove garlic, minced
4 cups hot cooked rice

Makes 4 servings

Prep Time:
10 minutes

Cook Time:
20 minutes

1. Place fish in 2-quart shallow baking dish.

2. Mix soup, broth, salsa, lime juice, cilantro, oregano and garlic powder. Pour over fish. Bake at 400°F. for 20 minutes or until fish flakes easily when tested with a fork. Serve over rice.

Scallop and Artichoke Heart Casserole

Makes 4 servings

1 package (9 ounces) frozen artichoke hearts, cooked and drained
1 pound scallops
1 teaspoon canola or vegetable oil
¼ cup chopped red bell pepper
¼ cup sliced green onion tops
¼ cup all-purpose flour

2 cups low-fat (1%) milk
1 teaspoon dried tarragon leaves, crushed
¼ teaspoon salt
¼ teaspoon white pepper
1 tablespoon chopped fresh parsley
Dash paprika

Cut large artichoke hearts lengthwise into halves. Arrange artichoke hearts in even layer in 8-inch square baking dish.

Rinse scallops; pat dry with paper towel. If scallops are large, cut into halves. Arrange scallops evenly over artichokes.

Preheat oven to 350°F. Heat oil in medium saucepan over medium-low heat. Add bell pepper and green onions; cook and stir 5 minutes or until tender. Stir in flour. Gradually stir in milk until smooth. Add tarragon, salt and white pepper; cook and stir over medium heat 10 minutes or until sauce boils and thickens.

Pour hot sauce over scallops. Bake, uncovered, 25 minutes or until bubbling and scallops are opaque. Sprinkle with chopped parsley and paprika before serving.

Tuna Tortilla Roll-Ups

Makes 6 servings

1 can (10¾ ounces) condensed
   cream of celery soup
1 cup milk
1 can (9 ounces) tuna, drained
   and flaked
1 package (10 ounces) frozen
   broccoli spears, thawed,
   drained and cut into 1-inch
   pieces

1 cup (4 ounces) shredded
   Cheddar cheese
1⅓ cups *French's*® French Fried
   Onions, divided
6 (7-inch) flour or corn tortillas
1 medium tomato, chopped

Note:

A tortilla is a round,
thin unleavened
Mexican bread that is
baked on a griddle. It
can be made of either
corn or wheat flour,
water and a little salt.

Preheat oven to 350°F. In small bowl, combine soup and milk; set aside. In medium bowl, combine tuna, broccoli, ½ cup cheese and ⅔ *cup* French Fried Onions; stir in ¾ cup soup mixture. Divide tuna mixture evenly among tortillas; roll up tortillas. Place, seam-side down, in lightly greased 13×9-inch baking dish. Stir tomato into remaining soup mixture; pour down center of roll-ups. Bake, covered, at 350°F for 35 minutes or until heated through. Top center of roll-ups with remaining cheese and ⅔ *cup* onions; bake, uncovered, 5 minutes or until onions are golden brown.

Microwave Directions: *Use corn tortillas only. Prepare soup mixture and roll-ups as above; place roll-ups, seam-side down, in 12×8-inch microwave-safe dish. Stir tomato into remaining soup mixture; pour down center of roll-ups. Cook, covered, on HIGH 15 to 18 minutes or until heated through. Rotate dish halfway through cooking time. Top center of roll-ups with remaining cheese and ⅔ cup onions; cook, uncovered, 1 minute or until cheese melts. Let stand 5 minutes.*

Lemony Dill Salmon and Shell Casserole

Makes 6 servings

Nonstick cooking spray
1½ cups sliced mushrooms
⅓ cup sliced green onions
1 clove garlic, minced
2 cups fat-free (skim) milk
3 tablespoons all-purpose flour
1 tablespoon grated lemon peel
¾ teaspoon dried dill weed

¼ teaspoon salt
⅛ teaspoon black pepper
1½ cups frozen green peas
1 can (7½ ounces) salmon,
    drained and flaked
6 ounces uncooked medium
    shell pasta, cooked, rinsed
    and drained

1. Preheat oven to 350°F.

2. Spray medium nonstick saucepan with cooking spray; heat over medium heat until hot. Add mushrooms, onions and garlic; cook and stir 5 minutes or until vegetables are tender.

3. Combine milk and flour in medium bowl until smooth. Stir in lemon peel, dill weed, salt and pepper. Stir into saucepan; heat over medium-high heat 5 to 8 minutes or until thickened, stirring constantly. Remove saucepan from heat. Stir in peas, salmon and pasta. Pour pasta mixture into 2-quart casserole.

4. Bake, covered, 35 to 40 minutes. Serve immediately. Garnish as desired.

Bacon-Tuna Parmesano

½ cup milk
2 tablespoons margarine or
   butter
1 package (4.8 ounces) PASTA
   RONI® Parmesano
1 package (10 ounces) frozen
   peas

1 can (6⅛ ounces) white tuna in
   water, drained, flaked
4 slices crisply cooked bacon,
   crumbled
½ cup sliced green onions

Makes 4 servings

Microwave Directions

1. In round 3-quart microwaveable glass casserole, combine 1⅔ cups water, milk and margarine. Microwave, uncovered, on HIGH 4 to 5 minutes or until boiling.

2. Stir in pasta, Special Seasonings, frozen peas, tuna, bacon and onions.

3. Microwave, uncovered, on HIGH 9 to 10 minutes or until peas are tender, stirring after 3 minutes.

4. Cover; let stand 3 to 4 minutes. Sauce will thicken upon standing. Stir before serving.

Note:

To cook bacon in the microwave, place the bacon slices, in a single layer between paper towels on a microwaveable rack or plate. Microwave at HIGH about 1 minute per slice. Be careful when removing cooked bacon from the microwave because the bacon grease can get extremely hot.

Crab and Corn Enchilada Casserole

Makes 6 servings

Spicy Tomato Sauce (recipe follows), divided
10 to 12 ounces fresh crabmeat or flaked or chopped surimi crab
1 package (10 ounces) frozen corn, thawed and drained
1½ cups (6 ounces) shredded reduced-fat Monterey Jack cheese, divided
1 can (4 ounces) diced mild green chilies
12 (6-inch) corn tortillas
1 lime, cut into 6 wedges
Sour cream (optional)

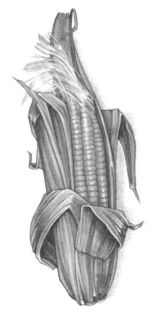

Preheat oven to 350°F. Prepare Spicy Tomato Sauce.

Combine 2 cups Spicy Tomato Sauce, crabmeat, corn, 1 cup cheese and chilies in medium bowl. Cut each tortilla into 4 wedges. Place one-third of tortilla wedges in bottom of shallow 3- to 4-quart casserole, overlapping to make solid layer. Spread half of crab mixture on top. Repeat with another layer tortilla wedges, remaining crab mixture and remaining tortillas. Spread remaining 1 cup Spicy Tomato Sauce over top; cover.

Bake 30 to 40 minutes or until heated through. Sprinkle with remaining ½ cup cheese; bake uncovered 5 minutes or until cheese melts. Squeeze lime over individual servings. Serve with sour cream, if desired.

Spicy Tomato Sauce

2 cans (15 ounces each) no-salt-added stewed tomatoes, undrained or 6 medium tomatoes
2 teaspoons olive oil
1 medium onion, chopped
1 tablespoon minced garlic
2 tablespoons chili powder
2 teaspoons ground cumin
2 teaspoons dried oregano leaves, crushed
1 teaspoon ground cinnamon
¼ teaspoon red pepper flakes
¼ teaspoon ground cloves

Place tomatoes with juice in food processor or blender; process until finely chopped. Set aside.

Heat oil over medium-high heat in large saucepan or Dutch oven. Add onion and garlic. Cook and stir 5 minutes or until onion is tender. Add chili powder, cumin, oregano, cinnamon, red pepper flakes and cloves. Cook and stir 1 minute. Add tomatoes; reduce heat to medium-low. Simmer, uncovered, 20 minutes or until sauce is reduced to 3 to 3¼ cups. *Makes about 3 cups sauce*

Shrimp Casserole

Makes 4 servings

¾ pound raw medium Florida
    shrimp, peeled, deveined
⅓ cup chopped celery
¼ cup chopped onion
¼ cup chopped green bell
    pepper
3 tablespoons margarine
1 can (10¾ ounces) condensed
    cream of celery soup

½ cup dry stuffing mix
1 hard-boiled egg, chopped
⅓ cup sliced water chestnuts
1 tablespoon lemon juice
¼ teaspoon salt
¼ cup (1 ounce) shredded
    Cheddar cheese

Microwave Directions

Halve large shrimp. In 1½-quart shallow casserole, combine shrimp, celery, onion, bell pepper and margarine. Cover; cook on HIGH 4 minutes, stirring after 2 minutes. Stir in soup, stuffing mix, egg, water chestnuts, lemon juice and salt. Cover; cook on HIGH 4 minutes. Sprinkle with cheese; cook, uncovered, on HIGH 1 minute.

Favorite recipe from **Florida Department of Agriculture and Consumer Services, Bureau of Seafood and Aquaculture**

Sicilian Fish and Rice Bake

Makes 6 servings

Prep Time:
6 minutes

Cook Time:
58 minutes

Stand Time:
5 minutes

3 tablespoons olive or
    vegetable oil
¾ cup chopped onion
½ cup chopped celery
1 clove garlic, minced
½ cup uncooked long-grain
    white rice
2 cans (14.5 ounces each)
    CONTADINA® Recipe Ready
    Diced Tomatoes, undrained

1 teaspoon salt
1 teaspoon ground black
    pepper
½ teaspoon granulated sugar
⅛ teaspoon cayenne pepper
1 pound firm white fish
¼ cup finely chopped fresh
    parsley

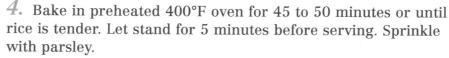

1. Heat oil in large skillet. Add onion, celery and garlic; sauté for 2 to 3 minutes or until vegetables are tender.

2. Stir in rice; sauté for 5 minutes or until rice browns slightly. Add undrained tomatoes, salt, black pepper, sugar and cayenne pepper; mix well.

3. Place fish in bottom of greased 12×7½-inch baking dish. Spoon rice mixture over fish; cover with foil.

4. Bake in preheated 400°F oven for 45 to 50 minutes or until rice is tender. Let stand for 5 minutes before serving. Sprinkle with parsley.

No-Fuss Tuna Quiche

1 unbaked 9-inch deep-dish
  pastry shell
1½ cups low-fat milk
3 eggs
⅓ cup chopped green onions
1 tablespoon chopped drained
  pimiento
1 teaspoon dried basil leaves,
  crushed
½ teaspoon salt
1 (3-ounce) pouch of STARKIST®
  Premium Albacore or
  Chunk Light Tuna
½ cup (2 ounces) shredded low-
  fat Cheddar cheese
8 spears (4 inches each)
  broccoli

Preheat oven to 450°F. Bake pastry shell for 5 minutes; remove to rack to cool. *Reduce oven temperature to 325°F.* For filling, in large bowl whisk together milk and eggs. Stir in onions, pimiento, basil and salt. Fold in tuna and cheese. Pour into prebaked pastry shell. Bake at 325°F for 30 minutes.

Meanwhile, in saucepan, steam broccoli spears over simmering water for 5 minutes. Drain; set aside. After 30 minutes baking time, arrange broccoli spears, spoke-fashion, over quiche. Bake 25 to 35 minutes more or until knife inserted 2 inches from center comes out clean. Let stand for 5 minutes. Cut into 8 wedges, centering broccoli spear in each wedge.

Tip: *If desired, 1 cup chopped broccoli can be added to the filling before baking.*

Note:

Tuna is the name given to a vast number of similar-tasting fish that like to swim in both the Mediterranean and the Pacific. Sizes range from the enormous bluefin that weighs up to 1600 pounds to the can-bound albacore that weighs in at 6 to 15 pounds.

Creamy "Crab" Fettuccine

Makes 6 servings

1 pound imitation crabmeat
   sticks
6 ounces uncooked fettuccine
3 tablespoons margarine or
   butter, divided
1 small onion, chopped
2 ribs celery, chopped
½ medium red bell pepper,
   chopped
2 cloves garlic, minced

1 cup reduced-fat sour cream
1 cup reduced-fat mayonnaise
1 cup (4 ounces) shredded
   sharp Cheddar cheese
2 tablespoons chopped fresh
   parsley
¼ teaspoon salt
⅛ teaspoon black pepper
½ cup cornflake crumbs
   Fresh chives (optional)

1. Preheat oven to 350°F. Spray 2-quart square baking dish with nonstick cooking spray. Cut crabmeat into bite-size pieces. Cook pasta according to package directions until al dente. Drain and set aside.

2. Meanwhile, melt 1 tablespoon margarine in large skillet over medium-high heat. Add onion, celery, bell pepper and garlic; cook and stir 2 minutes or until vegetables are tender.

3. Combine sour cream, mayonnaise, cheese, parsley, salt and black pepper in large bowl. Add crabmeat, pasta and vegetable mixture, stirring gently to combine. Pour into prepared dish.

4. Melt remaining 2 tablespoons margarine. Combine cornflake crumbs and margarine in small bowl; sprinkle evenly over casserole.

5. Bake, uncovered, 30 minutes or until hot and bubbly. Garnish with chives, if desired.

Fish a la Paolo

1 (16-ounce) jar NEWMAN'S
OWN® Medium Salsa
1 (10-ounce) package frozen
chopped spinach, thawed,
drained and squeezed dry
(or favorite mild vegetable)
2 tablespoons capers
1 tablespoon lemon juice

1 pound firm fresh fish, such
as scrod fillets, cut into
4 pieces
1 tablespoon butter, cut into
small pieces
1 large tomato, thinly sliced
½ cup fresh cilantro leaves,
chopped

Makes 4 servings

Preheat oven to 400°F. Mix salsa with spinach, capers and lemon juice; place in bottom of 11×7-inch baking dish. Place fish on top. Dot fish with butter and top with tomato slices. Bake 25 minutes. Remove from oven and top with chopped cilantro.

Tuna-Noodle Casserole

1 tablespoon butter
¾ cup diced onion
1 can cream of mushroom soup
1 cup milk
3 cups hot cooked egg noodles
2 cans tuna, drained and flaked
1¼ cups frozen peas

1 jar diced pimientos, drained
1 tablespoon lemon juice
¼ teaspoon salt
¼ teaspoon black pepper
½ cup fresh bread crumbs
½ cup grated BELGIOIOSO®
Parmesan Cheese

Makes 4 servings

Preheat oven to 450°F. Melt butter in medium saucepan over medium-high heat. Add onion; sauté 3 minutes. Add soup and milk. Cook 3 minutes, whisking constantly. Combine soup mixture, noodles, tuna, peas, pimientos, lemon juice, salt and pepper in 2-quart casserole. Combine bread crumbs and BelGioioso Parmesan Cheese in separate bowl; sprinkle on top of tuna mixture. Bake at 450°F for 15 minutes or until bubbly.

Louisiana Seafood Bake

Makes 4 servings

⅔ cup uncooked regular rice
1 cup sliced celery
1 cup water
1 can (14½ ounces) whole
    tomatoes, undrained and
    cut up
1 can (8 ounces) tomato sauce
1⅓ cups *French's®* French Fried
    Onions, divided
1 teaspoon *Frank's® RedHot®*
    Cayenne Pepper Sauce
½ teaspoon garlic powder

¼ teaspoon dried oregano,
    crumbled
¼ teaspoon dried thyme,
    crumbled
½ pound white fish, thawed if
    frozen and cut into 1-inch
    chunks
1 can (4 ounces) shrimp,
    drained
⅓ cup sliced pitted ripe olives
¼ cup (1 ounce) grated
    Parmesan cheese

Preheat oven to 375°F. In 1½-quart casserole, combine uncooked rice, celery, water, tomatoes, tomato sauce, *⅔ cup* French Fried Onions and the seasonings. Bake, covered, at 375°F for 20 minutes. Stir in fish, shrimp and olives. Bake, covered, 20 minutes or until heated through. Top with cheese and remaining *⅔ cup* onions; bake, uncovered, 3 minutes or until onions are golden brown.

Microwave Directions: *In 2-quart microwave-safe casserole, prepare rice mixture as above. Cook, covered, on HIGH for 15 minutes, stirring rice halfway through cooking time. Add fish, shrimp and olives. Cook, covered, 12 to 14 minutes or until rice is cooked. Stir casserole halfway through cooking time. Top with cheese and remaining onions; cook, uncovered, 1 minute. Let stand 5 minutes.*

Flounder Fillets over Zesty Lemon Rice

Makes 6 servings

¼ cup butter
3 tablespoons fresh lemon juice
2 teaspoons chicken bouillon
    granules
½ teaspoon black pepper
1 cup cooked rice

1 package (10 ounces) frozen
    chopped broccoli, thawed
1 cup (4 ounces) shredded
    sharp Cheddar cheese
1 pound flounder fillets
½ teaspoon paprika

1. Preheat oven to 375°F. Spray 2-quart casserole with nonstick cooking spray.

2. Melt butter in small saucepan over medium heat. Add lemon juice, bouillon granules and pepper; cook and stir 2 minutes or until bouillon granules dissolve.

3. Combine rice, broccoli, cheese and ¼ cup lemon sauce in medium bowl; spread on bottom of prepared dish. Place fillets over rice mixture. Pour remaining lemon sauce over fillets.

4. Bake, uncovered, 20 minutes or until fish flakes easily when tested with fork. Sprinkle evenly with paprika.

Note:

When storing fresh fish, wrap it tightly in plastic wrap. If possible, place the package on ice and store it in the coldest part of the refrigerator. Be sure that melting ice drains away from the fish. If the flesh comes in contact with moisture, it may become discolored. Fresh fish should be used within a day of purchase.

Impossibly Easy Salmon Pie

Makes 8 servings

1 can (7½ ounces) salmon packed in water, drained and deboned
½ cup grated Parmesan cheese
¼ cup sliced green onions
1 jar (2 ounces) chopped pimientos, drained
½ cup low-fat (1%) cottage cheese
1 tablespoon lemon juice

1½ cups low-fat (1%) milk
¾ cup reduced-fat baking and pancake mix
2 whole eggs
2 egg whites *or* ¼ cup egg substitute
¼ teaspoon salt
¼ teaspoon dried dill weed
¼ teaspoon paprika (optional)

1. Preheat oven to 375°F. Spray 9-inch pie plate with nonstick cooking spray. Combine salmon, Parmesan cheese, onions and pimientos in prepared pie plate; set aside.

2. Combine cottage cheese and lemon juice in blender or food processor; blend until smooth. Add milk, baking mix, whole eggs, egg whites, salt and dill. Blend 15 seconds. Pour over salmon mixture. Sprinkle with paprika, if desired.

3. Bake 35 to 40 minutes or until lightly golden and knife inserted halfway between center and edge comes out clean. Cool 5 minutes before serving. Garnish as desired.

Kid's Favorite Tuna Casserole

¾ pound VELVEETA®
    Pasteurized Prepared
    Cheese Product, cubed
⅔ cup milk
1 package (3 ounces)
    PHILADELPHIA® Cream
    Cheese, cubed

3 cups (6 ounces) medium
    noodles, cooked, drained
1 package (10 ounces) frozen
    peas, thawed, drained
1 can (6 ounces) tuna, drained,
    flaked
1 cup crushed potato chips

Makes 4 to 6 servings

Prep Time:
15 minutes

Cook Time:
25 minutes

**Microwave Cook
Time:**
8 minutes

• Preheat oven to 350°F.

• Stir together VELVEETA, milk and cream cheese in saucepan over low heat until VELVEETA is melted.

• Stir in noodles, peas and tuna. Spoon into 2-quart casserole. Top with chips.

• Bake 20 to 25 minutes or until thoroughly heated.

Microwave Directions: *Reduce milk to 3 tablespoons. Microwave VELVEETA, milk and cream cheese in 2-quart casserole on HIGH 3 to 4 minutes or until VELVEETA is melted, stirring after 2 minutes. Stir in noodles, peas and tuna. Microwave 3 to 4 minutes or until thoroughly heated, stirring after 2 minutes. Top with chips.*

Seafood Lasagna

Makes 8 to 10 servings

1 package (16 ounces) lasagna noodles
2 tablespoons margarine
1 large onion, finely chopped
1 package (8 ounces) cream cheese, cut into ½-inch pieces, at room temperature
1½ cups cream-style cottage cheese
2 teaspoons dried basil leaves
½ teaspoon salt
⅛ teaspoon black pepper
1 egg, lightly beaten
2 cans (10¾ ounces each) cream of mushroom soup
⅓ cup milk
1 clove garlic, minced
½ pound bay scallops, rinsed and patted dry
½ pound flounder fillets, rinsed, patted dry and cut into ½-inch cubes
½ pound medium raw shrimp, peeled and deveined
½ cup dry white wine
1 cup (4 ounces) shredded mozzarella cheese
2 tablespoons grated Parmesan cheese

1. Cook lasagna noodles according to package directions; drain.

2. Melt margarine in large skillet over medium heat. Cook onion in hot margarine until tender, stirring frequently. Stir in cream cheese, cottage cheese, basil, salt and pepper; mix well. Stir in egg; set aside.

3. Combine soup, milk and garlic in large bowl until well blended. Stir in scallops, fish fillets, shrimp and wine.

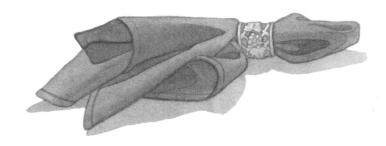

4. Preheat oven to 350°F. Grease 13×9-inch baking pan.

5. Place layer of noodles in prepared pan, overlapping noodles. Spread half the cheese mixture over noodles. Place layer of noodles over cheese mixture and top with half the seafood mixture. Repeat layers. Sprinkle with mozzarella and Parmesan cheeses.

6. Bake 45 minutes or until bubbly. Let stand 10 minutes before cutting.

Crab and Brown Rice Casserole

1 pound Florida blue crab meat, fresh, or thawed frozen 3 eggs, lightly beaten 1 cup mayonnaise 1 cup cooked brown rice	¾ cup evaporated milk ¾ cup (3 ounces) shredded Cheddar cheese ¼ teaspoon hot pepper sauce	**Makes 6 servings**

Preheat oven to 350°F. Grease 1½-quart casserole; set aside. Remove and discard any pieces of cartilage from crab meat. Set crab meat aside.

Combine eggs, mayonnaise, brown rice, milk, cheese and hot pepper sauce in large bowl. Stir in crab meat. Bake 30 to 35 minutes or until knife inserted 1 inch from center comes out clean.

Favorite recipe from **Florida Department of Agriculture and Consumer Services, Bureau of Seafood and Aquaculture**

Easy Tuna & Pasta Pot Pie

Makes 5 servings

Prep and Cook Time:
28 minutes

Note:

Canned tuna is
precooked and is
packed in either water
or oil. Like other food
products, it is available
in various quality
grades. Fancy is the
highest grade,
containing large pieces
of meat; followed by
chunk, with smaller
pieces; and finally
flake, which contains
even smaller bits
and pieces.

1 tablespoon butter
1 large onion, chopped
1½ cups cooked small shell pasta
    or elbow macaroni
1 can (10¾ ounces) condensed
    cream of celery or
    mushroom soup, undiluted
1 cup frozen peas, thawed

1 can (6 ounces) tuna in water,
    drained and flaked into
    pieces
½ cup sour cream
½ teaspoon dried dill weed
¼ teaspoon salt
1 package (7.5 ounces)
    buttermilk biscuits

1. Preheat oven to 400°F. Melt butter in medium ovenproof skillet over medium heat. Add onion; cook and stir 5 minutes.

2. Stir in pasta, soup, peas, tuna, sour cream, dill and salt; mix well. Cook 3 minutes or until hot. Press mixture down in skillet to form even layer.

3. Unwrap biscuit dough; arrange individual biscuits over tuna mixture. Bake 15 minutes or until biscuits are golden brown and tuna mixture is bubbly.

Tip: *If you do not have an ovenproof skillet, cook ingredients in skillet as directed through step 2, but do not press mixture down in skillet. Lightly grease 1½- to 2-quart baking dish. Spread hot pasta mixture in prepared dish; press down to form even layer. Proceed with step 3 as directed.*

Herb-Baked Fish & Rice

1½ cups hot chicken bouillon
½ cup uncooked regular rice
¼ teaspoon Italian seasoning
¼ teaspoon garlic powder
1 package (10 ounces) frozen
    chopped broccoli, thawed
    and drained
1⅓ cups *French's®* French Fried
    Onions, divided

1 tablespoon grated Parmesan
    cheese
1 pound unbreaded fish fillets,
    thawed if frozen
    Paprika (optional)
½ cup (2 ounces) shredded
    Cheddar cheese

Preheat oven to 375°F. In 12×8-inch baking dish, combine hot bouillon, uncooked rice and seasonings. Bake, covered, at 375°F for 10 minutes. Top with broccoli, *⅔ cup* French Fried Onions and the Parmesan cheese. Place fish fillets diagonally down center of dish; sprinkle fish lightly with paprika. Bake, covered, at 375°F for 20 to 25 minutes or until fish flakes easily with fork. Stir rice. Top fish with Cheddar cheese and remaining *⅔ cup* French Fried Onions; bake, uncovered, 3 minutes or until onions are golden brown.

<u>Microwave Directions:</u> *In 12×8-inch microwave-safe dish, prepare rice mixture as above, except reduce bouillon to 1¼ cups. Cook, covered, on HIGH 5 minutes, stirring halfway through cooking time. Stir in broccoli, ⅔ cup onions and the Parmesan cheese. Arrange fish fillets in single layer on top of rice mixture; sprinkle fish lightly with paprika. Cook, covered, on MEDIUM (50-60%) 18 to 20 minutes or until fish flakes easily with fork and rice is done. Rotate dish halfway through cooking time. Top fish with Cheddar cheese and remaining ⅔ cup onions; cook, uncovered, on HIGH 1 minute or until cheese melts. Let stand 5 minutes.*

Mediterranean-Style Tuna Noodle Casserole

Makes 6 to 8 servings

1 tablespoon Lucini Premium Select extra virgin olive oil
4 cloves garlic, minced
2 large onions, chopped (1½ cups)
12 ounces mushrooms, chopped (4 cups)
2 large tomatoes, chopped
1 red bell pepper, diced (1 cup)
1 green bell pepper, diced (1 cup)
1 cup chopped fresh cilantro leaves *or* ¼ cup dried oregano leaves

2 tablespoons dried marjoram or oregano leaves
1 to 2 teaspoons ground red pepper
1 pound JARLSBERG LITE™ cheese, shredded (4 cups)
1 (16-ounce) can black-eyed peas, rinsed and drained
2 (7-ounce) cans tuna, drained and flaked
6 ounces cooked pasta (tricolor rotelle, bows or macaroni)

Note:

The word sauté is derived from the French word *sauter,* meaning "to jump." Sautéing is the technique of rapidly cooking or browning food in a small amount of fat in a skillet or sauté pan.

Preheat oven to 350°F. Heat oil in large skillet; sauté garlic until golden. Add onions; sauté until transparent, about 2 minutes on medium-high heat.

Add mushrooms, tomatoes and bell peppers; cook and stir 3 to 5 minutes or until mushrooms begin to brown. Add cilantro, marjoram and ground red pepper.

Toss with cheese, peas, tuna and pasta. Pour into greased baking dish. Bake, covered, 45 minutes or until cooked through.

You Say Potato...

CHAPTER SIX

Potato & Cauliflower Bake

Makes 10 servings

Note:

When purchasing cauliflower, choose firm, heavy heads with compact florets. The leaves should be crisp and green without signs of yellowing. Avoid heads that have a speckled appearance or brown spots. A medium head of cauliflower weighs about two pounds.

4 cups frozen country-style
   hash browns
1 large head cauliflower, cut
   into small florets (about
   4 cups)
2 cups (8 ounces) shredded
   Cheddar cheese, divided

1 cup chopped onion
¼ cup diced red bell pepper
1¾ cups HIDDEN VALLEY® The
   Original Ranch® Dressing,
   divided
½ cup sour cream
½ cup plain dry bread crumbs

Mix together hash browns, cauliflower, 1 cup cheese, onion and
bell pepper in a large mixing bowl. Whisk together 1½ cups
dressing and sour cream. Pour over potato mixture; mix well.
Transfer potato mixture to a 2-quart baking dish. Mix together
remaining 1 cup cheese, ¼ cup dressing and bread crumbs.
Sprinkle on top of casserole. Bake at 350°F. for 60 minutes,
until browned, bubbly and cauliflower is tender. Let stand for
10 minutes before serving.

Sweet 'n' Sassy Potato Casserole

3 pounds sweet potatoes, peeled and cut into 1-inch pieces
3 Anjou pears or tart apples, peeled and cut into 1-inch pieces
½ cup packed light brown sugar
½ cup maple or pancake syrup
2 tablespoons *Frank's® RedHot®* Cayenne Pepper Sauce
2 teaspoons ground cinnamon
¼ teaspoon ground allspice
2 tablespoons unsalted butter

Makes 8 servings

Prep Time: *25 minutes*

Cook Time: *35 minutes*

1. Place sweet potatoes in large saucepan; cover with water. Bring to a boil. Cook 10 to 15 minutes or until tender. Drain. Place potatoes and pears in greased 3-quart baking dish.

2. Preheat oven to 400°F. Combine sugar, maple syrup, *Frank's RedHot* Sauce and spices in medium bowl. Pour over potatoes and pears. Dot with butter. Cover tightly.

3. Bake 30 to 35 minutes or until heated through and pears are tender. Baste mixture with sauce occasionally. Sprinkle with chopped toasted almonds, if desired.

Vegetable Cobbler

Cobbler

PAM® No-Stick Cooking Spray
1 medium butternut squash, peeled and cut into 1½-inch pieces
3 medium red potatoes, unpeeled and cut into 1½-inch pieces
3 medium parsnips, peeled and cut into 1-inch pieces
1 medium red onion, cut into 6 wedges
¼ cup WESSON® Vegetable Oil
1 tablespoon chopped fresh dill weed
1 teaspoon salt
¾ cup homemade chicken stock or canned chicken broth
½ cup milk
1 (15-ounce) can pears, cut into 1-inch pieces, juice reserved
1 tablespoon cornstarch
4 cups broccoli florets
1 teaspoon grated fresh lemon peel

Topping

1¾ cups all-purpose baking mix
¾ cup shredded Cheddar cheese
½ cup cornmeal
1 tablespoon chopped fresh dill weed
¾ teaspoon coarsely ground pepper
¾ cup milk

Cobbler

Preheat oven to 400°F. Spray 13×9×2-inch baking dish with PAM® Cooking Spray. In prepared baking dish, toss *all* vegetables *except* broccoli with Wesson® Oil, 1 tablespoon dill and salt to coat. Bake, covered, 40 to 45 minutes. Meanwhile, in saucepan, combine stock, milk, reserved pear juice and cornstarch; blend well. Bring to a boil. Add broccoli and lemon peel and cook until slightly thick; set aside.

Topping

In small bowl, combine *all* topping ingredients; mix with fork until well blended.

Stir vegetables in baking dish. Add pears; gently mix. Pour broccoli sauce evenly over vegetables. Drop 12 heaping spoonfuls of topping evenly over vegetables. Bake, uncovered, for 15 minutes or until topping is golden.

Spirited Sweet Potato Casserole

2½ pounds sweet potatoes
2 tablespoons reduced-calorie
   margarine
⅓ cup low-fat (1%) or fat-free
   (skim) milk
¼ cup packed brown sugar
2 tablespoons bourbon or apple
   juice

1 teaspoon ground cinnamon
1 teaspoon vanilla
2 egg whites
½ teaspoon salt
⅓ cup chopped pecans

Makes 8 servings

1. Preheat oven to 375°F. Bake potatoes 50 to 60 minutes or until very tender. Cool 10 minutes; leave oven on. Scoop pulp from warm potatoes into large bowl; discard potato skins. Add margarine to bowl; mash with potato masher until potatoes are fairly smooth and margarine has melted. Stir in milk, brown sugar, bourbon, cinnamon and vanilla; mix well.

2. Beat egg whites with electric mixer at high speed until soft peaks form. Add salt; beat until stiff peaks form. Gently fold egg whites into sweet potato mixture.

3. Spray 1½-quart soufflé dish with nonstick cooking spray. Spoon sweet potato mixture into dish; top with pecans.

4. Bake 30 to 35 minutes or until soufflé is puffed and pecans are toasted. Serve immediately.

Potatoes and Leeks au Gratin

Makes 6 to 8 servings

5 tablespoons butter, divided
2 large leeks, sliced
2 tablespoons minced garlic
2 pounds baking potatoes, peeled (about 4 medium)
1 cup heavy cream
1 cup milk
3 eggs

2 teaspoons salt
¼ teaspoon white pepper
2 to 3 slices dense day-old white bread, such as French or Italian
2 ounces Parmesan cheese
Fresh chives for garnish

Note:

Leeks are a member of the onion family. The smaller the leek, the more tender it will be. Leeks over 1½ inches in diameter can be tough and woody. To prepare them, trim off the roots and remove any withered outer leaves. Cut off the leaf tops down to where the dark green begins to pale. The green tops are too tough to eat but may be used to flavor stocks.

1. Preheat oven to 375°F. Generously butter shallow oval 10-cup baking dish with 1 tablespoon butter; set aside.

2. Melt 2 tablespoons butter in large skillet over medium heat. Add leeks and garlic. Cook and stir 8 to 10 minutes or until leeks are softened. Remove from heat; set aside.

3. Cut potatoes crosswise into ¹⁄₁₆-inch-thick slices. Layer half of potato slices in prepared baking dish. Top with half of leek mixture. Repeat layers with remaining potato slices and leek mixture. Whisk cream, milk, eggs, salt and pepper in medium bowl until well blended; pour evenly over leek mixture.

4. To prepare bread crumbs, tear bread slices into 1-inch pieces and place in food processor or blender; process until fine crumbs form. Measure ¾ cup crumbs. Grate cheese into small bowl; stir in bread crumbs. Melt remaining 2 tablespoons butter in small saucepan; pour over crumbs, tossing to blend thoroughly. Sprinkle crumb mixture evenly over cream mixture.

5. Bake 50 to 60 minutes or until top is golden and potatoes are tender. Let stand 5 to 10 minutes before serving. Garnish, if desired.

Roasted Potatoes and Pearl Onions

3 pounds red potatoes, well-
   scrubbed and cut into
   1½-inch cubes
1 package (10 ounces) pearl
   onions, peeled
2 tablespoons olive oil

2 teaspoons dried basil leaves
   or thyme leaves
1 teaspoon paprika
¾ teaspoon salt
¾ teaspoon dried rosemary
¾ teaspoon black pepper

Makes 8 servings

1. Preheat oven to 400°F. Spray large shallow roasting pan (do not use glass baking dish or potatoes will not brown) with nonstick cooking spray.

2. Add potatoes and onions to pan; drizzle with oil. Combine basil, paprika, salt, rosemary and pepper in small bowl; mix well. Sprinkle over potatoes and onions; toss well to coat lightly with oil and seasonings.

3. Bake 20 minutes; toss well. Continue baking 15 to 20 minutes or until potatoes are browned and tender.

Festive Potato and Squash Casserole

Makes 8 to 10 servings

3 pounds large baking potatoes, pricked with a fork
2 butternut squash (2½ pounds)
1 cup milk
¼ teaspoon ground nutmeg

1 teaspoon dried fines herbes
1¾ cups shredded JARLSBERG cheese, divided
Salt and freshly ground black pepper to taste

Bake potatoes and squash in 350°F oven until done, about 1¼ to 1½ hours. (Place foil under squash to prevent drips in oven.)

Scoop potato pulp into large bowl. Peel and seed squash. Using potato masher, mash squash with potatoes, milk, nutmeg and dried fines herbes.

Stir 1¼ cups cheese into squash mixture. Spoon mixture into low 2- or 2½-quart baking dish and sprinkle with remaining ½ cup cheese. Bake at 350°F for 30 to 40 minutes or until heated through and beginning to brown.

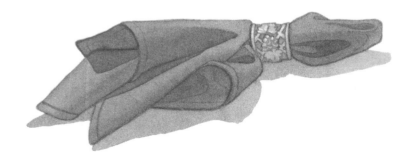

Crispy Potatoes au Gratin

Makes 6 servings

4 baking potatoes, peeled and
   sliced ⅛ inch thick
   (2½ pounds)
2 cups *French's*® French Fried
   Onions, divided
2 cups half-and-half
¾ cup ricotta cheese

¾ teaspoon salt
¼ teaspoon garlic powder
⅛ teaspoon ground black
   pepper
¾ cup shredded white Cheddar
   or Swiss cheese

Prep Time:
10 minutes

Cook Time:
about 1 hour

1. Preheat oven to 375°F. Arrange potatoes and *1 cup* French
Fried Onions in greased 13×9-inch baking dish. Combine half-
and-half, ricotta cheese, salt, garlic powder and pepper; whisk
until well combined. Pour over potatoes; stir gently.

2. Bake, uncovered, 50 minutes or until potatoes are tender.

3. Sprinkle with Cheddar cheese and remaining *1 cup* onions.
Bake 3 minutes or until cheese is melted and onions are golden.

<u>Tip:</u> *If desired, stir in 2 cups diced ham along with ricotta cheese
mixture.*

Baked Apple & Sweet Potato Casserole

Makes 6 servings

6 sweet potatoes
3 Michigan Apples
2 tablespoons melted butter, divided
½ cup orange juice

¼ cup rum
¼ cup packed dark brown sugar
⅛ teaspoon ground cinnamon
⅛ teaspoon ground allspice

Note:

Sweet potatoes are not truly a potato. This tuberous root is actually a member of the morning glory family. Although the words yam and sweet potato are sometimes used interchangeably, they are two distinct vegetables. Canned and frozen sweet potatoes are available, but are often mislabeled as yams.

Preheat oven to 350°F. Boil or steam potatoes until tender. Remove skin and cut lengthwise into slices. Peel and core Michigan Apples; slice into rings. Grease 9×6-inch baking dish with 1 tablespoon butter. Layer potatoes and apples in dish. Combine orange juice, rum, brown sugar, cinnamon and allspice in medium bowl. Pour juice mixture over potato-apple layers. Drizzle with remaining 1 tablespoon butter. Bake 30 minutes or until brown, glazed and liquid is absorbed.

Favorite recipe from **Michigan Apple Committee**

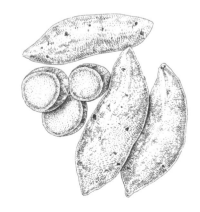

Harvest Vegetable Scallop

4 medium carrots, thinly sliced
1 package (10 ounces) frozen
    chopped broccoli, thawed
    and drained
1⅓ cups *French's®* French Fried
    Onions, divided
5 small red potatoes, sliced
    ⅛ inch thick

1 jar (8 ounces) pasteurized
    processed cheese spread
¼ cup milk
    Freshly ground black pepper
    Seasoned salt

Makes 6 servings

Preheat oven to 375°F. In 12×8-inch baking dish, combine carrots, broccoli and ⅔ *cup* French Fried Onions. Tuck potato slices into vegetable mixture at an angle. Dot vegetables evenly with cheese spread. Pour milk over vegetables; sprinkle with seasonings as desired. Bake, covered, at 375°F for 30 minutes or until vegetables are tender. Top with remaining ⅔ *cup* onions; bake, uncovered, 3 minutes or until onions are golden brown.

Microwave Directions: *In 12×8-inch microwavable dish, prepare vegetables as above. Top with cheese spread, milk and seasonings as above. Cook, covered, at HIGH 12 to 14 minutes or until vegetables are tender, rotating dish halfway through cooking time. Top with remaining onions; cook, uncovered, 1 minute. Let stand 5 minutes.*

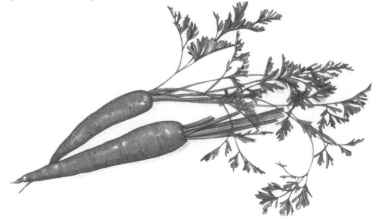

Roasted Savory Potatoes

Makes 4 to 6 servings

½ cup mayonnaise
1 teaspoon LAWRY'S® Garlic
   Powder with Parsley
½ to ¾ teaspoon LAWRY'S®
   Seasoned Pepper
½ teaspoon LAWRY'S®
   Seasoned Salt

¼ teaspoon dried rosemary,
   crushed (optional)
2 medium russet potatoes, cut
   into ¼-inch-thick slices
½ cup sliced green onion
¼ cup (1 ounce) grated
   Parmesan cheese

In 9-inch square glass baking dish, combine mayonnaise,
seasonings and rosemary. Add potatoes and onion; stir gently to
coat. Sprinkle with cheese. Cover and bake in 350°F oven
45 minutes; uncover. Bake 5 minutes longer to brown.

Serving Suggestion: *Serve with grilled meat, fish or poultry.*

Potato 'n' Onion Bake

Makes 4 servings

1 pound all-purpose or baking
   potatoes, thinly sliced
2 medium onions, thinly sliced
2 tablespoons BERTOLLI® Olive
   Oil
½ teaspoon salt

½ teaspoon ground black
   pepper
2 cups RAGÚ® Chunky
   Gardenstyle Pasta Sauce
3 tablespoons grated Parmesan
   cheese

Preheat oven to 400°F. In 2-quart baking dish, layer ½ of the
potatoes, onions, oil, salt and pepper; repeat layers. Bake covered
20 minutes or until potatoes are tender. Remove cover; pour
Ragú® Chunky Gardenstyle Pasta Sauce over potato mixture;
sprinkle with Parmesan cheese. Bake an additional 10 minutes
or until heated through.

Vegetable Casserole

8 potatoes, peeled and cooked
    until tender
1 cup milk
¾ cup (1½ sticks) unsalted
    butter, divided
1 package (about 16 ounces)
    frozen spinach, cooked

Salt and pepper
1 pound carrots, sliced and
    cooked until tender
1 pound string beans, cut into
    1-inch pieces and cooked
    until tender
½ teaspoon paprika

Makes 10 to 12 servings

1. Preheat oven to 375°F. Lightly grease 4-quart casserole or roasting pan.

2. Mash potatoes with milk and ½ cup butter until creamy. Set aside.

3. Spread spinach in casserole and dot with 1 tablespoon butter; season with salt and pepper.

4. Layer half of potatoes over spinach, followed by carrots and string beans. Dot with another 1 tablespoon butter; season with salt and pepper.

5. Layer remaining half of potatoes on top. Dot with remaining 2 tablespoons butter and sprinkle with paprika. Bake 1 hour until heated through and lightly browned.

Grated Potato and Blue Cheese Casserole

Makes 6 servings

2 teaspoons butter or
   margarine
1½ cups finely chopped red
   onions
8 ounces Neufchâtel cheese,
   softened
¼ to ⅓ cup finely crumbled
   domestic blue cheese

¾ cup heavy cream
1 tablespoon minced fresh
   thyme *or* 1 teaspoon dried
   thyme leaves, crushed
½ teaspoon salt
2 pounds baking potatoes
   (about 4 medium)

1. Preheat oven to 350°F. Grease 11×7-inch baking dish; set aside.

2. Melt butter in large skillet over medium heat; add onions. Cook and stir about 5 minutes or until onions are softened and translucent. Remove from heat; set aside to cool in small bowl.

3. Beat Neufchâtel cheese in large bowl with electric mixer at medium speed until fluffy. Add blue cheese; beat until blended. Beat in cream, thyme and salt at low speed until mixture is fairly smooth. (There will be some small lumps.) Add cooled onions; beat until blended. Set aside.

4. Peel potatoes, then grate 1 potato into cheese mixture with large-holed section of metal grater. Fold into cheese mixture with rubber spatula (this prevents potato from turning brown). Repeat with remaining potatoes, 1 at a time.

5. Pour mixture into prepared baking dish; cover with foil. Bake 45 minutes. Uncover; bake 15 to 20 minutes more until crisp around edges.

6. Turn oven to broil. Broil casserole, 6 inches from heat, 3 to 5 minutes until top is golden brown.

7. Remove from oven; let stand 5 minutes before serving.

Sweet Potato Gratin

Makes 4 to 6 servings

3 tablespoons olive oil, divided
2 cloves garlic, finely chopped
1½ pounds sweet potatoes (yam variety), peeled and sliced ¼ inch thick
⅔ cup chicken broth
Salt
White pepper

½ cup BLUE DIAMOND® Blanched Whole Almonds, chopped
½ cup fresh white bread crumbs
½ cup (2 ounces) shredded Swiss cheese
2 tablespoons chopped fresh parsley

Grease 8-inch square baking pan with 1 tablespoon oil. Sprinkle pan with garlic. Layer sweet potato slices in pan. Pour broth over potatoes. Season with salt and pepper to taste. Cover and bake at 375°F 30 minutes. Meanwhile, combine almonds, bread crumbs, cheese, parsley, ¼ teaspoon salt and ⅛ teaspoon pepper. Toss with remaining 2 tablespoons oil. Sprinkle over hot potatoes and bake, uncovered, 20 minutes longer or until top is golden.

One Potato, Two Potato

Russets, also called russet Burbank or Idaho, have a high starch and low moisture content. They are popular for baking and for French fries. They are large (up to 18 ounces each) and oval with rough brown skin.

Long whites are all-purpose potatoes with thin, pale brown skin. They can be fried, baked or boiled. They average 8 ounces each.

Round whites and round reds, also called boiling potatoes, are good for boiling and mashing because of their lower starch and higher moisture content. They are small potatoes with a smooth light tan or red skin.

Yukon gold potatoes have a thin skin and flesh that is yellow or buttery gold. They are low in starch and high in moisture content which makes them ideal for mashing.

New potatoes are young potatoes. They may be any variety, but most often are round reds. New potatoes have a very thin, wispy skin, a crisp, waxy texture and are available in a wide range of sizes.

Mediterranean-Style Roasted Vegetables

Makes 6 servings

1½ pounds red potatoes
1 tablespoon plus
    1½ teaspoons olive oil,
    divided
1 red bell pepper
1 yellow or orange bell pepper
1 small red onion

2 cloves garlic, minced
½ teaspoon salt
¼ teaspoon black pepper
1 tablespoon balsamic vinegar
¼ cup chopped fresh basil
    leaves

1. Preheat oven to 425°F. Spray large shallow metal roasting pan with nonstick cooking spray. Cut potatoes into 1½-inch chunks; place in pan. Drizzle 1 tablespoon oil over potatoes; toss to coat. Bake 10 minutes.

2. Cut bell peppers into 1½-inch chunks. Cut onion through core into ½-inch wedges. Add bell peppers and onion to pan. Drizzle remaining 1½ teaspoons oil over vegetables; sprinkle with garlic, salt and black pepper. Toss well to coat. Return to oven; bake 18 to 20 minutes or until vegetables are browned and tender, stirring once.

3. Transfer to large serving bowl. Drizzle vinegar over vegetables; toss to coat. Add basil; toss again. Serve warm or at room temperature with additional black pepper, if desired.

Potato-Turnip Pudding

3 pounds potatoes, peeled
2 pounds turnips, peeled
2 large onions, peeled
½ cup dry bread crumbs
½ cup FILIPPO BERIO® Olive Oil
3 eggs, lightly beaten
1 teaspoon white pepper

½ teaspoon salt
½ teaspoon ground sumac* or
   paprika

*Sumac can be found in Middle Eastern or specialty food shops.

Makes 12 to 15 servings

Preheat oven to 350°F. Lightly grease 13×9-inch pan with olive oil. Shred potatoes, turnips and onions in food processor using grater disk or by hand using metal grater. Discard any liquid that accumulates. (Grated potatoes will discolor quickly. If grating by hand, reserve grated potatoes in bowl of ice water to slow discoloration. Drain potatoes well before combining with other ingredients.) In large bowl, combine potatoes, turnips, onions, bread crumbs, olive oil, eggs, pepper, salt and sumac. Spoon into prepared dish. Bake 1 hour or until top is crusty and brown but center is still moist.

Note:

Choose turnips that are about 2 inches in diameter. Larger turnips have a coarse texture and less sweet flavor. Select ones that are firm and heavy for their size with smooth, unblemished skin. Avoid turnips that are soft, shriveled and have many root hairs.

Campbell's® Scalloped Potato-Onion Bake

Makes 6 servings

Prep Time:
15 minutes

Cook Time:
1 hour 15 minutes

1 can (10¾ ounces)
CAMPBELL'S® Condensed
Cream of Celery Soup *or*
98% Fat Free Cream of
Celery Soup
½ cup milk
Dash pepper

4 medium potatoes (about
1¼ pounds), thinly sliced
1 small onion, thinly sliced
(about ¼ cup)
1 tablespoon margarine *or*
butter
Paprika

1. Mix soup, milk and pepper. In 1½-quart casserole layer *half* the potatoes, onion and soup mixture. Repeat layers. Dot with margarine. Sprinkle with paprika.

2. Cover and bake at 400°F. for 1 hour. Uncover and bake 15 minutes more or until potatoes are tender.

Tip: *For a variation and dash of color, add ¼ cup chopped fresh parsley in step 1.*

Party Potatoes

1 bag (32 ounces) Southern-style hash browns
2 cans (10¾ ounces each) condensed cream of potato soup, undiluted
2 cups (16 ounces) sour cream

2 cups (8 ounces) shredded Cheddar cheese
¾ red onion, finely chopped
¼ cup (½ stick) butter, sliced
Parmesan cheese (optional)

1. Preheat oven to 350°F. Grease 13×9-inch baking dish.

2. Combine hash browns, soup, sour cream, Cheddar cheese and onion in large bowl. Spoon evenly into baking dish and pat down.

3. Arrange butter slices on top and sprinkle with Parmesan cheese, if desired.

4. Cover with foil; bake 60 minutes. Remove foil and bake an additional 10 minutes or until browned.

Note:

Organisms that cause food-borne illness thrive at temperatures between 40° and 140°F. If you have leftovers, chill them quickly. Do not transfer a large pot of food directly from the range to the refrigerator. Divide it into several smaller containers so that it chills quickly.

Potato Patch Pie

Makes 8 main-dish servings

Crust

Unbaked 9-inch Classic CRISCO® Double Crust (recipe follows)

Filling

2 tablespoons all-purpose flour
1 teaspoon instant chopped onion
½ teaspoon dry mustard
¼ teaspoon dried oregano leaves
⅛ teaspoon garlic powder
4 medium new red potatoes (about one pound)

1 (10-ounce) package frozen chopped broccoli, thawed and drained on paper towels
1 (2-ounce) jar sliced pimento, drained
8 slices (¾ ounce each) Swiss pasteurized process cheese food, divided
⅓ pound cooked ham, trimmed and cut into ½-inch chunks

Topping

1 tablespoon skim milk
2 teaspoons grated Parmesan cheese

1. Follow directions for preparing and rolling double crust.

2. For filling, in small bowl, combine flour, onion, mustard, oregano and garlic powder; set aside. Peel and thinly slice 2 potatoes into bottom of unbaked 9-inch pie shell. Sprinkle with 1 tablespoon flour mixture. Spoon broccoli over potatoes. Sprinkle pimento over top. Sprinkle remaining flour mixture over top of vegetables. Place 3 slices cheese on top of vegetables. Break fourth slice into quarters. Fill in spaces. Sprinkle ham over cheese. Peel and thinly slice remaining potatoes over ham. Top with remaining cheese slices.

3. Heat oven to 400°F. Moisten edge of bottom crust with water. Lift top crust onto filled pie. Fold top edge under bottom crust; flute or make rope edge. Cut slits or design in top crust to allow steam to escape while baking.

4. Bake pie 35 minutes; then remove from oven.

5. For topping, brush top crust with milk and sprinkle with Parmesan cheese. Cover edge of crust with foil to prevent over-browning. Return to oven for 10 minutes. Let stand 10 to 15 minutes before cutting and serving.

Classic Crisco® Double Crust

2 cups all-purpose flour
1 teaspoon salt
¾ CRISCO® Stick or ¾ cup
    CRISCO® all-vegetable
    shortening
	5 tablespoons cold water (or
	    more as needed)

1. Spoon flour into measuring cup and level. Combine flour and salt in medium bowl.

2. Cut in ¾ cup shortening using pastry blender or 2 knives until all flour is blended to form pea-size chunks.

3. Sprinkle with water, 1 tablespoon at a time. Toss lightly with fork until dough forms a ball. Divide dough in half.

4. Press dough between hands to form 5- to 6-inch "pancake." Flour rolling surface and rolling pin lightly. Roll both halves of dough into circle. Trim one circle of dough 1 inch larger than upside-down 9-inch pie plate. Carefully remove trimmed dough. Set aside to reroll and use for pastry cutout garnish, if desired.

5. Fold dough into quarters. Unfold and press into pie plate. Trim edge even with plate. Add desired filling to unbaked crust. Moisten pastry edge with water. Lift top crust onto filled pie. Trim ½ inch beyond edge of pie plate. Fold top edge under bottom crust. Flute. Cut slits in top crust to allow steam to escape. Follow baking directions given for that recipe.

Makes 1 (9-inch) double crust

New-Fashioned SPAM™ Scalloped Potatoes

Makes 6 servings

Nonstick cooking spray
1 (10¾-ounce) can 99% fat-free condensed cream of mushroom soup
½ cup skim milk
1 (2-ounce) jar diced pimiento, drained
¼ teaspoon black pepper
1 (12-ounce) can SPAM® Lite, cubed

1 cup chopped onion
½ cup frozen peas
4½ cups thinly sliced peeled potatoes
2 tablespoons dry bread crumbs
1 tablespoon chopped fresh parsley

Note:

To scallop refers to the technique of preparing a food by slicing it into small pieces and layering it in a casserole with a creamy sauce. The finished dish may be topped with cracker or bread crumbs before baking.

Preheat oven to 350°F. Spray 2-quart casserole with nonstick cooking spray. In medium bowl, combine soup, milk, pimiento and pepper. In casserole, layer half each of SPAM®, onion, peas, potatoes and sauce. Repeat layers. Cover. Bake 1 hour or until potatoes are nearly tender. Combine bread crumbs and parsley; sprinkle over casserole. Bake, uncovered, 15 minutes longer or until potatoes are tender. Let stand 10 minutes before serving.

Carrie's Sweet Potato Casserole

Topping (recipe follows)
3 pounds sweet potatoes,
   cooked and peeled
½ cup (1 stick) butter, softened
1 teaspoon vanilla

½ cup sugar
2 eggs, beaten
½ cup evaporated milk
1 cup pecans, chopped

Makes 8 to 12 servings

1. Prepare Topping; set aside. Preheat oven to 350°F. Grease 13×9-inch baking dish.

2. Mash sweet potatoes with butter in large bowl. Beat with electric mixer until light and fluffy.

3. One at a time, add vanilla, sugar, eggs and evaporated milk, beating after each addition. Spread in prepared baking dish. Spoon Topping over potatoes and sprinkle with pecans.

4. Bake 25 minutes or until heated through. Serve hot.

Topping: *Combine 1 cup packed light brown sugar, ½ cup all-purpose flour and ⅓ cup melted butter in medium bowl.*

Note:

This casserole works well and looks pretty in individual serving dishes. Lightly grease 8 (6-ounce) oven-proof ramekins and fill almost to the top with sweet potato mixture. Top as directed in recipe and bake 20 minutes at 350°F or until heated through.

Potato Gorgonzola Gratin

Makes 4 to 6 servings

1 pound (2 medium-large)
Colorado baking potatoes,
unpeeled and very thinly
sliced, divided
Salt and black pepper
Ground nutmeg
½ medium onion, thinly sliced
1 medium tart green apple,
such as pippin or Granny
Smith, unpeeled, cored and
very thinly sliced

1 cup low-fat milk or half-and-
half
¾ cup (3 ounces) Gorgonzola or
other blue cheese,
crumbled
2 tablespoons freshly grated
Parmesan cheese

Preheat oven to 400°F. In 8- or 9-inch square baking dish,
arrange half the potatoes. Season generously with salt and
pepper; sprinkle lightly with nutmeg. Top with onion and apple.
Arrange remaining potatoes on top. Season again with salt and
pepper; add milk. Cover dish with aluminum foil. Bake 30 to
40 minutes or until potatoes are tender. Remove foil; top with
both cheeses. Bake, uncovered, 10 to 15 minutes or until top is
lightly browned.

Favorite recipe from **Colorado Potato Administrative Committee**

Potato Bacon Casserole

Makes 6 servings

4 cups frozen shredded hash
    brown potatoes
½ cup finely chopped onion
8 ounces bacon or turkey
    bacon, cooked and
    crumbled*
1 cup (4 ounces) shredded
    cheddar cheese
1 can (12 fluid ounces) NESTLÉ®
    CARNATION® Evaporated
    Milk or NESTLÉ®
    CARNATION® Evaporated
    Lowfat Milk

1 egg, lightly beaten or ¼ cup
    egg substitute
1½ teaspoons seasoned salt

*May substitute with 1 package (2.1 ounces)
precooked bacon slices, cut into small pieces.

PREHEAT oven to 350°F. Grease 8-inch square baking dish.

LAYER ½ potatoes, ½ onion, ½ bacon and ½ cheese in prepared baking dish; repeat layers. Combine evaporated milk, egg and seasoned salt in small bowl. Pour evenly over potato mixture; cover.

BAKE for 55 to 60 minutes. Uncover; bake for an additional 5 minutes. Let stand for 10 to 15 minutes before serving.

Oven Roasted Mushrooms and New Potatoes

Makes 4 servings

1½ pounds new potatoes, scrubbed and cut into ½-inch chunks (about 4½ cups)

2 tablespoons vegetable oil

1 pound fresh white mushrooms, halved or quartered if large (about 5 cups)

1 red bell pepper, cut in ½-inch chunks

1 teaspoon minced garlic

½ cup sliced green onions

1 teaspoon salt

½ teaspoon thyme leaves, crushed

¼ teaspoon black pepper

Preheat oven to 450°F. Toss potatoes with vegetable oil in 13×9×2-inch baking pan; bake uncovered, 10 minutes. Stir in mushrooms, bell pepper and garlic; bake uncovered, about 15 minutes until potatoes are almost tender. Stir in green onions, salt, thyme and black pepper; bake about 10 minutes longer or until vegetables are tender.

Favorite recipe from **Mushroom Council**

Gratin of Two Potatoes

Makes 6 servings

2 large baking potatoes (about
1¼ pounds)
2 large sweet potatoes (about
1¼ pounds)
1 tablespoon unsalted butter
1 large sweet or yellow onion,
thinly sliced and separated
into rings
2 teaspoons all-purpose flour

1 cup fat-free reduced-sodium
chicken broth
½ teaspoon salt
¼ teaspoon white pepper *or*
⅛ teaspoon ground red
pepper
¾ cup freshly grated Parmesan
cheese

1. Cook baking potatoes in large pot of boiling water 10 minutes. Add sweet potatoes; return to a boil. Simmer potatoes, uncovered, 25 minutes or until tender. Drain; cool under cold running water.

2. Meanwhile, melt butter in large nonstick skillet over medium-high heat. Add onion; cover and cook 3 minutes or until wilted. Uncover; cook over medium-low heat 10 to 12 minutes or until tender, stirring occasionally. Sprinkle with flour; cook 1 minute, stirring frequently. Add chicken broth, salt and pepper; bring to a boil over high heat. Reduce heat and simmer, uncovered, 2 minutes or until sauce thickens, stirring occasionally.

3. Preheat oven to 375°F. Spray 13×9-inch baking dish with nonstick cooking spray. Peel potatoes; cut crosswise into ¼-inch slices. Layer half of baking and sweet potato slices in prepared dish. Spoon half of onion mixture evenly over potatoes. Repeat layering with remaining potatoes and onion mixture. Cover with foil. Bake 25 minutes or until heated through.

4. Preheat broiler. Uncover potatoes; sprinkle evenly with cheese. Broil, 5 inches from heat, 3 to 4 minutes or until cheese is bubbly and light golden brown.

Potato Nugget Casserole

Makes 10 servings

Note:

Canned evaporated milk, both whole and skim, has about 60% of the water removed. It is then sealed in cans and heat treated. It is convenient to keep on hand because it does not require refrigeration until after it is opened. Evaporated milk should not be confused with sweetened condensed milk.

2 pounds frozen potato
   nuggets
1 can (10¾ ounces) condensed
   cream of celery soup,
   undiluted
1 can (10¾ ounces) condensed
   cream of mushroom soup,
   undiluted

1 can (10¾ ounces) condensed
   Cheddar cheese soup,
   undiluted
1 can (about 5 ounces)
   evaporated milk
2 cups (8 ounces) shredded
   mozzarella cheese
2 cups (8 ounces) shredded
   Cheddar cheese

1. Preheat oven to 350°F. Spread potatoes in 13×9-inch casserole; set aside.

2. Mix soups and evaporated milk in large saucepan. Bring to a boil, stirring occasionally. Pour over potatoes and mix until well combined.

3. Bake 45 minutes. Remove from oven; sprinkle cheeses evenly over casserole. Bake 5 minutes or until cheeses melt.

Versatile Veggies

CHAPTER SEVEN

Pasta with Roasted Vegetables

Makes 4 servings

Note:

Generally, fresh Brussels sprouts are removed from their stalks and sold by the pound or in cardboard containers covered with cellophane. At farmers' markets, they also may be found still attached to their stalks. These sprouts are fresher and have better flavor. Do not remove them from the stalk until just before cooking.

1 (2-pound) butternut squash, peeled, seeded and cut into 1-inch cubes
1 (10-ounce) container fresh Brussels sprouts, each cut into halves
1 small bulb fennel (about 8 ounces), trimmed, halved and thinly sliced
¼ cup olive oil
3 large cloves garlic, peeled and halved lengthwise
¾ teaspoon salt
½ teaspoon dried oregano leaves
8 ounces penne *or* ziti pasta
¼ cup pumpkin seeds
1½ teaspoons TABASCO® brand Pepper Sauce
½ cup grated Parmesan cheese

Preheat oven to 450°F. In roasting pan, combine squash, Brussels sprouts, fennel, olive oil, garlic, salt and oregano. Bake 20 minutes, stirring occasionally.

Meanwhile, prepare penne according to package directions. During last 2 minutes of roasting vegetables, add pumpkin seeds to vegetables. Continue cooking until seeds are lightly toasted.

To serve, toss cooked, drained pasta with roasted vegetables, TABASCO® Sauce and Parmesan cheese to mix well.

Eggplant Parmesan

½ cup olive or vegetable oil
1 medium eggplant (about
    1½ pounds), peeled, sliced
1 carton (15 ounces) ricotta
    cheese
1 can (15 ounces) CONTADINA®
    Italian-Style Tomato Sauce

1 clove garlic, minced
½ teaspoon dried oregano
    leaves, crushed
½ cup CONTADINA Seasoned
    Bread Crumbs
2 tablespoons grated Parmesan
    cheese

Makes 6 servings

Prep Time:
20 minutes

Cook Time:
30 minutes

1. Heat oil in large skillet. Add eggplant; cook for 2 to 3 minutes on each side or until tender. Remove from oil with slotted spoon. Drain on paper towels.

2. Place half of eggplant slices in greased 12×7½-inch baking dish. Spoon half of ricotta cheese over eggplant.

3. Combine tomato sauce, garlic and oregano in small bowl. Pour half of tomato sauce mixture over ricotta cheese.

4. Combine bread crumbs and Parmesan cheese in separate small bowl; sprinkle half over top of sauce mixture. Repeat layers.

5. Bake in preheated 350°F oven for 30 minutes or until sauce is bubbly.

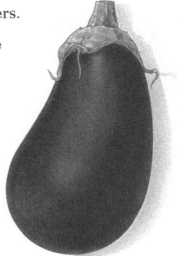

Broccoli Casserole with Crumb Topping

Makes 6 servings

2 slices day-old white bread, coarsely crumbled (about 1¼ cups)
½ cup shredded mozzarella cheese (about 2 ounces)
2 tablespoons chopped fresh parsley (optional)
2 tablespoons BERTOLLI® Olive Oil

1 clove garlic, finely chopped
6 cups broccoli florets and/or cauliflowerets
1 envelope LIPTON® RECIPE SECRETS® Onion Soup Mix
1 cup water
1 large tomato, chopped

1. In small bowl, combine bread crumbs, cheese, parsley, 1 tablespoon oil and garlic; set aside.

2. In 12-inch skillet, heat remaining 1 tablespoon oil over medium heat and cook broccoli, stirring frequently, 2 minutes.

3. Stir in onion soup mix blended with water. Bring to a boil over high heat. Reduce heat to low and simmer uncovered, stirring occasionally, 8 minutes or until broccoli is almost tender. Add tomato and simmer 2 minutes.

4. Spoon vegetable mixture into 1½-quart casserole; top with bread crumb mixture. Broil 1½ minutes or until crumbs are golden and cheese is melted.

Green Beans with Blue Cheese and Roasted Peppers

1 bag (20 ounces) frozen cut
   green beans
½ jar (about 3 ounces) roasted
   red pepper strips, drained
   and slivered
⅛ teaspoon salt
⅛ teaspoon white pepper

4 ounces cream cheese
½ cup milk
¾ cup blue cheese (3 ounces),
   crumbled
½ cup Italian-style bread crumbs
1 tablespoon margarine or
   butter, melted

Preheat oven to 350°F. Spray 2-quart oval casserole with nonstick cooking spray.

Combine green beans, red pepper strips, salt and pepper in prepared dish.

Place cream cheese and milk in small saucepan; heat over low heat, stirring until melted. Add blue cheese; stir only until combined. Pour cheese mixture over green bean mixture and stir until green beans are coated.

Combine bread crumbs and margarine in small bowl; sprinkle evenly over casserole.

Bake, uncovered, 20 minutes or until hot and bubbly.

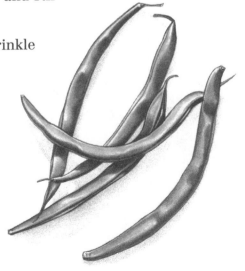

Stuffed Tomatoes

Makes 6 side-dish servings

3 large ripe red tomatoes, cored
Salt
2 tablespoons olive oil, divided
1 pound BOB EVANS® Italian Roll Sausage
1 cup chopped green bell pepper
½ medium onion, finely chopped
2 cloves garlic, minced
½ cup hot milk

1 cup dried bread crumbs
1 egg, beaten
4 tablespoons chopped fresh parsley, divided
1 teaspoon dried basil leaves
1 teaspoon dried oregano leaves
Black pepper to taste
1 cup (4 ounces) shredded mozzarella cheese
¼ cup grated Parmesan cheese

With core side up, cut each tomato in half horizontally; remove seeds. Sprinkle interior of tomatoes lightly with salt to help remove moisture. Place tomato halves, cut sides down, on paper towels to drain about 15 minutes.

Preheat oven to 350°F. Grease baking dish with 1 tablespoon olive oil. Heat remaining tablespoon olive oil in large skillet over medium heat. Add tomato halves and cook 4 minutes on each side. Remove tomatoes from skillet and place, cut sides up, in prepared baking dish. Crumble sausage into same skillet. Add bell pepper, onion and garlic; cook until sausage is browned and onion is tender. Transfer sausage mixture to medium bowl with slotted spoon. Stir in milk and bread crumbs; let cool slightly. Add egg, 2 tablespoons parsley, basil and oregano. Season with salt and black pepper to taste. Divide mixture evenly among tomato halves and bake 10 minutes. Remove from the oven; sprinkle with mozzarella cheese. Top with Parmesan cheese. Place tomatoes under broiler until cheese is melted and golden brown. Garnish with remaining 2 tablespoons parsley and serve hot. Refrigerate leftovers.

Scalloped Apples & Onions

1 medium onion, thinly sliced
4 tablespoons butter, melted, divided
5 red or green apples, cored and thinly sliced

8 ounces (1½ cups) pasteurized process cheese, cut into small pieces, divided
2 cups *French's*® French Fried Onions, divided

Makes 6 side-dish servings

Prep Time:
15 minutes

Cook Time:
about 30 minutes

1. Preheat oven to 375°F. Sauté onion in 2 tablespoons butter in medium skillet over medium-high heat 3 minutes or until tender. Add apples and sauté 5 minutes or until apples are tender.

2. Stir 1 cup cheese, *1 cup* French Fried Onions and remaining melted butter into apple mixture. Transfer to greased 9-inch deep dish pie plate.

3. Bake, uncovered, 20 minutes or until heated through. Top with remaining cheese and onions. Bake 5 minutes or until cheese is melted.

Tip: *To save time and cleanup, apple mixture may be baked in a heatproof skillet if desired. Wrap skillet handle in heavy-duty foil.*

Variation: *For added Cheddar flavor, substitute French's® Cheddar French Fried Onions for the original flavor.*

Note:

Process cheese (or pasteurized process cheese) is made by grinding together different lots of cheese, some ripe, others "green." Water can be added along with chemical emulsifiers, and then the mixture is heated. The advantage of process cheese is that it melts easily and smoothly.

Spinach Bake

Makes 6 servings

Prep Time:
10 minutes

Bake Time:
55 minutes

2 packages (10 ounces each)
  frozen chopped spinach,
  thawed, well drained
2 eggs, beaten
1 can (10¾ ounces) condensed
  cream of mushroom soup
1 medium onion, chopped
1 cup KRAFT® Shredded Sharp
  Cheddar Cheese

⅔ cup MIRACLE WHIP® *or*
  MIRACLE WHIP LIGHT®
  Dressing
½ cup bread crumbs
2 tablespoons butter *or*
  margarine, melted

MIX spinach, eggs, soup, onion, cheese and dressing.

SPOON spinach mixture into greased 10×6-inch or 8-inch square baking dish. Mix crumbs and butter; sprinkle over spinach mixture.

BAKE at 350°F for 45 to 55 minutes or until thoroughly heated.

Campbell's® Vegetable Lasagna

1 package (10 ounces) frozen chopped broccoli

1 small red *or* green pepper, chopped (about ½ cup)

1 medium carrot, chopped (about ⅓ cup)

1 small onion, chopped (about ¼ cup)

1 can (10¾ ounces) CAMPBELL'S® Condensed Broccoli Cheese Soup `or 98% Fat Free Broccoli Cheese Soup

½ cup milk

¼ cup grated Parmesan cheese

6 lasagna noodles, cooked and drained

1½ cups shredded mozzarella cheese (6 ounces)

Makes 6 servings

Prep Time:
20 minutes

Cook and Stand Time:
40 minutes

1. In medium saucepan place broccoli, pepper, carrot and onion. Cover with water. Over medium-high heat, heat to a boil. Reduce heat to low. Cover and cook 5 minutes or until tender. Drain.

2. Mix soup, milk and Parmesan cheese. Set aside.

3. In 2-quart shallow baking dish spread ½ *cup* soup mixture. Top with *3* lasagna noodles, ½ *cup* soup mixture, ¾ *cup* mozzarella cheese and *1½ cups* vegetable mixture. Repeat layers. Top with remaining soup mixture.

4. Bake at 400°F. for 20 minutes. Uncover and bake 10 minutes more or until hot. Let stand 10 minutes.

Fall Cranberry Nut Squash

Makes 4 servings

Prep Time:
7 minutes

Cook Time:
45 minutes

2 medium acorn squash
½ cup packed light brown sugar
⅓ cup PETER PAN® Honey
    Roasted Creamy Peanut
    Butter
2 tablespoons butter

1 teaspoon finely shredded
    fresh orange peel
1 teaspoon vanilla
¼ teaspoon ground cinnamon
¼ teaspoon ground allspice
½ cup dried cranberries

Preheat oven to 350°F. Cut off ends of squash, then cut horizontally into halves; remove seeds. Place halves, cut sides up, in 11×7×2-inch baking pan. In bowl, stir together sugar, peanut butter, butter, orange peel, vanilla, cinnamon and allspice. Spoon mixture into and onto squash halves. Bake, covered, 30 minutes. Sprinkle 2 tablespoons cranberries over each squash half. Bake, uncovered, 10 to 15 minutes or until squash is tender.

Cheesy Corn Bake

Makes 6 servings

3 eggs, well beaten
1 can (16 ounces) creamed corn
¾ cup unseasoned dry bread
    crumbs
¾ cup (3 ounces) shredded
    Cheddar cheese
½ medium green bell pepper,
    chopped

½ cup hot milk
1 tablespoon chopped onion
1 teaspoon LAWRY'S®
    Seasoned Salt
¾ teaspoon LAWRY'S®
    Seasoned Pepper
¼ teaspoon LAWRY'S® Garlic
    Powder with Parsley

In large bowl, combine all ingredients. Pour into ungreased 2-quart casserole. Bake in 350°F oven 1 hour. Let stand 10 minutes before serving.

Serving Suggestion: *Serve topped with prepared LAWRY'S® Original Style Spaghetti Sauce for extra flavor.*

Herbed Cauliflower Casserole

Makes 5 (¾-cup) servings

5 cups cauliflower florets
(about 1¼ pounds)
1 tablespoon margarine, melted
1 small red bell pepper, cored,
seeded and quartered
2 tablespoons water
3 large tomatoes, peeled,
seeded and coarsely
chopped

2 to 3 teaspoons chopped fresh
tarragon
½ teaspoon chopped fresh
parsley
⅓ cup (about 9 to 10) coarsely
crushed unsalted saltine
crackers

1. Preheat oven to 450°F. Toss cauliflower with margarine in large bowl; place cauliflower and bell pepper, cut sides down, in one layer in shallow baking pan. Add water to pan. Roast vegetables 15 minutes; *reduce oven temperature to 425°F.* Continue roasting 25 to 28 minutes until cauliflower is tender and golden brown and bell pepper skin has blistered. Remove bell pepper pieces to plate and transfer cauliflower to 11×7-inch baking dish. *Reduce oven temperature to 400°F.*

2. Place tomatoes in food processor or blender. Remove and discard skin from bell pepper. Add bell pepper to food processor; process until smooth. Add tarragon and parsley; blend well.

3. Pour tomato sauce over cauliflower; bake 10 minutes or until cauliflower is hot and bubbly. Sprinkle with cracker crumbs just before serving. Garnish, if desired.

Roasted Red Pepper & Tomato Casserole

Makes 6 servings

1 jar (12 ounces) roasted red
    peppers, drained
1½ teaspoons red wine vinegar
1 teaspoon olive oil
1 clove garlic, minced
¼ teaspoon salt
¼ teaspoon black pepper

⅓ cup grated Parmesan cheese,
    divided
3 medium tomatoes (about
    1½ pounds), sliced
½ cup (about 1 ounce) herb-
    flavored croutons, crushed

Note:

Tomatoes should never
be refrigerated before
cutting because cold
temperatures cause
their flesh to become
mealy and lose flavor.
Store them at room
temperature. Ripening
can be hastened by
placing them in a
paper bag.

Microwave Directions

1. Combine red peppers, vinegar, oil, garlic, salt and black
pepper in food processor; process using on/off pulsing action
1 minute until slightly chunky. Reserve 2 tablespoons cheese for
garnish. Stir remaining cheese into red pepper mixture.

2. Arrange tomato slices in 8-inch round microwavable baking
dish; microwave at HIGH 1 minute. Spoon red pepper mixture on
top; microwave at HIGH 2 to 3 minutes or until tomatoes are
slightly soft.

3. Sprinkle with reserved cheese and croutons.

Broccoli-Stuffed Shells

Makes 4 servings

1 tablespoon butter or
    margarine
¼ cup chopped onion
1 cup ricotta cheese
1 egg
2 cups chopped cooked broccoli
    or 1 package (10 ounces)
    frozen chopped broccoli,
    thawed and well drained
1 cup (4 ounces) shredded
    Monterey Jack cheese

20 jumbo pasta shells
1 can (28 ounces) crushed
    tomatoes with added purée
1 packet (1 ounce) HIDDEN
    VALLEY® The Original
    Ranch® Salad Dressing &
    Seasoning Mix
¼ cup grated Parmesan cheese

Preheat oven to 350°F. In small skillet, melt butter over medium heat. Add onion; cook until onion is tender but not browned. Remove from heat; cool. In large bowl, stir ricotta cheese and egg until well blended. Add broccoli and Monterey Jack cheese; mix well. In large pot of boiling water, cook pasta shells 8 to 10 minutes or just until tender; drain. Rinse under cold running water; drain again. Stuff each shell with about 2 tablespoons broccoli-cheese mixture.

In medium bowl, combine tomatoes, sautéed onion and salad dressing & seasoning mix; mix well. Pour one third of the tomato mixture into 13×9-inch baking dish. Arrange filled shells in dish. Spoon remaining tomato mixture over top. Sprinkle with Parmesan cheese. Bake, covered, until hot and bubbly, about 30 minutes.

Vegetable Gratin

Makes 6 to 8 servings

2 tablespoons olive oil
3 small *or* 1 large zucchini,
    sliced into ¼-inch slices
⅛ teaspoon *each* salt, thyme,
    rosemary and freshly
    ground black pepper,
    divided
1 (6.5-ounce) packages
    ALOUETTE® Savory
    Vegetable

2 cups fresh broccoli florets
2 small yellow squash, sliced
1 small onion, sliced
1 cup crushed BRETON® Wheat
    Crackers

• Preheat oven to 350°F. Place oil in medium-sized gratin or shallow baking dish.

• Layer zucchini in prepared dish.

• Sprinkle zucchini lightly with half each of salt, thyme, rosemary and pepper.

• Place 3 tablespoons Alouette on top of zucchini.

• Layer with broccoli, yellow squash, onion, remaining seasonings and Alouette until dish is filled.

• Sprinkle with cracker crumbs; cover with foil and bake 20 minutes.

• Remove foil and bake another 20 minutes. Brown lightly under broiler 1 to 2 minutes.

• Serve hot or at room temperature.

<u>Hint:</u> *A delicious way to liven up vegetables! Great with grilled chicken or steak.*

Zucchini Bake

⅔ cup QUAKER® Oat Bran hot cereal, uncooked
½ teaspoon dried Italian seasoning
¼ teaspoon black pepper
1 egg white
1 tablespoon water
2 medium zucchini, sliced ¾ inch thick, quartered (about 3 cups)

1 small onion, chopped
⅔ cup low-sodium tomato sauce
2 teaspoons olive oil
2 teaspoons grated Parmesan cheese
¼ cup (1 ounce) shredded part-skim mozzarella cheese

Heat oven to 375°F. Lightly spray 8-inch square baking dish with nonstick cooking spray or oil lightly. In large plastic food storage bag, combine oat bran, Italian seasoning and pepper; mix well. In shallow dish, lightly beat egg white and water. Coat zucchini with oat bran mixture; shake off excess. Dip into egg mixture, then coat again with oat bran mixture. Place zucchini in prepared dish; sprinkle with onion. Spoon combined tomato sauce and oil over vegetables. Sprinkle with Parmesan cheese. Bake 30 minutes or until zucchini is crisp-tender; top with mozzarella cheese. Serve warm.

Microwave Directions: *In large plastic food storage bag, combine oat bran, Italian seasoning and pepper; mix well. In shallow dish, lightly beat egg white and water. Coat zucchini with oat bran mixture; shake off excess. Dip into egg mixture, then coat again with oat bran mixture. Place zucchini in 8-inch square microwavable dish; sprinkle with onion. Spoon combined tomato sauce and oil over vegetables. Sprinkle with Parmesan cheese. Microwave at HIGH (100% power) 5½ to 6½ minutes or until zucchini is crisp-tender, rotating dish ½ turn after 3 minutes. Sprinkle with mozzarella cheese. Let stand 3 minutes before serving. Serve warm.*

Note:

Once purchased, unwashed, fresh zucchini can be kept in the refrigerator in a perforated plastic bag for up to 5 days. Just before using, rinse the zucchini under cold running water and scrub it lightly with a vegetable brush.

Green Bean and Onion Casserole

Makes 6 servings

Prep Time:
5 minutes

Cook Time:
30 minutes

1 jar (1 pound) RAGÚ® Cheese Creations!® Classic Alfredo Sauce
2 packages (9 ounces each) frozen green beans, thawed
1 can (2.8 ounces) French fried onions

¼ teaspoon ground white pepper
1 tablespoon grated Parmesan cheese (optional)

1. Preheat oven to 350°F. In 1½-quart casserole, combine Ragú Cheese Creations! Sauce, green beans, ½ of the onions and pepper; sprinkle with cheese.

2. Bake uncovered 25 minutes or until hot and bubbling. Top with remaining onions and bake an additional 5 minutes.

Apple & Carrot Casserole

Makes 6 servings

6 large carrots, sliced
4 large apples, peeled, quartered, cored and sliced
5 tablespoons all-purpose flour
1 tablespoon packed brown sugar

½ teaspoon ground nutmeg
1 tablespoon margarine
½ cup orange juice
½ teaspoon salt (optional)

Preheat oven to 350°F. Cook carrots in large saucepan in boiling water 5 minutes; drain. Layer carrots and apples in large casserole. Combine flour, sugar and nutmeg; sprinkle over top. Dot with margarine; pour orange juice over flour mixture. Sprinkle with salt, if desired. Bake 30 minutes or until carrots are tender.

Indonesian Honey-Baked Beans

Makes 8 servings

2 cans (15 ounces each) white beans, drained
2 apples, pared and diced
1 small onion, diced
⅔ cup honey
½ cup golden raisins

⅓ cup sweet pickle relish
1 tablespoon prepared mustard
1 teaspoon curry powder or to taste
Salt to taste

Combine all ingredients in 2½-quart casserole. Add enough water just to cover. Bake at 300°F about 1½ hours, adding more water if needed.

Favorite recipe from **National Honey Board**

Harvesting Nature's Bounty

Follow these purchasing tips so that you can enjoy fresh vegetables at their peak of flavor.

Asparagus: **Choose firm, straight spears with closed, compact tips. The stalks should be crisp, not wilted, woody or dry.**

Broccoli: **Look for tightly closed, compact, dark green to purplish-green florets on firm yet tender stalks. Avoid those with yellow flowers, wilted leaves and tough stems.**

Carrots: **Choose firm, well-shaped carrots with a deep orange color. Avoid those that are flabby, soft, cracked or shriveled.**

Cauliflower: **Look for a creamy-white head with tightly packed, crisp florets. The leaves should be bright green. Avoid heads with brown spots.**

Corn: **Choose corn with fresh, moist green husks; the cob should be well filled with bright, plump milky kernels. Kernels should be tightly packed together in even rows.**

Green Beans: **Look for vivid green, crisp beans without scars. Avoid bruised or large beans.**

Onions: **Choose firm, well-shaped onions with dry skins. Avoid those with sprouts.**

Zucchini: **Look for glossy, dark green skin and firm flesh. Avoid zucchini with any brown spots or those longer than 8 inches.**

Confetti Scalloped Corn

Makes 6 servings

1 egg, beaten
1 cup skim milk
1 cup coarsely crushed saltine crackers (about 22 two-inch square crackers), divided
¼ teaspoon salt
⅛ teaspoon pepper
1 can (16½ ounces) cream-style corn

¼ cup finely chopped onion
1 jar (2 ounces) chopped pimiento, drained
1 tablespoon CRISCO® Oil*
1 tablespoon chopped fresh parsley

*Use your favorite Crisco Oil product.

Note:

Pimientos are large, heart-shaped red sweet peppers, about 3½ inches long and 2½ inches wide. They are sweeter in flavor than red bell peppers.

1. Heat oven to 350°F.

2. Combine egg, milk, ⅔ cup cracker crumbs, salt and pepper in medium bowl. Stir in corn, onion and pimiento. Pour into ungreased 1-quart casserole.

3. Combine remaining ⅓ cup cracker crumbs with oil in small bowl. Toss to coat. Sprinkle over corn mixture.

4. Bake at 350°F for 1 hour or until knife inserted in center comes out clean. *Do not overbake.* Sprinkle with parsley. Let stand 5 to 10 minutes before serving. Garnish, if desired.

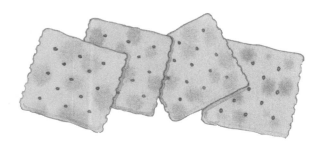

Mediterranean Strata

2 pounds green zucchini or
    yellow squash, cut into
    ¼-inch slices
1 cup ricotta cheese
3 eggs
1½ cups milk, heavy cream or
    half-and-half
1 cup minced fresh basil
    (2 bunches)

2 tablespoons all-purpose flour
1 tablespoon minced garlic
1 cup shredded mozzarella
    cheese
1 cup *French's®* French Fried
    Onions

Makes 6 servings

Prep Time:
15 minutes

Cook Time:
about 1 hour

1. Preheat oven to 350°F. Place zucchini and *2 tablespoons water* into 2-quart microwave-safe baking dish. Cover with vented plastic wrap. Microwave on HIGH 3 minutes or until just tender; drain well.

2. Whisk together ricotta cheese, eggs, milk, basil, flour, garlic and *½ teaspoon salt* in large bowl. Pour over zucchini. Bake, uncovered, 50 minutes or until custard is just set.

3. Sprinkle with mozzarella cheese and French Fried Onions. Bake 5 minutes until onions are golden. Garnish with diced red bell pepper, if desired.

<u>Tip:</u> *You may substitute 8 ounces crumbled feta cheese for the ricotta cheese. Omit salt.*

Pepperidge Farm®
Florentine Casserole

Makes 6 servings

Prep Time:
10 minutes

Cook Time:
35 minutes

4 cups PEPPERIDGE FARM®
   Herb Seasoned Stuffing
1 tablespoon margarine *or*
   butter, melted
1 can (10¾ ounces)
   CAMPBELL'S® Condensed
   Cream of Celery Soup *or*
   98% Fat Free Cream of
   Celery Soup

½ cup sour cream *or* plain
   yogurt
1 teaspoon onion powder
1 package (about 10 ounces)
   frozen chopped spinach,
   thawed
¼ cup grated Parmesan cheese

1. Mix ½ *cup* stuffing and margarine. Set aside.

2. Mix soup, sour cream, onion powder, spinach and cheese. Add remaining stuffing. Mix lightly. Spoon into 1½-quart casserole. Sprinkle reserved stuffing mixture over top.

3. Bake at 350°F. for 35 minutes or until hot.

<u>Tip:</u> *To thaw spinach, microwave on HIGH 3 minutes, breaking apart with fork halfway through heating.*

Eggplant, Tomato & Cheese Casserole

1 small eggplant, peeled
5 tablespoons olive oil
2 medium onions, thinly sliced
½ teaspoon LAWRY'S® Garlic
    Powder with Parsley
½ teaspoon LAWRY'S®
    Seasoned Salt
¼ teaspoon LAWRY'S®
    Seasoned Pepper

¼ teaspoon red pepper flakes
2 to 2½ teaspoons dried basil
3 medium tomatoes, cored and
    thinly sliced
½ cup (4 ounces) farmer's
    cheese
¾ cup heavy cream

Makes 6 servings

Slice eggplant crosswise into ¼-inch slices. Sprinkle with salt and layer on paper towels to remove moisture. Let stand 30 minutes then rinse and pat dry. In large skillet, heat 1 tablespoon olive oil. Add onions, Garlic Powder with Parsley, Seasoned Salt, Seasoned Pepper and red pepper flakes and cook over medium-high heat until onions are soft. Add 1 teaspoon basil. Place 2 tablespoons olive oil in 11-inch au gratin dish or shallow casserole. Layer ½ onion mixture in bottom of dish, then overlap slices of ½ eggplant and ½ tomatoes. Top with remaining onion mixture, then remaining eggplant and tomatoes. Bake in 400°F oven, covered, 10 minutes. Drizzle with remaining 2 tablespoons olive oil and continue baking another 30 minutes; basting from time to time with accumulated pan juices. Remove from oven and let stand at room temperature for several hours. (Can be refrigerated at this point; however, return to room temperature before completing and serving.) In blender or food processor fitted with steel knife, beat together farmer's cheese and heavy cream. Add remaining basil. Spread over eggplant-tomato mixture. Place under broiler until cheese is melted and slightly browned, about 5 minutes.

<u>Hint:</u> *Any type of soft French cheese can be used including goat's cheese, triple cream cheese, camembert and soft herb type cheese.*

Cheesy Broccoli 'n Mushroom Bake

Makes 6 to 8 servings

Prep Time:
10 minutes

Bake Time:
35 minutes

2 packages (10 ounces each) frozen broccoli spears, thawed
1 can (10¾ ounces) condensed cream of mushroom soup
½ cup MIRACLE WHIP® Salad Dressing

½ cup milk
1 cup KRAFT® Shredded Cheddar Cheese
½ cup coarsely crushed croutons

• ARRANGE broccoli in 12×8-inch baking dish. `

• WHISK together soup, salad dressing and milk. Pour over broccoli. Sprinkle with cheese and croutons.

• BAKE at 350°F for 30 to 35 minutes or until thoroughly heated.

Creamy Spinach Italiano

Makes 4 servings

Prep Time:
10 minutes

Cook Time:
35 minutes

1 cup ricotta cheese
¾ cup half-and-half or milk
2 packages (10 ounces each) frozen chopped spinach, thawed and squeezed dry
1⅓ cups *French's®* French Fried Onions, divided

½ cup chopped roasted red pepper
¼ cup chopped fresh basil
¼ cup grated Parmesan cheese
1 teaspoon garlic powder
¼ teaspoon salt

1. Preheat oven to 350°F. Whisk together ricotta cheese and half-and-half in large bowl until well combined. Stir in spinach, ⅔ *cup* French Fried Onions, red pepper, basil, Parmesan, garlic powder and salt. Pour mixture into greased deep-dish 9-inch pie plate.

2. Bake for 25 minutes or until heated through; stir. Sprinkle with remaining ⅔ *cup* onions. Bake for 5 minutes or until onions are golden.

Autumn Casserole

Makes 6 (½-cup) servings

¼ cup fat-free reduced-sodium chicken broth or water
2 cups sliced mushrooms
2 cups washed, stemmed and chopped fresh spinach
1 cup diced red bell pepper
1 clove garlic, minced
1 cup cooked spaghetti squash

¼ teaspoon salt
¼ teaspoon black pepper
⅛ teaspoon dried Italian seasoning
⅛ teaspoon red pepper flakes (optional)
¼ cup grated Parmesan cheese

1. Preheat oven to 350°F. Spray 1-quart casserole with nonstick cooking spray.

2. Heat chicken broth in medium saucepan. Add mushrooms, spinach, bell pepper and garlic. Cook 10 minutes or until vegetables are tender, stirring frequently. Stir in squash. Add salt, black pepper, Italian seasoning and red pepper flakes, if desired.

3. Spoon into prepared casserole. Sprinkle with cheese. Bake 5 to 10 minutes or until cheese melts.

<u>Hint:</u> *For 1 cup cooked spaghetti squash, place half small spaghetti squash in microwavable dish and add ¼ cup water. Microwave at HIGH 8 to 10 minutes or until squash is tender when pierced with a fork. Discard seeds and scrape out strands of squash. Or, bake in preheated 350°F oven 45 minutes or until tender.*

Baked Tomato Risotto

Makes 6 servings

1 jar (28 ounces) spaghetti
   sauce
1 can (14 ounces) chicken broth
2 cups halved sliced zucchini
1 can (4 ounces) sliced
   mushrooms

1 cup arborio rice
2 cups (8 ounces) shredded
   mozzarella cheese

Note:

Risotto is a classic rice dish of northern Italy. It is easy to make but requires a special short-grain, high-starch rice. Arborio is the most readily available. Never rinse arborio rice before cooking since you don't want to wash off the starchy coating that makes the finished dish creamy.

Preheat oven to 350°F. Spray 3-quart casserole with nonstick cooking spray.

Combine spaghetti sauce, broth, zucchini, mushrooms and rice in prepared dish.

Bake, covered, 30 minutes. Remove from oven and stir casserole. Cover and bake 15 to 20 minutes or until rice is tender. Remove from oven; sprinkle evenly with cheese. Bake, uncovered, 5 minutes or until cheese is melted.

Easy Spinach-Zucchini Pie

1 to 2 medium zucchini (each
about 8 inches long)
Hot water
2 packages (10 ounces each)
frozen chopped spinach,
thawed and well drained
½ cup sour cream
1 package (3 ounces) cream
cheese, softened
¼ cup (1 ounce) grated
Parmesan cheese

3 tablespoons dry bread
crumbs
1 egg, slightly beaten
½ teaspoon garlic salt
½ teaspoon dried basil,
crumbled
1⅓ cups *French's*® French Fried
Onions, divided
½ cup (2 ounces) shredded
Cheddar cheese

Preheat oven to 375°F. Using sharp knife, trim off 1 side of
zucchini to form a straight edge. Starting at straight edge, cut
zucchini lengthwise into eight thin strips (about ⅛ inch thick).
Place zucchini strips in shallow dish filled with hot water about
3 minutes to soften; drain. In large bowl, using fork, thoroughly
combine spinach, sour cream, cream cheese, Parmesan cheese,
bread crumbs, egg, seasonings and ⅔ *cup* French Fried Onions.
Line bottom and side of 9-inch pie plate or quiche dish with
zucchini strips, allowing 3 inches of each strip to hang over edge.
Spoon spinach mixture evenly into pie plate. Fold zucchini strips
over spinach mixture, tucking ends into center of mixture. Cover
pie plate with foil. Bake, covered, at 375°F for 40 minutes or
until zucchini is tender. Top center of pie with Cheddar cheese
and remaining ⅔ *cup* onions; bake, uncovered, 3 minutes or
until onions are golden brown.

New England Baked Beans

Makes 4 to 6 servings

½ pound uncooked navy beans
¼ pound salt pork, trimmed
   Water
1 small onion, chopped
2 cloves garlic, minced
3 tablespoons packed light
   brown sugar
3 tablespoons maple syrup

3 tablespoons unsulphured
   molasses
½ teaspoon salt
½ teaspoon dry mustard
⅛ teaspoon black pepper
½ bay leaf
⅓ cup canned diced tomatoes,
   well drained

1. Rinse beans thoroughly in colander under cold running water. Place in large bowl; cover with 4 inches water. Let stand at least 8 hours, then rinse and drain.

2. Cut pork into 4 (¼-inch-thick) slices. Score pork with tip of sharp knife, taking care not to cut completely through pork; set aside.

3. Bring 3 cups water to a boil in 1-quart saucepan. Place pork in water; boil 1 minute. Remove from saucepan to medium plate. Slice and set aside.

4. Place beans in heavy, 3-quart saucepan. Cover beans with 2 inches cold water. Bring beans to a boil over high heat. Reduce heat to low; simmer, covered, 30 to 35 minutes or until tender. Drain, reserving liquid.

5. Preheat oven to 350°F. Line bottom of large casserole with ½ of pork slices. Spoon beans over pork slices.

6. Place 2 cups reserved bean liquid into 1½-quart saucepan. Bring to a boil over high heat. Add onion, garlic, brown sugar, maple syrup, molasses, salt, mustard, pepper and bay leaf; simmer 2 minutes. Stir in tomatoes; cook 1 minute. Pour onion mixture over beans in casserole. Top with remaining pork slices.

7. Cover casserole with foil. Bake 2½ hours. Remove cover; bake 30 minutes or until thickened. Skim fat from surface.

8. Discard pork slices and bay leaf before serving. Garnish with fresh parsley, if desired.

Tomato-Bread Casserole

Makes 8 to 10 servings

- ½ pound loaf French bread, sliced
- 3 tablespoons butter or margarine, softened
- 1 can (14½ ounces) whole peeled tomatoes, cut up
- 1½ pounds fresh tomatoes, thinly sliced
- 1 cup lowfat cottage or ricotta cheese
- ¼ cup olive or vegetable oil
- ¾ teaspoon LAWRY'S® Seasoned Salt
- ½ teaspoon dried oregano, crushed
- ½ teaspoon LAWRY'S® Garlic Powder with Parsley
- ½ cup Parmesan cheese

Spread bread slices with butter; cut into large cubes. Arrange on jelly-roll pan. Toast in 350°F oven about 7 minutes. Place ½ of cubes in greased 13×9×2-inch baking dish. Drain canned tomatoes, reserving liquid. Top bread cubes with ½ of fresh tomato slices, ½ reserved tomato liquid, ½ of cottage cheese, ½ of oil, ½ of canned tomatoes, ½ of Seasoned Salt, ½ of oregano and ½ of Garlic Powder with Parsley. Repeat layers. Sprinkle with Parmesan cheese. Bake, covered, in 350°F oven 40 minutes. Uncover and bake 5 minutes longer to brown top.

Serving Suggestion: *Sprinkle with parsley. Serve with any grilled or baked meat, fish or poultry entrée.*

Broccoli and Onion Casserole

Makes 6 servings

1 large onion
¾ cup fat-free low-sodium
  chicken broth
1¼ pounds broccoli

½ teaspoon black pepper,
  divided
Dash paprika

Preheat oven to 375°F. Cut onion into quarters, then crosswise into thin slices. Bring onion and chicken broth to a boil in medium saucepan over high heat. Reduce heat to low. Simmer, covered, 5 minutes or until onion is fork-tender. Remove onion to small bowl with slotted spoon, leaving broth in saucepan. Set aside.

Trim broccoli, removing tough part of stems. Cut into florets with ½-inch stems. Peel remaining broccoli stems; cut into ¼-inch-thick slices.

Spread half of broccoli in 8-inch square baking dish or 2-quart casserole. Spread half of onion slices on broccoli. Sprinkle with ¼ teaspoon pepper. Repeat layers.

Pour reserved broth over vegetables. Cover tightly with foil. Bake 25 minutes or until broccoli is tender. *Do not stir.* Drain liquid; sprinkle with paprika before serving.

Snappy Waistline Eggplant Bake

Makes 10 (4-ounce) servings

PAM® No-Stick Cooking Spray
3 tablespoons WESSON® Canola Oil, divided
4 cups peeled and cubed eggplant, cut into 1½-inch pieces
½ cup diced onion
1 can (14.5 ounces) HUNT'S® Diced Tomatoes with Basil, Garlic & Oregano

2 tablespoons finely chopped fresh parsley
1 teaspoon sugar
⅛ teaspoon pepper
1 cup fat free seasoned large croutons, slightly crushed
½ cup shredded Provolone
½ cup shredded low fat Cheddar cheese

Note:

Eggplant becomes bitter with age. Purchase them within a few days of using. Store unwashed eggplant in a cool, dry place for a day or two, or in a plastic bag in the refrigerator for up to five days.

1. Preheat oven to 350°F.

2. Spray 11×7×2-inch baking dish with PAM® Cooking Spray.

3. In large skillet, heat *2 tablespoons* Wesson® Oil until hot. Sauté eggplant 5 to 7 minutes or until tender; spoon into baking dish.

4. In same skillet, heat *remaining* oil and sauté onion. Stir in Hunt's® Diced Tomatoes, parsley, sugar and pepper; bring to a boil.

5. Evenly pour tomato mixture over eggplant. Top with croutons and cheeses.

6. Bake, uncovered, for 30 minutes or until cheese is brown and juices are bubbly.

Original Green Bean Casserole

Makes 6 servings

Prep Time:
5 minutes

Cook Time:
35 minutes

1 can (10¾ ounces) condensed cream of mushroom soup
¾ cup milk
⅛ teaspoon ground black pepper
2 packages (9 ounces each) frozen cut green beans, thawed*

1⅓ cups *French's®* French Fried Onions, divided

*Substitute 2 cans (14½ ounces each) cut green beans, drained, for frozen green beans.

1. Preheat oven to 350°F. Combine soup, milk and pepper in 1½-quart casserole; stir until well blended. Stir in beans and ⅔ *cup* French Fried Onions.

2. Bake, uncovered, 30 minutes or until hot; stir. Sprinkle with remaining ⅔ *cup* onions. Bake 5 minutes or until onions are golden brown.

Microwave Directions: *Prepare green bean mixture as above; pour into 1½-quart microwave-safe casserole. Cover with vented plastic wrap. Microwave on HIGH 8 to 10 minutes or until heated through, stirring halfway through cooking time. Uncover. Top with remaining onions. Cook 1 minute until onions are golden. Let stand 5 minutes.*

Substitution: *You can substitute 4 cups cooked, cut fresh green beans for the frozen or canned.*

Easy Italian Vegetable Pasta Bake

3 cups mostaccioli, cooked, drained 1 jar (27½ ounces) light pasta sauce 1 package (8 ounces) KRAFT® 2% Milk Shredded Reduced Fat Mozzarella Cheese, divided	2 cups thinly sliced mushrooms 2 cups sliced halved yellow squash 2 cups sliced halved zucchini	**Makes 6 servings** **Prep Time:** *15 minutes* **Bake Time:** *25 minutes*

MIX mostaccioli, pasta sauce, 1 cup of the cheese and vegetables in large bowl.

SPOON into 13×9-inch baking dish. Top with remaining cheese.

BAKE at 375°F for 20 to 25 minutes or until thoroughly heated.

SPAM™ Cheesy Broccoli Bake

1 (10-ounce) package frozen chopped broccoli 1 (10¾-ounce) can Cheddar cheese soup ½ cup sour cream	1 (12-ounce) can SPAM® Classic, cubed 1½ cups cooked white rice ½ cup buttered bread crumbs	**Makes 4 to 6 servings**

Heat oven to 350°F. Cook broccoli according to package directions. Drain well. In medium bowl, combine soup and sour cream. Add broccoli, SPAM® and rice to soup mixture. Spoon into 1½-quart casserole. Sprinkle with bread crumbs. Bake 30 to 35 minutes or until thoroughly heated.

Fresh Vegetable Casserole

Makes 4 to 6 servings

8 small new potatoes
8 baby carrots
1 small cauliflower, broken into florets
4 stalks asparagus, cut into 1-inch pieces
3 tablespoons butter or margarine

3 tablespoons all-purpose flour
2 cups milk
Salt
Black pepper
¾ cup (3 ounces) shredded Cheddar cheese
Chopped fresh cilantro

Note:

When cooking with cheese, use a low temperature and cook it slowly as high temperatures cause it to become rubbery. Cheese that is shredded or cut into very small pieces will melt quickly when added to a hot liquid. Often the liquid mixture can be removed from the heat and the cheese stirred in.

1. Cook vegetables until crisp-tender. Arrange vegetables in buttered 2-quart casserole. Preheat oven to 350°F.

2. To make sauce, melt butter in medium saucepan over medium heat. Stir in flour until smooth. Gradually stir in milk. Cook until thickened, stirring constantly. Season to taste with salt and pepper. Add cheese, stirring until cheese is melted. Pour sauce over vegetables and sprinkle with cilantro. Bake 15 minutes or until heated through.

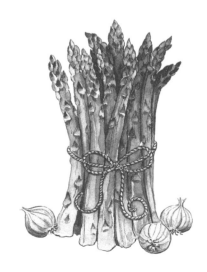

Eggplant Squash Bake

½ cup chopped onion
1 clove garlic, minced
   Nonstick olive oil cooking
   spray
1 cup part-skim ricotta cheese
1 jar (4 ounces) diced
   pimientos, drained
¼ cup grated Parmesan cheese
2 tablespoons fat-free (skim)
   milk
1½ teaspoons dried marjoram
¾ teaspoon dried tarragon
¼ teaspoon salt
¼ teaspoon ground nutmeg

¼ teaspoon black pepper
1 cup no-sugar-added meatless
   spaghetti sauce, divided
½ pound eggplant, peeled and
   cut into thin crosswise
   slices
6 ounces zucchini, cut in half
   then lengthwise into thin
   slices
6 ounces yellow summer
   squash, cut in half then
   lengthwise into thin slices
2 tablespoons shredded part-
   skim mozzarella cheese

Microwave Directions

1. Combine onion and garlic in medium microwavable bowl. Spray lightly with cooking spray. Microwave at HIGH 1 minute.

2. Add ricotta, pimientos, Parmesan, milk, marjoram, tarragon, salt, nutmeg and pepper. Spray 9- or 10-inch round microwavable baking dish with cooking spray. Spread ⅓ cup spaghetti sauce in bottom of dish.

3. Layer half of eggplant, zucchini and squash in dish; top with ricotta mixture. Layer remaining eggplant, zucchini and summer squash over ricotta mixture. Top with remaining ⅔ cup spaghetti sauce.

4. Cover with vented plastic wrap. Microwave at HIGH 17 to 19 minutes or until vegetables are tender, rotating dish every 6 minutes. Top with mozzarella cheese. Let stand 10 minutes before serving.

Broccoli & Cheddar Noodle Casserole

Makes 6 servings

Prep Time:
25 minutes

Cook Time:
25 minutes

1 package (12 ounces) dry wide egg noodles
3 tablespoons margarine or butter, divided
2 cups chopped onions
4 cups broccoli flowerets
1 can (14.5 ounces) CONTADINA® Stewed Tomatoes, undrained
1 can (6 ounces) CONTADINA Tomato Paste

1 package (1½ ounces) spaghetti sauce seasoning mix
2 cups water
1 teaspoon garlic salt
1½ cups (6 ounces) shredded Cheddar cheese
½ cup CONTADINA Seasoned Italian Bread Crumbs

1. Cook noodles according to package directions; drain.

2. Meanwhile, melt 2 tablespoons margarine in 5-quart saucepan; sauté onions until tender.

3. Stir in broccoli, undrained tomatoes, tomato paste, seasoning mix, water and garlic salt. Bring to a boil. Reduce heat; simmer, uncovered, for 10 minutes, stirring occasionally. Stir in cooked noodles.

4. Layer half of the noodle mixture in 13×9×2-inch baking dish. Sprinkle with cheese. Layer with remaining noodle mixture.

5. Melt remaining 1 tablespoon margarine; stir in crumbs. Sprinkle over casserole; cover and bake in preheated 350°F oven 20 minutes. Uncover; bake 5 minutes.

Campbell's® Creamed Onion Bake

4 tablespoons margarine *or* butter	1 can (10¾ ounces) CAMPBELL'S® Condensed Cream of Mushroom Soup *or* 98% Fat Free Cream of Mushroom Soup
1½ cups PEPPERIDGE FARM® Corn Bread Stuffing	
2 tablespoons chopped fresh parsley *or* 2 teaspoons dried parsley flakes	¼ cup milk
	1 cup frozen peas
3 large onions, cut in half and sliced (about 3 cups)	1 cup shredded Cheddar cheese (4 ounces)

Makes 6 servings

Prep Time:
15 minutes

Cook Time:
30 minutes

1. Melt *2 tablespoons* margarine and mix with stuffing and parsley. Set aside.

2. In medium skillet over medium heat, heat remaining margarine. Add onions and cook until tender.

3. Stir in soup, milk and peas. Spoon into 2-quart shallow baking dish. Sprinkle cheese and stuffing mixture over soup mixture.

4. Bake at 350°F. for 30 minutes or until hot.

Pasta Primavera Casserole

Makes 6 servings

Prep Time:
15 minutes

Cook Time:
40 minutes

8 ounces uncooked rotini pasta
1 jar (12 ounces) chicken gravy
½ cup milk
1⅓ cups *French's®* French Fried
Onions, divided
1 small zucchini, thinly sliced
1 tomato, chopped
1 cup frozen peas, thawed and
drained

1 cup (4 ounces) shredded
mozzarella cheese
½ cup grated Parmesan cheese
2 tablespoons minced fresh
basil *or* 1 teaspoon dried
basil leaves

Note:

**Primavera is an
Italian word meaning
"springtime." It is used
as a term in the title of
recipes that contain
fresh spring
vegetables, either
raw or blanched.**

Preheat oven to 350°F. Grease 2-quart oblong baking dish. Cook pasta according to package directions using shortest cooking time. Drain. Return pasta to saucepan.

Add gravy, milk, *⅔ cup* French Fried Onions, zucchini, tomato, peas, cheeses and basil to pasta; toss lightly. Spoon into prepared baking dish.

Bake, uncovered, 35 minutes or until heated through, stirring halfway through cooking time. Top with remaining *⅔ cup* onions. Bake, uncovered, 5 minutes or until onions are golden brown.

Tasty
Brunch
Favorites

CHAPTER EIGHT

Apple Brunch Strata

Makes 8 servings

½ pound sausage, casing removed
4 cups cubed French bread
2 cups diced peeled Michigan Apples
¼ cup sliced green onions
⅓ cup sliced black olives
1½ cups (6 ounces) shredded sharp Cheddar cheese

2 cups reduced-fat milk
8 eggs
2 teaspoons spicy brown mustard
½ teaspoon salt
¼ teaspoon black pepper
Paprika

1. Brown sausage in skillet over medium-high heat. Drain on paper towels; set aside.

2. Spray 13×9×2-inch baking dish with nonstick cooking spray. Layer half of bread cubes in bottom of dish. Crumble sausage over bread. Top with Michigan Apples, green onions, olives and cheese. Place remaining bread on top.

3. Mix milk, eggs, mustard, salt and pepper in medium bowl; pour over bread. Cover with foil and refrigerate 4 hours or overnight.

4. Preheat oven to 350°F. Bake, covered, 45 minutes. Remove foil and bake 15 minutes or until center is set. Let stand 15 minutes before serving. Sprinkle with paprika, if desired.

Tip: *Suggested Michigan Apple varieties to use include Empire, Gala, Golden Delicious, Ida Red, Jonagold, Jonathan, McIntosh and Rome.*

Variation: *Substitute 1 can (20 ounces) sliced Michigan Apples, drained and chopped for fresh Apples.*

Favorite recipe from **Michigan Apple Committee**

Baked Ham & Cheese Monte Cristo

6 slices bread, divided
2 cups (8 ounces) shredded
    Cheddar cheese, divided
1⅓ cups *French's®* French Fried
    Onions, divided
1 package (10 ounces) frozen
    broccoli spears, thawed,
    drained and cut into 1-inch
    pieces

2 cups (10 ounces) cubed
    cooked ham
5 eggs
2 cups milk
½ teaspoon ground mustard
½ teaspoon seasoned salt
¼ teaspoon coarsely ground
    black pepper

Makes 6 to 8 servings

Preheat oven to 325°F. Cut 3 bread slices into cubes; place in greased 12×8-inch baking dish. Top bread with 1 cup cheese, ⅔ *cup* French Fried Onions, the broccoli and ham. Cut remaining bread slices diagonally into halves. Arrange bread halves down center of casserole, overlapping slightly, crusted points all in one direction. In medium bowl, beat eggs, milk and seasonings; pour evenly over casserole. Bake, uncovered, at 325°F for 1 hour or until center is set. Top with remaining 1 cup cheese and ⅔ *cup* onions; bake, uncovered, 5 minutes or until onions are golden brown. Let stand 10 minutes before serving.

Note:

There are many different types of eggs, but the chicken egg is most commonly used in cooking. The color of the egg shell (white or brown) is determined by the breed of the chicken. The color of the shell does not affect flavor, quality, nutrients or cooking characteristics of the egg.

French Toast Strata

Makes 6 servings

4 ounces day-old French or Italian bread, cut into ¾-inch cubes (4 cups)
⅓ cup golden raisins
1 package (3 ounces) cream cheese, cut into ¼-inch cubes
3 eggs

1½ cups milk
½ cup maple-flavored pancake syrup
1 teaspoon vanilla
2 tablespoons sugar
1 teaspoon ground cinnamon
Additional maple-flavored pancake syrup (optional)

1. Spray 11×7-inch baking dish with nonstick cooking spray. Place bread cubes in even layer in prepared dish; sprinkle raisins and cream cheese evenly over bread.

2. Beat eggs in medium bowl with electric mixer at medium speed until blended. Add milk, ½ cup pancake syrup and vanilla; mix well. Pour egg mixture evenly over bread mixture. Cover; refrigerate at least 4 hours or overnight.

3. Preheat oven to 350°F. Combine sugar and cinnamon in small bowl; sprinkle evenly over strata.

4. Bake, uncovered, 40 to 45 minutes or until puffed, golden brown and knife inserted in center comes out clean. Cut into squares and serve with additional pancake syrup, if desired.

Serving Suggestion: *Serve with fresh fruit compote.*

Breakfast Sausage Casserole

4 cups cubed day-old bread
2 cups (8 ounces) shredded
　　sharp cheddar cheese
2 cans (12 fluid ounces *each*)
　　NESTLÉ® CARNATION®
　　Evaporated Milk
10 eggs, lightly beaten

1 teaspoon dry mustard
¼ teaspoon onion powder
　　Ground black pepper to taste
1 package (16 ounces) fresh
　　breakfast sausage, cooked,
　　drained and crumbled

Makes 10 to
12 servings

GREASE 13×9-inch baking dish. Place bread in prepared baking dish. Sprinkle with cheese. Combine evaporated milk, eggs, dry mustard, onion powder and pepper in medium bowl. Pour evenly over bread and cheese. Sprinkle with sausage. Cover; refrigerate overnight.

PREHEAT oven to 325°F.

BAKE for 55 to 60 minutes or until cheese is golden brown. Cover with foil if top browns too quickly.

Pace® Festive Breakfast Casserole

Makes 6 servings

Prep and Chill Time:
2 hours 15 minutes

Cook Time:
45 minutes

Note:

To check if an egg is fresh, place it in a bowl of cold water. A fresh egg will sink, a stale egg will float.

8 ounces bulk pork sausage
6 cups white bread cut in cubes
   (about 8 slices)
1½ cups shredded Cheddar
   cheese (6 ounces)

1 cup PACE® Picante Sauce *or*
   Chunky Salsa
4 eggs
¾ cup milk

1. In medium skillet over medium-high heat, cook sausage until browned, stirring to separate meat. Pour off fat.

2. In 2-quart shallow baking dish arrange sausage. Top with bread cubes and cheese. Mix picante sauce, eggs and milk. Pour over bread and cheese making sure all bread is moistened. Cover and refrigerate 2 hours or overnight.

3. Uncover. Bake at 350°F. for 45 minutes or until knife inserted in center comes out clean.

Three Cheese Asparagus and Leeks Bread Pudding

PAM® No-Stick Cooking Spray
⅓ cup WESSON® Vegetable Oil
3 small leeks, washed and cut into ½-inch slices
1 pound asparagus, washed and cut into ½-inch pieces
½ cup *each:* chopped fresh basil and parsley
1 tablespoon fresh grated lemon peel
2½ cups milk
1 pint (2 cups) heavy cream

5 eggs
¼ pound *each:* grated Fontina, Parmesan and Provolone cheeses
1½ teaspoons garlic salt
½ teaspoon cayenne pepper
½ teaspoon coarse ground black pepper
1 to 1½ pounds sourdough bread, cut into 1-inch cubes and lightly toasted

Makes 8 to 10 servings

Prep Time:
20 minutes

Cook Time:
50 to 60 minutes

Preheat oven to 375°F. Spray a 4-quart oval baking dish (at least 2-inches deep) with PAM® Cooking Spray; set aside. In a large skillet, heat Wesson® Oil until hot. Sauté leeks, asparagus, basil, parsley and lemon peel until leeks are tender (about 10 minutes). Meanwhile, in a large bowl, whisk together milk, cream, and eggs. Stir in cheeses, garlic salt, cayenne, pepper, black pepper, sautéed vegetables and bread; toss until well coated. Spoon bread mixture into baking dish and bake 50 to 60 minutes or until top is crusty brown and a knife inserted in center comes out clean. If pudding looks too brown before it's finished, cover loosely with foil. Cool 7 minutes before serving.

<u>Hint:</u> *This recipe is perfect to prepare hours ahead of time or even the day before. Simply, sauté the vegetables and refrigerate. Then mix together the remaining ingredients except the bread in a large bowl and refrigerate until ready to bake. At the last minute, toss the bread with all ingredients and bake. It's a real time saver!*

Make-Ahead Breakfast Casserole

Makes 10 to 12 servings

2½ cups seasoned croutons
1 pound BOB EVANS® Original Recipe Roll Sausage
2¼ cups milk
4 eggs
1 (10½-ounce) can condensed cream of mushroom soup
1 (10-ounce) package frozen chopped spinach, thawed and squeezed dry
1 (4-ounce) can mushrooms, drained and chopped

1 cup (4 ounces) shredded sharp Cheddar cheese
1 cup (4 ounces) shredded Monterey Jack cheese
¼ teaspoon dry mustard
Fresh herb sprigs and carrot strips (optional)
Picante sauce or salsa (optional)

Spread croutons on bottom of greased 13×9-inch baking dish. Crumble sausage into medium skillet. Cook over medium heat until browned, stirring occasionally. Drain off any drippings. Spread over croutons. Whisk milk and eggs in large bowl until blended. Stir in soup, spinach, mushrooms, cheeses and mustard. Pour egg mixture over sausage and croutons. Refrigerate overnight. Preheat oven to 325°F. Bake egg mixture 50 to 55 minutes or until set and lightly browned on top. Garnish with herb sprigs and carrot strips, if desired. Serve hot with picante sauce, if desired. Refrigerate leftovers.

Hash Brown Bake

Makes 4 servings

1 packet (1 ounce) HIDDEN VALLEY® The Original Ranch® Salad Dressing & Seasoning Mix
1¼ cups milk
3 ounces cream cheese
6 cups hash browns, frozen shredded potatoes
1 tablespoon bacon bits
½ cup shredded sharp Cheddar cheese

In blender, combine salad dressing & seasoning mix, milk and cream cheese. Pour over potatoes and bacon bits in 9-inch baking dish. Top with cheese. Bake at 350°F for 35 minutes.

Albacore Quiche

Makes 6 servings

1 (9-inch) pie shell or 1 refrigerated (½ of 15-ounce package) pie crust
1 (3-ounce) pouch of STARKIST® Premium Albacore Tuna
⅓ cup chopped green onions
¾ cup shredded Cheddar or Swiss cheese or a combination of cheeses
3 eggs
1¼ cups half-and-half or milk
½ teaspoon dried basil or dill weed
¼ teaspoon ground black pepper

Prep Time:
60 minutes

Line pie shell with foil; fill with pie weights, dry beans or rice. Bake in 375°F oven 10 minutes. Remove foil and pie weights; place tuna, onions and cheese in pie shell. In medium bowl, combine eggs, half-and-half and seasonings; pour over pie shell. Continue baking 40 to 50 more minutes or until quiche is set and knife inserted near center comes out clean. Cool slightly before serving.

Vegetable Cheese Frittata

Makes 6 servings

½ cup fresh green beans, cut into 1-inch pieces
1 small onion, chopped
3 tablespoons butter or margarine
¼ red bell pepper, chopped
¼ cup sliced fresh mushrooms

¼ cup dry bread crumbs
½ cup prepared HIDDEN VALLEY® The Original Ranch® Dressing
6 eggs, beaten
⅓ cup shredded Cheddar cheese
¼ cup grated Parmesan cheese

Preheat oven to 350°F. In medium saucepan, steam green beans over boiling water until crisp-tender, about 4 minutes. In medium skillet, sauté onion in butter until onion is softened; stir in beans, red pepper and mushrooms. Fold vegetables, bread crumbs and salad dressing into eggs. Pour into buttered quiche dish. Sprinkle with cheeses. Bake until set, about 25 minutes.

Note: *Substitute chopped tomatoes, diced green chili peppers, sliced black olives, chopped zucchini or any vegetable combination for green beans, onion and mushrooms.*

Easy Crab-Asparagus Pie

4 ounces crabmeat, shredded
12 ounces fresh asparagus, cut
  into pieces and cooked
½ cup chopped onion, cooked
1 cup (4 ounces) shredded
  Monterey Jack cheese
¼ cup (1 ounce) grated
  Parmesan cheese

Black pepper
¾ cup all-purpose flour
¾ teaspoon baking powder
½ teaspoon salt
2 tablespoons butter or
  margarine, chilled
1½ cups milk
4 eggs, lightly beaten

Makes 6 servings

1. Preheat oven to 350°F. Lightly grease 10-inch quiche dish or pie plate.

2. Layer crabmeat, asparagus and onion in prepared dish; top with cheeses. Season with pepper.

3. Combine flour, baking powder and salt in large bowl. With pastry blender or 2 knives, cut in butter until mixture forms coarse crumbs. Stir in milk and eggs; pour over vegetables and cheeses.

4. Bake 30 minutes or until filling is puffed and knife inserted near center comes out clean. Serve hot.

Note:

Asparagus can be steamed or boiled. To boil asparagus, in a large saucepan, bring water to a boil and then add the asparagus pieces. Boil 4 to 6 minutes or until crisp-tender. Drain in a colander.

Sour Cream Chicken Quiche

Makes 1 (9-inch) pie

Note:

When making pies and quiches, it's important to choose the right pie plate. Heat-resistant glass or dull-finished metal pie plates provide the best browning. A shiny pan reflects heat, so the bottom crust can turn out underbaked and soggy. If you choose a nonstick pie plate be sure the crust is secured over the edge. The nonstick coating won't hold it in place as well, and it could slide down the sides when the crust shrinks in the oven.

Crust
Classic CRISCO® Single Crust
(recipe follows)

Filling
2 tablespoons CRISCO® Stick or
2 tablespoons CRISCO®
all-vegetable shortening
2 tablespoons chopped green
bell pepper
2 tablespoons chopped onion
1 cup cubed cooked chicken

1 tablespoon all-purpose flour
¼ teaspoon salt
Dash nutmeg
Dash black pepper
½ cup shredded sharp Cheddar
cheese
¼ cup shredded Swiss cheese
2 eggs, lightly beaten
¾ cup milk
¾ cup dairy sour cream

1. For crust, prepare as directed. Do not bake. Heat oven to 400°F.

2. For filling, melt Crisco in small skillet. Add green pepper and onion. Cook on medium-high heat 3 minutes, stirring frequently. Add chicken and flour. Cook and stir 2 minutes. Spread in bottom of unbaked pie crust. Sprinkle with salt, nutmeg and black pepper. Top with Cheddar cheese and Swiss cheese.

3. Combine eggs, milk and sour cream in medium bowl. Stir until smooth. Pour carefully over cheese.

4. Bake at 400°F for 20 minutes. *Reduce oven temperature to 350°F.* Bake 30 to 35 minutes or until knife inserted near center comes out clean. *Do not overbake.* Cool 10 minutes before cutting and serving. Refrigerate leftover pie.

Classic Crisco® Single Crust

1⅓ cups all-purpose flour	½ CRISCO® Stick or ½ cup
½ teaspoon salt	CRISCO® all-vegetable
	shortening
	3 tablespoons cold water

1. Spoon flour into measuring cup and level. Combine flour and salt in medium bowl.

2. Cut in shortening using pastry blender or 2 knives until all flour is blended to form pea-size chunks.

3. Sprinkle with water, 1 tablespoon at a time. Toss lightly with fork until dough forms a ball.

4. Press dough between hands to form 5- to 6-inch "pancake." Flour rolling surface and rolling pin lightly. Roll dough into circle. Trim circle 1 inch larger than upside-down 9-inch pie plate. Carefully remove trimmed dough. Set aside to reroll and use for pastry cutout garnish, if desired.

5. Fold dough into quarters. Unfold and press into pie plate. Fold edge under. Flute.   *Makes 1 (9-inch) single crust*

Summer Sausage 'n' Egg Wedges

Makes 6 servings

4 eggs, beaten
⅓ cup milk
¼ cup all-purpose flour
½ teaspoon baking powder
⅛ teaspoon garlic powder
2½ cups (10 ounces) shredded
    Cheddar or mozzarella
    cheese, divided

1½ cups diced HILLSHIRE FARM®
    Summer Sausage
1 cup cream-style cottage
    cheese with chives

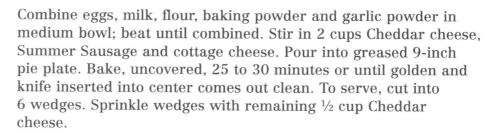

Preheat oven to 375°F.

Combine eggs, milk, flour, baking powder and garlic powder in medium bowl; beat until combined. Stir in 2 cups Cheddar cheese, Summer Sausage and cottage cheese. Pour into greased 9-inch pie plate. Bake, uncovered, 25 to 30 minutes or until golden and knife inserted into center comes out clean. To serve, cut into 6 wedges. Sprinkle wedges with remaining ½ cup Cheddar cheese.

Tip: Here's a simple do-ahead garlic bread and a great accompaniment to your favorite Hillshire Farm meal: Cut a 1 pound loaf of French bread into 1-inch slices. Spread with a mixture of ½ cup soft butter and ¼ teaspoon garlic powder. Sprinkle with salt, pepper and paprika. Reassemble the loaf and wrap in heavy-duty foil. Heat in a 350°F oven for 15 to 20 minutes.

Parmesan and Roasted Red Pepper Strata

Makes 6 servings

1 loaf (16 ounces) French bread, cut into ½-inch-thick slices
2 jars (7½ ounces each) roasted red peppers, drained and cut into ½-inch pieces
1 cup grated Parmesan cheese
1 cup sliced green onions
3 cups (12 ounces) shredded mozzarella cheese

8 eggs
¾ cup reduced-fat (2%) milk
1 container (7 ounces) prepared pesto
2 teaspoons minced garlic
¾ teaspoon salt

1. Grease 13×9-inch baking dish. Arrange half of bread slices in single layer on bottom of prepared baking dish. Top bread with half of red peppers, ½ cup Parmesan, ½ cup green onions and 1½ cups mozzarella. Repeat layers with remaining bread, red peppers, Parmesan, green onions and mozzarella.

2. Combine eggs, milk, pesto, garlic and salt in medium bowl; whisk to combine. Pour egg mixture evenly over strata. Cover and refrigerate overnight.

3. Preheat oven to 375°F. Bake, uncovered, 30 minutes or until hot and bubbly.

<u>Hint:</u> *If time allows, let the strata stand at room temperature about 15 minutes before baking.*

Pepperidge Farm® French Toast Casserole

Makes 8 servings

Prep and Chill Time:
1 hour 15 minutes

Cook Time:
50 minutes

1 loaf (16 ounces) PEPPERIDGE FARM® Cinnamon Swirl Bread, any variety, cut into cubes (about 8 cups)

6 eggs
3 cups milk
2 teaspoons vanilla extract
Confectioners' sugar

1. In greased 3-quart shallow baking dish arrange bread cubes. Mix eggs, milk and vanilla. Pour over bread. Cover and refrigerate 1 hour or overnight.

2. Uncover. Bake at 350°F. for 50 minutes or until golden. Sprinkle with confectioners' sugar. Serve with pancake syrup if desired.

<u>Tip:</u> *This quick-to-assemble breakfast casserole can be refrigerated overnight for a special morning treat.*

Spinach Pie

Makes 6 servings

1 tablespoon olive oil
1 pound fresh spinach, washed, drained and stems removed
1 medium potato, cooked and mashed

2 eggs, beaten
¼ cup cottage cheese
¼ cup grated BELGIOIOSO® Romano Cheese
Salt

Preheat oven to 350°F. Grease 8-inch round cake pan with olive oil. Tear spinach into bite-sized pieces. Combine spinach, potato, eggs, cottage cheese and BelGioioso Romano Cheese in large bowl. Spoon mixture into prepared pan. Bake 15 to 20 minutes or until set. Season to taste with salt.

Pinwheel Cheese Quiche

2 tablespoons margarine or
    butter
2 cups sliced mushrooms
6 green onions, sliced (about
    2 cups)
1 package (8 ounces)
    refrigerated crescent rolls,
    separated into 8 triangles

1 envelope LIPTON® RECIPE
    SECRETS® Savory Herb
    with Garlic Soup Mix
½ cup half-and-half
4 eggs, beaten
1 cup (about 4 ounces)
    shredded Monterey Jack or
    mozzarella cheese

**Makes about
6 servings**

Preheat oven to 375°F.

In 12-inch skillet, melt margarine over medium heat and cook
mushrooms and green onions, stirring occasionally, 5 minutes or
until tender. Remove from heat and set aside.

In 9-inch pie plate sprayed with nonstick cooking spray, arrange
crescent roll triangles in spoke pattern with narrow tips hanging
over rim of pie plate about 2 inches. Press dough onto bottom and
up side of pie plate sealing edges to form full crust.

In medium bowl, combine savory herb with garlic soup mix, half-
and-half and eggs. Stir in cheese and mushroom mixture. Pour
into prepared pie crust. Bring tips of dough over filling towards
center. Bake uncovered 30 minutes or until knife inserted in
center comes out clean.

Chilies Rellenos Casserole

Makes 4 servings

3 eggs, separated
¾ cup milk
¾ cup all-purpose flour
½ teaspoon salt
1 tablespoon butter or
   margarine
½ cup chopped onion
2 cans (7 ounces each) whole
   green chilies, drained

8 slices (1 ounce each)
   Monterey Jack cheese, cut
   into halves
Garnishes: sour cream, sliced
   green onions, pitted ripe
   olive slices, guacamole and
   salsa

1. Preheat oven to 350°F.

2. Combine egg yolks, milk, flour and salt in blender or food processor container. Cover; process until smooth. Pour into bowl; let stand until ready to use.

3. Melt butter in small skillet over medium heat. Add onion; cook and stir until tender.

4. Pat chilies dry with paper towels. Slit each chili lengthwise and carefully remove seeds. Place 2 halves of cheese and 1 tablespoon onion in each chili; reshape chilies to cover cheese. Place in single layer in greased 13×9-inch baking dish.

5. In small clean bowl, beat egg whites until soft peaks form; fold into yolk mixture. Pour over chilies.

6. Bake 20 to 25 minutes or until casserole is puffed and knife inserted in center comes out clean. Broil 4 inches below heat 30 seconds or until top is golden brown. Serve with desired garnishes.

Country Fare Breakfast with Wisconsin Fontina

¼ cup butter
2 cups frozen hash brown
   potatoes
¼ cup finely chopped onion
6 eggs, beaten
2 tablespoons milk
¾ teaspoon salt

⅛ teaspoon pepper
¼ cup chopped fresh parsley,
   divided
1 cup (4 ounces) shredded
   Wisconsin Fontina cheese,
   divided
1 cup cubed cooked turkey

Melt butter in 10-inch ovenproof skillet; add potatoes and onion.
Cook, covered, over medium heat 15 minutes until tender and
lightly browned; stir occasionally. Beat together eggs, milk, salt
and pepper; stir in 3 tablespoons parsley and ½ cup cheese. Pour
egg mixture over potatoes; sprinkle with turkey. Bake, uncovered,
in preheated 350°F oven for 20 minutes or until eggs are set.
Sprinkle remaining ½ cup cheese over eggs; return to oven for
about 2 minutes until cheese is melted. Remove from oven and
garnish with remaining parsley. Cut into wedges and serve with
salsa, if desired.

Hint: *Ham can be substituted for turkey.*

Favorite recipe from **Wisconsin Milk Marketing Board**

Note:

**Refrigerate eggs
immediately after
purchasing. To prevent
them from absorbing
odors from other
foods, store them in
the original carton. For
best flavor, use eggs
within a week after
purchasing. However,
they will keep for five
weeks after the
packing date without
loss of nutrients or
functional properties.**

Italian Vegetable Strata

Makes 8 servings

Prep Time:
10 minutes

Cook Time:
50 minutes

1 loaf Italian bread
1⅓ cups *French's®* French Fried
   Onions, divided
1 cup (4 ounces) shredded
   mozzarella cheese, divided
1 small zucchini, thinly sliced
1 red bell pepper, sliced

5 eggs
2½ cups milk
⅓ cup (1½ ounces) grated
   Parmesan cheese
½ teaspoon *each* dried oregano
   and basil leaves

1. Preheat oven to 350°F. Grease 3-quart shallow baking dish. Cut enough slices of bread, ½ inch thick, to arrange single layer in bottom of dish, overlapping slices if necessary. Layer ⅔ *cup* French Fried Onions, ⅔ *cup* mozzarella cheese, zucchini and bell pepper over bread.

2. Beat eggs, milk, Parmesan cheese, oregano, basil, ½ *teaspoon salt* and ¼ *teaspoon black pepper* in medium bowl. Pour over layers. Sprinkle with remaining ⅓ *cup* mozzarella cheese. Let stand 10 minutes.

3. Bake 45 minutes or until knife inserted in center comes out clean. Sprinkle with remaining ⅔ *cup* onions. Bake 5 minutes or until onions are golden. Cool on wire rack 10 minutes. Cut into squares to serve.

Sausage and Broccoli Noodle Casserole

Makes 6 servings

1 jar (1 pound) RAGÚ® Cheese Creations!® Classic Alfredo Sauce

⅓ cup milk

1 pound sweet Italian sausage, cooked and crumbled

1 package (9 ounces) frozen chopped broccoli, thawed

8 ounces egg noodles, cooked and drained

1 cup shredded Cheddar cheese (about 4 ounces)

¼ cup chopped roasted red peppers

Prep Time:
15 minutes

Cook Time:
30 minutes

1. Preheat oven to 350°F. In large bowl, combine Ragú® Cheese Creations!® Sauce and milk. Stir in sausage, broccoli, noodles, ¾ cup cheese and roasted peppers.

2. In 13×9-inch baking dish, evenly spread sausage mixture. Sprinkle with remaining ¼ cup cheese.

3. Bake 30 minutes or until heated through.

Tip: *Substitute sausage with equal amounts of vegetables for a hearty vegetarian entrée.*

SPAM™ Breakfast Burritos

Makes 6 servings

1 (12-ounce) can SPAM® Classic, cubed
4 eggs
2 tablespoons milk
1 tablespoon butter
1 cup (4 ounces) shredded Cheddar cheese, divided

1 cup (4 ounces) shredded Monterey Jack cheese, divided
6 (6-inch) flour tortillas
CHI-CHI'S® Salsa or Taco Sauce

Heat oven to 400°F. In medium bowl, beat together SPAM®, eggs and milk. Melt butter in large skillet; add egg mixture. Cook, stirring, to desired doneness. Divide SPAM™ mixture and half of cheeses evenly among tortillas. Roll up tortillas; place seam side down in 12×8-inch baking dish. Sprinkle remaining cheeses over top of burritos. Bake 5 to 10 minutes or until cheese is melted. Serve with salsa.

Brunch Strata

Makes 6 servings

1 can (10¾ ounces) condensed cream of celery soup
2 cups cholesterol-free egg substitute *or* 8 eggs
1 cup fat-free (skim) milk
1 can (4 ounces) sliced mushrooms (optional)
¼ cup sliced green onions

1 teaspoon dry mustard
½ teaspoon salt (optional)
¼ teaspoon black pepper
6 slices reduced-fat white bread, cut into 1-inch cubes
4 links reduced-fat precooked breakfast sausage, thinly sliced

Preheat oven to 350°F. Combine soup, egg substitute, milk, mushrooms, green onions, mustard, salt and pepper in medium bowl; mix well. Spray 2-quart baking dish with nonstick cooking spray. Combine bread cubes, sausage and soup mixture; toss to coat. Bake 35 to 40 minutes or until set.

Hash Brown Casserole

Makes 12 servings

3 cartons (4 ounces *each*) cholesterol-free egg product or 6 eggs, well beaten
1 can (12 fluid ounces) NESTLÉ® CARNATION® Evaporated Milk
1 teaspoon salt
½ teaspoon ground black pepper

1 package (30 ounces) frozen shredded hash brown potatoes
2 cups (8 ounces) shredded cheddar cheese
1 medium onion, chopped
1 small green bell pepper, chopped
1 cup diced ham (optional)

PREHEAT oven to 350°F. Grease 13×9-inch baking dish.

COMBINE egg product, evaporated milk, salt and black pepper in large bowl. Add potatoes, cheese, onion, bell pepper and ham; mix well. Pour mixture into prepared baking dish.

BAKE for 60 to 65 minutes or until set.

<u>Hint:</u> *For a lower fat version of this recipe, use cholesterol-free egg product, substitute NESTLÉ® CARNATION® Evaporated Fat Free Milk for Evaporated Milk and 10 slices turkey bacon, cooked and chopped, for the diced ham. Proceed as above.*

Note:

Processed liquid egg products are available refrigerated and frozen. Cholesterol-free products generally contain egg whites, nonfat milk, emulsifiers, stabilizers, gums and color. These products can be substituted for whole eggs in cooking and baking. Pasteurized liquid eggs that contain both whites and yolks are also available.

Feta Brunch Bake

Makes 4 servings

1 medium red bell pepper
2 bags (10 ounces each) fresh
 spinach, washed and
 stemmed
6 eggs
6 ounces crumbled feta cheese

⅓ cup chopped onion
2 tablespoons chopped fresh
 parsley
¼ teaspoon dried dill weed
 Dash black pepper

Preheat broiler. Place bell pepper on foil-lined broiler pan. Broil, 4 inches from heat, 15 to 20 minutes or until blackened on all sides, turning every 5 minutes with tongs. Place in paper bag; close bag and set aside to cool about 15 to 20 minutes. To peel pepper, cut around core, twist and remove. Cut in half and peel off skin with paring knife; rinse under cold water to remove seeds. Cut into ½-inch pieces.

To blanch spinach, heat 1 quart water in 2-quart saucepan over high heat to a boil. Add spinach. Return to a boil; boil 2 to 3 minutes until crisp-tender. Drain and immediately plunge into cold water. Drain; let stand until cool enough to handle. Squeeze spinach to remove excess water. Finely chop with chef's knife.

Preheat oven to 400°F. Grease 1-quart baking dish. Beat eggs in large bowl with electric mixer at medium speed until foamy. Stir in bell pepper, spinach, cheese, onion, parsley, dill weed and black pepper. Pour egg mixture into prepared dish. Bake 20 minutes or until set. Let stand 5 minutes before serving. Garnish as desired.

Potato-Ham Scallop

Makes 6 servings

2 cups cubed HILLSHIRE FARM®
 Ham
6 potatoes, peeled and thinly
 sliced
¼ cup chopped onion
⅓ cup all-purpose flour

Salt and black pepper to taste
2 cups milk
3 tablespoons bread crumbs
1 tablespoon butter or
 margarine, melted

Preheat oven to 350°F.

Place ½ of Ham in medium casserole. Cover with ½ of potatoes
and ½ of onion. Sift ½ of flour over onions; sprinkle with salt and
pepper. Repeat layers with remaining ham, potatoes, onion, flour,
salt and pepper. Pour milk over casserole. Bake, covered,
1¼ hours. Combine bread crumbs and butter in small bowl;
sprinkle over top of casserole. Bake, uncovered, 15 minutes or
until topping is golden brown.

How Much of This = That?

If you don't have:	Use:
1 cup buttermilk	1 tablespoon lemon juice or vinegar plus milk to equal 1 cup (stir; let stand 5 minutes)
1 tablespoon cornstarch	2 tablespoons all-purpose flour or 2 teaspoons arrowroot
1 small clove garlic	⅛ teaspoon garlic powder
1 cup tomato sauce	½ cup tomato paste plus ½ cup water
1 cup whole milk	1 cup skim milk plus 2 tablespoons melted butter
1 cup sour cream	1 cup plain yogurt

Vegetable Medley Quiche

Makes 6 servings

Nonstick cooking spray
2 cups frozen diced potatoes with onions and peppers, thawed
1 can (10¾ ounces) reduced-fat condensed cream of mushroom soup, divided
1 (16-ounce) package frozen mixed vegetables (such as zucchini, carrots and beans), thawed and drained

1 cup cholesterol-free egg substitute *or* 4 eggs
½ cup grated Parmesan cheese, divided
¼ cup fat-free (skim) milk
¼ teaspoon dried dill weed
¼ teaspoon dried thyme leaves
¼ teaspoon dried oregano leaves
Dash salt and pepper

1. Preheat oven to 400°F. Spray 9-inch pie plate with nonstick cooking spray; press potatoes onto bottom and side of pan to form crust. Spray potatoes lightly with nonstick cooking spray. Bake 15 minutes.

2. Combine half of soup, mixed vegetables, egg substitute and half of cheese in small bowl; mix well. Pour egg mixture into potato shell; sprinkle with remaining cheese. *Reduce oven temperature to 375°F.* Bake 35 to 40 minutes or until set.

3. Combine remaining soup, milk and seasonings in small saucepan; mix well. Simmer over low heat 5 minutes or until heated through. Serve sauce with quiche.

Betty Jo's Sausage and Cheese Grits

PAM® No-Stick Cooking Spray
1 pound mild or hot cooked
  sausage, crumbled and
  drained
1½ cups grits
2½ cups shredded Cheddar
  cheese

3 tablespoons WESSON®
  Vegetable Oil
1½ cups milk
3 eggs, slightly beaten

Makes 6 to 8 servings

Preheat oven to 350°F. Lightly spray a 13×9×2-inch baking dish with PAM® Cooking Spray. Evenly spread crumbled sausage on bottom of dish; set aside. Bring 4½ cups water to a boil in a large saucepan. Stir in grits and lower heat. Cook 5 minutes until thickened, stirring occasionally. Add cheese and Wesson® Oil; stir until cheese has melted. Stir in milk and eggs; blend well. Evenly spoon mixture over sausage; bake, uncovered, 1 hour or until grits have set.

Note:

Grits, also known as hominy grits, are a cereal made of dried, milled corn kernels. Quick-cooking grits are finely ground so they cook in less than 5 minutes instead of the 20 to 30 minutes required for regular grits. Instant grits have been precooked and dehydrated. Regular, quick-cooking and instant grits should be stored in a tightly sealed container and placed in a cool, dry place.

Cheddar and Leek Strata

Makes 12 servings

8 eggs, lightly beaten
2 cups milk
½ cup ale or beer
2 cloves garlic, minced
¼ teaspoon salt
¼ teaspoon black pepper
1 loaf (16 ounces) sourdough
    bread, cut into ½-inch
    cubes

2 small leeks, coarsely chopped
1 red bell pepper, chopped
1½ cups (6 ounces) shredded
    Swiss cheese
1½ cups (6 ounces) shredded
    sharp Cheddar cheese
Fresh sage sprigs for garnish

1. Combine eggs, milk, ale, garlic, salt and black pepper in large bowl. Beat until well blended.

2. Place ½ of bread cubes on bottom of greased 13×9-inch baking dish. Sprinkle ½ of leeks and ½ of bell pepper over bread cubes. Top with ¾ cup Swiss cheese and ¾ cup Cheddar cheese. Repeat layers with remaining ingredients, ending with Cheddar cheese.

3. Pour egg mixture evenly over top. Cover tightly with plastic wrap or foil. Weigh top of strata down with slightly smaller baking dish. Refrigerate strata at least 2 hours or overnight.

4. Preheat oven to 350°F. Bake, uncovered, 40 to 45 minutes or until center is set. Garnish with fresh sage, if desired. Serve immediately.

Ham and Egg Enchiladas

Makes 4 servings

2 tablespoons butter
1 small red bell pepper, chopped
3 green onions with tops, sliced
½ cup diced ham
8 eggs
8 (7- to 8-inch) flour tortillas
2 cups (8 ounces) shredded Colby-Jack cheese or Pepper-Jack cheese, divided

1 can (10 ounces) enchilada sauce
½ cup prepared salsa
Sliced avocado, fresh cilantro and red pepper slices for garnish

1. Preheat oven to 350°F.

2. Melt butter in large nonstick skillet over medium heat. Add bell pepper and onions; cook and stir 2 minutes. Add ham; cook and stir 1 minute.

3. Lightly beat eggs with wire whisk in medium bowl. Add eggs to skillet; cook until eggs are set, but still soft, stirring occasionally.

4. Spoon about ⅓ cup egg mixture evenly down center of each tortilla; top with 1 tablespoon cheese. Roll tortillas up and place seam side down in shallow 11×7-inch baking dish.

5. Combine enchilada sauce and salsa in small bowl; pour evenly over enchiladas.

6. Cover enchiladas with foil; bake 20 minutes. Uncover; sprinkle with remaining cheese. Continue baking 10 minutes or until enchiladas are hot and cheese is melted. Garnish, if desired. Serve immediately.

Ranch Quiche Lorraine

Makes 8 servings

2 cups crushed butter-flavored crackers
6 tablespoons butter or margarine, melted
2 cups shredded Swiss cheese
4 eggs
2 cups heavy cream

1 packet (1.2 ounces) HIDDEN VALLEY® The Original Ranch® Dressing with Bacon
1 tablespoon dehydrated minced onion

Note:

Genuine Swiss cheese from Switzerland is known as Emmentaler. It is easy enough to produce the holes in the cheese, but difficult to produce the fine, nutty flavor that is its trademark. This characteristic flavor is said to be derived from the quality of the grasses on which the cattle feed.

Preheat oven to 375°F. In medium bowl, combine crackers and butter. Press crumb mixture evenly into 10-inch pie pan or quiche dish. Bake until golden, about 7 minutes. Remove and cool pan on wire rack.

Increase oven temperature to 425°F. Sprinkle cheese over cooled pie crust. In medium bowl, whisk eggs until frothy. Add cream, salad dressing mix and onion. Pour egg mixture over cheese. Bake 15 minutes; *reduce temperature to 350°F* and continue baking until knife inserted in center comes out clean, about 20 minutes longer. Cool on wire rack 10 minutes before slicing.

Ham and Cheese Bread Pudding

1 small loaf (8 ounces) sourdough, country French or Italian bread, cut into 1-inch-thick slices

3 tablespoons butter or margarine, softened

8 ounces ham or smoked ham, cubed

2 cups (8 ounces) shredded mild or sharp Cheddar cheese

3 eggs

2 cups milk

1 teaspoon dry mustard

½ teaspoon salt

⅛ teaspoon white pepper

1. Grease 11×7-inch baking dish. Spread 1 side of each bread slice with butter. Cut into 1-inch cubes; place on bottom of prepared dish. Top with ham; sprinkle with cheese.

2. Beat eggs in medium bowl. Whisk in milk, mustard, salt and pepper. Pour egg mixture evenly over bread mixture. Cover; refrigerate at least 6 hours or overnight.

3. Preheat oven to 350°F.

4. Bake bread pudding, uncovered, 45 to 50 minutes or until puffed and golden brown and knife inserted in center comes out clean. Garnish, if desired. Cut into squares. Serve immediately.

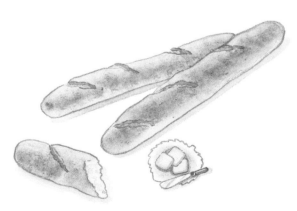

Roasted Pepper and Sourdough Brunch Casserole

Makes 8 servings

3 cups sourdough bread cubes
1 jar (12 ounces) roasted pepper strips, drained
4 ounces (1 cup) shredded reduced-fat sharp Cheddar cheese
4 ounces (1 cup) shredded reduced-fat Monterey Jack cheese

1 cup nonfat cottage cheese
12 ounces cholesterol-free egg substitute
1 cup fat-free (skim) milk
¼ cup chopped fresh cilantro
¼ teaspoon black pepper

1. Spray 11×9-inch baking dish with nonstick cooking spray. Place bread cubes in dish. Arrange roasted peppers evenly over bread cubes. Sprinkle Cheddar and Monterey Jack cheeses over peppers.

2. Place cottage cheese in food processor or blender; process until smooth. Add egg substitute; process 10 seconds. Combine cottage cheese mixture and milk in small bowl; pour over ingredients in baking dish. Sprinkle with cilantro and black pepper. Cover with plastic wrap; refrigerate 4 to 12 hours.

3. Preheat oven to 375°F. Bake, uncovered, 40 minutes or until hot and bubbly and golden brown on top.

Chile, Egg & Cheese Casserole

1 tablespoon WESSON®
   Vegetable Oil, divided
½ cup *each:* chopped green bell
   pepper, red bell pepper and
   yellow bell pepper
1 cup chopped onion
2 jalapeño peppers, seeded and
   minced
3 containers (8 ounces each) fat
   free egg substitute (or
   12 eggs)

1 teaspoon salt
10 corn tortillas, torn into bits
1 can (14.5 ounces) HUNT'S®
   Diced Tomatoes in Juice
1½ cups low fat shredded
   Cheddar cheese, divided
   PAM® No-Stick Cooking Spray
1 tablespoon chopped fresh
   cilantro

1. Preheat oven to 400°F.

2. In large skillet, heat ½ *tablespoon* of Wesson® Oil over medium-high heat. Sauté bell peppers, onion and jalapeños until tender, about 5 minutes.

3. Meanwhile, in large mixing bowl, combine egg substitute and salt; stir in tortillas. When vegetables are cooked, stir into egg mixture.

4. Pour *remaining* oil into skillet; heat over medium heat. Add egg mixture and cook about 2 minutes, or until eggs are halfway cooked; remove from heat. Stir in Hunt's® Diced Tomatoes in Juice and ¾ *cup* cheese.

5. Transfer egg mixture to 13×9×2-inch baking dish, lightly sprayed with PAM® Cooking Spray. Top with *remaining* cheese.

6. Bake, uncovered, about 25 minutes, or until lightly browned. Sprinkle with cilantro.

Hash Brown Frittata

Makes 6 servings

1 (10-ounce) package BOB EVANS® Skinless Link Sausage
6 eggs
1 (12-ounce) package frozen hash brown potatoes, thawed

1 cup (4 ounces) shredded Cheddar cheese
⅓ cup whipping cream
¼ cup chopped green and/or red bell pepper
¼ teaspoon salt
Dash black pepper

Preheat oven to 350°F. Cut sausage into bite-size pieces. Cook in small skillet over medium heat until lightly browned, stirring occasionally. Drain off any drippings. Whisk eggs in medium bowl; stir in sausage and remaining ingredients. Pour into greased 2-quart casserole dish. Bake, uncovered, 30 minutes or until eggs are almost set. Let stand 5 minutes before cutting into squares; serve hot.

Ham 'n Egg Special Strata

Makes 6 to 8 servings

¼ cup butter
2 cups sliced fresh mushrooms
1 medium onion, chopped
2 cups diced cooked ham
8 slices white bread, cubed
4 eggs
2½ cups milk

2 cups (8 ounces) shredded cheddar cheese
1 tablespoon prepared mustard
1 teaspoon LAWRY'S® Seasoned Salt
Dash LAWRY'S® Seasoned Pepper

In medium skillet, heat butter. Add mushrooms and onion and cook over medium-high heat until tender; stir in ham. In 13×9×2-inch baking dish, place bread cubes; arrange ham mixture over bread. In medium bowl, combine remaining ingredients; mix well. Pour over bread cubes, making sure all are moistened. Cover; refrigerate overnight. Bake, uncovered, in 325°F oven 55 to 60 minutes. Serve immediately.

Potato and Egg Pie

Makes 6 servings

1 package (20 ounces) frozen
  O'Brien hash brown
  potatoes, thawed
⅓ cup WESSON® Vegetable Oil
1½ tablespoons chopped fresh
  parsley
1 package (12 ounces) bulk
  breakfast sausage, cooked,
  crumbled and drained
¾ cup shredded Swiss cheese

¾ cup shredded Pepper-Jack
  cheese
1 can (4 ounces) sliced
  mushrooms, drained
½ cup milk
4 eggs, beaten
1 teaspoon garlic salt
¼ teaspoon pepper
4 to 6 thin tomato slices

Preheat oven to 425°F. In a medium bowl, combine potatoes and
Wesson® Oil; blend to coat. Press mixture into a 10-inch pie dish.
Bake for 30 minutes or until golden brown; remove from oven.
Reduce oven temperature to 350°F. Meanwhile, in a large bowl,
combine 1 tablespoon parsley and *remaining* ingredients *except*
tomato slices; blend well. Pour into potato crust. Bake for
25 minutes or until eggs are set. Place tomato slices over pie
and top with *remaining* parsley. Bake 5 to 7 minutes longer.

Note:

Slice tomatoes with
a serrated knife, if
possible. Otherwise,
puncture the skin with
the point of a sharp
utility knife and
then slice.

Spinach and Cheese Brunch Squares

Makes 8 main-course servings

Prep Time:
20 minutes

Cook Time:
50 minutes

Stand Time:
10 minutes

1 box (11 ounces) pie crust mix
⅓ cup cold water
1 package (10 ounces) frozen chopped spinach, thawed and well drained
1⅓ cups *French's*® French Fried Onions
1 cup (4 ounces) shredded Swiss cheese

1 container (8 ounces) low-fat sour cream
5 eggs
1 cup milk
1 tablespoon *French's*® Bold n' Spicy Brown Mustard
½ teaspoon salt
⅛ teaspoon ground black pepper

Preheat oven to 450°F. Line 13×9×2-inch baking pan with foil; spray with nonstick cooking spray. Combine pie crust mix and water in large bowl until moistened and crumbly. Using floured bottom of measuring cup, press mixture firmly into bottom of prepared pan. Prick with fork. Bake 20 minutes or until golden. *Reduce oven temperature to 350°F.*

Layer spinach, French Fried Onions and cheese over crust. Combine sour cream, eggs, milk, mustard, salt and pepper in medium bowl; mix until well blended. Pour over vegetable and cheese layers. Bake 30 minutes or until knife inserted in center comes out clean. Let stand 10 minutes. Cut into squares* to serve.

*To serve as appetizers, cut into 2-inch squares.

Tip: *The next time you make omelets, create onion omelets! Sprinkle French Fried Onions across the omelet before folding.*

Hearty Breakfast Custard Casserole

1 pound (2 medium-large)
    Colorado baking potatoes
Salt and black pepper
8 ounces low-fat bulk pork
    sausage, cooked and
    crumbled *or* 6 ounces finely
    diced lean ham *or* 6 ounces
    turkey bacon, cooked and
    crumbled
⅓ cup julienne-sliced roasted
    red pepper *or* 1 jar
    (2 ounces) sliced pimientos,
    drained

3 eggs
1 cup low-fat milk
3 tablespoons chopped fresh
    chives or green onion tops
    or ¾ teaspoon dried thyme
    or oregano leaves
Salsa and low-fat sour cream
    or plain yogurt (optional)

Heat oven to 375°F. Grease 8- or 9-inch square baking dish or other small casserole. Peel potatoes and slice very thinly; arrange half of potatoes in baking dish. Sprinkle with salt and black pepper. Cover with half of sausage. Arrange remaining potatoes on top; sprinkle with salt and black pepper. Top with remaining sausage and roasted red pepper. Beat eggs, milk and chives until blended. Pour over potatoes. Cover baking dish with foil and bake 35 to 45 minutes or until potatoes are tender. Uncover and bake 5 to 10 minutes more. Serve with salsa and sour cream, if desired.

Favorite recipe from **Colorado Potato Administrative Committee**

Mushroom & Onion Egg Bake

Makes about 6 servings

1 tablespoon vegetable oil
4 green onions, chopped
4 ounces mushrooms, sliced
1 cup low-fat cottage cheese
1 cup sour cream

6 eggs
2 tablespoons all-purpose flour
¼ teaspoon salt
⅛ teaspoon black pepper
Dash hot pepper sauce

Note:

Mushrooms are members of the fungus family. They grow on decaying material and are reproduced from spores. Mushrooms have grown wild since ancient times, surviving wherever there is decaying material to support their growth. There are thousands of mushroom species varying by color, shape, size and flavor.

1. Preheat oven to 350°F. Grease shallow 1-quart baking dish.

2. Heat oil in medium skillet over medium heat. Add onions and mushrooms; cook until tender. Set aside.

3. In blender or food processor, process cottage cheese until almost smooth. Add sour cream, eggs, flour, salt, black pepper and hot pepper sauce; process until combined. Stir in onions and mushrooms. Pour into greased dish. Bake about 40 minutes or until knife inserted near center comes out clean.

Egg & Sausage Casserole

Makes 6 servings

½ pound pork sausage
3 tablespoons margarine or
  butter, divided
2 tablespoons all-purpose flour
¼ teaspoon salt
¼ teaspoon black pepper

1¼ cups milk
2 cups frozen hash brown
  potatoes
4 eggs, hard-boiled and sliced
½ cup cornflake crumbs
¼ cup sliced green onions

Preheat oven to 350°F. Spray 2-quart oval baking dish with nonstick cooking spray.

Crumble sausage into large skillet; brown over medium-high heat until no longer pink, stirring to separate meat. Drain sausage on paper towels. Discard fat and wipe skillet with paper towel.

Melt 2 tablespoons margarine in same skillet over medium heat. Stir in flour, salt and pepper until smooth. Gradually stir in milk; cook and stir until thickened. Add sausage, potatoes and eggs; stir to combine. Pour into prepared dish.

Melt remaining 1 tablespoon margarine. Combine cornflake crumbs and melted margarine in small bowl; sprinkle evenly over casserole.

Bake, uncovered, 30 minutes or until hot and bubbly. Sprinkle with onions.

Ham & Cheese Grits Soufflé

Makes 4 to 6 servings

3 cups water
¾ cup quick-cooking grits
½ teaspoon salt
½ cup (2 ounces) shredded
   mozzarella cheese

2 ounces ham, finely chopped
2 tablespoons minced chives
2 eggs, separated
   Dash hot pepper sauce

1. Preheat oven to 375°F. Grease 1½-quart soufflé dish or deep casserole.

2. Bring water to a boil in medium saucepan. Stir in grits and salt. Cook, stirring frequently, about 5 minutes or until thickened. Stir in cheese, ham, chives, egg yolks and hot pepper sauce.

3. In small clean bowl, beat egg whites until stiff but not dry; fold into grits mixture. Pour into prepared dish. Bake about 30 minutes or until puffed and golden. Serve immediately.

Say Cheese!

There are hundreds of types of cheese available today, each with its own distinctive flavor and texture. Many factors affect the flavor and texture of cheese, but the list can be simplified to include three main elements: the milk source, the cheesemaking process and the aging procedure.

All cheese is made from animal milk (either cow's, goat's or sheep's) and is either fresh or ripened.

Fresh unripened cheese includes cottage cheese, ricotta and cream cheese.

Ripened cheese is classified according to texture; soft-ripened, semi-soft, semi-firm and firm (or hard). In general, the longer the aging process, the firmer the cheese.

Soft-ripened cheeses: feta, Brie, and blue cheeses such as Gorgonzola and Roquefort

Semi-soft cheeses: Monterey Jack, Muenster and Gouda

Semi-firm cheeses: Cheddar and Swiss

Firm cheeses: Parmesan and Romano

South-of-the-Border Quiche Squares

1 pound BOB EVANS® Zesty
  Hot Roll Sausage
1 (8-ounce) package
  refrigerated crescent dinner
  roll dough
1 cup (4 ounces) shredded
  Monterey Jack cheese,
  divided
1 cup (4 ounces) shredded
  Cheddar cheese, divided
½ cup diced green chiles

½ cup chopped green onions
1 cup diced fresh or drained
  canned tomatoes
8 eggs, beaten
1 cup half-and-half
1 cup milk
2 tablespoons Dijon mustard
1 tablespoon chopped fresh
  parsley
½ teaspoon chili powder

Preheat oven to 350°F. Crumble and cook sausage in medium skillet over medium heat until browned. Drain well on paper towels. Unroll dough and press perforations together. Press dough on bottom and 1 inch up sides of greased 13×9×2-inch baking pan. Bake 8 minutes or until light golden. Remove from oven; sprinkle with half of cheeses. Top with chiles, onions, tomatoes, sausage and remaining cheeses. Blend eggs, half-and-half, milk, mustard, parsley and chili powder in medium bowl. Pour mixture evenly over cheese layer. Bake 25 to 30 minutes or until set. Cool 5 minutes before cutting into 8 (4-inch) squares. Serve hot. Refrigerate leftovers.

Chile Cheese Puff

Makes 8 servings

¾ cup all-purpose flour
1½ teaspoons baking powder
9 eggs
1 pound (16 ounces) shredded
    Monterey Jack cheese
2 cups (16 ounces) 1% milkfat
    cottage cheese

2 cans (4 ounces each) diced
    green chilies, drained
1½ teaspoons sugar
¼ teaspoon salt
⅛ teaspoon hot pepper sauce
1 cup salsa

Note:

The heat of chili peppers comes from a substance known as capsaicin located in the seeds, in the veins (the thin inner membranes to which the seeds are attached) and in the parts nearest the veins.

Preheat oven to 350°F. Spray 13×9-inch baking dish with nonstick cooking spray.

Combine flour and baking powder in small bowl.

Whisk eggs in large bowl until blended; add Monterey Jack, cottage cheese, chilies, sugar, salt and hot pepper sauce. Add flour mixture; stir just until combined. Pour into prepared dish.

Bake, uncovered, 45 minutes or until egg mixture is set. Let stand 5 minutes before serving. Serve with salsa.

Make-Ahead Brunch Bake

Makes 6 servings

1 pound bulk pork sausage
6 eggs, beaten
2 cups light cream or half-and-half
½ teaspoon salt

1 teaspoon ground mustard
1 cup (4 ounces) shredded Cheddar cheese
1⅓ cups *French's*® French Fried Onions

Crumble sausage into large skillet. Cook over medium-high heat until browned; drain well. Stir in eggs, cream, salt, mustard, *½ cup* cheese and *⅔ cup* French Fried Onions; mix well. Pour into greased 12×8-inch baking dish. Refrigerate, covered, 8 hours or overnight. Bake, uncovered, at 350°F for 45 minutes or until knife inserted in center comes out clean. Top with remaining cheese and onions; bake, uncovered, 5 minutes or until onions are golden brown. Let stand 15 minutes before serving.

Weekend Brunch Casserole

Makes 6 to 8 servings

1 pound BOB EVANS® Original Recipe Roll Sausage
1 can (8 ounces) refrigerated crescent dinner rolls
2 cups (8 ounces) shredded mozzarella cheese

4 eggs, beaten
¾ cup milk
¼ teaspoon salt
⅛ teaspoon black pepper

Preheat oven to 425°F. Crumble sausage into medium skillet. Cook over medium heat until browned, stirring occasionally. Drain off any drippings. Line bottom of greased 13×9-inch baking dish with crescent roll dough, firmly pressing perforations to seal. Sprinkle with sausage and cheese. Combine remaining ingredients in medium bowl until blended; pour over sausage. Bake 15 minutes or until set. Let stand 5 minutes before cutting into squares; serve hot. Refrigerate leftovers.

Mexican Quiche

Makes 8 servings

1 cup (4 ounces) shredded
4 cheese Mexican blend
1 large green or red bell pepper, chopped
1 can (4 ounces) ORTEGA® Diced Green Chiles
2 large green onions, sliced
1 *unbaked* 9-inch (4-cup volume) frozen deep-dish pie shell

4 eggs, lightly beaten
¾ cup ORTEGA® Salsa-Homestyle
¾ cup NESTLÉ® CARNATION® Evaporated Milk
Garnish Suggestions: ORTEGA® Salsa-Homestyle, sour cream, sliced green onions, diced tomatoes

PREHEAT oven to 375°F.

SPRINKLE cheese, bell pepper, chiles and green onions onto bottom of pie shell. Combine eggs, salsa and evaporated milk in small bowl until blended. Pour into pie shell.

BAKE for 40 to 45 minutes or until knife inserted halfway between center and edge comes out clean. Cool on wire rack for 15 minutes. Garnish as desired.

Spinach Sensation

Makes 6 servings

½ pound bacon slices
1 cup (8 ounces) sour cream
3 eggs, separated
2 tablespoons all-purpose flour
⅛ teaspoon black pepper
1 package (10 ounces) frozen
   chopped spinach, thawed
   and squeezed dry

½ cup (2 ounces) shredded
   sharp Cheddar cheese
½ cup dry bread crumbs
1 tablespoon margarine or
   butter, melted

1. Preheat oven to 350°F. Spray 2-quart round baking dish with nonstick cooking spray.

2. Place bacon in single layer in large skillet; cook over medium heat until crisp. Remove from skillet; drain on paper towels. Crumble and set aside.

3. Combine sour cream, egg yolks, flour and pepper in large bowl; set aside. Beat egg whites in medium bowl with electric mixer at high speed until stiff peaks form. Stir ¼ of egg whites into sour cream mixture; fold in remaining egg whites.

4. Arrange half of spinach in prepared dish. Top with half of sour cream mixture. Sprinkle ¼ cup cheese over sour cream mixture. Sprinkle bacon over cheese. Repeat layers, ending with remaining ¼ cup cheese.

5. Combine bread crumbs and margarine in small bowl; sprinkle evenly over cheese. Bake, uncovered, 30 to 35 minutes or until egg mixture is set. Let stand 5 minutes before serving.

Easy Morning Strata

Makes 10 to 12 servings

1 pound BOB EVANS® Original Recipe Roll Sausage
8 eggs
10 slices bread, cut into cubes (about 10 cups)
3 cups milk
2 cups (8 ounces) shredded Cheddar cheese
2 cups (8 ounces) sliced fresh mushrooms
1 (10-ounce) package frozen cut asparagus, thawed and drained
2 tablespoons butter or margarine, melted
2 tablespoons all-purpose flour
1 tablespoon dry mustard
2 teaspoons dried basil leaves
1 teaspoon salt

Crumble sausage into large skillet. Cook over medium heat until browned, stirring occasionally. Drain off any drippings. Whisk eggs in large bowl. Add sausage and remaining ingredients; mix well. Spoon into greased 13×9-inch baking dish. Cover; refrigerate 8 hours or overnight. Preheat oven to 350°F. Bake 60 to 70 minutes or until knife inserted near center comes out clean. Let stand 5 minutes before cutting into squares; serve hot. Refrigerate leftovers.

Serving Suggestion: *Serve with sliced fresh plums.*

Easy
6-Ingredient
Dinners

CHAPTER NINE

One-Dish Chicken Florentine

Makes 4 servings

Prep Time:
5 minutes

Cook Time:
40 minutes

4 boneless, skinless chicken
   breast halves (about
   1¼ pounds)
1 jar (1 pound 10 ounces)
   RAGÚ® Old World Style®
   Pasta Sauce
1½ cups water

1¼ cups uncooked regular or
   converted rice
1 package (10 ounces) frozen
   chopped spinach, thawed
1 cup shredded mozzarella
   cheese (about 4 ounces)

Note:

**If you skin and debone
your own chicken
breasts, be sure to
reserve both the bones
and skin. Let these
scraps collect in a
plastic bag in your
freezer and soon you'll
have enough to make
flavorful homemade
chicken stock.**

1. Preheat oven to 375°F. Season chicken, if desired, with salt and pepper.

2. In 13×9-inch baking dish, combine Ragú Pasta Sauce, water, rice and spinach. Arrange chicken on uncooked rice mixture.

3. Bake uncovered 30 minutes. Sprinkle with cheese and bake an additional 10 minutes or until chicken is thoroughly cooked. Let stand 10 minutes before serving.

Hamburger Casserole Olé

1 pound lean ground beef or
  ground turkey
1 package (1¼ ounces) taco
  seasoning mix
1 cup water
1 box (9 ounces) BIRDS EYE®
  frozen Cut Green Beans

½ cup shredded sharp Cheddar
  cheese
½ cup shredded mozzarella
  cheese

Makes 4 servings

Prep Time:
15 minutes

Cook Time:
25 to 30 minutes

• Preheat oven to 325°F.

• Brown beef; drain excess fat. Add taco mix and water; cook over low heat 8 to 10 minutes or until liquid has been absorbed.

• Meanwhile, cook green beans according to package directions; drain.

• Spread meat in greased 13×9-inch baking pan. Spread beans over meat. Sprinkle with cheeses.

• Bake 15 to 20 minutes or until hot and cheese is melted.

<u>Serving Suggestion:</u> *Serve over tortillas or corn chips and top with sour cream, chopped avocado, chopped lettuce and/or chopped tomatoes.*

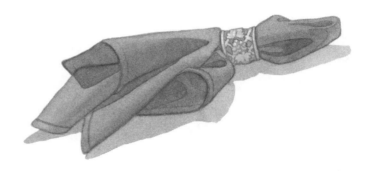

Classic Chicken Biscuit Pie

Makes 8 servings

Prep Time:
10 minutes

Cook Time:
30 minutes

12 TYSON® Individually Fresh
  Frozen® Boneless, Skinless
  Chicken Tenderloins
4 cups water
2 boxes UNCLE BEN'S®
  COUNTRY INN® Chicken
  Flavored Rice

1 can (10¾ ounces) condensed
  cream of chicken soup
1 bag (16 ounces) frozen mixed
  vegetables
1 container (12 ounces)
  refrigerated buttermilk
  biscuits

PREP: Preheat oven to 400°F. CLEAN: Wash hands. Remove protective ice glaze from frozen chicken by holding under cool running water 1 to 2 minutes. Cut chicken into 1-inch pieces. CLEAN: Wash hands.

COOK: In large saucepan, combine chicken, water, rice, contents of seasoning packets, soup and mixed vegetables; mix well. Bring to a boil. Cover, reduce heat; simmer 10 minutes or until internal juices of chicken run clear. (Or insert instant-read meat thermometer in thickest part of chicken. Temperature should read 170°F.) Place in 13×9-inch baking pan; top with biscuits. Bake 10 to 12 minutes or until biscuits are deep golden brown.

SERVE: Serve immediately.

CHILL: Refrigerate leftovers immediately.

Chicken and Asparagus Stir-Fry

1 cup uncooked rice
2 tablespoons vegetable oil
1 pound boneless skinless
    chicken breasts, cut into
    ½-inch-wide strips
2 medium red bell peppers, cut
    into thin strips

½ pound fresh asparagus,* cut
    diagonally into 1-inch
    pieces
½ cup bottled stir-fry sauce

For stir-frying, select thin stalks of asparagus and cut them on the diagonal—they will cook more quickly.

Makes 4 servings

Prep and Cook Time:
18 minutes

1. Cook rice according to package directions. Keep hot.

2. Heat oil in wok or large skillet over medium-high heat until hot. Stir-fry chicken 3 to 4 minutes or until chicken is no longer pink in center.

3. Stir in bell peppers and asparagus; reduce heat to medium. Cover and cook 2 minutes or until vegetables are crisp-tender, stirring once or twice.

4. Stir in sauce. Serve immediately with rice.

Hearty Buffalo-Style Vegetable Soup

Makes 6 servings

Prep Time:
5 minutes

Cook Time:
10 minutes

2 cans (10½ ounces *each*)
  chicken or beef broth
3 tablespoons *Frank's® RedHot®*
  Cayenne Pepper Sauce
1 bag (16 ounces) frozen
  vegetables

1½ cups diced cooked chicken or
  Polish sausage
6 thick slices French bread
3 tablespoons blue cheese,
  crumbled

1. Combine broth, *2½ cups water* and *Frank's RedHot* Sauce in large saucepan. Heat to boiling. Add vegetables and chicken. Reduce heat to medium-low. Cook, covered, 7 minutes or until vegetables are tender.

2. Preheat oven broiler. Toast bread slightly on both sides. Top one side with blue cheese. Place under broiler until cheese is melted and bread is crisp.

3. Ladle soup into warm bowls. Top each bowl with 1 blue cheese toast.

Groovy Angel Hair Goulash

1 pound lean ground beef
2 tablespoons margarine or
    butter
1 (4.8-ounce) package PASTA
    RONI® Angel Hair Pasta
    with Herbs

1 (14½-ounce) can diced
    tomatoes, undrained
1 cup frozen or canned corn,
    drained

Makes 4 servings

Prep Time:
5 minutes

Cook Time:
15 minutes

1. In large skillet over medium-high heat, brown ground beef.
Remove from skillet; drain. Set aside.

2. In same skillet, bring 1½ cups water and margarine to a boil.

3. Stir in pasta; cook 1 minute or just until pasta softens slightly.
Stir in tomatoes, corn, beef and Special Seasonings; return to
a boil. Reduce heat to medium. Gently boil uncovered, 4 to
5 minutes or until pasta is tender, stirring frequently. Let stand
3 to 5 minutes before serving.

Note:

Goulash, or *gulyás,*
is a Hungarian stew
prepared with meat,
most often beef, and
vegetables. It is
usually seasoned
with Hungarian
paprika, served over
buttered egg noodles
and topped with
sour cream.

Stir-Fried Pork with Oranges and Snow Peas

Makes 4 servings

Prep and Cook Time:
20 minutes

1 cup uncooked rice
1 tablespoon vegetable oil
1 pound lean boneless pork, cut
    into ¼-inch-wide strips

½ pound snow peas, trimmed
½ cup bottled stir-fry sauce
1 can (11 ounces) mandarin
    orange sections, drained

1. Cook rice according to package directions.

2. Heat oil in wok or large skillet over high heat until hot. Stir-fry pork 3 minutes or until brown.

3. Add snow peas; stir-fry 2 to 3 minutes or until crisp-tender. Add stir-fry sauce; stir until well blended. Gently stir in orange sections. Serve with rice.

<u>Hint:</u> *For an extra boost of orange flavor, stir in 2 tablespoons frozen orange juice concentrate with the stir-fry sauce.*

SPAM™ Vegetable Hash

½ cup chopped onion
2 tablespoons butter or
   margarine
2 cups frozen cubed hash
   brown potatoes, thawed

1 (12-ounce) can SPAM® Classic,
   cubed
1 (10-ounce) package frozen
   peas and carrots, thawed
½ teaspoon black pepper

Makes 4 to 6 servings

In large skillet over medium-high heat, sauté onion in butter until tender. Stir in potatoes. Cook, stirring occasionally, until potatoes are lightly browned. Stir in SPAM®, peas and carrots and pepper. Cook, stirring occasionally, until thoroughly heated.

Spicy Quick and Easy Chili

1 pound ground beef
1 large clove garlic, minced
1 can (15¼ ounces)
   DEL MONTE® Whole Kernel
   Golden Sweet Corn,
   drained

1 can (16 ounces) kidney beans,
   drained
1½ cups salsa, mild, medium or
   hot
1 can (4 ounces) diced green
   chiles, undrained

Makes 4 servings

Prep and Cook Time:
15 minutes

1. Brown meat with garlic in large saucepan; drain.

2. Add remaining ingredients. Simmer, uncovered, 10 minutes, stirring occasionally. Sprinkle with chopped green onions, if desired.

Velveeta® Chicken Enchilada Casserole

Makes 6 servings

Prep Time:
15 minutes

Bake Time:
35 minutes

2 cups chopped cooked chicken
1 can (10¾ ounces) condensed
   cream of chicken soup
½ pound (8 ounces) VELVEETA®
   Mexican Pasteurized
   Process Cheese Spread
   with Jalapeño Peppers, cut
   up

8 corn tortillas (6 inch)
½ cup TACO BELL® HOME
   ORIGINALS®* Thick 'N
   Chunky Salsa

**TACO BELL and HOME ORIGINALS are
registered trademarks owned and licensed by
Taco Bell Corp.*

Note:

Enchiladas are Mexican entrées prepared by rolling softened corn tortillas around a filling of shredded meat, chicken or cheese. They are baked with a topping of sauce and usually cheese. This casserole has all the flavor of traditional enchiladas without all the work of having to roll them up!

1. Mix chicken, soup and VELVEETA.

2. Spread 1 cup of the chicken mixture on bottom of 12×8-inch baking dish; cover with 4 of the tortillas. Top with ¼ cup of the salsa and 1 cup of the remaining chicken mixture. Repeat layers with 4 tortillas, remaining ¼ cup salsa and remaining chicken mixture.

3. Bake, uncovered, at 350°F for 30 to 35 minutes or until thoroughly heated. Top with additional salsa, if desired.

Teriyaki Chicken Medley

2 cups cooked white rice (about ¾ cup uncooked)

2 cups (10 ounces) cooked chicken, cut into strips

1⅓ cups *French's®* French Fried Onions, divided

1 package (12 ounces) frozen bell pepper strips, thawed and drained*

1 jar (12 ounces) chicken gravy

3 tablespoons teriyaki sauce

Or, substitute 2 cups sliced bell peppers for frozen pepper strips.

Prep Time:
10 minutes

Cook Time:
31 minutes

Preheat oven to 400°F. Grease 2-quart oblong baking dish. Press rice into bottom of prepared dish.

Combine chicken, ⅔ *cup* French Fried Onions, bell pepper strips, gravy and teriyaki sauce in large bowl; mix well. Pour mixture over rice layer. Cover; bake 30 minutes or until heated through. Top with remaining ⅔ *cup* onions. Bake 1 minute or until onions are golden.

Chicken Parmesan Noodle Bake

Makes 4 servings

Prep and Cook Time:
35 minutes

1 package (12 ounces) extra-wide noodles
4 boneless, skinless chicken breast halves
¼ teaspoon rosemary, crushed
2 cans (14½ ounces each) DEL MONTE® Diced Tomatoes with Basil, Garlic & Oregano

½ cup (2 ounces) shredded mozzarella cheese
¼ cup (1 ounce) grated Parmesan cheese

1. Preheat oven to 450°F.

2. Cook noodles according to package directions; drain.

3. Meanwhile, sprinkle chicken with rosemary; season with salt and pepper, if desired. Arrange chicken in 13×9-inch baking dish. Bake, uncovered, 20 minutes or until chicken is no longer pink in center. Drain; remove chicken from dish.

4. Drain tomatoes, reserving liquid. In large bowl, toss reserved liquid with noodles; place in baking dish. Top with chicken and tomatoes; sprinkle with cheeses.

5. Bake 10 minutes or until heated through. Sprinkle with additional Parmesan cheese and garnish, if desired.

Southern BBQ Chicken and Rice

1½ cups water
1 cup UNCLE BEN'S® ORIGINAL
   CONVERTED® Brand Rice
1 cup barbecue sauce, divided

4 TYSON® Individually Fresh
   Frozen® Chicken Half
   Breasts
1 package (6 half ears) frozen
   corn on the cob

Makes 4 servings

Prep Time:
none

Cook Time:
40 to 45 minutes

COOK: CLEAN: Wash hands. In large skillet, combine water, rice, ¾ cup barbecue sauce and chicken. Bring to a boil. Cover, reduce heat; simmer 25 minutes. Add corn; cook 15 to 20 minutes or until internal juices of chicken run clear. (Or insert instant-read meat thermometer in thickest part of chicken. Temperature should read 170°F.) Spoon remaining ¼ cup barbecue sauce over chicken. Remove from heat; let stand 5 minutes or until liquid is absorbed.

SERVE: Serve with extra barbecue sauce and corn bread, if desired.

CHILL: Refrigerate leftovers immediately.

Campbell's® Garlic Mashed Potatoes & Beef Bake

Makes 4 servings

Prep Time:
10 minutes

Cook Time:
20 minutes

1 pound ground beef
1 can (10¾ ounces)
   CAMPBELL'S® Condensed
   Cream of Mushroom with
   Roasted Garlic Soup
1 tablespoon Worcestershire
   sauce

1 bag (16 ounces) frozen
   vegetable combination
   (broccoli, cauliflower,
   carrots), thawed
3 cups hot mashed potatoes

1. In medium skillet over medium-high heat, cook beef until browned, stirring to separate meat. Pour off fat.

2. In 2-quart shallow baking dish mix beef, ½ *can* soup, Worcestershire and vegetables.

3. Stir remaining soup into potatoes. Spoon potato mixture over beef mixture. Bake at 400°F. for 20 minutes or until hot.

Salsa Corn Soup with Chicken

Makes 8 servings

3 quarts chicken broth
2 pounds boneless skinless
   chicken breasts, cooked
   and diced
2 packages (10 ounces each)
   frozen whole kernel corn,
   thawed

4 jars (11 ounces each)
   NEWMAN'S OWN® All
   Natural Salsa
4 large carrots, diced

Bring chicken broth to a boil in Dutch oven. Add chicken, corn, Newman's Own® Salsa and carrots. Bring to a boil. Reduce heat and simmer until carrots are tender.

Shrimp and Vegetables with Lo Mein Noodles

2 tablespoons vegetable oil
1 pound medium shrimp, peeled
2 packages (21 ounces each) frozen lo mein stir-fry mix with sauce

Fresh cilantro
1 small wedge cabbage
¼ cup peanuts, chopped

Makes 6 servings

Prep and Cook Time:
20 minutes

1. Heat oil in wok or large skillet over medium-high heat. Add shrimp; stir-fry 3 minutes or until shrimp are pink and opaque. Remove shrimp from wok to medium bowl. Set aside.

2. Remove sauce packet from stir-fry mix. Add frozen vegetables and noodles to wok; stir in sauce. Cover and cook 7 to 8 minutes, stirring frequently.

3. While vegetable mixture is cooking, chop enough cilantro to measure 2 tablespoons. Shred cabbage.

4. Stir shrimp, cilantro and peanuts into vegetable mixture; heat through. Serve immediately with cabbage.

Note:

Since medium shrimp

do not require

deveining, substitute

them for large shrimp

whenever possible

to save valuable

preparation time.

Wisconsin Cheese Pasta Casserole

Makes 6 to 8 servings

1 pound spaghetti or fettuccine, broken into 3-inch pieces
1 quart (4 cups) prepared spaghetti sauce
½ cup plus ⅓ cup grated Wisconsin Romano cheese, divided

1¾ cups (7 ounces) sliced or shredded Wisconsin Colby cheese
1½ cups (6 ounces) shredded Wisconsin Mozzarella cheese

Prepare pasta according to package instructions; drain. Toss warm pasta with prepared spaghetti sauce to coat. Add ½ cup Romano cheese to mixture and mix well. Spread half of sauced pasta into bottom of 13×9×2-inch baking dish. Cover with 1 cup Colby cheese. Spread remaining pasta over cheese. Top with remaining ¾ cup Colby cheese. Sprinkle with remaining ⅓ cup Romano cheese and Mozzarella cheese. Bake at 350°F for 35 to 40 minutes or until top is lightly browned and casserole is bubbly. Remove from heat and let stand at least 10 minutes before serving.

Favorite recipe from **Wisconsin Milk Marketing Board**

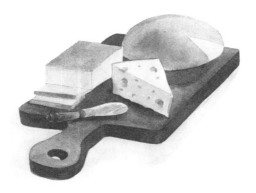

Mexican Lasagna

1 jar (1 pound 10 ounces)
   RAGÚ® Old World Style®
   Pasta Sauce
1 pound ground beef
1 can (15¼ ounces) whole
   kernel corn, drained

4½ teaspoons chili powder
6 (8½-inch) flour tortillas
2 cups shredded Cheddar
   cheese (about 8 ounces)

Makes 8 servings

Prep Time:
20 minutes

Cook Time:
40 minutes

1. Preheat oven to 350°F. Set aside 1 cup Ragú Pasta Sauce. In 10-inch skillet, brown ground beef over medium-high heat; drain. Stir in remaining Ragú Pasta Sauce, corn and chili powder.

2. In 13×9-inch baking dish, spread 1 cup sauce mixture. Arrange two tortillas over sauce, overlapping edges slightly. Layer half the sauce mixture and ⅓ of the cheese over tortillas; repeat layers, ending with tortillas. Spread tortillas with reserved sauce.

3. Bake 30 minutes, then top with remaining cheese and bake an additional 10 minutes or until sauce is bubbling and cheese is melted.

Tip: *Substitute refried beans for ground beef for a meatless main dish.*

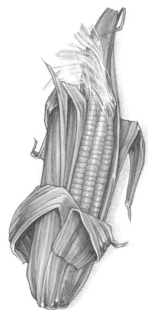

By-the-Sea Casserole

Makes 6 servings

Prep Time:
10 minutes

Cook Time:
15 minutes

1 bag (16 ounces) BIRDS EYE®
frozen Mixed Vegetables
2 cans (6 ounces each) tuna in
water, drained
1 cup uncooked instant rice

1 can (10¾ ounces) cream of
celery soup
1 cup 1% milk
1 cup cheese-flavored fish-
shaped crackers

Microwave Directions

• In medium bowl, combine vegetables and tuna.

• Stir in rice, soup and milk.

• Place tuna mixture in 1½-quart microwave-safe casserole dish; cover and microwave on HIGH 6 minutes. Stir; microwave, covered, 6 to 8 minutes more or until rice is tender.

• Stir casserole and sprinkle with crackers.

Green Chile Chicken Enchiladas

2 cups shredded cooked
    chicken
1½ cups (6 ounces) shredded
    Mexican cheese blend or
    Cheddar cheese, divided
½ cup HIDDEN VALLEY® The
    Original Ranch® Dressing

¼ cup sour cream
2 tablespoons canned diced
    green chiles, rinsed and
    drained
4 (9 to 10-inch) flour tortillas,
    warmed

Makes 4 servings

Mix together chicken, ¾ cup cheese, dressing, sour cream and green chiles in medium bowl. Divide evenly down center of each tortilla. Roll up tortillas and place, seam side down, in 9-inch baking dish. Top with remaining ¾ cup cheese. Bake at 350°F. for 20 minutes or until cheese is melted and lightly browned.

Any Way You Slice It

Good quality, sharp knives are absolutely essential in the kitchen. Most good knives are made from a combination of carbon steel and stainless steel. Carbon steel is superior for holding a sharp edge; however, it pits and stains easily. Mixing carbon steel with stainless steel makes a sturdier and easier to maintain blade. Knives are available with wood or hardened plastic handles. Wooden handles must be periodically oiled and protected from long exposure to water and heat. Good cutlery should be washed by hand as dishwashers are often too hot.

A high quality knife has a full tang, meaning that the blade runs the entire length of the handle. It should be securely riveted to the handle in several places. Every kitchen needs at least three knives: a paring knife, utility knife and chef's knife.

A *paring knife* has a short 3- or 4-inch-long blade. It is used for peeling and slicing fruit and vegetables, chopping herbs and other fine work.

A *utility knife* has a 6-inch-long blade. It is a general purpose knife for slicing fruit, vegetables, meat, poultry, fish and cheese.

A *chef's knife* has a wide, slightly curved blade from 7 to 12 inches long. This knife is used primarily for chopping food using a rocking motion.

Beef Teriyaki Stir-Fry

Makes 4 servings

Prep and Cook Time:
22 minutes

1 cup uncooked rice
1 pound beef sirloin, thinly
  sliced
½ cup teriyaki marinade, divided
2 tablespoons vegetable oil,
  divided

1 medium onion, halved and
  sliced
2 cups frozen green beans,
  rinsed and drained

1. Cook rice according to package directions, omitting salt.

2. Combine beef and ¼ cup marinade in medium bowl; set aside.

3. Heat ½ tablespoon oil in wok or large skillet over medium-high heat until hot. Add onion; stir-fry 3 to 4 minutes or until crisp-tender. Remove from wok to medium bowl.

4. Heat ½ tablespoon oil in wok. Stir-fry beans 3 minutes or until crisp-tender and hot. Drain off excess liquid. Add beans to onions in bowl.

5. Heat remaining 1 tablespoon oil in wok. Drain beef, discarding marinade. Stir-fry beef about 3 minutes or until browned. Stir in vegetables and remaining ¼ cup marinade; cook and stir 1 minute or until heated through. Serve with rice.

Broccoli, Chicken and Rice Casserole

1 box UNCLE BEN'S® COUNTRY INN® Broccoli Rice Au Gratin
2 cups boiling water
4 TYSON® Individually Fresh Frozen® Boneless, Skinless Chicken Breasts

¼ teaspoon garlic powder
2 cups frozen broccoli
1 cup shredded Cheddar cheese

Makes 4 servings

Prep Time:
none

Cook Time:
40 minutes

COOK: Preheat oven to 425°F. In 13×9-inch baking pan, combine rice and contents of seasoning packet. Add boiling water; mix well. CLEAN: Wash hands. Add chicken, sprinkle with garlic powder; cover and bake 30 minutes. Add broccoli and cheese; bake, covered, 8 to 10 minutes or until internal juices of chicken run clear. (Or insert instant-read meat thermometer in thickest part of chicken. Temperature should read 170°F.)

SERVE: Serve hot out of the oven with yeast rolls, if desired.

CHILL: Refrigerate leftovers immediately.

Pork Chops and Yams

Makes 4 servings

4 pork chops (½ inch thick)
2 tablespoons oil
2 (16-ounce) cans yams or
    sweet potatoes, drained
¾ cup SMUCKER'S® Orange
    Marmalade or Apricot
    Preserves

½ large green bell pepper, cut
    into strips
2 tablespoons minced onion

1. Brown pork chops in oil over medium heat.

2. Place yams in 1½-quart casserole. Stir in marmalade, bell pepper and onion. Layer pork chops over yam mixture. Cover and bake at 350°F for 30 minutes or until pork chops are tender.

Italian Pasta Bake

Makes 6 servings

Prep Time:
10 minutes

Bake Time:
20 minutes

1 pound ground beef *or* Italian
    sausage
4 cups cooked mostaccioli *or*
    penne pasta
1 jar (28 to 30 ounces)
    spaghetti sauce (about
    2¾ cups)

¾ cup KRAFT® 100% Grated
    Parmesan Cheese, divided
2 cups KRAFT® Shredded Low-
    Moisture Part-Skim
    Mozzarella Cheese

BROWN meat in large skillet; drain.

STIR in mostaccioli, spaghetti sauce and ½ cup of the Parmesan cheese. Spoon into 13×9-inch baking dish. Top with mozzarella cheese and remaining ¼ cup Parmesan cheese.

BAKE at 375°F for 20 minutes.

Easy Beef Skillet Dinner

1 pound ground beef
1 medium onion, chopped
1 small green bell pepper,
    chopped (optional)
1 jar (1 pound 10 ounces)
    RAGÚ® Robusto!™ Pasta
    Sauce

2 cans (14½ ounces each) beef
    broth
2 cups uncooked rotelle or
    spiral pasta

Prep Time:
10 minutes

Cook Time:
25 minutes

1. In 12-inch nonstick skillet, brown ground beef over medium-high heat; drain. Add onion and green pepper and cook, stirring occasionally, 3 minutes or until vegetables are tender. Remove ground beef mixture and set aside.

2. In same skillet, bring Ragú Pasta Sauce and broth to a boil. Stir in uncooked pasta. Reduce heat to low and simmer covered, stirring occasionally, 12 minutes or until pasta is tender.

3. Return ground beef mixture to skillet and cook, stirring occasionally, 2 minutes or until heated through.

Note:

Every kitchen needs several spoons for stirring and mixing. Spoons are available in plastic, wood and metal. Choose plastic or wood for nonstick surfaces, because metal will scratch these surfaces. Select spoons that are made in a single piece; joints break and are more difficult to clean.

Cheeseburger Macaroni Stew

Makes 6 servings

Prep Time:
5 minutes

Cook Time:
15 minutes

1 pound ground beef
1 can (28 ounces) crushed
   tomatoes in purée
1½ cups uncooked elbow
   macaroni

2 tablespoons *French's®*
   Worcestershire Sauce
1 cup shredded Cheddar cheese
1½ cups *French's®* French Fried
   Onions

1. Cook meat in large nonstick skillet over medium-high heat until browned and no longer pink; drain.

2. Add tomatoes, macaroni and *1½ cups water*. Bring to boiling. Boil, partially covered, 10 minutes until macaroni is tender. Stir in Worcestershire.

3. Sprinkle with cheese and French Fried Onions.

Tip: *For a Southwestern flavor, add 2 tablespoons chili powder to ground beef and substitute 2 tablespoons Frank's® RedHot Sauce for the Worcestershire.*

Chicken di Napolitano

1 tablespoon olive oil
2 boneless, skinless chicken
    breasts (about 8 ounces)
1 can (14½ ounces) diced
    tomatoes, undrained
1¼ cups water

1 box UNCLE BEN'S® COUNTRY
    INN® Rice Pilaf
¼ cup chopped fresh basil *or*
    1½ teaspoons dried basil
    leaves

Makes 2 servings

1. Heat oil in large skillet. Add chicken, cook over medium-high heat 8 to 10 minutes or until lightly browned on both sides.

2. Add tomatoes, water, rice and contents of seasoning packet. Bring to a boil. Cover; reduce heat and simmer 15 to 18 minutes or until chicken is no longer pink in center and liquid is absorbed.

3. Stir in basil. Slice chicken and serve over rice.

Tip: *For more flavor, substitute diced tomatoes with Italian herbs or roasted garlic for diced tomatoes.*

Chili Stew

Makes 4 servings

Prep Time:
2 minutes

Cook Time:
7 to 10 minutes

1 box (10 ounces) BIRDS EYE®
  frozen Sweet Corn
2 cans (15 ounces each) chili

1 can (14 ounces) stewed
  tomatoes
Chili powder

• In large saucepan, cook corn according to package directions; drain.

• Stir in chili and tomatoes; cook until heated through.

• Stir in chili powder to taste.

<u>Serving Suggestion:</u> *Serve with your favorite corn bread or sprinkle with shredded Cheddar cheese.*

Pizza Casserole

Makes 6 to 8 servings

1 pound BOB EVANS® Italian
  Roll Sausage
12 ounces wide noodles, cooked
  according to package
  directions
2 (14-ounce) jars pepperoni
  pizza sauce

2 cups (8 ounces) shredded
  Cheddar cheese
2 cups (8 ounces) shredded
  mozzarella cheese
6 ounces sliced pepperoni

Preheat oven to 350°F. Crumble and cook sausage in medium skillet over medium heat until browned. Drain on paper towels. Layer half of noodles in lightly greased 13×9-inch casserole dish. Top with half of sausage, half of pizza sauce, half of cheeses and half of pepperoni. Repeat layers with remaining ingredients, reserving several pepperoni slices for garnish on top of casserole. Bake 35 to 40 minutes. Refrigerate leftovers.

Penne Tuna Casserole

1 package (16 ounces) uncooked BARILLA® Mini Penne
1 jar (26 ounces) BARILLA® Lasagna & Casserole Sauce
2 cans (6 ounces each) tuna, drained and separated into chunks

1½ cups shredded mozzarella cheese
3 tablespoons grated Parmesan cheese
Chopped fresh parsley, for garnish

Makes 4 to 6 servings

Preheat oven to 350°F.

Prepare penne according to package directions; drain.

Combine penne with BARILLA® sauce and tuna in 12×8-inch casserole; mix well. Sprinkle with cheeses and bake 40 minutes or until heated through and cheeses are melted. Place casserole under broiler briefly to brown cheese, if desired. Garnish with chopped parsley, if desired. Serve immediately.

Variation: *Substitute cooked shrimp, or sliced or diced cooked chicken for tuna.*

Serving Suggestion: *Serve with freshly steamed asparagus, sautéed green and yellow squash or a fresh salad.*

Note:

Semi-soft cheeses, like mozzarella and Muenster are easier to shred if they are cold. Place them in the freezer for 10 to 15 minutes before shredding.

Chicken Divan

Makes 4 servings

⅔ cup milk
2 tablespoons margarine or
   butter
1 package (4.8 ounces) PASTA
   RONI® Four Cheese Flavor
   with Corkscrew Pasta

2 cups chopped cooked chicken
   or turkey
2 cups broccoli flowerets
½ cup croutons, coarsely
   crushed

Microwave Directions

1. In round 3-quart microwaveable glass casserole, combine 1½ cups water, milk and margarine. Microwave, uncovered, on HIGH 4 to 5 minutes or until boiling.

2. Stir in pasta, Special Seasonings, chicken and broccoli.

3. Microwave, uncovered, on HIGH 12 to 13 minutes, stirring after 6 minutes.

4. Let stand 4 to 5 minutes or until desired consistency. Sauce will be thin, but will thicken upon standing. Stir before serving.

5. Sprinkle with croutons.

Quick & Easy Meatball Soup

Makes 4 to 6 servings

1 package (15 to 18 ounces) frozen Italian sausage meatballs without sauce

2 cans (about 14 ounces each) Italian-style stewed tomatoes

2 cans (about 14 ounces each) beef broth

1 can (about 14 ounces) mixed vegetables

½ cup uncooked rotini or small macaroni

½ teaspoon dried oregano leaves

1. Thaw meatballs in microwave oven according to package directions.

2. Place remaining ingredients in large saucepan. Add meatballs. Bring to a boil. Reduce heat; cover and simmer 15 minutes or until pasta is tender.

Baked SPAM® & Tortellini Casserole

Makes 6 servings

1 (30-ounce) jar spaghetti sauce

1 (12-ounce) can SPAM® Classic, cubed

1 (10-ounce) package refrigerated cheese tortellini

½ cup chopped onion

1 cup (4 ounces) shredded mozzarella cheese

Heat oven to 375°F. In 2½-quart casserole combine all ingredients except cheese; mix gently. Bake, covered, 50 to 60 minutes or until tortellini are tender, stirring halfway through baking time. During last 5 minutes of baking, uncover and top with cheese.

One-Dish Chicken Bake

Makes 4 servings

Prep Time:
10 minutes

Bake Time:
35 minutes

1 package (6 ounces) STOVE TOP® Stuffing Mix for Chicken

4 boneless skinless chicken breast halves (about 1¼ pounds)

1 can (10¾ ounces) condensed cream of mushroom soup

⅓ cup BREAKSTONE® or KNUDSEN® Sour Cream or milk

1. **STIR** stuffing crumbs, contents of Stuffing Mix Pouch, 1½ cups hot water and ¼ cup margarine, cut-up, just until moistened; set aside.

2. **PLACE** chicken in 12×8-inch baking dish. Mix soup and sour cream; pour over chicken. Top with stuffing.

3. **BAKE** at 375°F for 35 minutes or until chicken is cooked through.

Oriental Beef with Vegetables

1 pound lean ground beef or
   ground turkey
1 large onion, coarsely chopped
2 cloves garlic, minced
2½ cups (8 ounces) frozen mixed
   vegetable medley, such as
   carrots, broccoli and red
   peppers, thawed

½ cup stir-fry sauce
1 can (3 ounces) chow mein
   noodles

Makes 4 servings

1. Cook ground beef and onion in wok or large skillet over medium heat until beef is no longer pink, stirring to separate meat. Spoon off fat.

2. Add garlic; stir-fry 1 minute. Add vegetables; stir-fry 2 minutes or until heated through.

3. Add stir-fry sauce; stir-fry 30 seconds or until hot. Serve over chow mein noodles.

Note:

When purchasing fresh garlic, choose firm, dry heads with tightly closed cloves and smooth skin. Avoid garlic with sprouting green shoots. Store the garlic, unwrapped, in a cool, dry, dark place with good ventilation for 2 to 3 months.

Fettuccine with Chicken Breasts

Makes 8 servings

12 ounces uncooked fettuccine
  or egg noodles
1 cup HIDDEN VALLEY® The
  Original Ranch® Dressing
⅓ cup Dijon mustard

8 boneless, skinless chicken
  breast halves, pounded thin
½ cup butter
⅓ cup dry white wine

Cook fettuccine according to package directions; drain. Preheat oven to 425°F. Stir together dressing and mustard; set aside. Pour fettuccine into oiled baking dish. Sauté chicken in butter in large skillet until no longer pink in center. Transfer cooked chicken to bed of fettuccine. Add wine to skillet; cook until reduced to desired consistency. Drizzle over chicken. Pour reserved dressing mixture over chicken. Bake at 425°F. about 10 minutes, or until dressing forms golden brown crust.

Monterey Black Bean Tortilla Supper

Makes 5 to 6 servings

1 pound ground beef, browned
  and drained
1½ cups bottled salsa
1 (15-ounce) can black beans,
  drained
4 (8-inch) flour tortillas

2 cups (8 ounces) shredded
  Wisconsin Monterey Jack
  cheese*

*For authentic Mexican flavor, substitute
2 cups shredded Wisconsin Queso Blanco.

Heat oven to 400°F. Combine ground beef, salsa and beans. In lightly greased 2-quart round casserole, layer one tortilla, ⅔ cup meat mixture and ½ cup cheese. Repeat layers three more times. Bake 30 minutes or until heated through.

Favorite recipe from **Wisconsin Milk Marketing Board**

Oriental Chicken & Rice

1 (6.9-ounce) package RICE-A-RONI® Chicken Flavor
2 tablespoons margarine or butter
1 pound boneless, skinless chicken breasts, cut into thin strips

¼ cup teriyaki sauce
½ teaspoon ground ginger
1 (16-ounce) package frozen Oriental-style mixed vegetables

Prep Time:
5 minutes

Cook Time:
25 minutes

1. In large skillet over medium heat, sauté rice-vermicelli mix with margarine until vermicelli is golden brown.

2. Slowly stir in 2 cups water, chicken, teriyaki sauce, ginger and Special Seasonings; bring to a boil. Reduce heat to low. Cover; simmer 10 minutes.

3. Stir in vegetables. Cover; simmer 5 to 10 minutes or until rice is tender and chicken is no longer pink inside. Let stand 3 minutes.

Tip: *Use pork instead of chicken and substitute ¼ cup orange juice for ¼ cup of the water.*

Pork and Peach Bake

Makes 4 servings

1 (6-ounce) package stuffing
  mix
½ cup SMUCKER'S® Peach
  Preserves, divided
4 pork chops (½ inch thick)

2 tablespoons oil
1 (8-ounce) can sliced peaches,
  drained
Parsley

Note:

**Peaches are classified
as freestone, meaning
that the pit is easily
removed from the
flesh, and clingstone,
meaning that the flesh
adheres to the pit and
must be cut away.
Nearly all varieties sold
fresh in markets are
freestone. Clingstone
peaches are used for
commercial purposes,
although they can
sometimes be found at
farmers' markets.**

Make stuffing mix according to package directions, decreasing water by ¼ cup; stir in ¼ cup preserves. Spoon stuffing into *ungreased* 1-quart casserole.

Brown pork chops in oil over medium heat. Arrange pork chops and peaches over stuffing. Spoon remaining ¼ cup preserves over chops.

Cover and bake at 350°F for 45 minutes to 1 hour or until pork chops are tender. Garnish with parsley.

Quick 'n' Easy Home-Style Beans

2 cans (16 ounces each) pork and beans
¼ cup *French's®* Classic Yellow® Mustard
¼ cup packed light brown sugar
2 tablespoons *French's®* Worcestershire Sauce

1½ cups shredded Cheddar cheese
1½ cups *French's®* French Fried Onions

Makes 6 servings

Prep Time:
5 minutes

Cook Time:
5 minutes

1. Combine beans, mustard, sugar and Worcestershire in medium skillet. Cook over medium heat until hot and bubbly.

2. Top with cheese and French Fried Onions. Cover and cook until cheese melts.

3. Serve with grilled or broiled hot dogs.

Broccoli Beef

2 tablespoons vegetable oil
1 teaspoon chopped shallots
10 ounces sliced beef

6 tablespoons LEE KUM KEE® Stir-Fry Sauce, LEE KUM KEE® Spicy Stir-Fry Sauce or LEE KUM KEE® Stir-Fry Sauce Kung Pao, divided
1 cup cooked broccoli florets

Makes 4 servings

Heat skillet over medium heat. Add oil. Sauté shallots. Add beef and 2 tablespoons Stir-Fry Sauce; stir-fry. When beef is half done, add broccoli and remaining 4 tablespoons Stir-Fry Sauce. Cook and stir until beef is done and broccoli is tender and heated through.

Herbed Chicken & Vegetables

Makes 4 servings

Prep Time:
10 minutes

Cook Time:
40 minutes

2 medium all-purpose potatoes,
   thinly sliced (about
   1 pound)
2 medium carrots, sliced
4 bone-in chicken pieces (about
   2 pounds)

1 envelope LIPTON® RECIPE
   SECRETS® Savory Herb
   with Garlic Soup Mix
⅓ cup water
1 tablespoon BERTOLLI® Olive
   Oil

1. Preheat oven to 425°F. In broiler pan without the rack, place potatoes and carrots; arrange chicken on top. Pour soup mix blended with water and oil over chicken and vegetables.

2. Bake uncovered 40 minutes or until chicken is thoroughly cooked and vegetables are tender.

Slow Cooker Method: *Place all ingredients in slow cooker, arranging chicken on top; cover. Cook on HIGH 4 hours or LOW 6 to 8 hours.*

Broccoli-Fish Roll-Ups

1 can (10¾ ounces) cream of
broccoli soup
½ cup fat-free (skim) milk
2 cups seasoned stuffing
crumbs

¾ pound flounder (4 medium
pieces)
1 box (10 ounces) broccoli
spears, thawed
Paprika

Makes 4 servings

Prep and Cook Time:
30 minutes

1. Preheat oven to 375°F. Grease 9×9-inch baking pan. Combine soup and milk in medium bowl. Set aside ½ cup soup mixture.

2. Combine stuffing crumbs and remaining soup mixture. Pat into prepared pan.

3. Place fish on clean work surface. Arrange 1 broccoli spear across narrow end of fish. Starting at narrow end, gently roll up fish. Place over stuffing mixture, seam side down. Repeat with remaining fish and broccoli.

4. Arrange any remaining broccoli spears over stuffing mixture. Spoon reserved ½ cup soup mixture over broccoli-fish roll-ups. Sprinkle with paprika.

5. Bake 20 minutes or until fish flakes easily when tested with fork.

Variation: *Asparagus spears and cream of asparagus soup may be substituted for broccoli spears and cream of broccoli soup.*

Creamy Mac & Cheese Alfredo

Makes 4 servings

Prep Time:
10 minutes

Cook Time:
25 minutes

8 ounces elbow macaroni,
   cooked and drained
1 jar (1 pound) RAGÚ® Cheese
   Creations!® Classic Alfredo
   Sauce

¾ cup chicken broth
¼ cup plain dry bread crumbs
2 tablespoons grated Parmesan
   cheese (optional)

1. Preheat oven to 350°F. In large bowl, combine hot macaroni, Ragú Cheese Creations! Sauce and broth. Season, if desired, with salt and pepper.

2. In 1-quart baking dish, spoon macaroni mixture; sprinkle with bread crumbs and cheese. Bake uncovered 25 minutes or until heated through.

Quick Corn, Potato and Frank Soup

Makes 6 servings

2 cans (about 15 ounces each)
   cream-style corn
2 cans (10½ ounces each)
   condensed chicken broth
2 cups frozen ready-to-cook
   hash browned potatoes
   with onions and peppers

½ teaspoon hot pepper sauce
1 package (12 ounces) HEBREW
   NATIONAL® Beef Franks,
   Reduced Fat Beef Franks or
   97% Fat Free Beef Franks
½ cup sliced green onions,
   including tops

Combine corn, broth, potatoes with onions and peppers, and hot sauce in large saucepan. Bring to a boil over high heat. Slice franks crosswise into ½-inch pieces; stir into broth mixture. Simmer, uncovered, 10 to 12 minutes. Stir in onions; simmer 3 minutes.

Mexican-Style Chicken

1 package (6 ounces) STOVE
   TOP® Stuffing Mix for
   Chicken
4 boneless skinless chicken
   breast halves (about
   1¼ pounds)

1 cup salsa
1 cup (4 ounces) KRAFT®
   Natural Shredded Cheddar
   Cheese

Makes 4 servings

Prep Time:
10 minutes

Bake Time:
40 minutes

1. **STIR** Stuffing Mix Pouch, 1½ cups hot water and ¼ cup margarine, cut-up just until moistened.

2. **SPOON** stuffing in 12×8-inch baking dish. Top with chicken. Pour salsa over chicken; sprinkle with cheese.

3. **BAKE** at 375°F for 40 minutes or until chicken is cooked through.

Note:

There is no one definition of salsa. Its ingredients vary depending on the region in which it is made, and on the use for which it is intended. It does, however, always contain tomatoes and chilies in some form or another.

Baked Pasta Primavera Casserole

Makes 6 servings

Prep Time:
10 minutes

Cook Time:
30 minutes

1 jar (1 pound 10 ounces)
RAGÚ® Old World Style®
Pasta Sauce
2 cups shredded mozzarella
cheese (about 8 ounces)
½ cup grated Parmesan cheese

1 bag (16 ounces) frozen Italian-
style vegetables, thawed
8 ounces ziti or penne pasta,
cooked and drained

1. Preheat oven to 350°F. In large bowl, combine Ragú Pasta Sauce, 1 cup mozzarella cheese and Parmesan cheese. Stir in vegetables and hot pasta.

2. In 2½-quart casserole, spoon pasta mixture; sprinkle with remaining 1 cup mozzarella cheese.

3. Bake uncovered 30 minutes or until heated through.

Cajun Chicken Bayou

2 cups water
1 can (10 ounces) diced
   tomatoes and green chilies,
   undrained

1 box UNCLE BEN'S CHEF'S
   RECIPE® Traditional Red
   Beans & Rice
2 boneless, skinless chicken
   breasts (about 8 ounces)

Makes 2 servings

1. In large skillet, combine water, tomatoes, beans & rice and contents of seasoning packet; mix well.

2. Add chicken. Bring to a boil. Cover; reduce heat and simmer 20 minutes or until chicken is no longer pink in center.

Hearty Shepherd's Pie

1½ pounds ground beef
2 cups *French's®* French Fried
   Onions
1 can (10¾ ounces) condensed
   tomato soup

2 teaspoons Italian seasoning
1 package (10 ounces) frozen
   mixed vegetables, thawed
3 cups hot mashed potatoes

Makes 6 servings

Prep Time:
10 minutes

Cook Time:
27 minutes

1. Preheat oven to 375°F. Cook meat in large oven-proof skillet until browned; drain. Stir in *1 cup* French Fried Onions, soup, *½ cup water,* seasoning and *¼ teaspoon each salt and pepper*.

2. Spoon vegetables over beef mixture. Top with mashed potatoes.

3. Bake 20 minutes or until hot. Sprinkle with remaining *1 cup* onions. Bake 2 minutes or until golden.

Lit'l Smokies 'n' Macaroni 'n' Cheese

Makes 8 servings

1 package (7¼ ounces) macaroni and cheese mix, prepared according to package directions
1 pound HILLSHIRE FARM® Lit'l Smokies
1 can (10¾ ounces) condensed cream of celery or mushroom soup, undiluted

⅓ cup milk
1 tablespoon minced parsley (optional)
1 cup (4 ounces) shredded Cheddar cheese

Preheat oven to 350°F.

Combine prepared macaroni and cheese, Lit'l Smokies, soup, milk and parsley, if desired, in medium bowl. Pour into small greased casserole. Sprinkle Cheddar cheese over top. Bake, uncovered, 20 minutes or until heated through.

Creamy Beef and Vegetable Casserole

1 pound lean ground beef
1 small onion, chopped
1 bag (16 ounces) BIRDS EYE®
   frozen Farm Fresh Mixtures
   Broccoli, Corn & Red
   Peppers

1 can (10¾ ounces) cream of
   mushroom soup

Makes 4 servings

Prep Time:
5 minutes

Cook Time:
10 to 15 minutes

• In medium skillet, brown beef and onion; drain excess fat.

• Meanwhile, in large saucepan, cook vegetables according to package directions; drain.

• Stir in beef mixture and soup. Cook over medium heat until heated through.

<u>Serving Suggestion:</u> *Serve over rice and sprinkle with ½ cup shredded Cheddar cheese.*

Note:

Dry onions can be

stored in a cool, dry

place with good air

circulation for up to

two months.

Campbell's® One-Dish Chicken & Rice Bake

Makes 4 servings

Prep Time:
5 minutes

Cook Time:
45 minutes

1 can (10¾ ounces)
CAMPBELL'S® Condensed
Cream of Mushroom Soup
or 98% Fat Free Cream of
Mushroom Soup
1 cup water*
¾ cup *uncooked* regular white
rice

¼ teaspoon paprika
¼ teaspoon pepper
4 skinless, boneless chicken
breast halves (about
1 pound)

*For creamier rice, increase water to 1⅓ cups.

1. In 2-quart shallow baking dish mix soup, water, rice, paprika and pepper. Place chicken on rice mixture. Sprinkle with additional paprika and pepper. **Cover.**

2. Bake at 375°F. for 45 minutes or until chicken is no longer pink and rice is done.

Savory
Homestyle
Stews

CHAPTER TEN

Southwestern-Style Beef Stew

Makes 8 servings

¼ cup all-purpose flour
1 teaspoon seasoned salt
¼ teaspoon ground black pepper
2 pounds beef stew meat, cut into bite-size pieces
2 tablespoons vegetable oil
1 large onion, cut into wedges
2 large cloves garlic, finely chopped
1 can (14½ ounces) stewed tomatoes, undrained

1 jar (16 ounces) ORTEGA® SALSA (any flavor)
1 cup beef broth
1 tablespoon ground oregano
1 teaspoon ground cumin
½ teaspoon salt
3 large carrots, peeled, cut into 1-inch slices
1 can (15 ounces) garbanzo beans, drained
1 cup frozen corn kernels

Note:

Applying a light coating of flour to food creates a dry surface. This helps the food brown better when frying or sautéing.

COMBINE flour, seasoned salt and pepper in medium bowl or large resealable plastic food-storage bag. Add meat; toss well to coat.

HEAT oil in large skillet over medium-high heat. Add meat, onion and garlic; cook for 5 to 6 minutes or until meat is browned on outside and onion is tender. Stir in tomatoes, salsa, broth, oregano, cumin and salt. Bring to a boil; cover. Reduce heat to low; cook, stirring occasionally, for 45 minutes or until meat is tender.

STIR in carrots, beans and corn. Increase heat to medium-low. Cook, stirring occasionally, for 30 to 40 minutes or until carrots are tender.

French-Style Pork Stew

1 package (6.2 ounces) long
  grain and wild rice
1 tablespoon vegetable oil
1 pork tenderloin (16 ounces),
  cut into ¾- to 1-inch cubes
1 medium onion, coarsely
  chopped
1 rib celery, sliced
2 tablespoons all-purpose flour
1½ cups chicken broth
½ package (16 ounces) frozen
  mixed vegetables (carrots,
  potatoes and peas)

1 jar (4.5 ounces) sliced
  mushrooms, drained
½ teaspoon dried basil leaves
¼ teaspoon dried rosemary
  leaves
¼ teaspoon dried oregano
  leaves
2 teaspoons lemon juice
⅛ teaspoon ground nutmeg
  Salt and black pepper

Makes 4 (1-cup) servings

Prep and Cook Time:
20 minutes

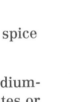

1. Prepare rice according to package directions, discarding spice packet, if desired.

2. While rice is cooking, heat oil in large saucepan over medium-high heat until hot. Add pork, onion and celery; cook 5 minutes or until pork is browned. Stir flour into chicken broth until dissolved; add to pork mixture. Cook over medium heat 1 minute, stirring constantly.

3. Stir in frozen vegetables, mushrooms, basil, rosemary and oregano; bring to a boil. Reduce heat to low; simmer, covered, 6 to 8 minutes or until pork is tender and barely pink in center. Stir in lemon juice, nutmeg, and salt and pepper to taste. Serve stew over rice.

Hearty Beef Barley Stew

Makes 6 servings

Prep Time:
10 minutes

Cook Time:
1 hour 40 minutes

1 tablespoon BERTOLLI® Olive Oil
1½ pounds beef stew meat
2 cups baby carrots
1 package (8 ounces) fresh mushrooms, sliced
2 cups (14½ ounces each) beef broth
1 can (14½ ounces) diced tomatoes, undrained
2 cups water
1 envelope LIPTON® RECIPE SECRETS® Onion Soup Mix
¾ cup barley
1 cup frozen peas

1. In 6-quart saucepot, heat oil over medium-high heat, brown beef, stirring occasionally, 4 minutes.

2. Stir in carrots, mushrooms, broth, tomatoes, water, soup mix and barley.

3. Bring to a boil over high heat. Reduce heat to medium-low and simmer, covered, 1½ hours, stirring occasionally. Stir in peas. Cook 5 minutes or until heated through.

Slow Cooker Method: *Layer carrots, mushrooms and beef in slow cooker. Combine broth, tomatoes, water, soup mix and barley. Pour over beef and vegetables. Cover. Cook on HIGH 5 to 6 hours or LOW 8 to 10 hours. Stir in peas and cook until heated through, about 5 minutes. Season, if desired, with salt and pepper.*

Garden-Vegetable Bulgur Stew

Makes 4 servings

1 tablespoon vegetable oil
1 large onion, chopped
2 medium tomatoes, peeled, seeded and chopped
2 medium carrots, thinly sliced
4 ounces fresh green beans, cut into 1-inch pieces
2 medium green onions, sliced
¾ cup canned chick-peas (garbanzo beans), drained
1 can (12 ounces) tomato juice
1 cup water
⅓ cup bulgur wheat
1 tablespoon dried mint leaves, crushed
1 teaspoon dried summer savory leaves, crushed
½ teaspoon salt
Dash black pepper
1 small zucchini, sliced
Sour cream for garnish
Fresh mint for garnish

1. Heat oil in 5-quart Dutch oven over medium heat. Cook and stir onion until tender. Stir tomatoes, carrots, green beans, green onions, chick-peas, tomato juice, water, bulgar, mint, savory, salt and pepper in Dutch oven. Bring to a boil over high heat. Reduce heat to medium-low; simmer, uncovered, about 20 minutes or until beans and carrots are slightly tender.

2. Add zucchini to vegetable mixture. Bring to a boil over high heat. Reduce heat to medium-low; simmer, uncovered, about 4 minutes or until zucchini is slightly tender.

3. Serve in bowls and garnish with dollops of sour cream and fresh mint, if desired.

California Stew

Makes 6 servings

2 pounds cubed beef or lamb
    stew meat, cut into 1-inch
    pieces
2 tablespoons salad oil
1 package (1⅝ ounces)
    LAWRY'S® Beef Stew
    Seasoning Mix
Water

1 cup dry red wine
12 small boiling onions, peeled
1 bunch carrots, peeled and cut
    into 1-inch pieces
3 medium zucchini, cut into
    1-inch pieces
2 large tomatoes, peeled and
    quartered

Note:

To peel tomatoes, first cut an "X" in the skin on the bottom of each tomato. Then place them, one at a time, in a saucepan of simmering water for about 10 seconds. Immediately plunge them into a bowl of cold water for another 10 seconds. The skins will peel off easily with a knife.

In large Dutch oven, brown meat in oil; drain fat. Add Beef Stew Seasoning Mix, 1 cup water and wine. Bring to a boil over medium-high heat; reduce heat to low, cover and simmer 1½ hours. Pierce each end of onions with fork to retain shape while cooking. Add onions and carrots to beef; cover and continue simmering 10 minutes. Add remaining ingredients, cover and continue simmering 20 minutes or until vegetables are tender.

Microwave Directions: *In 3-quart glass casserole dish, combine meat, Beef Stew Seasoning Mix, ½ cup water and wine. Cover with plastic wrap, venting one corner. Microwave on HIGH 10 minutes. Pierce each end of onions with fork to retain shape while cooking. Add all vegetables except tomatoes. Cover again and microwave on HIGH 10 minutes; stir and re-cover. Microwave at 50% power 45 minutes or until carrots are just tender. Stir in tomatoes during last 4 minutes.*

Home-Style Chicken and Sweet Potato Stew

4 boneless, skinless chicken
   breasts
   Garlic salt and pepper
½ cup all-purpose flour
¼ cup WESSON® Vegetable Oil
2 cups cubed, peeled sweet
   potatoes
1 cup chopped onion
1 (14.5-ounce) can HUNT'S®
   Stewed Tomatoes, lightly
   crushed

¾ cup homemade chicken stock
   or canned chicken broth
¾ cup apple cider
½ teaspoon dried dill weed
1 chicken bouillon cube
   Dash or two of GEBHARDT®
    Hot Pepper Sauce
   Salt to taste

Makes 4 servings

Rinse chicken and pat dry; cut into ½-inch pieces. Sprinkle with garlic salt and pepper. Place flour in plastic bag. Add chicken; shake until chicken is well coated. In large stockpot, heat Wesson® Oil. Add chicken; cook on both sides until golden brown. Remove chicken; set aside. In same pot, add sweet potatoes and onion; sauté until onion is tender. Stir in *remaining* ingredients *except* salt; blend well. Add browned chicken; bring to a boil. Reduce heat; cover and simmer 25 to 30 minutes or until chicken is no longer pink in center and potatoes are tender, stirring often. Salt to taste.

Hunter-Style Lamb Stew

Makes 4 servings

Prep Time:
15 minutes

Cook Time:
1 hour

1 pound boneless American
  lamb, cut into ¾-inch cubes
2 cloves garlic, minced
¾ cup apple juice or dry red
  wine
1 cup reduced-sodium chicken
  broth, divided
½ teaspoon dried rosemary,
  crushed

¼ teaspoon ground black
  pepper
⅛ teaspoon ground sage
2 tablespoons all-purpose flour
3 cups cooked linguini
1 to 2 tablespoons chopped
  fresh parsley

Spray skillet or large saucepan with nonstick cooking spray.
Cook and stir lamb cubes and garlic over medium-high heat until
lamb is evenly browned. Add apple juice, ½ cup broth, rosemary,
pepper and sage. Bring to a boil; reduce heat. Cover and simmer
about 1 hour or until lamb is tender. Combine remaining ½ cup
broth and flour. Stir into lamb mixture; cook and stir until
thickened and bubbly. Cook and stir 1 minute more. Serve lamb
mixture over hot cooked linguini. Sprinkle with parsley.

Favorite recipe from **American Lamb Council**

Hearty One-Pot Chicken Stew

12 TYSON® Individually Fresh
    Frozen® Boneless, Skinless
    Chicken Tenderloins
1 box UNCLE BEN'S CHEF'S
    RECIPE® Traditional Red
    Beans & Rice

1 can (14½ ounces) diced
    tomatoes, undrained
3 new red potatoes, unpeeled,
    cut into 1-inch pieces
2 carrots, sliced ½ inch thick
1 onion, cut into 1-inch pieces

Makes 4 servings

Prep Time:
10 minutes

Cook Time:
20 to 25 minutes

PREP: CLEAN: Wash hands. Remove protective ice glaze from frozen chicken by holding under cool running water 1 to 2 minutes. Cut into 1-inch pieces. CLEAN: Wash hands.

COOK: In large saucepan, combine chicken, beans and rice, contents of seasoning packet, 2¼ cups water, tomatoes, potatoes, carrots and onion. Bring to a boil. Cover, reduce heat; simmer 20 minutes or until internal juices of chicken run clear. (Or insert instant-read meat thermometer in thickest part of chicken. Temperature should read 170°F.)

SERVE: Serve with hot rolls, if desired.

CHILL: Refrigerate leftovers immediately.

Hearty Sausage Meatball Stew

Makes 6 to 8 servings

1 pound BOB EVANS® Italian Roll Sausage
2 eggs
½ cup dried bread crumbs
1 teaspoon Italian seasoning, divided
¾ teaspoon dried basil leaves, divided
½ teaspoon black pepper, divided
½ teaspoon seasoned salt
¼ cup olive oil
1 large onion, chopped
4 ribs celery, chopped

2 large carrots, cut into ½-inch-thick slices with crinkle cutter
2 medium zucchini, cut into ½-inch-thick circles with crinkle cutter
2 quarts (8 cups) chicken broth
2 (14½-ounce) cans diced tomatoes
8 ounces rotini, fusilli, gemelli or other pasta, cooked according to package directions
½ cup grated Romano cheese

To prepare meatballs, preheat oven to 400°F. Combine sausage, eggs, bread crumbs, ½ teaspoon Italian seasoning, ¼ teaspoon basil, ¼ teaspoon pepper and seasoned salt in medium bowl; mix well. Shape into 1-inch balls and place on ungreased baking sheet. Bake 25 minutes; let cool.

Heat oil in heavy-bottomed saucepan or Dutch oven. Add onion, celery and carrots; cook over medium heat until soft. Add zucchini; cover and cook 5 minutes. Add chicken broth and tomatoes; simmer 30 minutes. Add meatballs, rotini, remaining ½ teaspoon Italian seasoning, ½ teaspoon basil and ¼ teaspoon pepper; simmer 30 minutes more. Ladle into bowls; sprinkle each serving with 1 tablespoon Romano cheese. Refrigerate leftovers.

Italian Vegetable Stew

1 teaspoon BERTOLLI® Olive Oil
2 medium zucchini, halved
    lengthwise and thinly sliced
1 medium eggplant, chopped
1 large onion, thinly sliced
⅛ teaspoon ground black
    pepper

1 jar (1 pound 10 ounces)
    RAGÚ® Light Pasta Sauce
3 tablespoons grated Parmesan
    cheese
1 box (10 ounces) couscous

Makes 4 servings

Prep Time:
10 minutes

Cook Time:
25 minutes

1. In 12-inch nonstick skillet, heat oil over medium heat and cook zucchini, eggplant, onion and pepper, stirring occasionally, 15 minutes or until vegetables are golden.

2. Stir in Ragú Pasta Sauce and cheese. Bring to a boil over high heat. Reduce heat to low and simmer covered 10 minutes.

3. Meanwhile, prepare couscous according to package directions. Serve vegetable mixture over hot couscous.

Note:

Zucchini is the most popular summer squash. Distinguished by their edible skins and seeds, summer squash differ widely in skin color and shape. But the mild, delicate flavor found in all varieties makes them largely interchangeable in recipe use.

Jamaican Black Bean Stew

Makes 8 servings

2 cups brown rice
2 pounds sweet potatoes
3 pounds butternut squash
1 large onion, coarsely chopped
1 can (about 14 ounces)
   vegetable broth
3 cloves garlic, minced
1 tablespoon curry powder
1½ teaspoons allspice

½ teaspoon ground red pepper
¼ teaspoon salt
2 cans (15 ounces each) black
   beans, drained and rinsed
½ cup raisins
3 tablespoons fresh lime juice
1 cup diced tomato
1 cup diced, peeled cucumber

1. Prepare rice according to package directions. Peel sweet potatoes; cut into ¾-inch chunks to measure 4 cups. Peel squash; remove seeds. Cut flesh into ¾-inch cubes to measure 5 cups.

2. Combine potatoes, squash, onion, broth, garlic, curry powder, allspice, pepper and salt in Dutch oven. Bring to a boil; reduce heat to low. Simmer, covered, 5 minutes. Add beans and raisins. Simmer 5 minutes or just until sweet potatoes and squash are tender and beans are hot. Remove from heat; stir in lime juice.

3. Serve stew over brown rice and top with tomato and cucumber.

Carnival Pork Stew

Makes 8 servings

3 pounds lean boneless pork
   loin, cut into 2-inch pieces
   Salt and ground black pepper
2 tablespoons oil
8 ounces smoked ham, cut into
   ½-inch chunks
2 medium onions, chopped
2 stalks celery, chopped
2 green bell peppers, chopped
6 cloves garlic, minced
½ teaspoon dried thyme

1 (28-ounce) can whole
   tomatoes, undrained, cut
   up
¾ cup SMUCKER'S® Peach
   Preserves
1 cup water
1 tablespoon hot pepper sauce
1 cup uncooked long-grain rice
½ cup chopped fresh parsley
½ cup chopped green onions

Sprinkle pork with salt and black pepper. Heat oil in large Dutch oven. Add pork; cook 5 to 8 minutes or until well browned. Remove pork with slotted spoon; set aside.

Add ham, onions, celery, green peppers, garlic and thyme. Cook and stir over medium-high heat until vegetables are wilted, about 6 minutes. Add browned pork, tomatoes, preserves, water and hot pepper sauce. Cover and simmer for 45 minutes.

Add rice, parsley and green onions; stir to blend well. Cover and simmer 20 to 25 minutes or until rice is tender. Season to taste with salt and black pepper.

Harvest Veal Stew

Makes 6 servings

⅓ cup flour
2 teaspoons salt, divided
½ teaspoon dried tarragon
1½ pounds boneless veal
    shoulder, cut into 1-inch
    pieces
2 tablespoons olive oil
2 cups chicken broth
½ cup white wine or water

1 teaspoon TABASCO® brand
    Pepper Sauce
2 cups cauliflower pieces
2 cups butternut squash pieces
    (about 1 inch)
4 ounces green beans, cut into
    1½-inch pieces
Cooked egg noodles, tossed
    with butter and parsley

Note:

Because cauliflower acquires a strong odor with long storage, plan to use it within one week. Store it unwashed in a perforated plastic bag. Washed raw florets, tightly wrapped in plastic, will keep refrigerated for three to five days.

Combine flour, 1 teaspoon salt and tarragon in medium bowl; toss with veal until well coated. Heat oil in 5-quart saucepan over medium-high heat. Add veal; cook until well browned, turning occasionally. Add chicken broth, wine, TABASCO® Sauce and remaining 1 teaspoon salt; heat to boiling. Reduce heat to low; cover and simmer 45 minutes.

Add cauliflower, squash and green beans to saucepan; heat to boiling over high heat. Reduce heat to low; cover and simmer 15 minutes or until tender, stirring occasionally. Serve stew with noodles.

Dijon Lamb Stew

½ pound boneless lamb, cut
into small pieces*
½ medium onion, chopped
½ teaspoon dried rosemary
1 tablespoon olive oil
1 can (14½ ounces)
DEL MONTE® Stewed
Tomatoes - Italian Recipe

1 carrot, julienne cut
1 tablespoon Dijon mustard
1 can (15 ounces) white beans
or pinto beans, drained

*Top sirloin steak may be substituted for lamb.

Makes 4 servings

Prep Time:
10 minutes

Cook Time:
20 minutes

1. Brown meat with onion and rosemary in oil in large skillet over medium-high heat, stirring occasionally. Season with salt and pepper, if desired.

2. Add undrained tomatoes, carrot and mustard. Cover and cook over medium heat, 10 minutes; add beans.

3. Cook, uncovered, over medium heat 5 minutes, stirring occasionally. Garnish with sliced ripe olives and chopped parsley, if desired.

Chicken Peanut Stew

Makes 6 servings

Prep Time:
10 minutes

Cook Time:
35 minutes

1 (3- to 4-pound) chicken, cut
   up and skinned, if desired
1 onion, chopped
2 cloves garlic, minced
1 can (6 ounces) tomato paste

½ cup smooth peanut butter
¼ cup *Frank's® RedHot®* Cayenne
   Pepper Sauce
1 teaspoon curry powder
2 large carrots, diced

1. Heat *1 tablespoon oil* in large skillet until hot. Add chicken pieces; cook 10 minutes or until browned on both sides. Drain off all but 1 tablespoon fat. Add onion and garlic; cook and stir 3 minutes or until tender.

2. Combine *2 cups water,* tomato paste, peanut butter, *Frank's RedHot* Sauce and curry powder; whisk until well blended. Pour into skillet. Stir in carrots. Heat to boiling. Reduce heat to medium-low. Cook, partially covered, 20 minutes or until chicken is no longer pink near bone. Serve with hot cooked rice. Garnish with roasted peanuts, if desired.

Burgundy Beef Stew

¾ pound beef sirloin steak, cut into 1-inch cubes
1 cup diagonally sliced carrots
1 teaspoon minced garlic
¼ cup Burgundy or other dry red wine
2⅓ cups canned beef broth

1 can (14½ ounces) diced tomatoes, undrained
1 box UNCLE BEN'S® COUNTRY INN® Rice Pilaf
1 jar (15 ounces) whole pearl onions, drained

1. Generously spray large saucepan or Dutch oven with nonstick cooking spray. Heat over high heat until hot. Add beef; cook 2 to 3 minutes or until no longer pink. Stir in carrots, garlic and wine; cook 2 minutes.

2. Add broth, tomatoes, rice and contents of seasoning packet. Bring to a boil. Cover; reduce heat and simmer 10 minutes, stirring occasionally. Add onions; cook 10 minutes more or until rice is tender. Remove from heat and let stand, covered, 5 minutes.

<u>Variation:</u> *One 15-ounce can of drained sweet peas and pearl onions can be substituted for the pearl onions.*

Curried Eggplant, Squash & Chick-Pea Stew

Makes 2 servings

1 teaspoon olive oil
½ cup diced red bell pepper
¼ cup diced onion
1¼ teaspoons curry powder
1 clove garlic, minced
½ teaspoon salt
1¼ cups cubed peeled eggplant
¾ cup cubed peeled acorn or
    butternut squash

⅔ cup rinsed and drained
    canned chick-peas
½ cup vegetable broth or water
3 tablespoons white wine
    Hot pepper sauce (optional)
¼ cup lemon-flavored sugar-free
    yogurt
2 tablespoons chopped fresh
    parsley

Note:

Acorn squash is an acorn-shaped winter squash that weighs from one to three pounds. The skin is dark green with patches of orange. The flesh is a deep orange and has a sweet flavor.

1. Heat oil in medium saucepan over medium heat. Add bell pepper and onion; cook and stir 5 minutes. Stir in curry powder, garlic and salt. Add eggplant, squash, chick-peas, broth and wine to saucepan. Cover; bring to a boil. Reduce heat and simmer 20 to 25 minutes just until squash and eggplant are tender.

2. Season to taste with hot pepper sauce, if desired. Serve with yogurt and parsley.

Turkey Mushroom Stew

1 pound turkey cutlets
3 tablespoons butter or
    margarine
1 small onion, thinly sliced
2 tablespoons minced green
    onions with tops
½ pound mushrooms, sliced
2 to 3 tablespoons flour

1 cup half-and-half or milk
1 teaspoon dried tarragon
    leaves
1 teaspoon salt
    Black pepper to taste
½ cup frozen peas
½ cup sour cream (optional)
    Puff pastry shells (optional)

Place turkey cutlets between two sheets of waxed paper. Lightly pound with flat side of meat mallet to ¼-inch thickness. Cut into 4×1-inch strips; set aside.

Melt butter in 5-quart Dutch oven over medium heat. Cook and stir onions in hot butter until soft. Stir in mushrooms; cook 5 minutes. Remove vegetables with slotted spoon.

Cook and stir turkey in hot butter in same Dutch oven until almost done. Blend flour into half-and-half until smooth; stir into turkey. Add tarragon, salt and pepper. Return cooked vegetables to Dutch oven; stir in peas. Bring to a boil over medium heat. Reduce heat to low. Cover and simmer 15 to 20 minutes until turkey is fork-tender and peas are heated through. Remove from heat. For a richer flavor, stir in sour cream just before serving and serve in puff pastry shells, if desired.

Texas Beef Stew

Makes 4 servings

Prep Time:
5 minutes

Cook Time:
15 minutes

1 pound lean ground beef
1 small onion, chopped
1 can (28 ounces) crushed
    tomatoes with roasted
    garlic
1½ cups BIRDS EYE® frozen Farm
    Fresh Mixtures Broccoli,
    Cauliflower & Carrots

1 can (14½ ounces) whole new
    potatoes, halved
1 cup BIRDS EYE® frozen Sweet
    Corn
1 can (4½ ounces) chopped
    green chilies, drained
½ cup water

• In large saucepan, cook beef and onion over medium-high heat
until beef is well browned, stirring occasionally.

• Stir in tomatoes, vegetables, potatoes with liquid, corn, chilies
and water; bring to a boil.

• Reduce heat to medium-low; cover and simmer 5 minutes or
until heated through.

Serving Suggestion: *Serve over rice with warm crusty bread.*

Fruited Lamb Stew

Makes 4 servings

1 pound boneless lamb
2 tablespoons all-purpose flour
½ teaspoon salt
 Dash ground red pepper
2 tablespoons vegetable oil
1 small leek, sliced
3 cups chicken broth
½ teaspoon grated fresh ginger

8 ounces peeled baby carrots
¾ cup cut-up mixed dried fruit
 (half of 8-ounce package)
½ cup frozen peas
 Black pepper
1⅓ cups hot cooked couscous
 Fresh chervil for garnish
 (optional)

Preheat oven to 350°F. Cut lamb into ¾-inch cubes. Combine flour, salt and red pepper in medium bowl; toss lamb with flour mixture.

Heat oil in 5-quart ovenproof Dutch oven over medium-high heat. Add lamb; brown, stirring frequently. Add leek, chicken broth and ginger to Dutch oven. Bring to a boil over high heat. Cover; cook in oven 45 minutes.

Remove from oven; stir in carrots. Cover and cook in oven 30 minutes or until meat and carrots are almost tender.

Stir fruit and peas into stew. Cover and cook 10 minutes. If necessary, skim off fat with large spoon. Season with black pepper to taste. Serve stew in bowls; top with couscous. Garnish, if desired.

Hearty Sausage Stew

Makes 6 servings

¼ cup olive oil
4 carrots, chopped
1 onion, cut into quarters
1 cup chopped celery
2 cloves garlic, finely chopped
1 teaspoon finely chopped fennel
Salt and black pepper to taste
12 small new potatoes
1 pound mushrooms, cut into halves

2 cans (12 ounces each) diced tomatoes, undrained
1 can (8 ounces) tomato sauce
1 tablespoon dried oregano leaves
1 pound HILLSHIRE FARM® Polska Kielbasa,* sliced

Or use any variety Hillshire Farm® Smoked Sausage.

Note:

Celery is a good keeper. Store it in a plastic bag in the refrigerator for up to two weeks. If celery becomes limp or wilted, freshen it by soaking trimmed ribs in a bowl of ice water for about one hour.

Heat oil in heavy skillet over medium-high heat; add carrots, onion, celery, garlic, fennel, salt and pepper. Sauté until vegetables are soft. Add potatoes, mushrooms, tomatoes with liquid, tomato sauce and oregano; cook 20 minutes over low heat. Add Polska Kielbasa; simmer 15 minutes or until heated through.

Speedy Brunswick Stew

Makes 6 to 8 servings

8 boneless skinless chicken thighs, cut into bite-size pieces
1 teaspoon salt, divided
¼ teaspoon pepper
2 tablespoons vegetable oil
1 onion, cut lengthwise into ¼-inch slices
1 can (28 ounces) tomatoes, undrained, broken-up
2¼ cups water, divided
1 package (10 ounces) frozen lima beans
1 package (10 ounces) frozen whole kernel corn
1 tablespoon Worcestershire sauce
2 teaspoons chicken bouillon granules
1 teaspoon sugar
2 tablespoons all-purpose flour
2 tablespoons chopped fresh parsley

Sprinkle ¼ teaspoon salt and pepper over chicken. Heat oil in Dutch oven over medium-high heat. Add chicken and onion; cook and stir about 5 minutes.

Add tomatoes, 2 cups water, beans, corn, Worcestershire, bouillon granules, sugar and remaining ¾ teaspoon salt. Bring to a boil over high heat. Reduce heat to low. Cover and simmer 20 minutes or until chicken and vegetables are fork-tender.

Mix flour and remaining ¼ cup water in small bowl. Stir flour mixture into stew. Cook, stirring, until slightly thickened. Sprinkle with chopped parsley.

Favorite recipe from **Delmarva Poultry Industry, Inc.**

SPAM™ Stew with Buttermilk Topping

Makes 6 to 8 servings

1 (10¾-ounce) can cream of
chicken soup
½ cup milk
½ cup chopped onion
1 (3-ounce) package cream
cheese, cubed
¼ cup shredded carrot
¼ cup chopped celery
¼ cup (1 ounce) grated
Parmesan cheese
1 (12-ounce) can SPAM® Classic,
cubed

1 (10-ounce) package frozen cut
broccoli, cooked and
drained
1 cup buttermilk pancake mix
1 cup (4 ounces) shredded
Cheddar cheese
¼ cup milk
1 egg, beaten
1 tablespoon vegetable oil
¼ cup sliced almonds

Heat oven to 375°F. In large saucepan, combine soup, ½ cup milk,
onion, cream cheese, carrot, celery and Parmesan cheese. Cook
and stir until cream cheese is melted. Stir in SPAM® and broccoli;
heat thoroughly. Pour into 2-quart casserole. In medium bowl,
combine pancake mix and Cheddar cheese. In small bowl, stir
together ¼ cup milk, egg and oil. Add to pancake mix; stir until
combined. Spoon topping over SPAM™ mixture. Sprinkle with
almonds. Bake 20 to 25 minutes or until topping is golden brown.

Vegetable Stew Medley

Makes 12 servings

2 tablespoons CRISCO® Oil*
4 medium onions, thinly sliced
and separated into rings
3 medium green bell peppers,
cut into strips
2 cloves garlic, minced
4 medium zucchini, cut into
½-inch pieces
1 medium eggplant, cut into
½-inch pieces (about
1 pound)
1 can (14½ ounces) no-salt-
added whole tomatoes,
drained and chopped, or
4 or 5 fresh tomatoes,
peeled and quartered

1 teaspoon dried dill weed
¾ teaspoon dried basil leaves
½ teaspoon dried oregano
leaves
½ teaspoon black pepper
¼ teaspoon salt
1 package (9 ounces) frozen
peas
¼ cup lemon juice
2 tablespoons chopped fresh
parsley or 2 teaspoons
dried parsley

*Use your favorite Crisco Oil product.

1. Heat oil in Dutch oven (non-reactive or non-cast iron) on medium heat. Add onions, bell peppers and garlic. Cook and stir until tender.

2. Add zucchini and eggplant. Cook 5 minutes, stirring occasionally. Stir in tomatoes, dill weed, basil, oregano, black pepper and salt. Reduce heat to low. Cover. Simmer 20 minutes, stirring occasionally.

3. Stir in peas. Simmer 3 to 5 minutes or until peas are thawed and heated, stirring occasionally. Stir in lemon juice. Serve hot or chilled sprinkled with parsley.

Spicy African Chick-Pea and Sweet Potato Stew

Makes 4 servings

Spice Paste (recipe follows)
1½ pounds sweet potatoes, peeled and cubed
2 cups vegetable broth or water
1 can (16 ounces) plum tomatoes, undrained, chopped
1 can (16 ounces) chick-peas (garbanzo beans), drained and rinsed

1½ cups sliced fresh okra *or*
1 package (10 ounces) frozen cut okra, thawed
Yellow Couscous (recipe follows)
Hot pepper sauce
Fresh cilantro for garnish

Note:

Okra are slender, bright green pods filled with many small white seeds. Some pods are fuzzy. When cooked, okra develops a gumminess that makes it a good thickener for soups and stews.

1. Prepare Spice Paste.

2. Combine sweet potatoes, broth, tomatoes with juice, chick-peas, okra and Spice Paste in large saucepan. Bring to a boil over high heat. Reduce heat to low. Cover and simmer 15 minutes. Uncover; simmer 10 minutes or until vegetables are tender.

3. Meanwhile, prepare Yellow Couscous.

4. Serve stew with couscous and hot pepper sauce. Garnish, if desired.

Spice Paste

6 cloves garlic, peeled
1 teaspoon coarse salt
2 teaspoons sweet paprika
1½ teaspoons cumin seeds
1 teaspoon cracked black
   pepper

½ teaspoon ground ginger
½ teaspoon ground allspice
1 tablespoon olive oil

Process garlic and salt in blender or small food processor until garlic is finely chopped. Add remaining seasonings. Process 15 seconds. While blender is running, pour oil through cover opening; process until mixture forms paste.

Yellow Couscous

1 tablespoon olive oil
5 green onions, sliced
1⅔ cups water
⅛ teaspoon saffron threads *or*
   ½ teaspoon ground
   turmeric

¼ teaspoon salt
1 cup precooked couscous*

Check ingredient label for "precooked semolina."

Heat oil in medium saucepan over medium heat until hot. Add onions; cook and stir 4 minutes. Add water, saffron and salt. Bring to a boil. Stir in couscous. Remove from heat. Cover; let stand 5 minutes.

Makes 3 cups

Aromatic Asian Beef Stew

Makes 6 to 8 servings

4 tablespoons vegetable oil, divided
3 pounds beef stew meat, cut into 1¼-inch chunks
12 shallots, peeled
2 medium onions, chopped
4 cloves garlic, minced
3 cups water
2 tablespoons sugar
1½ teaspoons salt
1 teaspoon anise seeds
¼ teaspoon ground cinnamon
¼ teaspoon black pepper

2 bay leaves
1 pound white turnips (3 or 4) or 1 icicle radish or Japanese daikon, peeled and cut into wedges
1 pound carrots, cut into 1½-inch chunks
3 (2×½-inch) strips lemon peel
1 can (6 ounces) tomato paste Japanese daikon sprouts tied together with green onion top for garnish

1. Heat large wok over medium-high heat until hot. Drizzle 1 tablespoon oil into wok. Add ½ of beef; stir-fry 5 minutes or until browned. Remove to large bowl. Repeat with 1 tablespoon oil and remaining beef. Remove beef; set aside.

2. Heat 1 tablespoon oil in wok. Add shallots; stir-fry until browned. Remove to small bowl. Heat remaining 1 tablespoon oil in wok. Add onions and garlic; stir-fry 2 minutes.

3. Return beef and all juices to wok. Add water, sugar and seasonings. Cover; bring to a boil. Reduce heat to low; simmer 1¼ hours or until meat is almost tender.

4. Add turnips, carrots, shallots and lemon peel to beef. Cover; cook 30 minutes or until meat is tender, stirring occasionally. Remove and discard bay leaves and lemon peel. Stir tomato paste into stew. Cook and stir until sauce boils and thickens. Transfer to serving bowl. Garnish, if desired.

Fisherman's Stew

2 cups water
1 pound fish fillets (scrod,
    halibut, monkfish or cod),
    cut into 2-inch pieces
1 clove garlic, minced
1 tablespoon FILIPPO BERIO®
    Olive Oil
1 medium onion, chopped
¼ cup chopped almonds

¼ cup seasoned dry bread
    crumbs
2 cups vegetable broth or
    bouillon
2 medium tomatoes, diced
¼ teaspoon paprika
¼ teaspoon freshly ground
    black pepper
Salt

In large saucepan or Dutch oven, bring water to a boil over high heat. Add fish and garlic. Cover; reduce heat to low and simmer 15 minutes or until fish is opaque and flakes easily when tested with fork. Remove fish with slotted spoon; set aside. Reserve stock (about 2 cups).

Meanwhile, in small nonstick skillet, heat olive oil over medium heat until hot. Add onion; cook and stir 5 minutes or until softened. Add almonds and bread crumbs; cook and stir 3 to 5 minutes or until lightly browned. Add to reserved fish stock along with vegetable broth, tomatoes, paprika and pepper. Add fish; cover and cook until fish is heated through. Season to taste with salt. Serve hot.

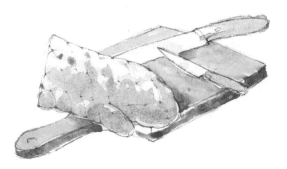

Catalonian Stew

Makes 6 servings

2 boneless skinless chicken
   breasts, cut into bite-size
   pieces
3 ounces pepperoni, diced
1 tablespoon vegetable oil
2 cans (15 ounces each) tomato
   sauce
3 cups chicken broth
1 cup pimiento-stuffed green
   olives, halved
2 tablespoons sugar

8 ounces uncooked rotini or
   other shaped pasta
⅓ cup chopped fresh parsley
⅛ teaspoon crushed saffron,
   optional
1 cup (4 ounces) SARGENTO®
   Fancy Mild or Sharp
   Cheddar Shredded Cheese
1 cup (4 ounces) SARGENTO®
   Fancy Monterey Jack
   Shredded Cheese

In Dutch oven, cook chicken and pepperoni in oil over medium heat until chicken is lightly browned, about 5 minutes; drain. Add tomato sauce, chicken broth, olives and sugar. Bring to a boil; reduce heat and simmer, covered, 15 minutes. Return to a boil. Add rotini, parsley and saffron, if desired; cover and cook an additional 15 minutes or until pasta is tender. Combine Cheddar and Monterey Jack cheeses in small bowl. Spoon stew into 6 individual ovenproof serving bowls; sprinkle evenly with cheese. Bake in preheated 350°F oven about 5 minutes or until cheese is melted.

New Orleans Stew

Makes 8 servings

2 green bell peppers, chopped
1 onion, chopped
3 ribs celery, chopped
2 tablespoons seafood
    seasoning
1 tablespoon dried marjoram
    leaves
    Salt and black pepper to taste

1 pound HILLSHIRE FARM® Hot
    Links,* sliced
4 ears corn on the cob, cut into
    quarters
1 pound unpeeled raw shrimp
    Seafood cocktail sauce

*Or use any variety Hillshire Farm Smoked Sausage.

Place bell peppers, onion and celery in large saucepan or Dutch oven; cover with water. Add seafood seasoning, marjoram, salt and black pepper to saucepan. Boil 10 to 15 minutes. Add Hot Links and corn to saucepan; boil 5 to 10 minutes. Add shrimp; boil 3 minutes. Remove pan from heat; let stand 5 minutes. Drain in colander. Serve with cocktail sauce.

A Passion for Pasta

Pasta makes a great accompaniment to stew! Commercially made pasta is available both dry and fresh.

Commercially made dry pasta begins with hard durum wheat and water. The ground durum wheat, or semolina, makes a firm, elastic dough that is sturdy enough to be shaped by machine. The dough is shaped by pushing it through a die or mold. It is then dried in commercial ovens. Dry pasta should be stored in a cool, dry place in a tightly covered container or tightly closed package. It will keep almost indefinitely.

Fresh pasta dough is made by mixing all-purpose wheat flour, whole eggs, salt and sometimes oil. It is blended, kneaded and rolled out by hand or machine. It is then cut into the desired widths. Commercially made fresh pasta is sold in bulk in Italian markets, or prepackaged in supermarkets. Fresh bulk pasta is very perishable. Refrigerate it tightly wrapped; use within 4 to 5 days. Prepackaged fresh pastas contain preservatives. These are stamped with a "use by" date. Frozen filled pasta is available in supermarkets and can be stored frozen up to 4 months. It should be cooked from the frozen state.

Greek-Style Chicken Stew

Makes 6 entrée servings

3 pounds skinless chicken
  breasts
All-purpose flour
Nonstick cooking spray
2 cups cubed peeled eggplant
2 cups sliced mushrooms
¾ cup coarsely chopped onion
  (about 1 medium)
2 cloves garlic, minced
1 teaspoon dried oregano
  leaves
½ teaspoon dried basil leaves

½ teaspoon dried thyme leaves
2 cups defatted low-sodium
  chicken broth
¼ cup dry sherry or additional
  defatted low-sodium
  chicken broth
¼ teaspoon salt
¼ teaspoon black pepper
1 can (14 ounces) artichoke
  hearts, drained
3 cups hot cooked wide egg
  noodles

1. Coat chicken very lightly with flour. Generously coat nonstick Dutch oven or large nonstick skillet with cooking spray; heat over medium heat until hot. Cook chicken 10 to 15 minutes or until browned on all sides. Remove chicken; drain fat from Dutch oven.

2. Add eggplant, mushrooms, onion, garlic, oregano, basil and thyme to Dutch oven; cook and stir over medium heat 5 minutes.

3. Return chicken to Dutch oven. Stir in chicken broth, sherry, salt and pepper; heat to a boil. Reduce heat to low and simmer, covered, about 1 hour or until chicken is no longer pink in center and juices run clear, adding artichoke hearts during last 20 minutes of cooking. Serve over noodles. Garnish as desired.

Herbed Pork and Vegetable Stew

4 boneless pork chops, cut into
 ¾-inch cubes
2 teaspoons olive oil
⅓ cup flour
2 (14½-ounce) cans beef broth
1 (14½-ounce) can diced
 tomatoes with garlic and
 onion
3 bay leaves
1 teaspoon dried marjoram
 leaves

½ teaspoon hot pepper sauce
¼ teaspoon salt
8 small new potatoes,
 quartered
1 (16-ounce) package baby
 carrots
1 (16-ounce) package small
 frozen pearl onions

Heat oven to 350°F. In a large nonstick skillet heat oil; cook pork, half at a time, for 2 to 3 minutes or until browned. Remove pork from skillet, reserving drippings. Transfer pork to a 4-quart casserole. Stir flour into drippings; stir in broth, tomatoes, bay leaves, marjoram, hot pepper sauce and salt. Cook and stir until thickened and bubbly. Stir the tomato mixture into the pork. Add the potatoes, carrots and onions. Bake, covered, for 55 to 60 minutes or until carrots are crisp-tender, stirring occasionally. Remove bay leaves. To serve, ladle into soup bowls.

Favorite recipe from **National Pork Board**

Barley Stew with Cornmeal-Cheese Dumplings

Makes 4 servings

2 cans (11½ ounces each) no-salt-added spicy vegetable juice cocktail
1 can (15½ ounces) butter beans, drained
1 can (14½ ounces) no-salt-added stewed tomatoes, undrained
1 cup sliced zucchini
1 cup sliced carrots
1 cup water
½ cup chopped peeled parsnip
⅓ cup quick pearl barley

1 bay leaf
2 tablespoons chopped fresh thyme
1½ tablespoons chopped fresh rosemary
⅓ cup all-purpose flour
⅓ cup cornmeal
1 teaspoon baking powder
¼ cup skim milk
1 tablespoon canola oil
⅓ cup (1½ ounces) shredded reduced-fat Cheddar cheese

Add vegetable juice, beans, tomatoes with juice, zucchini, carrots, water, parsnip, barley, bay leaf, thyme and rosemary to 3-quart saucepan. Bring to a boil over high heat. Reduce heat to medium-low. Cover; simmer 20 to 25 minutes or until tender, stirring occasionally. Remove and discard bay leaf.

Combine flour, cornmeal and baking powder in small bowl. Combine milk and oil in separate small bowl; stir into flour mixture. Stir in cheese. Drop dough by spoonfuls to make 4 mounds onto boiling stew. Cover; simmer 10 to 12 minutes or until wooden toothpick inserted near center of dumpling comes out clean.

Ranch-Style Beef Stew

2 pounds beef cubes, cut into ½-inch pieces
1 tablespoon BERTOLLI® Olive Oil
1 jar (1 pound 10 ounces) RAGÚ® Chunky Gardenstyle Pasta Sauce
1 can (14½ ounces) beef broth
½ cup pimento-stuffed green olives, halved
1 can (4 ounces) chopped green chilies, undrained
1 tablespoon dried oregano leaves, crushed

Prep Time:
10 minutes

Cook Time:
1 hour

1. Season beef, if desired, with salt and pepper. In 6-quart saucepot or Dutch oven, heat oil over medium-high heat and brown meat in two batches.

2. Stir in Ragú Pasta Sauce, broth, olives, chilies and oregano. Bring to a boil over high heat. Reduce heat to low and simmer covered, stirring occasionally, 1 hour or until beef is tender.

3. Serve, if desired, over hot cooked egg noodles or rice. Garnish, if desired, with chopped fresh cilantro.

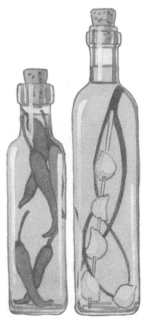

Mediterranean Stew

Makes 6 servings

8 ounces fresh okra *or*
  1 package (10 ounces)
  frozen cut okra, thawed
1 medium butternut or acorn
  squash
1 tablespoon olive oil
1½ cups chopped onions
1 clove garlic, minced
½ teaspoon ground cumin
½ teaspoon ground turmeric
¼ teaspoon ground cinnamon
¼ teaspoon ground red pepper
¼ teaspoon paprika
2 cups cubed unpeeled
  eggplant

2 cups sliced zucchini
1 medium carrot, sliced
1 can (8 ounces) tomato sauce
½ cup vegetable broth
1 can (15½ ounces) chick-peas
  (garbanzo beans), drained
1 medium tomato, chopped
⅓ cup raisins
  Salt
6 to 8 cups hot cooked
  couscous
  Minced fresh parsley for
  garnish

1. Wash okra under cold running water. Cut into ¾-inch slices.

2. Remove skin from butternut squash with vegetable peeler. Trim off stem. Cut squash lengthwise into halves; discard seeds. Cut flesh into 1-inch pieces.

3. Heat oil in Dutch oven over high heat until hot. Add onions and garlic; cook and stir 5 minutes or until tender. Stir in cumin, turmeric, cinnamon, red pepper and paprika; cook and stir 2 to 3 minutes.

4. Add okra, butternut squash, eggplant, zucchini, carrot, tomato sauce and broth. Bring to a boil over high heat. Reduce heat to low. Simmer, uncovered, 5 minutes.

5. Add chick-peas, tomato and raisins; simmer, covered, 30 minutes. Season to taste with salt. Serve over couscous. Garnish, if desired.

Sauerkraut Stew

2 pounds well-trimmed kosher flanken (beef short ribs)

1 package (2 pounds) HEBREW NATIONAL® Sauerkraut, undrained

2 cans (16 ounces each) diced tomatoes in juice, undrained

1 large potato, peeled, cut into ½-inch pieces

1¾ cups water, divided

½ teaspoon freshly ground black pepper

½ cup packed light brown sugar

2 tablespoons all-purpose flour

Combine flanken, sauerkraut, tomatoes with juice, potato, 1½ cups water and pepper in Dutch oven. Cover; bring to a boil over high heat. Reduce heat to low; simmer 2 hours or until meat is tender.

Transfer meat to cutting board; cool slightly. Skim fat from surface of stew; discard fat. Stir brown sugar into stew. Combine flour and remaining ¼ cup cold water in small glass measuring cup; stir into stew.

Discard bones and fat from meat; cut meat into ½-inch pieces. Stir into stew; simmer 5 minutes or until stew thickens.

Savory Bean Stew

Makes 6 (1-cup) servings

Prep and Cook Time: *30 minutes*

Note:

Polenta, an integral part of Northern Italian cuisine, is made from cornmeal. It is prepared by cooking cornmeal and water together to a thick spoonable consistency. Americans would call this dish "mush." When allowed to cool and become firm, it can be sliced or cut into squares and fried, broiled or baked.

1 tablespoon olive or vegetable oil
1 cup frozen vegetable blend (onions, celery, red and green bell peppers)
1 can (15½ ounces) chick-peas (garbanzo beans), rinsed and drained
1 can (15 ounces) pinto beans, rinsed and drained
1 can (15 ounces) black beans, rinsed and drained
1 can (14½ ounces) diced tomatoes with roasted garlic, undrained

¾ teaspoon dried thyme leaves
¾ teaspoon dried sage leaves
½ to ¾ teaspoon dried oregano leaves
¾ cup vegetable broth or chicken broth, divided
1 tablespoon all-purpose flour
Salt and black pepper

Polenta
3 cups water
¾ cup yellow cornmeal
¾ teaspoon salt

1. Heat oil in large saucepan over medium heat until hot. Add vegetable blend; cook and stir 5 minutes. Stir in beans, tomatoes with juice and herbs. Mix ½ cup vegetable broth and flour. Stir into bean mixture; bring to a boil. Boil, stirring constantly, 1 minute. Reduce heat to low; simmer, covered, 10 minutes. Add remaining ¼ cup broth to stew; season to taste with salt and black pepper.

2. While stew is simmering, prepare Polenta. Bring 3 cups water to a boil. Reduce heat to medium; gradually stir in cornmeal and salt. Cook 5 to 8 minutes or until cornmeal thickens and holds its shape, but is still soft. Season to taste with black pepper. Spread Polenta over plate and top with stew.

Santa Fe Taco Stew

1 tablespoon vegetable oil
½ cup diced onion
½ teaspoon LAWRY'S® Garlic Powder with Parsley
1 package (1.0 ounce) LAWRY'S® Taco Spices & Seasonings
1 can (28 ounces) diced tomatoes, undrained
1 can (15 ounces) pinto beans, drained
1 can (8¾ ounces) whole kernel corn, drained

1 can (4 ounces) diced green chiles, drained
1 cup beef broth
½ teaspoon cornstarch
1 pound pork butt or beef chuck, cooked and shredded
Dairy sour cream (garnish)
Tortilla chips (garnish)
Fresh cilantro (garnish)

In Dutch oven or large saucepan, heat oil. Add onion and Garlic Powder with Parsley and cook over medium-high heat 2 to 3 minutes until onion is tender. Add Taco Spices & Seasonings, tomatoes, beans, corn and chiles; mix well. In small bowl, gradually combine broth and cornstarch using wire whisk. Stir into stew. Add cooked meat. Bring to a boil over medium-high heat, stirring frequently. Reduce heat to low; cook, uncovered, 30 minutes, stirring occasionally. (Or, cook over low heat longer for a thicker stew.)

Serving Suggestion: *Garnish each serving with sour cream, tortilla chips and fresh cilantro, if desired.*

Hint: *Substitute 3 cups cooked, shredded chicken for pork or beef.*

Chunky Garden Stew

Makes 5 to 6 servings

Spicy Hot Sauce (recipe
  follows)
1 tablespoon olive or canola oil
3 medium Colorado Sangre red
  potatoes, cut into chunks
1 large carrot, sliced diagonally
1 medium onion, quartered
1 large yellow squash or
  zucchini, sliced
1 Japanese eggplant *or*
  ½ regular eggplant, cut into
  cubes
2 stalks celery, sliced
1 small red or green bell
  pepper, cut into chunks

1 teaspoon ground cinnamon
1 teaspoon coriander
1 teaspoon turmeric
½ teaspoon ground cumin
½ teaspoon ground cardamom
½ teaspoon salt
2 cans (14½ ounces each)
  vegetable broth
1 can (15 ounces) chick-peas,
  drained
⅔ cup raisins
6 cups hot cooked rice

Prepare Spicy Hot Sauce; set aside. Heat oil in Dutch oven over
medium-high heat. Add potatoes and carrot; cook and stir
5 minutes. Add onion, squash, eggplant, celery, bell pepper, spices
and salt; cook and stir 3 to 5 minutes. Add broth, chick-peas and
raisins; bring to a simmer. Simmer, covered, about 15 minutes or
until potatoes are tender. Serve vegetable stew over rice. Serve
with Spicy Hot Sauce.

Spicy Hot Sauce

⅓ cup chopped fresh cilantro
¼ cup water
1 tablespoon olive or canola oil
2 cloves garlic
½ teaspoon salt
½ teaspoon turmeric

¼ to ½ teaspoon ground red
   pepper
¼ teaspoon sugar
¼ teaspoon ground cumin
¼ teaspoon ground cardamom
¼ teaspoon ground coriander

Combine all ingredients in blender; process until smooth. Adjust flavors to taste.

Makes about ½ cup sauce

Favorite recipe from **Colorado Potato Administrative Committee**

Shrimp Creole Stew

1½ cups raw small shrimp,
   shelled
1 bag (16 ounces) BIRDS EYE®
   frozen Farm Fresh Mixtures
   Broccoli, Cauliflower & Red
   Peppers

1 can (14½ ounces) diced
   tomatoes
1½ teaspoons salt
1 teaspoon hot pepper sauce
1 teaspoon vegetable oil

Makes 4 servings

Prep Time:
5 minutes

Cook Time:
20 minutes

• In large saucepan, combine all ingredients.

• Cover; bring to a boil. Reduce heat to medium-low; simmer 20 minutes or until shrimp turn opaque.

Serving Suggestion: *Serve over Spanish or white rice and with additional hot pepper sauce for added zip.*

Carefree Golden Oven Stew

Makes 4 servings

4 small chicken breast halves, skinned
1 lemon, halved
½ teaspoon salt
Dash black pepper
1 Washington Golden Delicious apple, sliced
1 small onion, sliced lengthwise

1 cup mushrooms, halved
½ cup sliced carrots
⅔ cup chicken broth
¼ cup white wine
1 teaspoon dried tarragon leaves, crushed
1 teaspoon chopped fresh parsley

Note:

Store carrots in a plastic bag in the refrigerator's vegetable drawer. Avoid storing carrots with apples, pears or other fruits that produce ethylene gas when ripening, as this gas can give carrots a bitter taste.

Rub chicken with lemon and let stand 15 minutes. Sprinkle with salt and pepper. Place chicken breasts in 2-quart baking dish. Add apple, onion, mushrooms and carrots. In separate bowl combine chicken broth, wine and tarragon; pour over chicken mixture. Sprinkle with parsley. Bake, covered, at 350°F about 1 hour or until chicken is tender.

Favorite recipe from **Washington Apple Commission**

Spicy Zucchini-Pepper Stew

2 tablespoons olive oil
1 large onion, chopped
3 cloves garlic, chopped
1 to 2 teaspoons minced
    seeded jalapeño pepper*
2 jars (12 ounces each) roasted
    red peppers, drained
2 large tomatoes, diced
2 cups thinly sliced zucchini
    Grated peel of 1 lemon
1 teaspoon dried oregano
    leaves
1 teaspoon dried thyme leaves

½ teaspoon salt
¼ to ½ teaspoon saffron,
    crushed
    Black pepper to taste
2½ cups chicken broth or water
2 tablespoons water
3 tablespoons cornstarch
    Hot cooked rice

*Jalapeño peppers can sting and irritate the skin; wear rubber gloves when handling peppers and do not touch eyes. Wash hands after handling.

Heat oil in 5-quart Dutch oven over medium-high heat. Cook and stir onion, garlic and jalapeño until onion is soft. Add red peppers, tomatoes, zucchini, lemon peel, oregano, thyme, salt, saffron and black pepper. Cook and stir 5 minutes; add broth. Bring to a boil over high heat. Reduce heat to low. Cover and simmer 35 minutes.

Blend water into cornstarch in small cup until smooth. Stir into stew. Cook and stir until stew boils and sauce is slightly thickened. Serve over rice.

Sweet Potato Cranberry Stew

Makes 4 servings

2 teaspoons vegetable oil
1 pound lean pork, cut into
    1-inch strips
1 tablespoon brown sugar
2 sweet potatoes, peeled and
    cut into chunks

½ teaspoon ground allspice
¼ teaspoon black pepper
¾ cup canned chicken broth*
2 cups fresh cranberries

*One bouillon cube dissolved in ¾ cup water
can be substituted for canned chicken broth.*

Heat oil in medium saucepan over medium heat until hot. Add
pork and sugar. Cook and stir 10 minutes or until lightly browned.
Remove pork and set aside. Add sweet potatoes, allspice, pepper
and broth. Simmer, covered, over low heat 15 minutes. Add
cranberries and pork; simmer, covered, 15 minutes or until pork
is tender.

Favorite recipe from **The Sugar Association, Inc.**

Hearty Ground Beef Stew

Makes 6 servings

Prep Time:
5 minutes

Cook Time:
15 minutes

1 pound ground beef
3 cloves garlic, minced
1 package (16 ounces) Italian-
    style frozen vegetables
2 cups southern-style hash
    brown potatoes

1 jar (14 ounces) marinara
    sauce
1 can (10½ ounces) condensed
    beef broth
3 tablespoons *French's®*
    Worcestershire Sauce

1. Brown beef with garlic in large saucepan; drain. Add
remaining ingredients. Heat to boiling. Cover. Reduce heat to
medium-low. Cook 10 minutes or until vegetables are crisp-
tender.

2. Serve in warm bowls with garlic bread, if desired.

Oven-Baked Stew

Makes 8 servings

2 pounds boneless beef chuck
   or round steak, cut into
   1-inch cubes
¼ cup all-purpose flour
1⅓ cups sliced carrots
1 can (14 to 16 ounces) whole
   peeled tomatoes, undrained
   and chopped
1 envelope LIPTON® RECIPE
   SECRETS® Onion Soup
   Mix*

½ cup dry red wine or water
1 cup fresh or canned sliced
   mushrooms
1 package (8 ounces) medium
   or broad egg noodles,
   cooked and drained

*Also terrific with LIPTON® RECIPE SECRETS®
Beefy Onion, Onion-Mushroom or Beefy
Mushroom Soup Mix.

Prep Time:
15 minutes

Cook Time:
2 hours

1. Preheat oven to 425°F. In 2½-quart shallow casserole, toss beef with flour, then bake uncovered 20 minutes, stirring once.

2. *Reduce heat to 350°F.* Stir in carrots, tomatoes, soup mix and wine.

3. Bake covered 1½ hours or until beef is tender. Stir in mushrooms and bake covered an additional 10 minutes. Serve over hot noodles.

Slow Cooker Method: *Toss beef with flour and place in slow cooker. Add carrots, tomatoes, soup mix and wine. Cover. Cook on LOW 8 hours. Add mushrooms; cover and cook 30 minutes or until beef is tender. Serve over hot noodles.*

Moroccan Bean Stew

Makes 6 to 8 servings

1 pound baby lima beans,
  soaked overnight in
  2 quarts water (*or* boil
  2 minutes and allow to
  stand 1 hour)
2 cups orange juice
2 cups water
1 pound hot Italian sausage or
  spicy turkey sausage,
  cooked, drained and cut
  into ½-inch pieces

1 large onion, chopped
3 tablespoons dried fines
  herbes
4 chicken or beef bouillon
  cubes
1 tablespoon ground cinnamon
1 (10-ounce) package frozen
  peas, thawed
2 cups (8 ounces) shredded
  JARLSBERG LITE™ cheese

Note:

There are two distinct
varieties of lima beans.
Fordhooks are large,
slightly plump, pale
green beans with a full
flavor. Baby limas,
which are not
immature Fordhooks,
but a separate variety,
are half the size of
Fordhooks and
less plump.

Drain beans; cover with orange juice and water. Add sausage, onion, fines herbes, bouillon and cinnamon. Cover and simmer, stirring occasionally, 45 minutes or until beans are tender. (Recipe can be made ahead to this point and refrigerated.)

Bring to room temperature, if necessary. Heat gently to simmering. Remove from heat, stir in peas and cheese. Serve on white, wild, yellow or saffron rice with crisp green salad.

Sweet 'n' Sour Turkey Meatball Stew

Makes 6 servings

2 pounds ground turkey
¾ cup dry bread crumbs
½ cup chopped onion
⅓ cup chopped water chestnuts
1 clove garlic, minced
1 egg
½ teaspoon salt
½ teaspoon ground ginger
¼ teaspoon black pepper
4 tablespoons reduced-sodium soy sauce, divided
2 tablespoons vegetable oil
2 cups water

¼ cup apple cider vinegar
¼ cup sugar
1 can (20 ounces) pineapple chunks in juice, drained and juice reserved
1 medium green bell pepper, cut into ½-inch pieces
1 medium red bell pepper, cut into ½-inch pieces
Peel from 1 lemon, coarsely chopped
2 tablespoons cornstarch
Hot cooked rice (optional)

Combine turkey, bread crumbs, onion, water chestnuts, garlic, egg, salt, ginger, black pepper and 1 tablespoon soy sauce in large bowl; mix well. Shape into meatballs.*

Heat oil in 5-quart Dutch oven over medium heat. Brown meatballs in hot oil. Remove with slotted spoon. Discard fat. Combine water, vinegar, sugar and reserved pineapple juice in Dutch oven. Return meatballs to Dutch oven.

Bring to a boil over high heat. Reduce heat to low. Cover and simmer 20 to 25 minutes. Stir in pineapple, bell peppers and lemon peel. Simmer, uncovered, 5 minutes.

Blend remaining 3 tablespoons soy sauce into cornstarch in small bowl until smooth. Bring meatballs to a boil over medium-high heat; stir in cornstarch mixture. Cook 5 minutes or until mixture thickens, stirring constantly. Serve over rice, if desired.

*To quickly shape uniform meatballs, place meat mixture on cutting board; pat evenly into large square, 1 inch thick. With sharp knife, cut meat into 1-inch squares; shape each square into a ball.

Cordero Stew with Cornmeal Dumplings

Makes 6 servings

2 pounds lean lamb stew meat with bones, cut into 2-inch pieces *or* 1½ pounds lean boneless lamb, cut into 1½-inch cubes
1 teaspoon salt
½ teaspoon black pepper
2½ tablespoons vegetable oil, divided
1 large onion, chopped
1 clove garlic, minced
2 tablespoons tomato paste
2 teaspoons chili powder
1 teaspoon ground coriander
4 cups water

3 small potatoes, cut into 1½-inch chunks
2 large carrots, cut into 1-inch pieces
1 package (10 ounces) frozen corn
⅓ cup coarsely chopped celery leaves
½ cup all-purpose flour
½ cup yellow cornmeal
1 teaspoon baking powder
¼ teaspoon salt
2½ tablespoons cold butter or margarine
½ cup milk

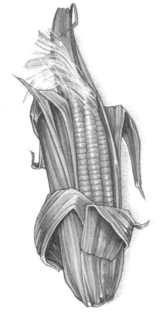

For stew, sprinkle meat with salt and pepper. Heat 2 tablespoons oil in 5-quart Dutch oven over medium-high heat. Add meat, a few pieces at a time, and cook until browned on all sides. Transfer meat to medium bowl. Heat remaining ½ tablespoon oil over medium heat in same Dutch oven. Add onion and garlic; cook until onion is tender. Stir in tomato paste, chili powder, coriander and water. Return meat to Dutch oven. Add potatoes, carrots, corn and chopped celery leaves. Bring to a boil. Cover; reduce heat and simmer 1 hour 15 minutes or until meat is tender.

During last 15 minutes of cooking, prepare cornmeal dumplings. Combine flour, cornmeal, baking powder and salt in medium bowl. Cut in butter with fingers, pastry blender or two knives until mixture resembles coarse crumbs. Make well in center; add milk all at once and stir with fork until mixture forms dough.

Drop dough onto stew, making six dumplings. Cover and simmer an additional 18 minutes or until dumplings are firm to the touch and wooden toothpick inserted in centers comes out clean.

Chicken Chick-Pea Stew

2 cloves garlic, minced
2 teaspoons vegetable oil
1 pound boneless skinless
    chicken breasts, cut into
    strips
1 onion, chopped
2 (15-ounce) cans chick-peas,
    drained
1 cup chicken stock *or*
    1 chicken bouillon cube
    dissolved in 1 cup water

2 tablespoons lemon juice
2 teaspoons sugar
1 teaspoon black pepper
¾ teaspoon dried tarragon
    leaves
2 tablespoons cornstarch
    (optional)
3 tablespoons water (optional)
2 cups fresh spinach torn into
    small pieces

**Makes 4 servings
(6 cups)**

In medium saucepan, cook and stir garlic in oil until brown. Add chicken and onion; cook 5 minutes. Add chick-peas, chicken stock, lemon juice, sugar, black pepper and tarragon. Simmer covered for 30 minutes over low heat. If stew is not thick enough, mix cornstarch with 3 tablespoons cold water until smooth. Add to stew and bring to a boil. Add spinach and cook 5 minutes over low heat.

Favorite recipe from **The Sugar Association, Inc.**

Black Bean & Pork Stew

Makes 8 servings

Note:

Oranges store well and can be purchased in large quantities according to need. One medium orange yields ⅓ to ½ cup juice. The rind of 1 medium orange yields 1 to 2 tablespoons grated peel.

2 (15-ounce) cans cooked black beans, rinsed and drained
2 cups water
1 pound boneless ham, cut into ¾-inch cubes
¾ pound BOB EVANS® Italian Dinner Link Sausage, cut into 1-inch pieces
¾ pound BOB EVANS® Smoked Sausage, cut into 1-inch pieces

1 pint cherry tomatoes, stems removed
1 medium onion, chopped
1 teaspoon red pepper flakes
6 cloves garlic, minced
⅛ teaspoon grated orange peel
Cornbread or rolls (optional)

Preheat oven to 350°F. Combine all ingredients except cornbread in large Dutch oven. Bring to a boil over high heat, skimming foam off if necessary. Cover; transfer to oven. Bake 30 minutes; uncover and bake 30 minutes more, stirring occasionally. Serve hot with cornbread, if desired, or cool slightly, then cover and refrigerate overnight. Remove any fat from surface. Reheat over low heat. Refrigerate leftovers.

Seafood Stew

2 tablespoons butter or
   margarine
1 cup chopped onion
1 cup green bell pepper strips
1 teaspoon dried dill weed
   Dash ground red pepper
1 can (14½ ounces) diced
   tomatoes, undrained
½ cup white wine
2 tablespoons lime juice
8 ounces swordfish steak, cut
   into 1-inch cubes

8 ounces bay or sea scallops,
   cut into quarters
1 bottle (8 ounces) clam juice
2 tablespoons cornstarch
2 cups frozen diced potatoes,
   thawed and drained
8 ounces frozen cooked
   medium shrimp, thawed
   and drained
½ cup whipping cream

Makes 6 servings

Prep and Cook Time:
20 minutes

1. Melt butter in Dutch oven over medium-high heat. Add onion, bell pepper, dill weed and red pepper; cook and stir 5 minutes or until vegetables are tender.

2. Reduce heat to medium. Add tomatoes with juice, wine and lime juice; bring to a boil. Add swordfish and scallops; cook and stir 2 minutes.

3. Combine clam juice and cornstarch in small bowl; stir until smooth.

4. Increase heat to high. Add potatoes, shrimp, whipping cream and clam juice mixture; bring to a boil. Season to taste with salt and black pepper.

<u>Serving Suggestion:</u> *For a special touch, garnish stew with fresh lemon wedges and basil leaves.*

Stick-to-Your-Ribs Hearty Beef Stew

Makes 6 to 8 servings

1½ pounds lean beef stew meat, cut into bite-size pieces
¼ cup all-purpose flour
½ teaspoon seasoned salt
⅓ cup WESSON® Vegetable Oil
2 medium onions, cut into 1-inch pieces
1 (14½-ounce) can beef broth
1 (8-ounce) can HUNT'S® Tomato Sauce
4 medium potatoes, peeled and cubed

5 stalks celery, cut into 1-inch pieces
6 carrots, peeled and cut into 1-inch pieces
1½ teaspoons salt
½ teaspoon Italian seasoning
½ teaspoon pepper
1 tablespoon cornstarch plus 2 tablespoons water

In a bag, toss beef with flour and seasoned salt until well coated. In a large Dutch oven, in hot Wesson® Oil, brown beef with onions until tender. Add *remaining* ingredients *except* cornstarch mixture; stir until well blended. Bring to a boil; reduce heat and simmer, covered, for 1 hour 15 minutes or until beef is tender. Stir cornstarch mixture; whisk into stew. Continue to cook an additional 10 minutes, stirring occasionally.

Zesty Lentil Stew

1 cup dried lentils
2 cups chopped peeled
   potatoes
1 can (14½ ounces) reduced-
   sodium chicken broth,
   defatted
1⅔ cups water
1½ cups chopped seeded
   tomatoes
1 can (11½ ounces) no-salt-
   added spicy vegetable juice
   cocktail
1 cup chopped onion
½ cup chopped carrot
½ cup chopped celery

2 tablespoons chopped fresh
   basil *or* 2 teaspoons dried
   basil leaves, crushed
2 tablespoons chopped fresh
   oregano *or* 2 teaspoons
   dried oregano leaves,
   crushed
1 to 2 tablespoons finely
   chopped jalapeño pepper*
¼ teaspoon salt

Jalapeño peppers can sting and irritate the skin; wear rubber gloves when handling peppers and do not touch eyes. Wash hands after handling.

Rinse lentils under cold water; drain. Combine lentils, potatoes, broth, water, tomatoes, vegetable juice cocktail, onion, carrot, celery, basil, oregano, jalapeño pepper and salt in 3-quart saucepan.

Bring to a boil over high heat. Reduce heat to medium-low. Cover; simmer 45 to 50 minutes or until lentils are tender, stirring occasionally.

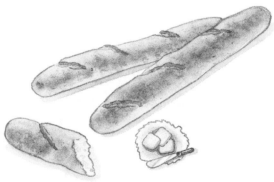

Hungarian Beef Stew

Makes 6 to 8 servings

¼ cup vegetable oil
1 medium onion, chopped
1 cup sliced mushrooms
2 teaspoons paprika
1 boneless beef sirloin steak,
    ½ inch thick, trimmed, cut
    into ½-inch pieces (about
    2 pounds)
½ cup beef broth

½ teaspoon caraway seeds
    Salt and black pepper to taste
2 tablespoons all-purpose flour
1 cup sour cream
    Hot buttered noodles
    (optional)
    Chopped fresh parsley for
    garnish

Note:

When purchasing fresh
mushrooms, choose
those that are firm and
evenly colored with
tightly closed caps.
Avoid ones that are
slimy or have any
soft dark spots.

Heat oil in 5-quart Dutch oven over medium-high heat. Cook and
stir onion and mushrooms in oil until onion is soft. Stir in paprika.
Remove with slotted spoon; set aside.

Brown half of beef in Dutch oven over medium-high heat. Remove
with slotted spoon; set aside. Brown remaining beef. Pour off
drippings. Return beef, onion and mushrooms to Dutch oven. Stir
in broth, caraway seeds, salt and pepper. Bring to a boil over high
heat. Reduce heat to low. Cover and simmer 45 minutes or until
beef is fork-tender.

Whisk flour into sour cream in small bowl. Whisk into stew. Stir
until slightly thickened. Do not boil. Serve over noodles. Garnish
with parsley.

Hot & Hearty
Soups

CHAPTER ELEVEN

Hoppin' John Soup

Makes 6 servings

Prep Time:
15 minutes

Cook Time:
20 minutes

4 strips uncooked bacon, chopped
1 large onion, chopped
2 cloves garlic, minced
2 cans (15 ounces each) black-eye peas, undrained
1 can (14½ ounces) reduced-sodium chicken broth
3 to 4 tablespoons *Frank's® RedHot®* Cayenne Pepper Sauce
1 teaspoon dried thyme leaves
1 bay leaf
2 cups cooked long grain rice (¾ cup uncooked rice)
2 tablespoons minced fresh parsley

1. Cook bacon, onion and garlic in large saucepan over medium-high heat 5 minutes or until vegetables are tender.

2. Add peas with liquid, broth, *½ cup water*, *Frank's RedHot* Sauce, thyme and bay leaf. Bring to a boil. Reduce heat to low; cook, covered, 15 minutes, stirring occasionally. Remove and discard bay leaf.

3. Combine rice and parsley in medium bowl. Spoon rice evenly into 6 serving bowls. Ladle soup over rice.

<u>Hint:</u> *For an attractive presentation, pack rice mixture into small ramekin dishes. Unmold into soup bowls. Ladle soup around rice.*

Harvest Soup

½ pound BOB EVANS® Special
   Seasonings Roll Sausage
1 large onion, finely chopped
2½ cups chicken broth
2 cups canned pumpkin
2 cups hot milk

1 teaspoon lemon juice
Dash ground nutmeg
Dash ground cinnamon
Salt and black pepper to taste
Chopped fresh parsley

Makes 6 to 8 servings

Crumble and cook sausage and onion in large saucepan until sausage is browned. Drain off any drippings. Add broth and bring to a boil. Stir in pumpkin; cover and simmer over low heat 15 to 20 minutes. Add milk, lemon juice, nutmeg, cinnamon, salt and pepper; simmer, uncovered, 5 minutes to blend flavors. Sprinkle with parsley before serving. Refrigerate leftovers.

Note:

Cinnamon comes from the dried bark of various laurel trees. The outer bark is peeled away, then the inner bark is rolled, pressed and dried.

Ground Beef, Spinach and Barley Soup

Makes 4 servings

12 ounces 95% lean ground beef
4 cups water
1 can (14½ ounces) no-salt-
    added stewed tomatoes,
    undrained
1½ cups thinly sliced carrots
1 cup chopped onion
½ cup quick-cooking barley
1½ teaspoons beef bouillon
    granules

1½ teaspoons dried thyme
    leaves, crushed
1 teaspoon dried oregano
    leaves, crushed
½ teaspoon garlic powder
¼ teaspoon black pepper
⅛ teaspoon salt
3 cups torn stemmed washed
    spinach leaves

Cook beef in large saucepan over medium heat until no longer pink, stirring to separate meat. Rinse beef under warm water; drain. Return beef to saucepan; add water, stewed tomatoes with juice, carrots, onion, barley, bouillon granules, thyme, oregano, garlic powder, pepper and salt.

Bring to a boil over high heat. Reduce heat to medium-low. Cover and simmer 12 to 15 minutes or until barley and vegetables are tender, stirring occasionally. Stir in spinach; cook until spinach starts to wilt.

Country Cream of Chicken Chowder

¼ cup CRISCO® Oil*
¼ cup finely chopped onion
¼ cup all-purpose flour
4 cups chicken broth
2 cups skim milk
1 bay leaf
3 cups frozen hash brown potatoes
1 package (10 ounces) frozen whole kernel corn
1 package (10 ounces) frozen cut green beans
1 package (10 ounces) frozen peas
1 package (10 ounces) frozen sliced carrots
1½ cups finely chopped cooked chicken
⅛ teaspoon pepper
2 tablespoons chopped fresh parsley *or* chives

Use your favorite Crisco Oil product.

Makes 10 servings

1. Heat oil in large saucepan on medium heat. Add onion. Cook and stir until tender. Stir in flour. Cook until bubbly. Stir in broth and milk gradually. Cook and stir until mixture is bubbly and slightly thickened. Add bay leaf.

2. Add potatoes, corn, beans, peas and carrots. Increase heat to medium-high. Bring mixture back to a boil. Reduce heat to low. Simmer 5 minutes or until beans are tender. Stir in chicken and pepper. Heat thoroughly. Remove bay leaf. Serve sprinkled with parsley.

Roasted Vegetable Soup

Makes 4 servings

Prep Time:
15 minutes

Cook Time:
25 minutes

Note:

To meet kosher standards and receive the kosher seal, commercial foods must be prepared under a rabbi's supervision. Kosher products are often marked by a K alone or a U or K in a circle. Kosher foods are available in most supermarkets.

2 baby eggplants (8 ounces), peeled and chopped
2 small zucchini, chopped
1 yellow squash, chopped
1 medium tomato, chopped
1 red bell pepper, seeded and chopped
1⅓ cups *French's®* French Fried Onions, divided
2 tablespoons olive oil

2 teaspoons minced garlic
1 teaspoon kosher salt or ½ teaspoon regular salt
3 cups chicken or vegetable broth
½ teaspoon dried thyme leaves
Garnish: heavy cream, zucchini and red bell pepper strips (optional)

1. Preheat oven to 400°F. Place vegetables in shallow roasting pan; toss with ⅔ *cup* French Fried Onions, oil, garlic and salt. Bake 20 minutes or until tender.

2. Place vegetables in food processor. Cover and process until smooth. Transfer to 2-quart saucepan. Stir in broth and thyme; heat through.

3. Spoon into serving bowls. If desired, swirl heavy cream into soup and garnish with vegetable strips. Serve with remaining onions.

Hodgepodge Gumbo

Makes 6 to 8 servings

2 to 3 pounds medium shrimp, uncleaned
½ pound bacon
4 cups diced fresh okra
2 onions, diced
½ cup chopped celery
½ cup chopped green bell pepper
⅓ cup all-purpose flour
1 can (6 ounces) tomato paste
1 teaspoon LAWRY'S® Garlic Powder with Parsley

2 pounds chicken wings
½ pound kielbasa sausage, sliced
1½ pounds crab, cleaned (optional)
2½ teaspoons LAWRY'S® Seasoned Salt
1 teaspoon LAWRY'S® Seasoned Pepper
Crushed red pepper to taste

Place shrimp in 2 quarts cold water; bring to a boil over medium-high heat. Remove and discard shells reserving water. In large skillet, cook bacon; drain, reserving ¼ cup grease in skillet. Add okra, onions, celery and bell pepper and cook over medium-high heat until tender; remove and set aside. In same skillet, combine flour and tomato paste; cook and stir until browned. Add Garlic Powder with Parsley while browning. Smooth out with 1 cup reserved shrimp water if necessary. In Dutch oven, combine bacon, vegetables, tomato paste mixture, remaining reserved shrimp water, chicken, sausage, crab, Seasoned Salt, Seasoned Pepper and red pepper. Bring to a boil over medium-high heat; reduce heat to low; cover and simmer 2 hours. Add shrimp; simmer 10 minutes.

<u>Serving Suggestion:</u> *Serve with hot white rice.*

Meatball & Pasta Soup

Makes 8 servings

Prep Time:
10 minutes

Cook Time:
15 minutes

2 cans (14½ ounces each) chicken broth
4 cups water
1 can (15 ounces) crushed tomatoes
1 package (15 ounces) frozen precooked Italian style meatballs, not in sauce

1 envelope LIPTON® RECIPE SECRETS® Onion Soup Mix
½ teaspoon garlic powder
1 cup uncooked mini pasta (such as conchigliette or ditalini)
4 cups fresh baby spinach leaves

1. In 6-quart saucepot, bring broth, water, crushed tomatoes, meatballs, soup mix and garlic powder to a boil over medium-high heat.

2. Add pasta and cook 5 minutes or until pasta is almost tender. Stir in spinach. Reduce heat to medium and simmer uncovered 2 minutes or until spinach is wilted and pasta is tender. Serve, if desired, with Parmesan cheese.

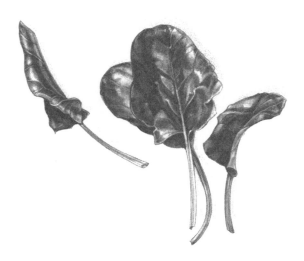

Native American Wild Rice Soup

Makes 12 servings

2 cups water
½ cup wild rice, uncooked, rinsed in cold water and drained
½ cup (1 stick) butter
1½ cups diced onions
8 ounces fresh button mushrooms, sliced
2 teaspoons fresh rosemary, stemmed, minced *or* ¾ teaspoon dried rosemary, crumbled

¾ cup flour
8 cups chicken broth
1 teaspoon salt
½ teaspoon freshly ground black pepper
1 cup whipping cream
2 tablespoons sherry or dry white wine

Place water in medium saucepan. Add wild rice and bring to a boil over medium heat. Reduce heat to low, cover and simmer about 45 minutes. Do not drain; set aside. Melt butter in 5-quart Dutch oven over medium heat. Add onions and mushrooms. Sauté about 3 minutes, until vegetables soften; add rosemary. Add flour gradually to mushroom mixture, cooking and stirring frequently over medium-high heat, until mixture boils. Add chicken broth; bring to a boil. Cook 1 minute; stir in reserved wild rice and any remaining liquid, salt and pepper. Stir in whipping cream and sherry; do not boil. Serve immediately.

Favorite recipe from **Wisconsin Milk Marketing Board**

Rosarita Refried Soup

Makes 12 (1-cup) servings

PAM® No-Stick Cooking Spray
1 cup diced onion
1 can (16 ounces) ROSARITA®
   Traditional No-Fat Refried
   Beans
6 cups fat free, low sodium
   chicken broth

1 can (14.5-ounce) HUNT'S®
   Diced Tomatoes in Juice
4 cups baked tortilla chips
½ cup shredded reduced fat
   Monterey Jack cheese
¼ cup chopped fresh cilantro

1. Spray a large saucepan with PAM® Cooking Spray. Sauté onion over low heat for 5 minutes.

2. Add Rosarita® Beans, broth and Hunt's® Tomatoes; mix well. Cook until heated through.

3. Place ½ *cup* tortilla chips in *each* bowl. Ladle soup into bowls. Garnish with cheese and cilantro.

Patrick's Irish Lamb Soup

1 tablespoon olive oil
1 medium onion, coarsely
    chopped
1½ pounds fresh lean American
    lamb boneless shoulder, cut
    into ¾-inch cubes
1 bottle (12 ounces) beer *or*
    ¾ cup water
1 teaspoon seasoned pepper

2 cans (14½ ounces each) beef
    broth
1 package (.93 ounce) brown
    gravy mix
3 cups cubed potatoes
2 cups thinly sliced carrots
2 cups shredded green cabbage
⅓ cup chopped fresh parsley
    (optional)

In 3-quart saucepan with cover, heat oil. Add onion and sauté until brown, stirring occasionally. Add lamb and sauté, stirring until browned. Stir in beer and pepper. Cover and simmer 30 minutes.

Mix in broth and gravy mix. Add potatoes and carrots; cover and simmer 15 to 20 minutes or until vegetables are tender. Stir in cabbage and cook just until cabbage turns bright green. Garnish with chopped parsley, if desired.

Favorite recipe from **American Lamb Council**

Note:

Beer is a low-alcohol beverage made by malting cereals (principally barley), adding flavor with hops and then fermenting the mixture. Yeast is added to start the fermentation process, which results in alcohol and carbon dioxide.

Ravioli Soup

Makes 4 servings

Prep and Cook Time:
15 minutes

1 package (9 ounces) fresh or frozen cheese ravioli or tortellini
¾ pound hot Italian sausage, crumbled
1 can (14½ ounces) DEL MONTE® Stewed Tomatoes - Italian Recipe

1 can (14½ ounces) beef broth
1 can (14½ ounces) DEL MONTE Italian Beans, drained
2 green onions, sliced

1. Cook pasta according to package directions; drain.

2. Meanwhile, cook sausage in 5-quart pot over medium-high heat until no longer pink; drain. Add undrained tomatoes, broth and 1¾ cups water; bring to a boil.

3. Reduce heat to low; stir in pasta, green beans and green onions. Simmer until heated through. Season with pepper and sprinkle with grated Parmesan cheese, if desired.

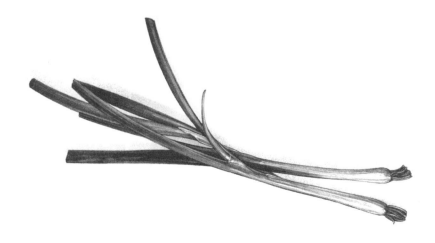

Cheddar Potato Chowder

Makes 4 servings

3 tablespoons margarine or
   butter
2 medium-size carrots, peeled
   and diced
2 medium-size ribs celery,
   thinly sliced
1 small onion, chopped
3 tablespoons all-purpose flour
¼ teaspoon dry mustard
¼ teaspoon paprika
¼ teaspoon ground pepper
2 cups milk

2 cups water
4 medium-size Idaho Potatoes
   (about 1¾ pounds), peeled
   and cut into ½-inch cubes
2 chicken-flavor bouillon cubes
   or envelopes
1½ cups shredded Cheddar
   cheese
4 slices bacon, cooked and
   crumbled (optional)
Chopped chives (optional)

In 3-quart saucepan over medium heat, melt margarine. Add carrots, celery and onion; cook until tender, about 10 minutes, stirring occasionally. Stir in flour, dry mustard, paprika and pepper; cook 1 minute.

Gradually add milk, water, potatoes and bouillon. Bring to a boil over high heat; reduce heat to low. Cover and simmer 10 minutes or until potatoes are tender.

Remove saucepan from heat; add cheese and stir just until melted. Top each serving with crumbled bacon and chopped chives, if desired.

Favorite recipe from **Idaho Potato Commission**

Shanghai Meatball Soup

Makes about 6 (1-cup) servings

Note:

Fresh ginger, also called gingerroot, is completely different from dry ground ginger. Buy it in small quantities and store it, unpeeled, tightly wrapped in the refrigerator for up to two weeks. To mince fresh ginger, cut a small chunk, peel the rough outer skin and put through a garlic press.

1 pound ground turkey
¾ cup QUAKER® Oats (quick or old fashioned, uncooked)
2 tablespoons lite soy sauce
1 tablespoon dry sherry (optional)
2 teaspoons sesame oil (optional)
1½ teaspoons minced fresh ginger
½ teaspoon black pepper

2 cans (14½ ounces each) reduced-salt chicken broth, divided
1 cup water
1½ cups halved pea pods or 1 (6-ounce) package frozen pea pods, thawed, cut in half
1 cup thinly sliced carrot strips
1½ cups bean sprouts
¼ cup thinly sliced green onions

Spray rack of broiler pan with no-stick cooking spray or oil lightly. Combine first seven ingredients and ¼ cup chicken broth; mix well. Shape into 1-inch meatballs; place on prepared rack. Broil 6 to 8 inches from heat 7 to 10 minutes or until cooked through. In 4-quart saucepan or Dutch oven, combine meatballs with water and remaining chicken broth; bring to a boil over high heat. Add pea pods and carrot strips; cook 1 to 2 minutes or until vegetables are crisp-tender. Turn off heat; add bean sprouts and green onions. Serve immediately.

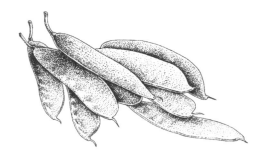

Hearty Mushroom Barley Soup

Nonstick cooking spray
1 teaspoon extra-virgin olive oil
2 cups chopped yellow onions
1 cup thinly sliced carrots
2 cans (about 14 ounces each) fat-free reduced-sodium chicken broth
1 can (10¾ ounces) 98% fat-free cream of mushroom soup
12 ounces sliced mushrooms

½ cup quick-cooking barley, uncooked
1 teaspoon reduced-sodium Worcestershire sauce
½ teaspoon dried thyme leaves
¼ cup finely chopped green onions
¼ teaspoon salt
¼ teaspoon black pepper

Makes 4 (1½-cup) servings

Heat Dutch oven or large saucepan over medium-high heat until hot. Coat with cooking spray. Add oil and tilt pan to coat bottom of pan. Add yellow onions; cook 8 minutes or until onions just begin to turn golden. Add carrots and cook 2 minutes.

Add chicken broth, cream of mushroom soup, mushrooms, barley, Worcestershire sauce and thyme; bring to a boil over high heat. Reduce heat to medium-low; cover and simmer 15 minutes, stirring occasionally. Stir in green onions, salt and pepper. Garnish as desired.

West Coast Bouillabaisse

Makes 6 servings

1 cup sliced onion
2 stalks celery, cut diagonally
    into slices
2 cloves garlic, minced
1 tablespoon vegetable oil
4 cups chicken broth
1 can (28 ounces) tomatoes
    with juice, cut up
1 can (6½ ounces) minced
    clams with juice
½ cup dry white wine
1 teaspoon Worcestershire
    sauce

½ teaspoon dried thyme,
    crushed
¼ teaspoon bottled hot pepper
    sauce
1 bay leaf
1 cup frozen cooked bay
    shrimp, thawed
1 (7-ounce) pouch of STARKIST®
    Premium Albacore or
    Chunk Light Tuna
  Salt and pepper to taste
6 slices lemon
6 slices French bread

In Dutch oven sauté onion, celery and garlic in oil for 3 minutes.
Stir in broth, tomatoes with juice, clams with juice, wine,
Worcestershire, thyme, hot pepper sauce and bay leaf. Bring to
a boil; reduce heat. Simmer for 15 minutes. Stir in shrimp and
tuna; cook for 2 minutes to heat. Remove bay leaf. Season with
salt and pepper. Garnish with lemon slices and serve with bread.

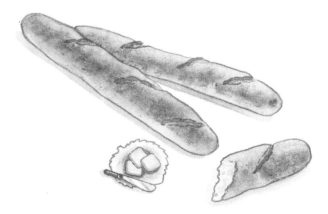

Minestrone

3 slices bacon, diced
½ cup chopped onion
1 large clove garlic, minced
2 cans (10½ ounces each) beef broth
1½ cups water
2 cans (15½ ounces each) Great Northern white beans, undrained
1 can (6 ounces) CONTADINA® Tomato Paste

1 teaspoon Italian herb seasoning
¼ teaspoon ground black pepper
2 medium zucchini, sliced
1 package (10 ounces) frozen mixed vegetables
½ cup elbow macaroni, uncooked
½ cup (2 ounces) grated Parmesan cheese (optional)

Makes 8 cups

Prep Time:
7 minutes

Cook Time:
28 minutes

1. Sauté bacon in large saucepan until crisp. Add onion and garlic; sauté until onion is tender.

2. Add broth, water, beans and liquid, tomato paste, Italian seasoning and pepper.

3. Reduce heat to low; simmer, uncovered, for 10 minutes. Add zucchini, mixed vegetables and macaroni. Return to a boil over high heat, stirring to break up vegetables.

4. Reduce heat to low; simmer for 8 to 10 minutes or until vegetables and macaroni are tender. Sprinkle with Parmesan cheese just before serving, if desired.

Tortilla Rice Soup

Makes 4 servings

Vegetable cooking spray
⅓ cup sliced green onions
4 cups chicken broth
2 cups cooked rice
1 can (10½ ounces) diced
    tomatoes with green chiles,
    undrained
1 cup cubed cooked chicken
    breast

1 can (4 ounces) chopped green
    chiles, undrained
1 tablespoon lime juice
    Salt to taste
    Tortilla chips
½ cup chopped tomato
½ avocado, cut into small cubes
4 lime slices for garnish
    Fresh cilantro for garnish

Note:

If you buy an avocado that is not fully ripe, put it in a brown paper bag and keep it at room temperature. It will soften within a day or two. When you are ready to eat it, cut it with a stainless steel knife and sprinkle it with lemon or lime juice to prevent it from discoloring.

Heat Dutch oven or large saucepan coated with cooking spray over medium-high heat until hot. Add onions; cook and stir until tender. Add broth, rice, tomatoes with juice, chicken and chiles with juice. Reduce heat to low; cover and simmer 20 minutes. Stir in lime juice and salt. Just before serving, pour into soup bowls; top with tortilla chips, chopped tomato and avocado. Garnish with lime slices and cilantro.

Favorite recipe from **USA Rice Federation**

Louisiana Shrimp and Chicken Gumbo

3 tablespoons vegetable oil
¼ cup flour
2 medium onions, chopped
1 cup chopped celery
1 large green bell pepper, chopped
2 cloves garlic, minced
3 cups chicken broth
1 (16-ounce) can whole tomatoes in juice, undrained

1 (10-ounce) package frozen sliced okra
1 bay leaf
1 teaspoon TABASCO® brand Pepper Sauce
¾ pound shredded cooked chicken
½ pound raw shrimp, peeled, deveined
Hot cooked rice

Makes 6 servings

Heat oil in large saucepan or Dutch oven. Add flour and cook over low heat until mixture turns dark brown and develops a nutty aroma, stirring frequently. Add onions, celery, bell pepper and garlic; cook 5 minutes or until vegetables are tender. Gradually add chicken broth. Stir in tomatoes with juice, okra, bay leaf and TABASCO® Sauce; bring to a boil. Add chicken and shrimp; cook 3 to 5 minutes or until shrimp turn pink. Remove bay leaf. Serve with rice.

Vegetable Soup with Delicious Dumplings

Makes 10 servings

Soup
- 2 tablespoons WESSON® Vegetable Oil
- 1 cup diced onion
- ¾ cup sliced celery
- 7 cups homemade chicken broth *or* 4 (14.5-ounce) cans chicken broth
- 2 (14.5-ounce) cans HUNT'S® Stewed Tomatoes
- ½ teaspoon garlic powder
- ½ teaspoon salt
- ½ teaspoon fines herbs seasoning
- ⅛ teaspoon pepper
- 1 (16-ounce) bag frozen mixed vegetables
- 1 (15.5-ounce) can HUNT'S® Red Kidney Beans, drained
- ⅓ cup uncooked long-grain rice

Dumplings
- 2 cups all-purpose flour
- 3 tablespoons baking powder
- 1 teaspoon salt
- ⅔ cup milk
- ⅓ cup WESSON® Vegetable Oil
- 1½ teaspoons chopped fresh parsley

Soup

In a large Dutch oven, heat 2 tablespoons Wesson® Oil. Add onion and celery; sauté until crisp-tender. Stir in *next 6* ingredients, ending with pepper; bring to a boil. Add vegetables, beans and rice. Reduce heat; cover and simmer 15 to 20 minutes or until rice is cooked and vegetables are tender.

Dumplings

Meanwhile, in a medium bowl, combine flour, baking powder and salt; blend well. Add milk, ⅓ cup Wesson® Oil and parsley; mix until batter forms a ball in the bowl. Drop dough by rounded tablespoons into simmering soup. Cook, covered, 10 minutes; remove lid and cook an additional 10 minutes.

Mulligatawny Soup

Makes 6 servings

2 tablespoons butter or
    margarine
1½ cups chopped onions
1 (10-ounce) package frozen
    mixed vegetables, thawed
2 tablespoons flour
2 teaspoons curry powder
1 teaspoon salt

½ teaspoon TABASCO® brand
    Pepper Sauce
¼ teaspoon ground cloves
1 quart (4 cups) water
1 (10½-ounce) can condensed
    chicken with rice soup
1 cup diced cooked chicken
1 cup chopped pared apple

Melt butter in large soup pot over medium heat. Add onions and
mixed vegetables; cook and stir about 5 minutes or just until
onion is tender. Stir in flour, curry powder, salt, TABASCO® Sauce
and cloves. Add water, soup, chicken and apple. Heat to boiling;
reduce heat to low and simmer, covered, 20 minutes. Ladle into
serving bowls. Serve with additional TABASCO® Sauce, if desired.

Mushroom and Rice Soup

Makes 4 servings

1 bag SUCCESS® Rice
2 tablespoons olive oil
2 cups sliced fresh mushrooms
1 cup chopped onion
1 cup diagonally sliced green
    onions

5 cups chicken broth
1 teaspoon pepper
1 teaspoon dried thyme leaves,
    crushed
1 tablespoon dry sherry

Prepare rice according to package directions.

Heat oil in large saucepan or Dutch oven over medium heat. Add
mushrooms and onions; cook and stir until tender. Add broth,
pepper and thyme. Reduce heat to low; simmer until thoroughly
heated, 5 to 7 minutes. Stir in rice and sherry; heat thoroughly,
stirring occasionally. Garnish, if desired.

Chicken Gumbo

Makes 6 to 8 servings

Prep Time:
10 minutes

Cook Time:
1 hour

4 TYSON® Fresh Skinless
  Chicken Thighs
4 TYSON® Fresh Skinless
  Chicken Drumsticks
¼ cup all-purpose flour
2 teaspoons Cajun or Creole
  seasoning blend
2 tablespoons vegetable oil
1 large onion, chopped
1 cup thinly sliced celery

3 cloves garlic, minced
1 can (14½ ounces) stewed
  tomatoes, undrained
1 can (14½ ounces) chicken
  broth
1 large green bell pepper, cut
  into ½-inch pieces
½ to 1 teaspoon hot pepper
  sauce or to taste

PREP: CLEAN: Wash hands. Combine flour and Cajun seasoning blend in reclosable plastic bag. Add chicken, 2 pieces at a time; shake to coat. Reserve excess flour mixture. CLEAN: Wash hands.

COOK: In large saucepan, heat oil over medium heat. Add chicken and brown on all sides; remove and set aside. Sauté onion, celery and garlic 5 minutes. Add reserved flour mixture; cook 1 minute, stirring frequently. Add tomatoes, chicken broth, bell pepper and hot sauce. Bring to a boil. Return chicken to saucepan; cover and simmer over low heat, stirring occasionally, 30 minutes or until internal juices of chicken run clear. (Or insert instant-read meat thermometer into thickest part of chicken. Temperature should read 180°F.)

SERVE: Serve in shallow bowls, topped with hot cooked rice, if desired.

CHILL: Refrigerate leftovers immediately.

Corn, Bacon & Rice Chowder

Makes 4 servings

1 package (7.2 ounces) RICE-A-RONI® Rice Pilaf
2 tablespoons margarine or butter
1 can (13¾ ounces) reduced-sodium or regular chicken broth
1½ cups frozen corn *or* 1 can (16 or 17 ounces) whole kernel corn, drained

1 cup milk
1 cup water
½ cup sliced green onions
2 slices crisply cooked bacon, crumbled

1. In 3-quart saucepan, sauté rice-pasta mix in margarine over medium heat, stirring frequently until pasta is lightly browned.

2. Stir in chicken broth and Special Seasonings; bring to a boil over high heat.

3. Cover; reduce heat. Simmer 8 minutes.

4. Stir in corn, milk, water and onions. Simmer, uncovered, 10 to 12 minutes, stirring occasionally. Stir in bacon before serving.

Cioppino

Makes about 14 cups

Prep Time:
30 minutes

Cook Time:
35 minutes

2 tablespoons olive or
vegetable oil
1½ cups chopped onions
1 cup chopped celery
½ cup chopped green bell
pepper
1 large clove garlic, minced
1 can (28 ounces) CONTADINA®
Recipe Ready Crushed
Tomatoes
1 can (6 ounces) CONTADINA
Tomato Paste
1 teaspoon Italian herb
seasoning

1 teaspoon salt
½ teaspoon ground black
pepper
2 cups water
1 cup dry red wine or chicken
broth
3 pounds white fish, shrimp,
scallops, cooked crab,
cooked lobster, clams
and/or oysters (in any
proportion)

1. Heat oil in large saucepan. Add onions, celery, bell pepper and garlic; sauté until vegetables are tender. Add tomatoes, tomato paste, Italian seasoning, salt, black pepper, water and wine.

2. Bring to a boil. Reduce heat to low; simmer, uncovered, for 15 minutes.

3. To prepare fish and seafood: scrub clams and oysters under running water. Place in ½-inch boiling water in separate large saucepan; cover. Bring to a boil. Reduce heat to low; simmer just until shells open, about 3 minutes. Set aside.

4. Cut crab, lobster, fish and scallops into bite-size pieces.

5. Shell and devein shrimp. Add fish to tomato mixture; simmer 5 minutes. Add scallops and shrimp; simmer 5 minutes.

6. Add crab, lobster and reserved clams; simmer until heated through.

Navy Bean and Ham Soup

Makes 4 to 6 servings

1 bag (16 ounces) navy beans
1 tablespoon vegetable oil
½ cup chopped onion
½ cup chopped celery
1 pound ham, diced
2 cups water
1 can (14½ ounces) chicken
    broth

2 bay leaves
2½ teaspoons LAWRY'S®
    Seasoned Salt
2 teaspoons LAWRY'S® Garlic
    Powder with Parsley
¾ teaspoon LAWRY'S®
    Seasoned Pepper

Wash beans and soak overnight, or for at least 4 hours. Pour off water from beans and rinse thoroughly. In soup pot or Dutch oven, heat oil. Add onion and celery and cook over medium-high heat until just tender. To pot, add drained beans and remaining ingredients. Bring to a boil over medium-high heat; reduce heat to low, cover and simmer 1 hour.

Soup's On!

Soup is a liquid, usually hot, but sometimes cold, that has been cooked with added ingredients, such as meat and vegetables. Depending on the ingredients, it can be served as a main course or a first course.

Bisque: A thick, rich soup that usually consists of puréed shellfish, such as lobster, shrimp or crayfish. Bisques can also be made from vegetables. Cream is added to bisques to make them smooth and thick.

Broth: A thin, clear liquid made from boiling meat, poultry or vegetables in water. Broth is often the basis for soups and stews.

Chowder: A thick and chunky type of milk- or cream-based soup closely associated with New England.

Consommé: A clear soup made from meat or poultry stock. The stock may be cooked further to reduce and concentrate it. Then it is clarified and strained to remove any sediment.

Stock: The flavorful liquid that results from the long simmering of meat, poultry or fish and bones in water. Vegetables, herbs and spices also contribute to the flavor. Stock is the basis for sauces, soups and stews.

Zesty Chicken & Vegetable Soup

Makes 4 to 6 servings

Prep Time:
5 minutes

Cook Time:
about 8 minutes

½ pound boneless skinless chicken breasts, cut into very thin strips
1 to 2 tablespoons *Frank's® RedHot®* Cayenne Pepper Sauce
4 cups chicken broth

1 package (16 ounces) frozen stir-fry vegetables
1 cup angel hair pasta, broken into 2-inch lengths *or* fine egg noodles
1 green onion, thinly sliced

Note:

A good soup pot is one that is heavy and conducts and distributes heat evenly. Copper is the ideal metal, though its cost puts it out of range for most cooks. Good alternatives are Calphalon, aluminum, or stainless steel with a copper or aluminum core.

1. Combine chicken and *Frank's RedHot* Sauce in medium bowl; set aside.

2. Heat broth to boiling in large saucepan over medium-high heat. Add vegetables and pasta; return to boiling. Cook 2 minutes. Stir in chicken mixture and green onion. Cook 1 minute or until chicken is no longer pink.

Tip: *For a change of pace, substitute 6 prepared frozen pot stickers for the pasta. Add to broth in step 2 and boil until tender.*

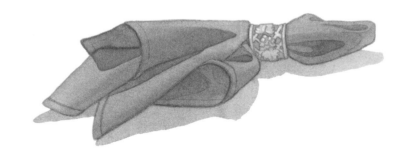

Creamy Crab Chowder

Makes 6 to 8 servings

1 tablespoon butter or
   margarine
1 cup finely chopped onion
2 cloves garlic, minced
1 cup finely chopped celery
½ cup finely chopped green bell
   pepper
½ cup finely chopped red bell
   pepper

3 cans (about 14 ounces each)
   chicken broth
3 cups diced peeled potatoes
1 package (10 ounces) frozen
   corn
2 cans (6½ ounces each) lump
   crabmeat
¼ teaspoon black pepper
½ cup half-and-half

Melt butter over medium heat in Dutch oven. Add onion and garlic. Cook and stir 6 minutes or until softened but not browned. Add celery and bell peppers. Cook 8 minutes or until celery is tender, stirring often.

Add broth and potatoes. Bring to a boil over high heat. Reduce heat to low and simmer 10 minutes. Add corn; cook 5 minutes or until potatoes are tender. Drain crabmeat and place in small bowl. Flake to break up large pieces. Add to Dutch oven. Stir in black pepper and half-and-half. Bring to a simmer. Do not boil. Serve hot.

Wisconsin Sausage Soup

Makes 8 to 10 servings

½ cup butter
1 onion, chopped
1 carrot, chopped
1 teaspoon minced garlic
1 cup all-purpose flour
2 cups chicken broth
2 cups milk
¾ cup beer
1 teaspoon Worcestershire sauce

½ teaspoon salt
½ teaspoon dry mustard
1 bay leaf
7 ounces Cheddar cheese, shredded
3 ounces Swiss cheese, shredded
½ pound HILLSHIRE FARM® Smoked Sausage

Melt butter in medium saucepan over medium heat. Add onion, carrot and garlic; sauté until softened. Add flour; cook 5 minutes, stirring often. Add chicken broth, milk, beer, Worcestershire sauce, salt, mustard and bay leaf. Reduce heat to low; cook until soup has thickened, whisking often.

Slowly whisk cheeses into soup until combined and smooth. Cut Smoked Sausage lengthwise into quarters, then slice into ½-inch pieces. Sauté sausage in small skillet over medium-high heat until heated through. Blot excess grease with paper towels; add sausage to soup. Serve soup hot.

Hearty Tortellini Soup

1 small red onion, chopped
2 medium carrots, chopped
2 ribs celery, thinly sliced
1 small zucchini, chopped
2 plum tomatoes, chopped
2 cloves garlic, minced
2 cans (14½ ounces each) chicken broth

1 can (15 to 19 ounces) red kidney beans, rinsed and drained
2 tablespoons *French's®* Worcestershire Sauce
1 package (9 ounces) refrigerated tortellini pasta

Makes 4 servings

Prep Time:
15 minutes

Cook Time:
10 minutes

1. Heat *2 tablespoons oil* in 6-quart saucepot or Dutch oven over medium-high heat. Add vegetables, tomatoes and garlic. Cook and stir 5 minutes or until vegetables are crisp-tender.

2. Add broth, *½ cup water,* beans and Worcestershire. Heat to boiling. Stir in pasta. Return to boiling. Cook 5 minutes or until pasta is tender, stirring occasionally. Serve with crusty bread and grated Parmesan cheese, if desired.

Mardi Gras Gumbo

Makes 4 servings

1 bag SUCCESS® Rice
1 can (14½ ounces) low-sodium
   chicken broth
1 can (10½ ounces) chicken
   gumbo soup

1 can (10½ ounces) condensed
   tomato soup
1 can (6 ounces) crabmeat,
   drained and flaked

Prepare rice according to package directions.

Combine remaining ingredients in medium saucepan. Bring to a boil over medium-high heat. Reduce heat to low. Stir in rice; heat thoroughly, stirring occasionally.

Mexican Fiesta Soup

Makes 8 (1½-cup) servings

3 cans (14½ ounces each)
   chicken broth
2 cups cubed cooked chicken
1 cup cubed peeled potatoes
1 cup chopped carrots
1 cup chopped onion
1 cup chopped celery
1 can (17 ounces) whole kernel
   corn, undrained
1 can (12 ounces) vegetable or
   tomato juice

1 cup tomato salsa
½ cup HOLLAND HOUSE®
   Vermouth Cooking Wine
1 can (4 ounces) chopped green
   chilies, undrained
¼ cup chopped fresh cilantro
   (optional)
Shredded Monterey Jack
   cheese (optional)
Tortilla chips (optional)

In large saucepan, combine chicken broth, chicken, potatoes, carrots, onion, celery, corn, vegetable juice, salsa, cooking wine, green chilies and cilantro, if desired, and place over medium-high heat. Bring to a boil; reduce heat. Simmer 20 to 30 minutes or until vegetables are tender. Serve with cheese and tortilla chips as garnishes, if desired.

New England Clam Chowder

4 ounces salt pork, diced
2 cups chopped onions
4 large potatoes, peeled and
    diced
4 (10-ounce) cans whole baby
    clams, drained (reserve
    liquid)

1½ teaspoons salt
1 teaspoon TABASCO® brand
    Pepper Sauce
4 cups half-and-half
3 cups milk
2 tablespoons butter or
    margarine

Cook salt pork in large saucepan until lightly browned. Remove and set aside. Add onions to drippings; cook until tender. Return salt pork to saucepan; add potatoes, reserved clam liquid, salt and TABASCO® Sauce. Simmer 20 to 25 minutes or until potatoes are tender. Add clams, half-and-half, milk and butter; cook until heated through. (Do not boil.)

Tip: *If fresh clams are available, scrub 7 dozen clams under running water and place in steamer or large covered kettle with 1½ cups water to cover bottom. Cook gently over medium heat about 10 minutes or until shells open. Stir clams once or twice while steaming. Remove clams from steamer and set aside to cool before removing meat. Continue cooking broth until reduced in volume to about 1½ cups. Set aside. Remove clams from shells; cut into ⅛-inch pieces and add to chowder as directed above.*

Note:

Traditional New England clam chowder is a milk- or cream-based soup, whereas Manhattan-style clam chowder is a tomato-based soup.

Oriental Chicken and Rice Soup

Makes 4 servings		

Prep Time:
10 minutes

Cook Time:
25 minutes

12 TYSON® Fresh Chicken Breast
   Tenders or Individually
   Fresh Frozen® Boneless,
   Skinless Chicken
   Tenderloins
1½ cups UNCLE BEN'S® Instant
   Rice

6 cups defatted reduced-
   sodium chicken broth
2 slices gingerroot (about
   ¼ inch thick)
½ cup chopped carrots
1 cup sliced pea pods
¼ cup chopped green onions

PREP: CLEAN: Wash hands. Remove protective ice glaze from frozen chicken by holding under cool running water 1 to 2 minutes. Cut into 1-inch pieces. CLEAN: Wash hands.

COOK: Heat chicken broth and gingerroot in large saucepan; add chicken. Simmer 5 minutes (8 minutes if using frozen chicken). Add carrots; simmer about 5 minutes or until internal juices of chicken run clear. (Or insert instant-read meat thermometer in thickest part of chicken. Temperature should read 170°F.) Stir in pea pods and rice. Remove from heat; cover. Let stand 5 minutes. Remove gingerroot.

SERVE: Sprinkle with green onions. Serve with herb bread and tea, if desired.

CHILL: Refrigerate leftovers immediately.

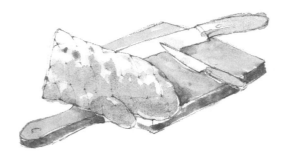

Butch's Black Bean Soup

Makes 8 servings

¼ cup olive oil
1 medium onion, diced
4 cloves garlic, minced
4 cups water
2 chicken-flavored bouillon
    cubes
1 large can (2 pounds 8 ounces)
    black beans, rinsed and
    drained
1 can (15 ounces) corn,
    undrained
1 medium potato, peeled and
    diced

3 ribs celery, diced
2 carrots, diced
1 cup uncooked rice or orzo
¼ cup fresh cilantro, minced
2 (11-ounce) jars NEWMAN'S
    OWN® Bandito Salsa
    (medium or hot) *or*
1 (26-ounce) jar NEWMAN'S
OWN® Diavolo Spicy
Simmer Sauce

Heat oil in large saucepan; cook and stir onion and garlic over high heat until onion is translucent. Add water and bouillon cubes; bring to a boil. Reduce heat to medium; add beans, corn, potato, celery, carrots, rice and cilantro. Stir in Newman's Own® Bandito Salsa and simmer until rice and vegetables are cooked, about 30 minutes.

Bounty Soup

Makes 4 servings

Prep and Cook Time:
30 minutes

Note:

Yellow crookneck squash is a summer squash with a slender curved neck and a slightly bulbous base. Summer squashes are available all year in supermarkets, but summer is their peak season.

½ pound yellow crookneck squash
2 cups frozen mixed vegetables
1 teaspoon dried parsley flakes
⅛ teaspoon dried rosemary
⅛ teaspoon dried thyme leaves
⅛ teaspoon salt
⅛ teaspoon black pepper
2 teaspoons vegetable oil

3 boneless skinless chicken breast halves (about ¾ pound), chopped
1 can (about 14 ounces) fat-free reduced-sodium chicken broth
1 can (14½ ounces) stewed tomatoes, undrained

1. Cut wide part of squash in half lengthwise, lay flat and cut crosswise into ¼-inch slices. Cut narrow part of squash into ¼-inch slices. Place squash, mixed vegetables, parsley, rosemary, thyme, salt and pepper in medium bowl.

2. Heat oil in large saucepan over medium-high heat. Add chicken; stir-fry 2 minutes. Stir in vegetables and seasonings. Add broth and tomatoes with juice, breaking large tomatoes apart. Cover; bring to a boil. Reduce heat to low. Cover; cook 5 minutes or until vegetables are tender.

<u>Serving Suggestion:</u> *Serve soup with grilled mozzarella cheese sandwiches.*

Potato Basil Soup

½ cup WESSON® Vegetable Oil
3 cups chopped celery
1½ cups chopped onions
1 teaspoon fresh minced garlic
1 quart chicken broth
3 to 4 cups peeled and diced
    russet potatoes (about
    3 large potatoes)

¼ cup chopped fresh parsley
¼ cup chopped fresh basil
¼ teaspoon black pepper
Grated Fontina cheese

Makes 8 cups

Prep Time:
10 minutes

Cook Time:
20 minutes

In large saucepan, heat Wesson® Oil until hot; sauté celery, onions and garlic until tender. Stir in chicken broth, potatoes, parsley, basil and pepper; bring to a boil and reduce heat. Simmer, covered, for 20 minutes or until potatoes are tender. Pour *half* of mixture into blender; purée until smooth. Set aside. Pour *remaining* soup into blender; blend until coarsely chopped. Combine both mixtures. Ladle soup into bowls; garnish with Fontina cheese and additional parsley if desired.

Tortellini Soup

3 cloves garlic, minced
1 tablespoon butter or
    margarine
1 can (48 ounces) COLLEGE
    INN® Chicken or Beef Broth
1 package (about 19 ounces)
    frozen cheese tortellini

1 package (10 ounces) frozen
    chopped spinach, thawed
2 cans (14½ ounces each)
    stewed tomatoes,
    undrained, cut into pieces
Grated Parmesan cheese

**Makes 8 to
10 servings (about
11 cups)**

In large saucepan, over medium-high heat cook garlic in butter for 1 to 2 minutes. Add broth and tortellini. Heat to a boil; reduce heat and simmer 10 minutes. Add spinach and tomatoes; simmer 5 minutes longer. Sprinkle each serving with cheese.

Turkey Vegetable Soup

Makes 4 servings

2½ pounds TURKEY WINGS
5 cups water
2 onions, quartered
1 carrot, cut into chunks
1 bay leaf
5 peppercorns
2 cubes low-sodium chicken
   bouillon
4 medium tomatoes, peeled
   and cut into quarters
1 cup green beans
1 medium zucchini, cut into
   ½- to ¾-inch slices
1 carrot, cut into ½-inch slices
1 stalk celery, cut into ½-inch
   slices

1 leek, thinly sliced
½ cup lima beans
3 tablespoons pearl barley
3 tablespoons fresh parsley,
   chopped *or* 1 tablespoon
   dry parsley
1½ teaspoons fresh oregano *or*
   ½ teaspoon dry oregano
1 clove garlic mashed with
   ¼ teaspoon salt
¾ teaspoon seasoned pepper
1 cup broccoli flowerettes
1 ear corn, cut into ½-inch
   slices
½ cup peas

1. In 5-quart saucepan, combine first seven ingredients. Bring to a boil over high heat. Skim off any foam. Reduce heat, cover and simmer for 1 to 1¼ hours or until turkey is tender.

2. Remove turkey from cooking liquid and allow to cool. Cut meat from bones, discard skin and bones. Cube meat.

3. Strain broth. Discard vegetables, seasonings and spices. Skim off any remaining fat. Return broth to saucepan.

4. Add tomatoes, green beans, zucchini, carrot, celery, leek, lima beans, barley, parsley, oregano, garlic mixture and seasoned pepper. Over high heat, bring mixture to a boil. Cover and reduce heat to a simmer. Cook 20 minutes.

5. Add turkey, broccoli, corn and peas; cook 5 minutes. Adjust seasoning to taste.

Favorite recipe from **National Turkey Federation**

Kaleidoscope Chowder

Makes 4 servings

3 cups water
3 large potatoes, peeled and diced
1 (26-ounce) jar NEWMAN'S OWN® Diavolo Sauce
2 large carrots, peeled and thinly sliced
1½ to 2 pounds assorted seafood, such as fish fillets, bay scallops, shrimp or clams

½ cup dry white wine
2 cups shredded fresh spinach leaves
1 yellow bell pepper, seeded and diced
Freshly grated Parmesan cheese

In large stockpot, bring water to a boil. Add potatoes; cook 5 minutes. Stir in Newman's Own® Diavolo Sauce and carrots. Bring to a boil; reduce heat and simmer 5 minutes.

Cut fish fillets into bite-size pieces. Peel and devein shrimp. Add seafood and wine to soup. Cook over medium-high heat, stirring often, until fish is opaque, 3 to 4 minutes. Add spinach and pepper; cover. Remove from heat and let stand until spinach and pepper are heated through, about 2 minutes. Serve with Parmesan cheese.

Tip: *This chowder is also excellent with diced cooked chicken breast.*

Italian Cupboard Soup

Makes 4 servings

2 boneless top loin pork chops, cubed
2 (14½-ounce) cans chicken broth
1 (15-ounce) can chopped tomatoes, undrained

1 (15-ounce) can cannellini or great Northern beans, drained
2 tablespoons dried minced onion
8 ounces fresh spinach leaves, torn

In deep saucepan, brown pork in small amount of oil; add chicken broth, tomatoes, beans and onion; bring to a boil, lower heat and simmer for 15 minutes; stir in spinach and cook 2 minutes.

Top each serving with grated Parmesan or Romano cheese.

Favorite recipe from **National Pork Board**

Zippy Lentil Soup

Makes 4 servings

2 teaspoons Lucini Premium Select extra virgin olive oil
1 cup chopped onion
2 teaspoons chopped garlic
½ cup pearl barley
2 (13¾-ounce) cans beef broth, defatted
1 (16-ounce) can crushed tomatoes

½ cup lentils
½ teaspoon dried marjoram leaves
¼ teaspoon black pepper
1 cup chopped celery
1½ cups (6 ounces) shredded JARLSBERG LITE™ cheese

Heat oil in large saucepan; sauté onion and garlic 2 minutes. Add barley; sauté 2 minutes. Add broth, tomatoes, lentils, marjoram and pepper; bring to a boil. Simmer, covered, 30 minutes. Add celery; simmer 10 minutes. Sprinkle about ¼ cup cheese over each serving.

Spicy Crab Soup

Makes 6 servings

1 pound crabmeat,* cooked, flaked and cartilage removed

1 can (28 ounces) crushed tomatoes in tomato purée, undrained

2 cups water

1 can (10¾ ounces) fat-free reduced-sodium chicken broth

¾ cup chopped celery

¾ cup diced onion

1 teaspoon seafood seasoning

¼ teaspoon lemon-pepper

1 package (10 ounces) frozen corn, thawed

1 package (10 ounces) frozen peas, thawed

Purchase flake-style or a mixture of flake and chunk crabmeat if purchasing blue crab or surimi blended seafood.

Combine tomatoes with purée, water, broth, celery, onion, seafood seasoning and lemon-pepper in 6-quart saucepan. Bring to a boil over high heat. Reduce heat to low. Cover and simmer 20 to 30 minutes. Add corn and peas; simmer 10 minutes more. Add crabmeat; simmer until heated through.

Favorite recipe from **National Fisheries Institute**

Note:

The English pea, also known as the green, shell or common garden pea, is a round seed of the legume family that grows in pods on a vine.

New Orleans Pork Gumbo

Makes 4 servings

Prep and Cook Time:
30 minutes

Note:

A Dutch oven is a large, heavy covered pot with two short handles which is used for the slow, moist cooking of a large quantity of food. They can range in size from 5 to 8 quarts. Pots larger than 8 quarts are generally referred to as stockpots.

1 pound pork loin roast
    Nonstick cooking spray
1 tablespoon margarine
2 tablespoons all-purpose flour
1 cup water
1 can (16 ounces) stewed
    tomatoes, undrained
1 package (10 ounces) frozen
    cut okra

1 package (10 ounces) frozen
    succotash
1 beef bouillon cube
1 teaspoon black pepper
1 teaspoon hot pepper sauce
1 bay leaf

1. Cut pork into ½-inch cubes. Spray large Dutch oven with cooking spray. Heat over medium heat until hot. Add pork; cook and stir 4 minutes or until pork is browned. Remove pork from Dutch oven.

2. Melt margarine in same Dutch oven. Stir in flour. Cook and stir until mixture is browned. Gradually whisk in water until smooth. Add pork and remaining ingredients. Bring to a boil. Reduce heat to low and simmer 15 minutes. Remove bay leaf before serving.

Grandma's Chicken Soup

Makes 8 servings

8 chicken thighs, skinned, fat trimmed
2 carrots, cut into ¼-inch slices
2 ribs celery, cut into ¼-inch slices
2 medium turnips, peeled and cubed
1 large onion, chopped

8 cups water
1½ teaspoons salt
¼ teaspoon pepper
¼ teaspoon poultry seasoning
⅛ teaspoon dried thyme leaves
1 cup wide egg noodles, uncooked

In large saucepan or Dutch oven, layer chicken, carrots, celery, turnips and onion. Add water, salt, pepper, poultry seasoning and thyme. Cook, covered, over medium heat until liquid boils. Reduce heat and simmer about 45 minutes or until chicken and vegetables are fork tender. Remove chicken; cool. Separate meat from bones; discard bones. Cut chicken into bite-size pieces. Heat soup mixture to boiling; stir in noodles. Cook, uncovered, about 5 to 7 minutes or until noodles are done. Stir in chicken.

Favorite recipe from **Delmarva Poultry Industry, Inc.**

Hearty Beef and Mushroom Soup

Makes 4 (1½-cup) servings

¾ pound sirloin beef sandwich steak
3 tablespoons butter or margarine, divided
1 small onion, chopped
1 package (6 ounces) sliced portobello mushrooms, cut into 1-inch chunks

1 large carrot, sliced
1 box UNCLE BEN'S® Brown & Wild Rice Mushroom Recipe
3 cans (14½ ounces each) beef broth
1 tablespoon chopped fresh parsley

1. Slice beef into 1-inch-wide strips; cut strips into 1-inch pieces.

2. Melt 2 tablespoons butter in large saucepan or Dutch oven over medium-high heat. Add onion and mushrooms; cook 2 minutes. Add remaining 1 tablespoon butter, beef and carrot; cook 2 minutes or until beef is no longer pink.

3. Add rice, contents of seasoning packet and broth. Bring to a boil. Cover; reduce heat and simmer 25 minutes or until rice is tender. Stir in parsley just before serving.

Tip: *If sliced portobello mushrooms are not available, substitute 2 medium portobello mushrooms cut into chunks. Or, substitute 6 ounces button mushrooms, cut into quarters.*

Manhattan Clam Chowder

2 pieces bacon, diced
1 large red bell pepper, diced
1 large green bell pepper, diced
1 rib celery, chopped
1 carrot, peeled and chopped
1 small onion, chopped
1 clove garlic, finely chopped
2 cups bottled clam juice
1 cup CLAMATO® Tomato
   Cocktail

2 medium potatoes, peeled and
   diced
1 large tomato, chopped
1 teaspoon oregano
½ teaspoon black pepper
2 cups fresh or canned clams,
   chopped (about 24 shucked
   clams)

In heavy 4-quart saucepan, sauté bacon, bell peppers, celery, carrot, onion and garlic over medium heat until tender, about 10 minutes. (Do not brown bacon.) Add clam juice, Clamato, potatoes, tomato, oregano and black pepper. Simmer 35 minutes or until potatoes are tender. Add clams; cook 5 minutes more.

Veg•All® Black Bean Soup

1 package (14 ounces) smoked
   sausage, cut into ½-inch
   slices
2 cans (15 ounces each)
   VEG·ALL® Original Mixed
   Vegetables

2 cans (15 ounces each) black
   beans with spices
1 can (14½ ounces) chicken
   broth

In large soup kettle, lightly brown sausage. Add Veg•All, beans, and chicken broth; heat until hot. Serve immediately.

Southwest Chicken Soup

Makes 4 to 6 servings

3 tablespoons vegetable oil
3 corn tortillas, cut into ½-inch
   strips
⅓ cup chopped onion
⅔ cup chopped green and red
   bell peppers
1 clove garlic, minced

¼ cup all-purpose flour
2 (12-ounce) cans chicken broth
2 cups cooked chicken, cubed
1 (15-ounce) can VEG·ALL®
   Mixed Vegetables, drained
2 teaspoons chili powder

Note:

Chili powder, cayenne pepper and red pepper flakes are all made from dried chilies. When using fresh, dried or ground chilies, keep in mind that the longer they are cooked, the hotter the dish will be.

1. Heat oil in large skillet; add tortilla strips and fry, stirring constantly, until golden. Drain on paper towel-lined plate.

2. Add onion and bell peppers to skillet; cook and stir until soft.

3. Add garlic and stir in flour; gradually stir in chicken broth.

4. Add remaining ingredients except tortilla strips; cook until thickened. Sprinkle with tortilla strips before serving.

Five-Alarm Chilis

CHAPTER TWELVE

Hearty Turkey Cannellini Chili

Makes 6 servings

Prep Time:
5 minutes

Cook Time:
30 minutes

Note:

By law, stick margarine must be 80 percent fat. It is sold salted and occasionally unsalted. Margarine can be used in place of butter for all cooking uses, although the flavor will be different.

1 pound ground turkey or ground beef
1 (6.9-ounce) package RICE-A-RONI® Chicken Flavor
2 tablespoons margarine or butter

1 (14½-ounce) can diced tomatoes with garlic and onion, undrained
1 tablespoon chili powder
1 (15-ounce) can cannellini beans, drained and rinsed

1. In large skillet over medium-high heat, cook ground turkey until no longer pink. Remove from skillet; drain. Set aside.

2. In same skillet over medium heat, sauté rice-vermicelli mix with margarine until vermicelli is golden brown.

3. Slowly stir in 2¼ cups water, tomatoes, chili powder and Special Seasonings; bring to a boil. Reduce heat to low. Cover; simmer 10 minutes.

4. Stir in beans and turkey; return to a simmer. Cover; simmer 5 to 7 minutes or until rice is tender.

Nell's Chili con Carne

2 tablespoons vegetable oil
2 cups diced onions
1 green bell pepper, seeded and chopped
3 cloves garlic, minced
2 pounds lean, coarsely ground beef
2 cups dried kidney beans, soaked overnight
1 jar (32 ounces) NEWMAN'S OWN® Spaghetti Sauce

2 to 3 cups water
2 to 3 tablespoons chili powder
1 teaspoon ground cumin
Salt and black pepper
1 cup chopped celery
1 can (8¾ ounces) whole kernel corn, drained
Sour cream and lime wedges (optional)

Heat oil in Dutch oven over medium-high heat. Add onions, bell pepper and garlic; cook and stir until vegetables are tender. Add beef; cook until browned. Add kidney beans, Newman's Own® Spaghetti Sauce, water, chili powder, cumin, salt and black pepper to taste. Simmer, uncovered, 1 hour, stirring frequently. Add celery and corn and simmer 1 hour. Garnish with sour cream and lime wedges, if desired.

Tip: *Three cups of cooked rice can be substituted for meat to make vegetarian chili.*

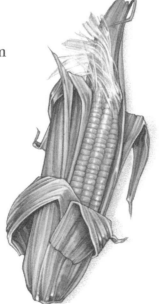

Chunky Chicken Chili

Makes 4 to 6 servings

Prep Time:
25 minutes

Cook Time:
30 minutes

1 pound boneless skinless chicken breast, cut into bite-sized pieces
1 cup chopped onion
½ cup chopped celery
½ cup chopped carrot
2 cloves garlic, minced
1 tablespoon vegetable oil
1 can (15½ ounces) dark red kidney beans, drained

1 can (27 ounces) FRANK'S® or SNOWFLOSS® Original Style Diced Tomatoes
1 cup MISSISSIPPI® Barbecue Sauce
1 can (8 ounces) tomato sauce
1 tablespoon chili powder
½ teaspoon ground cumin
1 green pepper, chopped

1. In large stockpot sauté chicken, onion, celery, carrot and garlic in oil. Cook and stir until chicken is no longer pink.

2. Stir in kidney beans, tomatoes, barbecue sauce, tomato sauce, chili powder and cumin.

3. Bring to a boil then reduce heat. Simmer, uncovered, 30 minutes, stirring occasionally.

4. Add green pepper and heat through before serving.

Chili á la Mexico

2 pounds ground beef
2 cups finely chopped onions
2 cloves garlic, minced
1 can (28 ounces) whole peeled
    tomatoes, undrained,
    coarsely chopped
1 can (6 ounces) tomato paste
1½ to 2 tablespoons chili powder

1 teaspoon ground cumin
¼ teaspoon salt
¼ teaspoon ground red pepper
    (optional)
¼ teaspoon ground cloves
    (optional)
Lime wedges and cilantro
    sprigs, for garnish

Brown beef in deep 12-inch skillet over medium-high heat 6 to
8 minutes, stirring to separate meat. Reduce heat to medium.
Pour off drippings. Add onions and garlic; cook and stir 5 minutes
or until onions are soft.

Stir in tomatoes with juice, tomato paste, chili powder, cumin,
salt, red pepper and cloves, if desired. Bring to a boil over high
heat. Reduce heat to low. Cover and simmer 30 minutes, stirring
occasionally. Ladle into bowls. Garnish with lime wedges and
cilantro.

Olive-Bean Chili

Makes 4 servings

Prep Time:
about 15 minutes

Cook Time:
about 10 minutes

3 tablespoons molasses
1½ teaspoons dry mustard
1½ teaspoons soy sauce
2 teaspoons olive oil
2 medium carrots, cut
    diagonally into ¼-inch
    slices
1 large onion, chopped
1 tablespoon chili powder
3 large tomatoes (1½ pounds),
    chopped

1 (15-ounce) can pinto beans,
    drained
1 (15-ounce) can kidney beans,
    drained
¾ cup California ripe olives,
    sliced
½ cup plain nonfat yogurt
    Crushed red pepper flakes

Combine molasses, mustard and soy sauce; set aside. Heat oil in large skillet; add carrots, onion, chili powder and ¼ cup water. Cook, covered, about 4 minutes or until carrots are almost tender. Uncover and cook, stirring, until liquid has evaporated. Add molasses mixture with tomatoes, pinto beans, kidney beans and olives. Cook, stirring gently, about 5 minutes or until mixture is hot and tomatoes are soft. Ladle chili into bowls; top with yogurt. Sprinkle with pepper flakes to taste.

Favorite recipe from **California Olive Industry**

Five-Way Cincinnati Chili

1 pound uncooked spaghetti, broken in half
1 pound ground chuck
2 cans (10 ounces each) tomatoes and green chilies, undrained
1 can (15 ounces) red kidney beans, drained
1 can (10½ ounces) condensed French onion soup

1¼ cups water
1 tablespoon chili powder
1 teaspoon sugar
½ teaspoon salt
¼ teaspoon ground cinnamon
½ cup chopped onion
½ cup (2 ounces) shredded Cheddar cheese

Makes 6 servings

Prep and Cook Time:
20 minutes

1. Cook pasta according to package directions; drain.

2. While pasta is cooking, cook beef in large saucepan or Dutch oven over medium-high heat until browned, stirring to separate meat; drain well. Add tomatoes with juice, beans, soup, water, chili powder, sugar, salt and cinnamon to saucepan; bring to a boil. Reduce heat to low. Simmer, uncovered, 10 minutes, stirring occasionally.

3. Serve chili over spaghetti; sprinkle with onion and cheese.

Note:

Serve this traditional chili your way or one of the ways Cincinnatians do— two-way over spaghetti, three-way with cheese, four-way with cheese and chopped onion or five-way with beans added to the chili.

Black Bean Vegetarian Chili

Makes 8 servings

1 tablespoon olive oil
2 onions, finely chopped, divided
1 green bell pepper, diced
1 teaspoon ground cumin
1 teaspoon minced garlic
1 to 2 canned chipotle peppers, stemmed, diced, seeds included*
4 cans (15 ounces each) black beans, rinsed and drained
1 can (15 ounces) corn kernels, drained

1 can (15 ounces) diced tomatoes, undrained
1 can (6 ounces) tomato paste plus 3 cans water
½ teaspoon salt
½ teaspoon black pepper
Sour cream

Chipotle peppers come in 7-ounce cans packed in adobo sauce. Use 1 pepper for mildly spicy chili, 2 for very spicy. Unused peppers may be frozen in small plastic bags for later use.

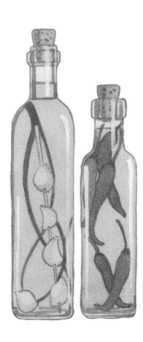

1. Heat olive oil in Dutch oven until hot. Reserve ½ cup chopped onions. Add remaining onions and bell pepper to Dutch oven; cook and stir 5 minutes or until soft. Add cumin; cook and stir about 10 seconds. Add garlic; cook and stir 1 minute.

2. Stir in chipotle peppers, black beans, corn, tomatoes with juice, tomato paste, water, salt and black pepper. Bring to a boil. Reduce heat and simmer 30 minutes.

3. Serve with sour cream, reserved onions and whole wheat flour tortillas, if desired.

Quick and Spicy Pork Chili

1 pound ground pork
1 medium onion, chopped
1 clove garlic, minced
1 (16-ounce) can kidney beans,
    drained
1 (14½-ounce) can Mexican-
    style diced tomatoes

1 (8-ounce) can tomato sauce
1 (8-ounce) can whole kernel
    corn, drained
2 tablespoons chili powder
1 tablespoon ground cumin
1 teaspoon salt
½ teaspoon black pepper

Makes 6 servings

Prep Time:
10 minutes

Cook Time:
15 minutes

In large saucepan, cook and stir pork with onion and garlic
until pork is no longer pink, about 6 minutes. Stir in remaining
ingredients; bring to a boil. Cover and simmer 15 minutes, until
flavors are blended and chili is hot. Serve with shredded Cheddar
cheese and warmed flour tortillas, if desired.

Favorite recipe from **National Pork Board**

Ragú® Chili

2 pounds ground beef
1 large onion, chopped
2 cloves garlic, finely chopped
1 jar (1 pound 10 ounces)
    RAGÚ® Robusto! Pasta
    Sauce

1 can (15 ounces) red kidney
    beans, rinsed and drained
2 tablespoons chili powder

Makes 8 servings

In 12-inch skillet, brown ground beef with onion and garlic over
medium-high heat; drain. Stir in remaining ingredients. Simmer
uncovered, stirring occasionally, 20 minutes. Serve, if desired,
with shredded Cheddar cheese.

<u>Hint:</u> *For spicier Ragú® Chili, stir in ½ teaspoon each ground
cumin and dried oregano.*

Chili con Carne

Makes 8 servings

1 tablespoon CRISCO® Oil*
1 cup chopped onion
1 cup chopped green bell
   pepper
1 pound ground beef round
1 can (28 ounces) whole
   tomatoes, undrained and
   chopped
1 can (8 ounces) tomato sauce

1 tablespoon chili powder
1 teaspoon salt
¼ teaspoon black pepper
   Dash of hot pepper sauce
   (optional)
1 can (30 ounces) kidney beans,
   undrained

Use your favorite Crisco Oil product.

Note:

Chili, often called chile
con carne (Spanish for
"chili with meat"), can
be traced back to
San Antonio where
these "bowls of red"
were sold in the
marketplace.

1. Heat oil in large saucepan or Dutch oven on medium heat.
Add onion and green pepper. Cook and stir until tender. Add
meat. Cook until browned, stirring occasionally. Stir in tomatoes,
tomato sauce, chili powder, salt, black pepper and hot pepper
sauce (if used). Bring to a boil. Reduce heat to low. Simmer
45 minutes, stirring occasionally.

2. Add beans. Heat thoroughly, stirring occasionally.

Glenn's Magic Chili

2½ pounds boneless beef, such as lean chuck or sirloin, cut into ¼-inch cubes, or lean coarsely ground beef
2 tablespoons Chef Paul Prudhomme's Meat Magic®
2 tablespoons chili powder
1 tablespoon dried oregano leaves
1½ teaspoons ground cumin
1 teaspoon salt
2 cups chopped peeled tomatoes
2 cups minced fresh onions
4 cups beef stock or water, divided

2 teaspoons minced garlic
1½ teaspoons Chef Paul Prudhomme's Magic Pepper Sauce™
6 whole jalapeño peppers with stems, about 4 ounces*
1 tablespoon corn flour or all-purpose flour
2 cups cooked pinto or red beans (optional)

*If fresh jalapeños are unavailable, use jarred jalapeño peppers, thoroughly rinsed and drained. For a spicier chili, chop jalapeños before adding.

In 4-quart saucepan, combine beef, Meat Magic®, chili powder, oregano, cumin and salt; stir well. Cover; cook over high heat 4 minutes. Stir well; re-cover and cook 1 minute. Stir in tomatoes and onions; re-cover and cook 10 minutes, stirring occasionally and scraping saucepan bottom well each time. Add 2 cups beef stock, garlic and Magic Pepper Sauce™, stirring well. Stir in jalapeños. Bring to a boil; reduce heat to low. Simmer 1 hour, stirring and scraping saucepan bottom occasionally. Remove any fat from top of chili mixture. In small bowl, stir together flour and 2 tablespoons liquid from chili mixture until well blended.

Add flour mixture, 1 cup beef stock and beans to chili mixture, stirring well. Simmer 40 minutes, stirring frequently. Add remaining 1 cup beef stock; cook and stir 20 minutes. Serve hot in bowls. Garnish as desired.

Chili Blanco

Makes 4 servings

½ pound diced turkey breast (optional)
1 tablespoon vegetable oil
½ cup diced celery
½ cup fresh or canned Anaheim chilies
½ cup chopped onion
1 can (16 to 19 ounces) white kidney beans, drained
2 cups water
1 cup diced fresh tomatoes
1 cup diced zucchini

½ teaspoon salt
½ teaspoon ground cumin
⅛ teaspoon black pepper
⅛ teaspoon ground cayenne pepper
Condiments: Shredded low fat cheese, chopped onion, chopped fresh cilantro and diced tomatoes
Corn or flour tortillas
Fresh Grape Salsa (recipe follows)

Brown turkey in oil in medium saucepan; drain. Add celery, chilies and onion; cook until tender. Add beans, water, tomatoes, zucchini, salt, cumin, black pepper and cayenne pepper; mix well. Bring to a boil; reduce heat and simmer 30 minutes. Serve with condiments, tortillas and Fresh Grape Salsa.

Fresh Grape Salsa

2 cups coarsely chopped California seedless grapes
½ cup chopped green onions
½ cup diced fresh or canned Anaheim chilies
2 tablespoons chopped fresh cilantro

2 tablespoons vinegar
1 clove garlic, minced
½ teaspoon salt
⅛ teaspoon hot pepper sauce

Combine all ingredients in medium bowl; mix well. Let stand at least 1 hour before serving. Drain off excess liquid before serving.

Makes about 3 cups

Favorite recipe from **California Table Grape Commission**

Green Flash Turkey Chili

Makes 6 servings

3 tablespoons olive oil, divided
3 large stalks celery, diced
1 large green bell pepper, diced
2 green onions, sliced
2 large cloves garlic, minced
1 pound ground turkey
4 cups canned white kidney
    beans, drained and rinsed

1½ cups water
⅓ cup TABASCO® brand Green
    Pepper Sauce
1¼ teaspoons salt
¼ cup chopped fresh parsley

Note:

Wash green onions thoroughly before trimming off the roots. Remove any wilted or discolored layers. The onions can then be sliced, chopped, cut into lengths or used whole.

Heat 2 tablespoons oil in large saucepan over medium heat. Add celery and green bell pepper; cook about 5 minutes or until crisp-tender. Add green onions and garlic; cook 5 minutes, stirring occasionally. Remove vegetables to plate with slotted spoon. Add remaining 1 tablespoon oil to saucepan; cook turkey over medium-high heat until well browned, stirring frequently.

Add vegetable mixture, kidney beans, water, TABASCO® Green Pepper Sauce and salt to saucepan. Heat to boiling over high heat. Reduce heat to low; cover and simmer 20 minutes, stirring occasionally. Uncover saucepan and simmer 5 minutes. Stir in parsley just before serving.

Texas-Style Chili

Makes 4½ cups

1½ pounds ground beef or cubed round steak
1 green bell pepper, diced
1 onion, diced
1 can (2.25 ounces) diced green chiles, drained
1 package (1.48 ounces) LAWRY'S® Spices & Seasonings for Chili
1½ tablespoons cornmeal

1 tablespoon chili powder
1 teaspoon sugar
¼ to ½ teaspoon cayenne pepper
1 can (14½ ounces) diced tomatoes, undrained
¾ cup water
Sour cream (optional)
Shredded cheddar cheese (optional)

In Dutch oven or large saucepan, cook beef until browned and crumbly; drain beef, reserving fat; set beef aside. In Dutch oven, heat reserved fat. Add bell pepper and onion; cook over medium-high heat 5 minutes or until vegetables are crisp-tender. Return beef to Dutch oven. Add chiles, Spices & Seasonings for Chili, cornmeal, chili powder, sugar and cayenne pepper; mix well. Stir in tomatoes and water. Bring to a boil over medium-high heat; reduce heat to low, cover, simmer 30 minutes, stirring occasionally.

Serving Suggestion: *Serve topped with sour cream or cheddar cheese, if desired.*

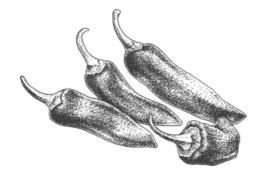

Chili Beef Mac

1 pound lean ground beef or
  ground turkey
4 teaspoons Mexican
  seasoning*
⅔ cup milk
1 (4.8-ounce) package PASTA
  RONI® Four Cheese Flavor
  with Corkscrew Pasta

1 medium green, red or yellow
  bell pepper, diced
½ cup salsa
¼ cup chopped fresh cilantro or
  sliced green onions

*2 teaspoons chili powder, 1 teaspoon ground
cumin and 1 teaspoon garlic salt can be
substituted.

Makes 4 servings

Prep Time:
5 minutes

Cook Time:
20 minutes

1. In large skillet over medium-high heat, cook ground beef and
Mexican seasoning for 5 minutes, stirring occasionally.

2. Add 1¼ cups water, milk, pasta, bell pepper, salsa and Special
Seasonings. Bring to a boil. Reduce heat to low. Cover; simmer
8 to 9 minutes or until pasta is tender. Stir in cilantro. Let stand
5 minutes before serving.

Pick a Chili Pepper

Chili peppers make up 90 percent of the
Capsicum family. There are over 100 varieties
of chili peppers in Mexico alone, each with
its own distinct flavor.

Anaheim chilies, also known as
California green chilies, are light green with
a mild flavor and a slight bite. They are
usually 4 to 6 inches long, about 1½ inches
wide and have a rounded tip.

Chipotle chilies are smoked, dried red
jalapeño peppers. They have a rich, smoky,
very hot flavor.

Jalapeño peppers are small, dark green
chilies, normally 2 to 3 inches long and
about ¾ of an inch wide with a blunt or
slightly tapered end. Their flavor varies from
hot to very hot. Ripe jalapeño peppers are
red and sweeter than the green jalapeño.

Poblano peppers are very dark green,
large triangular-shaped chilies with pointed
ends. Poblanos are 3½ to 5 inches long.
Their flavor ranges from mild to quite hot.

Serrano peppers are very small, medium-
green or red chilies with a very hot flavor.

A Honey of a Chili

Makes 6 servings

1 package (15 ounces) firm tofu
1 tablespoon vegetable oil
1 cup chopped onion
¾ cup chopped green bell
  pepper
2 cloves garlic, finely chopped
2 tablespoons chili powder
1 teaspoon ground cumin
1 teaspoon salt
½ teaspoon dried oregano

½ teaspoon crushed red pepper
  flakes
1 can (28 ounces) diced
  tomatoes, undrained
1 can (15½ ounces) red kidney
  beans, undrained
1 can (8 ounces) tomato sauce
¼ cup honey
2 tablespoons red wine vinegar

Note:

Honey is one of the only foods that will never go bad, no matter how long you keep it. Be sure to store it in a tightly closed jar in a cool, dry place. Do not refrigerate honey as it can become grainy and too thick to use.

Using a cheese grater shred tofu and freeze in zippered bag or airtight container. Thaw tofu; place in a strainer and press out excess liquid. In large saucepan or Dutch oven, heat oil over medium-high heat until hot; cook and stir onion, green pepper and garlic 3 to 5 minutes or until vegetables are tender and begin to brown. Stir in chili powder, cumin, salt, oregano and crushed red pepper. Stir in tofu; cook and stir 1 minute. Stir in diced tomatoes, kidney beans, tomato sauce, honey and vinegar. Bring to a boil; reduce heat and simmer, uncovered, 15 to 20 minutes, stirring occasionally.

Favorite recipe from **National Honey Board**

Tex-Mex Chicken & Rice Chili

1 package (6.8 ounces) RICE-A-RONI® Spanish Rice
2¾ cups water
2 cups chopped cooked chicken or turkey
1 can (15 or 16 ounces) kidney beans or pinto beans, rinsed and drained
1 can (14½ or 16 ounces) tomatoes or stewed tomatoes, undrained

1 medium green bell pepper, cut into ½-inch pieces
1½ teaspoons chili powder
1 teaspoon ground cumin
½ cup (2 ounces) shredded Cheddar or Monterey Jack cheese (optional)
Sour cream (optional)
Chopped cilantro (optional)

1. In 3-quart saucepan, combine rice-vermicelli mix, Special Seasonings, water, chicken, beans, tomatoes, green pepper, chili powder and cumin. Bring to a boil over high heat.

2. Reduce heat to low; simmer, uncovered, about 20 minutes or until rice is tender, stirring occasionally.

3. Top with cheese, sour cream and cilantro, if desired.

Soul City Chili

Makes about 10 servings (9½ cups)

2 pounds ground beef
½ teaspoon LAWRY'S® Seasoned Salt
½ teaspoon LAWRY'S® Seasoned Pepper
1 pound hot Italian sausage or kielbasa sausage, cut into bite-size pieces
2 cups water
1 can (15¼ ounces) kidney beans, undrained

1 can (14½ ounces) stewed tomatoes, undrained
2 packages (1.48 ounces each) LAWRY'S® Spices & Seasonings for Chili
½ cup hickory flavored barbecue sauce
¾ cup red wine

In Dutch oven, cook beef until browned and crumbly; drain fat. Add Seasoned Salt and Seasoned Pepper; mix well. Stir in sausage, water, beans, tomatoes, Spices & Seasonings for Chili and barbecue sauce. Bring to a boil over medium-high heat; reduce heat to low, simmer, uncovered, 20 minutes. Stir in wine. Heat through.

Serving Suggestion: *Top with diced green, yellow and red bell peppers and chopped onion. Perfect with crackers, too!*

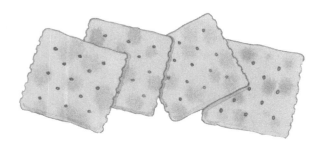

Spicy Vegetable Chili

Makes 4 servings

½ cup uncooked wheat berries
1 large onion, chopped
½ green bell pepper, chopped
½ yellow or red bell pepper, chopped
2 ribs celery, sliced
3 cloves garlic, minced
1 can (14½ ounces) chopped tomatoes
1 can (15 ounces) red kidney beans, rinsed and drained
1 can (15 ounces) chick-peas (garbanzo beans), rinsed and drained
¾ cup raisins
½ cup water
1 tablespoon chili seasoning blend or chili powder
1 teaspoon dried oregano leaves, crushed
1 tablespoon chopped fresh parsley
1½ teaspoons hot pepper sauce

1. Place wheat berries in small saucepan and cover with 2 cups water; let soak overnight. Bring to a boil over high heat. Reduce heat to low; cover and cook 45 minutes to 1 hour or until wheat berries are tender. Drain; set aside.

2. Spray large skillet or saucepan with nonstick cooking spray; heat over medium heat. Add onion; cover and cook 5 minutes. Add bell peppers, celery and garlic; cover and cook 5 minutes, stirring occasionally.

3. Add tomatoes, kidney beans, chick-peas, raisins, ½ cup water, chili seasoning, oregano and wheat berries to skillet; mix well. Bring to a boil over high heat. Reduce heat to low; simmer 25 to 30 minutes, stirring occasionally. Just before serving, stir in parsley and hot pepper sauce. Garnish, if desired.

Sock-it-to-'em Chili

Makes 6 servings

1 tablespoon vegetable oil
¾ pound ground turkey or lean ground beef
1 (8-ounce) package mushrooms, sliced
2 medium carrots, peeled and diced
1 large green bell pepper, seeded and diced
1 medium onion, diced

2 cloves garlic, minced
1½ teaspoons chili powder
½ teaspoon ground cumin
1 (26-ounce) jar NEWMAN'S OWN® Sockarooni Spaghetti Sauce
2 (15- to 19-ounce) cans black beans, undrained
1 cup water
1 medium zucchini, diced

Note:

Cumin is widely used in Mexican, Middle Eastern, North African and Indian cooking. Use it sparingly (or add a little at a time), as it is a potent spice and will dominate most other flavors in a dish.

Heat oil in 5-quart Dutch oven over medium-high heat until hot. Add turkey; cook and stir until no longer pink. Add mushrooms, carrots, pepper, onion, garlic, chili powder and cumin; cook until onion is tender, stirring frequently.

Stir in Newman's Own® Sockarooni Spaghetti Sauce, beans with their liquid and water; bring to a boil. Reduce heat to low; cover and simmer 20 minutes. Add zucchini; cook over medium-low heat, uncovered, 10 minutes or until zucchini is just tender. Serve hot.

White Bean Chili

Nonstick cooking spray
1 pound ground chicken
1½ cups coarsely chopped onions (about 2 medium)
3 cups coarsely chopped celery
3 cloves garlic, minced
4 teaspoons chili powder
1½ teaspoons ground cumin
¾ teaspoon ground allspice
¾ teaspoon ground cinnamon

½ teaspoon black pepper
1 can (16 ounces) whole tomatoes, undrained, coarsely chopped
1 can (15½ ounces) Great Northern beans, drained and rinsed
2 cups defatted low-sodium chicken broth

1. Spray large nonstick skillet with cooking spray; heat over medium heat until hot. Add chicken; cook and stir until browned, breaking into pieces with fork. Remove chicken; drain fat from skillet.

2. Add onions, celery and garlic to skillet; cook and stir over medium heat 5 to 7 minutes or until tender. Sprinkle with chili powder, cumin, allspice, cinnamon and pepper; cook and stir 1 minute.

3. Return chicken to skillet. Stir in tomatoes with juice, beans and chicken broth; heat to a boil. Reduce heat to low and simmer, uncovered, 15 minutes. Garnish as desired.

Fireball Vegetarian Chili

Makes 6 servings

Prep Time:
15 minutes

Cook Time:
25 minutes

1 onion, chopped
2 cloves garlic, minced
2 cans (15 to 19 ounces each)
   red kidney beans, rinsed
   and drained
1½ cups *each* coarsely chopped
   zucchini and carrots
1 can (15 ounces) crushed
   tomatoes in purée,
   undrained

1 can (7 ounces) whole kernel
   corn, drained
1 can (4½ ounces) chopped
   green chilies, drained
¼ cup *Frank's® RedHot®* Cayenne
   Pepper Sauce
1 tablespoon ground cumin

1. Heat *1 tablespoon oil* in large saucepot. Cook and stir onion and garlic 3 minutes or just until tender. Add remaining ingredients; stir until well blended.

2. Heat to boiling. Reduce heat to medium-low. Cook, partially covered, 20 minutes or until vegetables are tender and flavors are blended. Serve with hot cooked rice. Garnish with sour cream or shredded cheese, if desired.

Kahlúa® Turkey Chili Verde

3½ pounds turkey thighs
¼ cup olive oil
2 medium onions, chopped
1 large green bell pepper, chopped
12 large cloves garlic, peeled and chopped
2 tablespoons all-purpose flour
1 (28-ounce) can Italian tomatoes, drained and chopped
1 (14½-ounce) can chicken broth
1 (13-ounce) can tomatillos,* drained and mashed

1½ cups chopped fresh cilantro
4 (7-ounce) cans diced mild green chilies
½ cup KAHLÚA® Liqueur
2 jalapeño peppers, diced
5 teaspoons dried oregano leaves
2 teaspoons ground coriander seeds
2 teaspoons ground cumin
Salt, freshly ground black pepper and fresh lime juice

*Tomatillos (Mexican green tomatoes) can be found in the ethnic section of large supermarkets.

In large skillet, brown turkey thighs in olive oil over high heat, turning occasionally, about 15 minutes. Transfer to large roasting pan. Set aside. Discard all but ¼ cup drippings in skillet. Add onions, bell pepper and garlic; cook over medium heat until soft, about 10 minutes, stirring frequently. Add flour; cook and stir 3 to 4 minutes. Stir in tomatoes, chicken broth, tomatillos, cilantro, green chilies, Kahlúa®, jalapeño peppers, oregano, coriander and cumin. Bring to a boil. Pour over turkey thighs in roasting pan. Cover tightly with heavy foil; bake at 350°F, 1 hour.

Remove from oven; loosen foil. Set aside to cool. When cool enough to handle, remove skin and bones from turkey; discard. Cut meat into ½-inch cubes and place in large saucepan with sauce. Cook over medium heat until heated through. Season to taste with salt, pepper and lime juice. Serve hot; garnish as desired.

Chunky Ancho Chili with Beans

Makes 8 servings

5 dried ancho chilies
2 cups water
2 tablespoons lard or vegetable oil
1 large onion, chopped
2 cloves garlic, minced
1 pound lean boneless beef, cut into 1-inch cubes
1 pound lean boneless pork, cut into 1-inch cubes
1 to 2 fresh or canned jalapeño peppers,* stemmed, seeded and minced

1 teaspoon salt
1 teaspoon dried oregano
1 teaspoon ground cumin
½ cup dry red wine
3 cups cooked pinto beans *or* 2 cans (15 ounces each) pinto or kidney beans, drained

*Jalapeño peppers can sting and irritate the skin; wear rubber gloves when handling peppers and do not touch eyes. Wash hands after handling.

Rinse ancho chilies; remove stems, seeds and veins. Place in 2-quart pan with water. Bring to a boil; turn off heat and let stand, covered, 30 minutes or until chilies are soft. Pour chilies with liquid into blender or food processor container fitted with metal blade. Process until smooth; reserve.

Melt lard in 5-quart Dutch oven over medium heat. Add onion and garlic; cook until onion is tender. Add beef and pork; cook, stirring frequently, until meat is lightly browned. Add jalapeño peppers, salt, oregano, cumin, wine and ancho chili purée. Bring to a boil. Cover; reduce heat and simmer 1½ to 2 hours or until meat is very tender. Stir in beans. Simmer, uncovered, 30 minutes or until chili has thickened slightly.

Chilly Day Chili

Makes 8 servings (about 8 cups)

2 medium onions, chopped
1 green pepper, chopped
2 tablespoons vegetable oil
2 pounds lean ground beef
2 to 3 tablespoons chili powder
1 can (14½ ounces) tomatoes, cut into bite-size pieces

1 can (15 ounces) tomato sauce
½ cup HEINZ® Tomato Ketchup
1 teaspoon salt
¼ teaspoon black pepper
2 cans (15½ ounces each) red kidney beans, partially drained

In large saucepan or Dutch oven, cook and stir onions and green pepper in oil until tender. Add beef; cook until beef is no longer pink, stirring occasionally. Drain excess fat. Stir in chili powder, then add tomatoes, tomato sauce, ketchup, salt and black pepper. Simmer, uncovered, 30 minutes, stirring occasionally. Add kidney beans; simmer additional 15 minutes.

Hearty Chili

Makes 8 servings

2 pounds BOB EVANS® Original Recipe Roll Sausage
1½ cups chopped onions
1 (1¼-ounce) package chili seasoning
1 (30-ounce) can chili or kidney beans

3 cups tomato sauce
3 cups tomato juice
Hot pepper sauce to taste (optional)

Crumble sausage into large Dutch oven. Add onions. Cook over medium heat until sausage is browned, stirring occasionally. Drain off any drippings; stir in seasoning, then remaining ingredients. Bring to a boil over high heat. Reduce heat to low; simmer, uncovered, 30 minutes. Serve hot. Refrigerate leftovers.

Riverboat Chili

Makes 4 to 6 servings

Prep Time:
30 minutes

Cook Time:
2 hours

2 pounds lean ground beef
2 large onions, chopped
1 large green pepper, chopped
2 cans (14½ ounces each) FRANK'S® or SNOWFLOSS® Original Style Diced Tomatoes, undrained
1 can (14½ ounces) FRANK'S® or SNOWFLOSS® Stewed Tomatoes, undrained

⅓ cup MISSISSIPPI® Barbecue Sauce
2 bay leaves
3 whole cloves
2 teaspoons chili powder
½ teaspoon cayenne pepper
½ teaspoon paprika
4 cans (15½ ounces each) dark red kidney beans

1. Brown ground beef in large stock pot. Drain grease.

2. Add onions, green pepper, diced tomatoes, stewed tomatoes, barbecue sauce, bay leaves, cloves, chili powder, cayenne pepper and paprika. Stir well.

3. Add kidney beans and stir well.

4. Cover and simmer 2 hours, stirring occasionally.

Microwave Directions: *Crumble beef into large casserole dish. Cook uncovered about 6 minutes, stirring at least twice to break up meat. Drain grease. Add onions, green pepper, diced tomatoes, stewed tomatoes, barbecue sauce, bay leaves, cloves, chili powder, cayenne pepper and paprika. Cook 1 minute. Stir well. Add kidney beans and stir well. Cover and cook 15 to 20 minutes, stirring occasionally. Cover and let stand 5 minutes.*

Durango Chili

3 tablespoons vegetable oil, divided
1 pound lean ground beef
1 pound lean boneless beef, cut into ½-inch cubes
2 medium onions, chopped
1 green bell pepper, seeded and chopped
4 cloves garlic, minced
¼ cup tomato paste
3 to 5 fresh or canned jalapeño peppers,* stemmed, seeded and minced
2 bay leaves
5 tablespoons chili powder
1 teaspoon salt
1 teaspoon ground cumin
½ teaspoon black pepper
2 cans (14½ ounces each) tomatoes, undrained
1 bottle (12 ounces) beer
1 can (10¾ ounces) condensed beef broth *plus* 1 can water
2 cans (4 ounces each) diced green chilies, undrained
3 cups cooked pinto beans *or* 2 cans (15 ounces each) pinto or kidney beans, drained

Condiments

1 cup (4 ounces) shredded Cheddar cheese
½ cup sour cream
4 green onions with tops, sliced
1 can (2¼ ounces) sliced pitted ripe olives, drained

*Jalapeño peppers can sting and irritate the skin; wear rubber gloves when handling peppers and do not touch eyes. Wash hands after handling.

Note:

A garlic press is a hand tool that presses one or two cloves of garlic through small openings to mash them. Garlic presses can be difficult to clean, but the sooner they are cleaned after use, the easier it is.

Heat 1 tablespoon oil in 5-quart Dutch oven over medium-high heat. Add ground beef, stirring to separate meat; add cubed beef. Cook, stirring occasionally, until meat is lightly browned. Transfer meat and pan drippings to medium bowl. Heat remaining 2 tablespoons oil in Dutch oven over medium heat. Add onions, bell pepper and garlic; cook until tender. Stir in tomato paste, jalapeño peppers, bay leaves, chili powder, salt, cumin and black pepper. Chop tomatoes; add to Dutch oven. Add meat, beer, broth, water and green chilies. Bring to a boil. Reduce heat and simmer, partially covered, 2 hours or until meat is very tender and chili has thickened. Stir in beans. Simmer, uncovered, 20 minutes. For thicker chili, continue simmering, uncovered, until chili is of desired consistency. Discard bay leaves. Serve with condiments.

Turkey Chili with Black Beans

Makes 4 servings

1 pound ground turkey breast
1 can (about 14½ ounces)
    fat-free reduced-sodium
    chicken broth
1 large onion, finely chopped
1 green bell pepper, seeded and
    diced
2 teaspoons chili powder
½ teaspoon ground allspice

¼ teaspoon ground cinnamon
¼ teaspoon paprika
1 can (15 ounces) black beans,
    rinsed and drained
1 can (14 ounces) crushed
    tomatoes in tomato purée,
    undrained
2 teaspoons apple cider vinegar

1. Heat large nonstick skillet over high heat. Add turkey, chicken broth, onion and bell pepper. Cook and stir, breaking up turkey. Cook until turkey is no longer pink.

2. Add chili powder, allspice, cinnamon and paprika. Reduce heat to medium-low; simmer 10 minutes. Add black beans, tomatoes and vinegar; bring to a boil.

3. Reduce heat to low; simmer 20 to 25 minutes or until thickened to desired consistency. Garnish as desired.

Vegetarian Chili with Cornbread Topping

1 pound zucchini, halved and cut into ½-inch slices (about 4 cups)

1 red or green bell pepper, cut into 1-inch pieces

1 rib celery, thinly sliced

1 clove garlic, minced

2 cans (15 to 19 ounces each) kidney beans, rinsed and drained

1 can (28 ounces) crushed tomatoes in purée, undrained

¼ cup *Frank's® RedHot®* Cayenne Pepper Sauce

1 tablespoon chili powder

1 package (6½ ounces) cornbread mix plus ingredients to prepare mix

Prep Time:
20 minutes

Cook Time:
35 minutes

1. Preheat oven to 400°F. Heat *1 tablespoon oil* in 12-inch heatproof skillet* over medium-high heat. Add zucchini, bell pepper, celery and garlic. Cook and stir 5 minutes or until tender. Stir in beans, tomatoes, *Frank's RedHot* Sauce and chili powder. Heat to boiling, stirring.

2. Prepare cornbread mix according to package directions. Spoon batter on top of chili mixture, spreading to ½ inch from edges. Bake 30 minutes or until cornbread is golden brown and mixture is bubbly.

If handle of skillet is not heatproof, wrap in foil.

South of the Border Chili

Makes 4 servings

Prep and Cook Time:
45 minutes

4 large Idaho Potatoes, baked
1 tablespoon vegetable oil
12 ounces ground turkey
1 medium onion, diced
1 red or green bell pepper, diced
1 clove garlic, minced
1 tablespoon chili powder
1 can (15 ounces) red kidney beans, rinsed and drained

1 can (14½ ounces) stewed tomatoes, undrained
¼ cup water
½ teaspoon salt
2 tablespoons grated low-fat Cheddar cheese (optional)
2 tablespoons low-fat sour cream (optional)

1. In large nonstick skillet, over medium-high heat, heat oil. Add ground turkey; cook, stirring to break up large pieces, until lightly browned, about 5 minutes. With slotted spoon, remove turkey from skillet, set aside.

2. To skillet, add onion, bell pepper and garlic; cook until vegetables are tender-crisp, about 4 to 5 minutes. Add chili powder; cook, stirring, 1 minute.

3. Stir in kidney beans, stewed tomatoes with liquid, water and salt. Bring to a boil and reduce heat; simmer until thickened, about 10 to 12 minutes.

4. Halve potatoes lengthwise, cutting almost to base of each potato. Mash slightly with fork, leaving in skins. Spoon chili mixture over each potato, dividing evenly. Top with Cheddar cheese and sour cream, if desired.

Favorite recipe from **Idaho Potato Commission**

Two-Bean Chili

1 pound sweet Italian sausage, casing removed
1 pound ground beef
2 medium onions, chopped
1 large green bell pepper, chopped
3 cloves garlic, minced
¼ cup flour
3 tablespoons chili powder
2 teaspoons ground cumin
2 teaspoons dried basil leaves
2 teaspoons dried oregano leaves
1 teaspoon salt
2 (28-ounce) cans Italian-style tomatoes, undrained

3 tablespoons Worcestershire sauce
1¼ teaspoons TABASCO® brand Pepper Sauce
1 (20-ounce) can chick-peas, drained
1 (15½-ounce) can red kidney beans, drained
Sliced ripe olives, chopped onion, chopped green bell pepper, chopped tomato, shredded cheese and cooked rice (optional)

Note:

Worcestershire sauce is a dark, savory sauce developed in India and named after the English town, Worcester, where it was first bottled. It is made from a complex mix of ingredients, including anchovies, tamarind paste, molasses, onions, garlic and soy sauce.

Cook sausage, beef, onions, bell pepper and garlic in large heavy saucepan or Dutch oven about 20 minutes or until meats are browned and vegetables are tender; drain fat. Stir in flour, chili powder, cumin, basil, oregano and salt; cook 1 minute. Add tomatoes; break up with fork. Stir in Worcestershire sauce and TABASCO® Sauce. Cover and simmer 1 hour, adding water if necessary; stir occasionally. Stir in chick-peas and kidney beans. Cook until heated through. Serve with olives, onion, bell pepper, tomato, cheese and rice, if desired.

Hot Dogs with Chili

Makes 4 to 6 servings

½ pound HILLSHIRE FARM® Hot Dogs, cut into ½-inch slices
½ cup chopped onion
2 tablespoons chopped green pepper
½ teaspoon chili powder
2 tablespoons butter

2 cans (1 pound 4 ounces each) kidney beans, drained
1 can (10½ ounces) condensed tomato soup
1 teaspoon vinegar
½ teaspoon Worcestershire sauce

Sauté Hot Dogs, onion, green pepper and chili powder in butter until Hot Dogs are browned. Add remaining ingredients. Cover; cook over low heat 12 to 15 minutes. Stir often.

Chunky Chili con Carne

Makes 6 to 8 servings

2 pounds ground beef
1 cup chopped onion
1 tablespoon minced fresh garlic
1 can (14.5 ounces) HUNT'S® Whole Tomatoes
1 can (14.5 ounces) beef broth
1 can (6 ounces) HUNT'S® Tomato Paste

3 tablespoons GEBHARDT® Chili Powder
1 teaspoon ground cumin
½ teaspoon dried oregano
½ teaspoon cayenne pepper
1 teaspoon salt
1 can (30 ounces) chili beans

In large pot, brown meat with onion and garlic over medium heat; drain. Stir in tomatoes, broth, tomato paste, chili powder, cumin, oregano, cayenne pepper and salt; reduce heat to low and simmer 20 minutes. Stir in beans and simmer additional 10 minutes.

Chili Verde

Makes 4 servings

½ to ¾ pound boneless lean pork, cut into 1-inch cubes
1 large onion, halved and thinly sliced
6 cloves garlic, chopped or sliced
½ cup water
1 pound fresh tomatillos
1 can (about 14 ounces) chicken broth

1 can (4 ounces) diced mild green chilies
1 teaspoon ground cumin
1½ cups cooked navy or Great Northern beans or 1 can (15 ounces) Great Northern beans, rinsed and drained
½ cup lightly packed fresh cilantro, chopped
Sour cream

1. Place pork, onion, garlic and water in large saucepan. Cover; simmer over medium-low heat 30 minutes, stirring occasionally (add more water if necessary). Uncover; boil over medium-high heat until liquid evaporates and meat browns.

2. Stir in tomatillos and broth. Cover; simmer over medium heat 20 minutes or until tomatillos are tender. Pull tomatillos apart with 2 forks. Add chilies and cumin.

3. Cover; simmer over medium-low heat 45 minutes or until meat is tender and pulls apart easily. (Add more water or broth if necessary, to keep liquid at same level.) Add beans; simmer 10 minutes or until heated through. Stir in cilantro. Serve with sour cream.

Three-Bean Caribbean Chili

Makes 6 (1-cup) servings

1 tablespoon olive oil
1 large onion, chopped
2 cloves garlic, minced
1 jalapeño pepper,* seeded and minced
2 large red or green bell peppers, diced
1 tablespoon plus 2 teaspoons sweet paprika
1 tablespoon plus 2 teaspoons chili powder
2 teaspoons sugar
2 teaspoons ground cumin
½ teaspoon salt
¼ teaspoon ground cloves
3 cups water

1 can (6 ounces) tomato paste
1 can (15 ounces) red kidney beans, drained
1 can (15 ounces) cannellini beans, drained
1 can (15 ounces) black beans, drained
1 tablespoon balsamic vinegar
Mango Salsa (recipe follows)
Hot cooked brown rice
Fresh cilantro for garnish

*Jalapeño peppers can sting and irritate the skin; wear rubber gloves when handling peppers and do not touch eyes. Wash hands after handling.

1. Heat oil in large saucepan over medium heat until hot. Add onion and garlic; cook and stir 4 minutes. Add jalapeño and bell peppers; cook and stir 5 minutes or until tender.

2. Add paprika, chili powder, sugar, cumin, salt and cloves; cook and stir 1 minute.

3. Stir in water and tomato paste until well blended. Bring to a boil over high heat. Reduce heat to low. Cover and simmer 15 minutes. Stir in beans and vinegar; partially cover and simmer 15 minutes or until hot.

4. Meanwhile, prepare Mango Salsa.

5. Serve chili over rice. Top with Mango Salsa. Garnish, if desired.

Mango Salsa

1 large mango, peeled and cut
  into ¾-inch cubes
1 small firm ripe banana,
  peeled and cubed
3 tablespoons minced fresh
  cilantro

1 tablespoon thawed frozen
  orange juice concentrate
1 teaspoon balsamic vinegar

Combine mango, banana and cilantro in medium bowl. Stir
together juice concentrate and vinegar. Pour over fruit; toss.

Makes 1¼ cups

That's Using Your Bean

Beans, the seeded pods of legumes, are available in hundreds of varieties. These are some of the most common.

Black Bean: These small jet-black beans, also known as turtle beans, have an earthy, meaty flavor and mealy texture. They are available both dried and canned.

Chick-Pea: Also known as garbanzo or ceci beans, chick-peas are larger than green peas. They are round, irregularly shaped tan beans with a firm texture and mild, nutlike flavor. They are available both dried, canned, and in some parts of the country, fresh.

Great Northern Bean: These are large white beans which are similar in shape to lima beans, but with a delicate flavor. They are available both dried and canned.

Kidney Bean: This bean gets its name because of its shape. They have a firm texture and skins that range from very dark red to pink, and flesh that is cream colored. Kidney beans are noted for their robust flavor. Milder flavored white kidney beans, which are more difficult to find, are better known as cannellini beans. Kidney beans can be used interchangeably with pinto beans. Kidney beans, cannellini beans and pinto beans are available both dried and canned.

Navy Bean: Also called Yankee beans, navy beans are so named because they were a food staple for the U.S. Navy in the 1800's. These small oval-shaped white beans are the bean of choice for commercial baked beans and homemade navy bean soup. Navy beans are available both dried and canned.

Meaty Chili

Makes 6 servings

1 pound coarsely ground beef
¼ pound ground Italian sausage
1 large onion, chopped
2 medium ribs celery, diced
2 fresh jalapeño peppers,*
   chopped
2 cloves garlic, minced
1 can (28 ounces) whole peeled
   tomatoes, undrained, cut
   up
1 can (15 ounces) pinto beans,
   drained
1 can (12 ounces) tomato juice

1 cup water
¼ cup ketchup
1 teaspoon sugar
1 teaspoon chili powder
½ teaspoon salt
½ teaspoon ground cumin
½ teaspoon dried thyme leaves
⅛ teaspoon black pepper

Jalapeño peppers can sting and irritate the skin; wear rubber gloves when handling peppers and do not touch eyes. Wash hands after handling.

Cook beef, sausage, onion, celery, jalapeños and garlic in 5-quart Dutch oven over medium-high heat until meat is browned and onion is tender, stirring frequently.

Stir in tomatoes with juice, beans, tomato juice, water, ketchup, sugar, chili powder, salt, cumin, thyme and black pepper. Bring to a boil over high heat. Reduce heat to medium-low; simmer, uncovered, 30 minutes, stirring occasionally.

Ladle into bowls. Garnish, if desired.

California Turkey Chili

1¼ cups chopped onion
1 cup chopped green bell
　　pepper
2 cloves garlic, minced
3 tablespoons vegetable oil
1 can (28 ounces) kidney beans,
　　drained
1 can (28 ounces) stewed
　　tomatoes, undrained
1 cup red wine or water
3 cups cubed cooked California-
　　grown turkey

1 tablespoon chili powder
1 tablespoon chopped fresh
　　cilantro or 1 teaspoon dried
　　coriander
1 teaspoon crushed red pepper
½ teaspoon salt
　　Shredded Cheddar cheese
　　(optional)
　　Additional chopped onion
　　(optional)
　　Additional chopped fresh
　　cilantro (optional)

Cook and stir onion, green pepper, garlic in oil in large saucepan
over high heat until tender. Add beans, tomatoes with liquid,
wine, turkey, chili powder, cilantro, red pepper and salt. Cover;
simmer 25 minutes or until heated through. Top with cheese,
onion or cilantro, if desired.

Favorite recipe from **California Poultry Federation**

Bulgur Chili

Makes 4 servings

1 cup chopped onion
½ cup chopped celery
4 teaspoons sugar
2 tablespoons chili powder
1 tablespoon dried oregano
1 teaspoon ground cumin
1 teaspoon black pepper
2 teaspoons vegetable oil
⅔ cup uncooked bulgur

1½ cups water
1 can (28 ounces) tomatoes, crushed or stewed
1 can (14 ounces) black beans, rinsed and drained
1 can (14 ounces) cannellini or navy beans, rinsed and drained

In 3- to 4-quart saucepan, sauté onion, celery, sugar and seasonings in oil 5 minutes. Stir in bulgur and water. Simmer, covered, over low heat 10 minutes, stirring occasionally. Add tomatoes and beans. Simmer, covered, over low heat 15 to 20 minutes, stirring occasionally. Serve in warmed bowls.

Favorite recipe from **The Sugar Association, Inc.**

Vegetable Chili

Makes 4 to 6 servings

Prep Time:
5 minutes

Cook Time:
10 minutes

2 cans (15 ounces each) chunky chili tomato sauce
1 bag (16 ounces) BIRDS EYE® frozen Farm Fresh Mixtures Broccoli, Corn and Red Peppers

1 can (15½ ounces) red kidney beans
1 can (4½ ounces) chopped green chilies
½ cup shredded Cheddar cheese

• Combine tomato sauce, vegetables, beans and chilies in large saucepan; bring to a boil.

• Cook, uncovered, over medium heat 5 minutes.

• Sprinkle individual servings with cheese.

Pork and Wild Rice Chili

Makes 6 servings

1 pound boneless pork loin, cut into ½-inch cubes
1 onion, chopped
1 teaspoon vegetable oil
2 cans (14½ ounces each) chicken broth
1 can (18 ounces) white kernel corn, drained
2 cans (4 ounces each) chopped green chilies, drained

¾ cup uncooked California wild rice, rinsed
1 teaspoon ground cumin
½ teaspoon salt
½ teaspoon dried oregano leaves
1½ cups shredded Monterey Jack cheese (optional)
6 sprigs fresh cilantro (optional)

Cook and stir pork and onion in oil in large saucepan over high heat until onion is soft and pork is lightly browned. Add chicken broth, corn, green chilies, wild rice, cumin, salt and oregano. Cover and simmer 45 minutes or until rice is tender and grains have puffed open. Garnish with cheese and cilantro, if desired.

Favorite recipe from **California Wild Rice Advisory Board**

Note:

Sweet corn varieties can be golden yellow, white or a mixture of both. No matter which color, they all have that wonderfully sweet flavor of just-picked freshness.

Rick's Good-As-Gold Chili

Makes 4½ cups

½ cup vegetable oil
2 whole chicken breasts, split, skinned and boned
⅓ cup water
¼ cup instant minced onion
2 teaspoons instant minced garlic
1 can (15 ounces) tomato sauce
¾ cup beer
½ cup chicken broth
2 tablespoons chili powder
2 teaspoons ground cumin
1 teaspoon dried oregano leaves, crushed

1 teaspoon soy sauce
1 teaspoon Worcestershire sauce
¾ teaspoon salt
½ teaspoon paprika
½ teaspoon ground red pepper
¼ teaspoon turmeric
⅛ teaspoon rubbed sage
⅛ teaspoon dried thyme leaves, crushed
⅛ teaspoon dry mustard

1. Heat oil in large skillet over medium-high heat. Add chicken to skillet in single layer. Cook 10 minutes or until chicken is golden brown and no longer pink in center, turning once.

2. Meanwhile, stir water, onion and garlic in small bowl; let stand 10 minutes to soften.

3. When chicken is browned, remove from skillet and drain on paper towels.

4. When chicken cools slightly, cut into ¼-inch cubes on cutting board; set aside.

5. Drain drippings from skillet, reserving 2 tablespoons. Heat reserved drippings in skillet over medium-high heat. Add onion and garlic mixture; cook and stir 5 minutes or until onion and garlic are golden.

6. Add remaining ingredients except cubed chicken; stir well. Bring chili to a boil; reduce heat and simmer 20 minutes, stirring occasionally, until chili thickens slightly.

Winter White Chili

½ pound boneless pork loin *or* 2 boneless pork chops, cut into ½-inch cubes
½ cup chopped onion
1 teaspoon vegetable oil
1 (16-ounce) can navy beans, drained
1 (16-ounce) can chick peas, drained
1 (16-ounce) can white kernel corn, drained

1 (14½-ounce) can chicken broth
1 cup cooked wild rice
1 (4-ounce) can diced green chilies, drained
1½ teaspoons ground cumin
¼ teaspoon garlic powder
⅛ teaspoon hot pepper sauce
Chopped fresh parsley and shredded cheese

Makes 6 servings

Prep Time:
10 minutes

Cook Time:
25 minutes

In 4-quart saucepan, sauté pork and onion in oil over medium-high heat until onion is soft and pork is lightly browned, about 5 minutes. Stir in remaining ingredients except parsley and shredded cheese. Cover and simmer for 20 minutes. Serve each portion garnished with parsley and shredded cheese.

Favorite recipe from **National Pork Board**

Quick & Easy Chili

Makes 6 servings

1 pound ground beef
1 medium onion, chopped
2 cloves garlic, finely chopped
2 cans (15 ounces each) kidney,
    pinto or black beans,
    drained
1 jar (16 ounces) ORTEGA®
    SALSA (any flavor)
1 can (4 ounces) ORTEGA®
    Diced Green Chiles
2 teaspoons chili powder

½ teaspoon dried oregano,
    crushed
½ teaspoon ground cumin
    Topping suggestions:
    ORTEGA® SALSA, shredded
    Cheddar or Monterey Jack
    cheese, chopped tomatoes,
    sliced ripe olives, sliced
    green onions and sour
    cream

Note:

Chili powder is a spice
blend typically made
up of ground dried
chilies, cloves,
coriander, cumin,
garlic and oregano.

COOK beef, onion and garlic in large skillet over medium-high heat for 4 to 5 minutes or until beef is no longer pink; drain.

STIR in beans, salsa, chiles, chili powder, oregano and cumin. Bring to a boil. Reduce heat to low; cook, covered, for 20 to 25 minutes.

TOP as desired before serving.

Tex-Mex Chili

4 bacon slices, diced
2 pounds beef round steak, trimmed and cut into ½-inch cubes
1 medium onion, chopped
2 cloves garlic, minced
¼ cup chili powder
1 teaspoon dried oregano
1 teaspoon ground cumin
1 teaspoon salt
½ to 1 teaspoon ground red pepper
½ teaspoon hot pepper sauce
4 cups water
Additional chopped onion for garnish

Cook bacon in 5-quart Dutch oven over medium-high heat until crisp. Remove with slotted spoon; drain on paper towels. Add half of the steak to bacon drippings in Dutch oven; cook until lightly browned. Remove steak from Dutch oven. Repeat with remaining steak. Reduce heat to medium. Cook onion and garlic in pan drippings until onion is tender. Return steak and bacon to Dutch oven. Add chili powder, oregano, cumin, salt, ground red pepper, hot pepper sauce and water. Bring to a boil. Cover; reduce heat and simmer 1½ hours. Skim fat. Simmer, uncovered, 30 minutes or until steak is very tender and chili has thickened slightly. Serve in individual bowls. Garnish with additional chopped onion.

Rice and Chick-Pea Chili

Makes 4 servings

⅔ cup UNCLE BEN'S® ORIGINAL
    CONVERTED® Brand Rice
1 can (15 ounces) chick-peas,
    undrained
1 can (15 ounces) diced
    tomatoes, undrained
1 can (8 ounces) diced green
    chilies

1 cup frozen corn
¼ cup chopped fresh cilantro
1 tablespoon taco seasoning
½ cup (2 ounces) shredded
    reduced-fat Cheddar cheese

1. In medium saucepan, bring 1¾ cups water and rice to a boil. Cover; reduce heat and simmer 15 minutes.

2. Add remaining ingredients except cheese. Cook over low heat 10 minutes. Serve in bowls sprinkled with cheese.

Bandstand Chili

Makes 8 servings

Prep and Cook Time:
25 minutes

2 cups chopped cooked
    BUTTERBALL® Boneless
    Young Turkey
1 tablespoon vegetable oil
1½ cups chopped onions
1½ cups chopped red bell
    peppers
2 tablespoons mild Mexican
    seasoning*

1 clove garlic, minced
1 can (28 ounces) tomato purée
    with tomato bits
1 can (15½ ounces) light red
    kidney beans, undrained

*To make your own Mexican seasoning,
combine 1 tablespoon chili powder,
1½ teaspoons dried oregano and
1½ teaspoons ground cumin.

Heat oil in large skillet over medium heat until hot. Add onions, bell peppers, Mexican seasoning and garlic. Cook and stir 4 to 5 minutes. Add tomato purée and beans; stir in turkey. Reduce heat to low; simmer 5 minutes.

Texas Chili & Biscuits

Makes 4 to 6 servings

1 pound ground beef
1 package (about 1¾ ounces)
    chili seasoning mix
1 can (16 ounces) whole kernel
    corn, drained
1 can (14½ ounces) whole
    tomatoes, undrained and
    cut up

½ cup water
¾ cup biscuit baking mix
⅔ cup cornmeal
⅔ cup milk
1⅓ cups *French's®* French Fried
    Onions, divided
½ cup (2 ounces) shredded
    Monterey Jack cheese

Preheat oven to 400°F. In medium skillet, brown beef; drain. Stir in chili seasoning, corn, tomatoes and water; bring to a boil. Reduce heat; simmer, uncovered, 10 minutes. Meanwhile, in medium bowl, combine baking mix, cornmeal, milk and *⅔ cup* French Fried Onions; beat vigorously 30 seconds. Pour beef mixture into 2-quart casserole. Spoon biscuit dough in mounds around edge of casserole. Bake, uncovered, at 400°F for 15 minutes or until biscuits are light brown. Top biscuits with cheese and remaining *⅔ cup* onions; bake, uncovered, 1 to 3 minutes or until onions are golden brown.

Note:

The main ingredients for chili are cubed or coarsely ground beef and chili peppers or chili powder. The addition of beans can be highly controversial with chili aficionados. Whereas Texans generally do not add beans, others consider beans a necessity.

Spicy Tomato Chili with Red Beans

Makes 4 servings

1 tablespoon olive oil
1 cup chopped green bell
  pepper
1 cup chopped onion
1 cup sliced celery
1 clove garlic, minced
1 can (15 ounces) red beans,
  drained and rinsed

1 can (15 ounces) diced
  tomatoes, undrained
1 can (10 ounces) diced
  tomatoes with green chilies
1 can (8 ounces) low-sodium
  tomato sauce
8 (6-inch) corn tortillas

1. Preheat oven to 400°F.

2. Heat oil in large saucepan over medium heat until hot. Add bell pepper, onion, celery and garlic. Cook and stir 5 minutes or until onion is translucent.

3. Add remaining ingredients except tortillas. Bring to a boil; reduce heat to low. Simmer 15 minutes. Cut each tortilla into 8 wedges. Place on baking sheet; bake 8 minutes or until crisp. Crush half of tortilla wedges; place in bottom of soup bowls. Spoon chili over tortillas. Serve with remaining tortilla wedges.

Sizzling Skillet Dishes

CHAPTER THIRTEEN

Mediterranean Chicken and Rice

Makes 4 servings

Prep Time:
5 minutes

Cook Time:
30 minutes

4 TYSON® Fresh or Individually Fresh Frozen® Boneless, Skinless Chicken Breasts
2 cups UNCLE BEN'S® Instant Brown Rice
1 tablespoon olive oil
1 teaspoon minced garlic

1 can (15 ounces) diced tomatoes, undrained
1½ cups water
½ teaspoon dried oregano leaves
16 pitted kalamata olives
2 ounces feta cheese, crumbled

PREP: CLEAN: Wash hands. Remove protective ice glaze from frozen chicken by holding under cool running water 1 to 2 minutes. CLEAN: Wash hands.

COOK: In large nonstick skillet, heat olive oil and garlic; add chicken. Cook over medium heat 4 to 6 minutes (5 to 7 minutes if using frozen chicken) or until chicken is browned. Stir in tomatoes, water and oregano; cover. Reduce heat to low; simmer 10 minutes. Stir in rice; cover. Cook 10 minutes or until rice is cooked and internal juices of chicken run clear. (Or insert instant-read meat thermometer in thickest part of chicken. Temperature should read 170°F.) Stir in olives and sprinkle with cheese.

SERVE: For a complete Mediterranean-style meal, serve with a green salad tossed with Italian vinaigrette.

CHILL: Refrigerate leftovers immediately.

Szechuan Vegetable Lo Mein

2 cans (about 14 ounces each) vegetable or chicken broth
2 teaspoons minced garlic
1 teaspoon minced fresh ginger
¼ teaspoon red pepper flakes
1 package (16 ounces) frozen vegetable medley, such as broccoli, carrots, water chestnuts and red bell peppers

1 package (5 ounces) Oriental curly noodles or 5 ounces angel hair pasta, broken in half
3 tablespoons soy sauce
1 tablespoon dark sesame oil
¼ cup thinly sliced green onion tops

Makes 4 servings

Prep and Cook Time:
20 minutes

1. Combine broth, garlic, ginger and red pepper flakes in large deep skillet. Cover and bring to a boil over high heat.

2. Add vegetables and noodles to skillet; cover and return to a boil. Reduce heat to medium-low; simmer, uncovered, 5 to 6 minutes or until noodles and vegetables are tender, stirring occasionally.

3. Stir soy sauce and sesame oil into broth mixture; cook 3 minutes. Stir in green onions; ladle into bowls.

<u>Tip:</u> *For a heartier, protein-packed main dish, add 1 package (10½ ounces) extra-firm tofu, cut into ¾-inch pieces, to the broth mixture with the soy sauce and sesame oil.*

Spicy Tuna and Linguine with Garlic and Pine Nuts

Makes 4 to 6 servings

2 tablespoons olive oil
4 cloves garlic, minced
2 cups sliced mushrooms
½ cup chopped onion
½ teaspoon crushed red pepper
2½ cups chopped plum tomatoes
1 can (14½ ounces) chicken broth plus water to equal 2 cups
½ teaspoon salt
¼ teaspoon coarsely ground black pepper
1 package (9 ounces) uncooked fresh linguine
1 (7-ounce) pouch of STARKIST® Premium Albacore Tuna
⅓ cup chopped fresh cilantro
⅓ cup toasted pine nuts or almonds

Note:

Plum tomatoes, sometimes called Italian tomatoes, are small and oval in shape. Since they are fleshier than most globe tomatoes, they are a good choice for making sauces.

In 12-inch skillet, heat olive oil over medium-high heat; sauté garlic, mushrooms, onion and red pepper until golden brown. Add tomatoes, chicken broth mixture, salt and black pepper; bring to a boil.

Separate uncooked linguine into strands; place in skillet and spoon sauce over. Reduce heat to simmer; cook, covered, 4 more minutes or until cooked through. Toss gently; add tuna and cilantro and toss again. Sprinkle with pine nuts.

Quick Beef Bourguignonne

3 tablespoons all-purpose flour
½ teaspoon dried thyme
½ teaspoon ground black
pepper
¾ pound boneless sirloin or top
round steak, cut into 1-inch
pieces
2 tablespoons vegetable oil,
divided
3 cups (8 ounces) halved or
quartered crimini or white
mushrooms

⅓ cup thinly sliced shallots or
chopped onion
1 (14½-ounce) can beef broth
¼ cup water
¼ cup dry red wine or water
1 (4.8-ounce) package PASTA
RONI® Garlic Alfredo
¾ cup thinly sliced carrots

Prep Time:
15 minutes

Cook Time:
20 minutes

1. Combine flour, thyme and pepper in resealable plastic food storage bag. Add steak; shake to coat evenly with flour mixture.

2. In large skillet over medium-high heat, heat 1 tablespoon oil. Add steak; cook 3 minutes or until lightly browned on all sides. Remove from skillet; set aside.

3. In same skillet over medium heat, heat remaining 1 tablespoon oil. Add mushrooms and shallots; cook 3 minutes, stirring occasionally.

4. Add beef broth, ¼ cup water and wine; bring to a boil. Add pasta, steak, carrots and Special Seasonings. Reduce heat to medium. Simmer 5 minutes or until pasta is tender. Let stand 5 minutes before serving.

Bayou-Style Pot Pie

Makes 4 servings

Prep and Cook Time:
28 minutes

1 tablespoon olive oil
1 large onion, chopped
1 green bell pepper, chopped
1½ teaspoons minced garlic
8 ounces boneless skinless
   chicken thighs, cut into
   1-inch pieces
1 can (14½ ounces) stewed
   tomatoes, undrained

8 ounces fully cooked smoked
   sausage or kielbasa, thinly
   sliced
¾ teaspoon hot pepper sauce or
   to taste
2¼ cups buttermilk baking mix
¾ teaspoon dried thyme leaves
⅛ teaspoon black pepper
⅔ cup milk

1. Preheat oven to 450°F. Heat oil in medium ovenproof skillet over medium-high heat until hot. Add onion, bell pepper and garlic. Cook 3 minutes, stirring occasionally.

2. Add chicken and cook 1 minute. Add tomatoes with juice, sausage and hot pepper sauce. Cook, uncovered, over medium-low heat 5 minutes.

3. While chicken is cooking, combine baking mix, thyme and black pepper. Stir in milk. Drop batter by heaping tablespoonfuls in mounds over chicken mixture. Bake 14 minutes or until biscuits are golden brown and cooked through and chicken mixture is bubbly.

Hint: *You can use any of a variety of fully cooked sausages from your supermarket meat case. Andouille, a fairly spicy Louisiana-style sausage, is perfect for this dish.*

Greek Island Skillet

¾ **pound lean ground beef**
3 cups water
1 can (14 ounces) diced
  tomatoes, undrained
1 package KNORR® Recipe
  Classics™ Roasted Garlic
  Soup, Dip and Recipe Mix
2½ cups (8 ounces) uncooked
  pasta twists

1 package (10 ounces) frozen
  chopped spinach, thawed
  and drained
1 can (2.2 ounces) sliced ripe
  olives, drained (about
  ½ cup)
¼ **cup crumbled feta cheese or**
  grated Parmesan cheese
  (optional)

Makes 4 servings

Prep and Cook Time:
25 to 30 minutes

• In large skillet, sauté ground beef over medium-high heat
5 minutes or until lightly browned. Spoon off excess drippings.
Add water, tomatoes and recipe mix; bring to a boil.

• Stir in pasta and return to boiling; reduce heat, cover and
simmer 8 to 10 minutes or until pasta is tender, stirring
frequently.

• Stir in spinach and olives. Simmer 2 minutes or until heated
through. If desired, sprinkle with cheese.

Ham & Barbecued Bean Skillet

Makes 4 servings

Prep and Cook Time:
20 minutes

1 tablespoon vegetable oil
1 cup chopped onion
1 teaspoon minced garlic
1 can (15 ounces) red or pink kidney beans, rinsed and drained
1 can (15 ounces) cannellini or Great Northern beans, rinsed and drained

1 cup chopped green bell pepper
½ cup packed light brown sugar
½ cup catsup
2 tablespoons cider vinegar
2 teaspoons dry mustard
1 fully cooked smoked ham steak (about 12 ounces), cut ½ inch thick

1. Heat oil in large deep skillet over medium-high heat until hot. Add onion and garlic; cook 3 minutes, stirring occasionally.

2. Add kidney beans, cannellini beans, bell pepper, brown sugar, catsup, vinegar and mustard; mix well.

3. Trim fat from ham; cut into ½-inch pieces. Add ham to bean mixture; simmer over medium heat 5 minutes or until sauce thickens and mixture is heated through, stirring occasionally.

Pasta Beef & Zucchini Dinner

Makes 5 servings

1 pound extra-lean ground beef
1 medium onion, chopped
1 clove garlic, crushed
½ teaspoon salt
2 (14-ounce) cans ready-to-serve beef broth
1 teaspoon Italian seasoning
¼ teaspoon crushed red pepper
2 cups uncooked mini lasagna or rotini pasta

2 cups sliced zucchini (cut ⅜ inch thick)
1 tablespoon cornstarch
¼ cup water
3 plum tomatoes, each cut into 4 wedges
2 tablespoons grated Parmesan cheese

In large nonstick skillet, cook ground beef with onion, garlic and salt over medium heat 8 to 10 minutes or until beef is browned, stirring occasionally to break up beef into 1-inch crumbles. Remove beef mixture with slotted spoon; pour off drippings. Set beef aside.

Add broth, Italian seasoning and red pepper to same skillet. Bring to a boil; add pasta. Reduce heat to medium; simmer, uncovered, for 6 minutes, stirring occasionally. Add zucchini; continue cooking for an additional 6 to 8 minutes or until pasta is tender, yet firm. Push pasta and zucchini to side of skillet. Mix cornstarch with water and add to broth in skillet; bring to a boil. Return beef mixture to skillet. Add tomatoes; heat through, stirring occasionally. Spoon into serving dish; sprinkle with Parmesan cheese.

Favorite recipe from **North Dakota Wheat Commission**

Note:

The best known and most readily available variety of garlic is American garlic. It has white skin and a strong flavor. Use American garlic unless the recipe indicates otherwise.

Bistro Chicken Skillet

Makes 4 servings

Prep Time:
10 minutes

Cook Time:
30 minutes

1 (2- to 2½-pound) whole
chicken, cut into 8 pieces
2 teaspoons dried thyme
1 teaspoon paprika
1 teaspoon salt
½ teaspoon ground black
pepper
2 tablespoons olive oil
8 large whole cloves garlic,
peeled

¼ cup dry vermouth or water
2 tablespoons margarine or
butter
1 (4.6-ounce) package PASTA
RONI® Garlic & Olive Oil
with Vermicelli
1½ cups fresh asparagus, cut into
1½-inch pieces, or broccoli
florets
1 cup sliced carrots

1. Sprinkle meaty side of chicken with thyme, paprika, salt and
pepper. In large skillet over medium-high heat, heat oil. Add
chicken, seasoned-side down. Cook 5 minutes. Reduce heat to
medium-low; turn chicken over. Add garlic. Cover; cook 20 to
25 minutes or until chicken is no longer pink inside.

2. Meanwhile, in medium saucepan, bring 1½ cups water,
vermouth and margarine just to a boil. Stir in pasta, asparagus,
carrots and Special Seasonings. Reduce heat to medium. Gently
boil uncovered, 10 minutes or until pasta is tender, stirring
occasionally.

3. Remove chicken and garlic from skillet with slotted spoon.
Skim off and discard fat from skillet juices. Serve chicken, garlic
and reserved juices over pasta.

Indian Vegetable Curry

2 to 3 teaspoons curry powder
1 can (16 ounces) sliced
    potatoes, drained
1 bag (16 ounces) BIRDS EYE®
    frozen Farm Fresh Mixtures
    Broccoli, Cauliflower and
    Carrots

1 can (15 ounces) chick-peas,
    drained
1 can (14½ ounces) stewed
    tomatoes
1 can (13¾ ounces) vegetable
    or chicken broth
2 tablespoons cornstarch

**Makes about
6 servings**

Prep Time:
5 minutes

Cook Time:
15 minutes

• Stir curry powder in large skillet over high heat until fragrant, about 30 seconds.

• Stir in potatoes, vegetables, chick-peas and tomatoes; bring to a boil. Reduce heat to medium-high; cover and cook 8 minutes.

• Blend broth with cornstarch; stir into vegetables. Cook until thickened.

Serving Suggestion: *Add cooked chicken for a heartier main dish. Serve with white or brown rice.*

Florida Grapefruit Marinated Shrimp

Makes 4 servings

Note:

Grapefruit should be firm with shiny, smooth, thin skins. Fruit that feels heavy for its size is more likely to be juicy. Avoid lightweight grapefruit with rough skins.

1 cup frozen Florida grapefruit juice concentrate, thawed
2 cloves garlic, minced
3 tablespoons chopped fresh cilantro or parsley
2 teaspoons ketchup
1 tablespoon honey
¼ teaspoon crushed red pepper flakes
½ teaspoon salt
1 pound medium raw shrimp, shelled and deveined

2 teaspoons cornstarch
1 cup long-grain white rice
1 tablespoon olive oil
1 large red bell pepper, cut into strips
2 ribs celery, sliced diagonally into ¼-inch-thick slices
2 Florida grapefruit, peeled and sectioned
Fresh cilantro sprigs

Combine grapefruit juice concentrate, garlic, cilantro, ketchup, honey, red pepper flakes and salt in medium bowl. Stir in shrimp. Marinate 20 minutes, turning shrimp once. Drain shrimp, reserving marinade. Combine marinade with cornstarch. Meanwhile, prepare rice according to package directions. Heat oil over medium-high heat in large nonstick skillet; add shrimp. Cook and stir 2 to 3 minutes until shrimp turn pink and opaque. Add red bell pepper, celery and reserved marinade. Bring to a boil over high heat; boil until mixture thickens slightly, stirring constantly. Add grapefruit and heat 30 seconds. Garnish with fresh sprigs of cilantro.

Favorite recipe from **Florida Department of Citrus**

Apricot Ginger Glazed Chicken

2 tablespoons margarine or butter, divided
4 boneless, skinless chicken breast halves (about 1 pound)
1 (7.2-ounce) package RICE-A-RONI® Rice Pilaf

3 cups fresh or frozen broccoli flowerets
½ cup apricot jam
2 teaspoons Dijon mustard
½ teaspoon ground ginger

Makes 4 servings

Prep Time:
10 minutes

Cook Time:
30 minutes

1. In large skillet over medium heat, melt 1 tablespoon margarine. Add chicken; cook 5 minutes on each side or until browned. Remove from skillet; set aside.

2. In same skillet over medium heat, sauté rice-pasta mix with remaining 1 tablespoon margarine until pasta is golden brown. Slowly stir in 2 cups water and Special Seasonings; bring to a boil. Reduce heat to low. Cover; simmer 10 minutes.

3. Stir in broccoli. Place chicken over rice; return to a simmer. Cover; simmer 5 to 10 minutes or until rice is tender and chicken is no longer pink inside.

4. In small bowl, blend jam, mustard and ginger. Spoon 1 tablespoon glaze over each chicken breast and drizzle remaining glaze over rice. Cover; let stand 3 minutes before serving.

Tempting Tuna Parmesano

Makes 2 to 3 servings

Prep and Cook Time:
16 minutes

2 large cloves garlic
1 package (9 ounces)
    refrigerated fresh angel hair
    pasta
¼ cup butter or margarine
1 cup whipping cream
1 cup frozen peas

¼ teaspoon salt
1 can (6 ounces) white tuna in
    water, drained
¼ cup grated Parmesan cheese,
    plus additional for serving
Black pepper

1. Fill large deep skillet ¾ full with water. Cover and bring to a boil over high heat. Meanwhile, peel and mince garlic.

2. Add pasta to skillet; boil 1 to 2 minutes or until pasta is al dente. Do not overcook. Drain; set aside.

3. Add butter and garlic to skillet; cook over medium-high heat until butter is melted and sizzling. Stir in cream, peas and salt; bring to a boil.

4. Break tuna into chunks and stir into skillet with ¼ cup cheese. Return pasta to skillet. Cook until heated through; toss gently. Serve with additional cheese and pepper to taste.

Serving Suggestion: *Serve with a tossed romaine and tomato salad with Italian dressing.*

Lemon Chicken Rice

1 tablespoon olive oil
1 pound boneless, skinless
    chicken breast, cut into
    strips
1 clove garlic, crushed
1 cup uncooked rice*
1 can (14½ ounces) chicken
    broth

1 tablespoon grated lemon peel
½ teaspoon ground black
    pepper

*Recipe based on regular-milled long grain
white rice.

Heat oil in large skillet over medium-high heat until hot. Add chicken and garlic; cook and stir until browned. Stir in rice and broth. Cover and cook 15 minutes or until liquid is absorbed. Stir in lemon peel and pepper. Serve immediately.

Favorite recipe from **USA Rice Federation**

SPAM™ Skillet Dinner

3 medium zucchini
1 onion, thinly sliced
1 tablespoon vegetable oil
1 (12-ounce) can SPAM® Classic
3 medium potatoes, peeled,
    sliced
3 carrots, peeled, sliced

1 (16-ounce) can chopped
    tomatoes
¾ teaspoon garlic powder
½ teaspoon dried basil leaves
½ teaspoon dried oregano
    leaves

Cut zucchini into ½-inch slices. In large skillet, sauté zucchini and onion in oil 5 minutes. Cut SPAM® into 8 slices; halve each slice. Add potatoes, carrots and SPAM™ mixture to skillet; pour tomatoes over SPAM®. Sprinkle with garlic, basil and oregano. Cover; simmer 25 minutes or until potatoes are tender, stirring occasionally.

Honey-Dijon Chicken

Makes 4 servings

Prep Time:
10 minutes

Cook Time:
35 minutes

4 boneless, skinless chicken
  breast halves (about
  1 pound)
2 tablespoons all-purpose flour
3 tablespoons margarine or
  butter, divided

1 (6.9-ounce) package RICE-A-
  RONI® Chicken Flavor
1½ cups fresh or frozen sliced
  carrots
2 tablespoons honey
2 tablespoons Dijon mustard

1. Coat chicken with flour. In large skillet over medium heat, melt 2 tablespoons margarine. Add chicken; cook 5 minutes on each side or until browned. Remove from skillet; set aside.

2. In same skillet over medium heat, sauté rice-vermicelli mix with remaining 1 tablespoon margarine until vermicelli is golden brown.

3. Slowly stir in 2¼ cups water, carrots and Special Seasonings; bring to a boil. Place chicken over rice. Reduce heat to low. Cover; simmer 15 minutes.

4. In small bowl, combine honey and mustard. Drizzle over chicken. Simmer uncovered, 5 minutes or until rice is tender and chicken is no longer pink inside.

Note:

Honey is sold in one of three forms. Comb honey, taken directly from the hive, has the liquid honey still stored in the waxy comb, which is edible. Chunk honey includes small bits of the comb. By far the most common is extracted liquid honey, which has been removed from the comb, heated, strained, filtered and often pasteurized.

Spanish Rice

4 slices bacon, diced
1 medium green bell pepper,
    diced
1 small onion, chopped
1 large clove garlic, crushed
½ pound ground beef
2 cups canned stewed
    tomatoes, undrained

1 cup long grain rice, uncooked
1 cup water
1½ teaspoons TABASCO® brand
    Pepper Sauce
1 teaspoon salt

Makes 4 servings

Cook bacon until crisp in 12-inch skillet over medium-high heat,
stirring occasionally. With slotted spoon, remove to paper towels;
set aside. Cook green pepper, onion and garlic in drippings
remaining in skillet over medium heat until tender-crisp, about
5 minutes. Remove to bowl.

Cook ground beef in same skillet over medium-high heat until
well browned, stirring frequently. Drain. Add tomatoes with their
liquid, rice, water, TABASCO® Sauce, salt and green pepper
mixture. Bring to a boil over high heat; reduce heat to low. Cover
and simmer 20 minutes or until rice is tender, stirring
occasionally.

To serve, sprinkle mixture with cooked bacon.

Vegetable Pasta Italiano

Makes 6 servings

½ pound lean ground turkey
1 DOLE® Red Bell Pepper,
  seeded, sliced
1 tablespoon paprika
1 can (14½ ounces) crushed
  tomatoes
1 can (14½ ounces) reduced
  sodium chicken broth

2 cups uncooked bow tie pasta
2 cups DOLE® Broccoli, cut into
  florets
1 cup DOLE® Cauliflower, cut
  into florets
  Savory Topping (recipe
  follows)

• In 12-inch nonstick skillet, brown turkey 2 minutes.

• Stir in red pepper strips and paprika. Reduce heat to low, stirring 2 minutes longer.

• Stir in tomatoes, chicken broth and pasta. Bring to a boil. Reduce heat to low, cover and simmer 15 minutes. Arrange broccoli and cauliflower on top. Cover, simmer 10 minutes or until pasta is soft.

• Sprinkle with Savory Topping. Let stand 3 minutes before serving.

Savory Topping

¼ cup seasoned dry bread
  crumbs

¼ cup grated Parmesan cheese
¼ cup minced fresh parsley

• Combine all ingredients in small bowl; mix well.

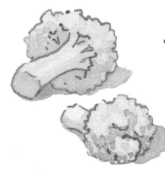

Tuscan Pot Pie

¾ pound sweet or hot Italian
 sausage
1 jar (26 to 28 ounces) chunky
 vegetable or mushroom
 spaghetti sauce
1 can (19 ounces) cannellini
 beans, rinsed and drained

½ teaspoon dried thyme leaves
1½ cups (6 ounces) shredded
 mozzarella cheese
1 package (8 ounces)
 refrigerated crescent dinner
 rolls

Makes 4 to 6 servings

Prep and Cook Time:
27 minutes

1. Preheat oven to 425°F. Remove sausage from casings. Brown
sausage in medium ovenproof skillet, stirring to separate meat.
Drain drippings.

2. Add spaghetti sauce, beans and thyme to skillet. Simmer
uncovered over medium heat 5 minutes. Remove from heat; stir
in cheese.

3. Unroll crescent dough; divide into triangles. Arrange in spiral
with points of dough towards center, covering sausage mixture
completely. Bake 12 minutes or until crust is golden brown and
meat mixture is bubbly.

Sausage and Eggplant Creole

Makes 6 to 8 servings

1½ pounds mild Italian sausage
1 large onion, chopped
1 green bell pepper, chopped
1 cup sliced celery
3 zucchini, halved lengthwise and cut into ½-inch slices
1 large eggplant, cut into 1-inch cubes
1 can (1 pound 12 ounces) whole tomatoes, cut up
1 teaspoon LAWRY'S® Garlic Salt

1 teaspoon LAWRY'S® Seasoned Salt
1 teaspoon LAWRY'S® Pinch of Herbs
1 teaspoon sugar
½ pound fresh mushrooms, sliced
½ pound Monterey Jack cheese, grated
¼ cup chopped fresh parsley (garnish)

In Dutch oven or large skillet, brown sausage until crumbly; drain fat. Add onion, green pepper, celery, zucchini, eggplant, tomatoes, Garlic Salt, Seasoned Salt, Pinch of Herbs, sugar and mushrooms; mix well. Bring to a boil over medium-high heat; reduce heat to low, cover and simmer 25 minutes, stirring occasionally. Top with cheese, cover and cook about 5 minutes or until cheese is melted.

Serving Suggestion: *Sprinkle with chopped fresh parsley. Serve over buttered noodles or rice.*

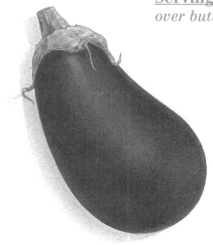

Skillet Pesto Tortellini

1¼ cups water
1¼ cups milk
1 envelope (1.2 ounces) creamy
   pesto sauce mix
1 package (16 ounces) frozen
   vegetable medley

1 package (12 ounces) frozen
   tortellini
Dash ground red pepper
½ cup (2 ounces) shredded
   mozzarella cheese

Makes 4 servings

Prep and Cook Time:
22 minutes

1. Blend water, milk and sauce mix in large deep skillet. Bring to a boil over high heat. Stir in vegetables, tortellini and ground red pepper; return to a boil.

2. Cook vegetables and tortellini, uncovered, over medium-high heat 8 to 10 minutes or until tortellini is tender and sauce has thickened, stirring occasionally.

3. Sprinkle with cheese just before serving.

Note:

Pesto, a green
uncooked sauce from
the Ligurian region of
Italy, is typically made
from fresh basil, garlic,
pine nuts, Parmesan
cheese and olive oil.

Jalapeño Chicken & Rice in a Skillet

Makes 4 servings

Prep Time:
5 minutes

Cook Time:
30 minutes

4 TYSON® Fresh or Individually Fresh Frozen® Boneless, Skinless Chicken Breasts
2 cups UNCLE BEN'S® Instant Rice
1 tablespoon olive oil
1 teaspoon minced garlic
2 cups defatted reduced-sodium chicken broth

1 can (15 ounces) black beans, rinsed and drained
1 to 2 teaspoons minced jalapeño pepper
½ teaspoon ground cumin
2 tablespoons chopped fresh cilantro

Note:

Regardless of the cooking method used, always cook chicken completely. Do not partially cook it and then store it to finish cooking later.

PREP: CLEAN: Wash hands. Remove protective ice glaze from frozen chicken by holding under cool running water 1 to 2 minutes. Pat dry. CLEAN: Wash hands.

COOK: In large nonstick skillet, heat olive oil and garlic; add chicken. Cook over medium heat 4 to 6 minutes (5 to 7 minutes if using frozen chicken) or until chicken is lightly browned. Stir in chicken broth, beans, jalapeño pepper and cumin; cover. Simmer 10 to 15 minutes or until internal juices of chicken run clear. (Or insert instant-read meat thermometer in thickest part of chicken. Temperature should read 170°F.) Stir in rice; cover. Let stand 5 minutes.

SERVE: Sprinkle with cilantro. Serve with lime wedges and salsa, if desired.

CHILL: Refrigerate leftovers immediately.

Skillet Spaghetti and Sausage

¼ pound mild or hot Italian
    sausage links, sliced
½ pound ground beef
¼ teaspoon dried oregano,
    crushed
4 ounces spaghetti, broken in
    half

1 can (14½ ounces)
    DEL MONTE® Diced
    Tomatoes with Basil, Garlic
    & Oregano
1 can (8 ounces) DEL MONTE
    Tomato Sauce
1½ cups sliced fresh mushrooms
2 stalks celery, sliced

Makes 4 to 6 servings

Prep Time:
5 minutes

Cook Time:
30 minutes

1. Brown sausage in large skillet over medium-high heat. Add beef and oregano; season to taste with salt and pepper, if desired.

2. Cook, stirring occasionally, until beef is browned; drain.

3. Add spaghetti, 1 cup water, undrained tomatoes, tomato sauce, mushrooms and celery. Bring to a boil, stirring occasionally.

4. Reduce heat; cover and simmer 12 to 14 minutes or until spaghetti is tender. Garnish with grated Parmesan cheese and chopped fresh parsley, if desired. Serve immediately.

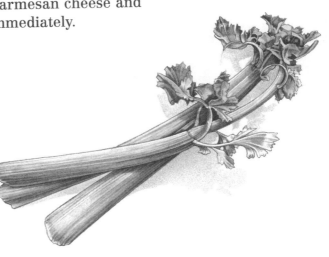

Superb Stroganoff

Makes 4 servings		

Prep Time:
5 minutes

Cook Time:
20 minutes

1 pound sirloin steak, cut into thin strips
2 tablespoons vegetable oil
½ cup chopped onion
1 can (4 ounces) mushrooms, drained

1 bag (16 ounces) BIRDS EYE® frozen Pasta Secrets Creamy Peppercorn
⅔ cup sour cream

• In large skillet, brown steak in oil over medium heat, stirring frequently.

• Stir in onion and mushrooms; cook 5 minutes or until onion is tender.

• Stir in Pasta Secrets and ¼ cup water; cover and cook over medium heat 5 minutes or until pasta is tender. Reduce heat to low; stir in sour cream. Cook until heated through.

Country Pork Skillet

Makes 4 servings		

4 boneless top loin pork chops, diced
1 (12-ounce) jar pork gravy

2 tablespoons ketchup
8 small red potatoes, diced
2 cups frozen mixed vegetables

In large skillet, brown pork cubes; stir in gravy, ketchup and potatoes; cover and simmer for 10 minutes. Stir in vegetables; cook for 10 to 15 minutes longer, until vegetables are tender.

Favorite recipe from **National Pork Board**

Chinese Skillet Chicken and Rice

Makes 4 servings

½ teaspoon red pepper flakes
½ teaspoon Chinese five-spice powder
¼ teaspoon white pepper
1 pound boneless skinless chicken breasts
2 teaspoons vegetable oil
1 large onion, chopped
2 cloves garlic, minced
1 cup uncooked white rice
1¼ cups fat-free reduced-sodium chicken broth

½ cup water
1 tablespoon reduced-sodium soy sauce
2 red bell peppers, sliced
1 cup fresh bean sprouts
1 cup sliced fresh mushrooms
¾ cup canned water chestnuts, drained
1 cup frozen peas, thawed
1 teaspoon minced fresh ginger

1. Combine red pepper flakes, five-spice powder and white pepper in small bowl. Rub onto all surfaces of chicken. Heat oil in large nonstick skillet over medium heat. Add chicken; cook 5 minutes. Turn chicken; cook 5 minutes. Remove and reserve.

2. Pour off all but 1 tablespoon drippings. Cook onion and garlic in drippings 3 minutes, stirring occasionally. Add rice; stir to coat. Stir in broth, water and soy sauce. Bring to a boil over high heat; reduce heat to medium.

3. Arrange chicken and bell peppers over rice in skillet. Cover and simmer 15 minutes or until most of the liquid is absorbed and chicken is cooked through. Remove from heat; stir bean sprouts, mushrooms, water chestnuts, peas and ginger into rice and chicken. Cover and let stand 10 minutes. Garnish with mushrooms and fresh herbs, if desired.

Saffron Chicken Risotto

Makes 4 servings

1½ pounds boneless, skinless
    chicken breast
¼ teaspoon salt
⅛ teaspoon white pepper
1 tablespoon olive oil
1 cup sliced fresh mushrooms
½ cup sliced green onions
½ cup chopped red bell pepper
½ cup chopped celery

1 tablespoon butter
1 cup uncooked rice
    Pinch of ground saffron
⅓ cup dry white wine
2 cups chicken broth
3 cups water
⅓ cup grated Parmesan cheese
⅓ cup sliced black olives
⅓ cup heavy cream

Cut chicken into 1-inch chunks; season with salt and white pepper. Heat oil in large skillet over medium-high heat until hot. Add chicken, mushrooms, onions, bell pepper and celery. Cook and stir until chicken is no longer pink in center. Remove chicken and vegetables; set aside. Melt butter in skillet until hot. Add rice and saffron; cook 2 to 3 minutes, stirring constantly. Add wine; stir until absorbed. Stir in 1 cup broth; cook, uncovered, until broth is absorbed, stirring frequently. Continue stirring and adding remaining 1 cup broth and water, one cup at a time; allow each cup to be absorbed before adding another, until rice is tender and has creamy consistency, about 25 to 30 minutes. Stir in cheese, olives, cream and chicken mixture; heat thoroughly. Serve immediately.

Tip: *Medium grain rice will yield the best consistency for risottos, but long grain rice can be used.*

Favorite recipe from **USA Rice Federation**

Zesty Chicken Succotash

1 (3- to 4-pound) chicken, cut
    up and skinned, if desired
1 onion, chopped
1 rib celery, sliced
¼ cup *Frank's® RedHot®* Cayenne
    Pepper Sauce

1 package (10 ounces) frozen
    lima beans
1 package (10 ounces) frozen
    whole kernel corn
2 tomatoes, coarsely chopped

Makes 6 servings

Prep Time:
10 minutes

Cook Time:
35 minutes

1. Heat *1 tablespoon oil* in large skillet until hot. Add chicken;
cook 10 minutes or until browned on both sides. Drain off all but
1 tablespoon fat. Add onion and celery; cook and stir 3 minutes or
until tender.

2. Stir in *¾ cup water*, **Frank's RedHot** Sauce and remaining
ingredients. Heat to boiling. Reduce heat to medium-low. Cook,
covered, 20 to 25 minutes or until chicken is no longer pink near
bone. Sprinkle with chopped parsley, if desired.

The Perfect Pan

Saucepan: **This round cooking utensil, with a deep straight or slightly flared side, a long handle and tight-fitting cover, is very versatile. It is used for cooking sauces, vegetables, grains and pasta, as well as reheating and melting. It should be made of a material that heats quickly and evenly, is easy to clean, nonreactive to acidic foods and not too heavy. Saucepans range in size from 2 cups to 4 quarts.**

Sauté pan: **The traditional sauté pan is a wide pan with a straight or slightly curved side that is slightly higher than a skillet and** has a long handle. This pan is designed for quick cooking over high heat. Use it for browning and stir-frying as well. A large skillet can be substituted for a sauté pan.

Skillet: **Also known as a frying pan, this round, shallow pan has a straight or slightly sloping side. It is most often used for frying and sautéing. When purchasing a skillet, choose a heavy pan that conducts heat evenly and has a tight fitting cover. Skillets range in size from 6 to 12 inches. A large skillet with a second short handle opposite the long handle is much easier to lift.**

Chuckwagon BBQ Rice Round-Up

Makes 4 servings

Prep Time:
5 minutes

Cook Time:
25 minutes

1 pound lean ground beef
1 (6.8-ounce) package RICE-A-RONI® Beef Flavor
2 tablespoons margarine or butter

2 cups frozen corn
½ cup prepared barbecue sauce
½ cup (2 ounces) shredded Cheddar cheese

1. In large skillet over medium-high heat, brown ground beef until well cooked. Remove from skillet; drain. Set aside.

2. In same skillet over medium heat, sauté rice-vermicelli mix with margarine until vermicelli is golden brown.

3. Slowly stir in 2½ cups water, corn and Special Seasonings; bring to a boil. Reduce heat to low. Cover; simmer 15 to 20 minutes or until rice is tender.

4. Stir in barbecue sauce and ground beef. Sprinkle with cheese. Cover; let stand 3 to 5 minutes or until cheese is melted.

Tip: *Salsa can be substituted for barbecue sauce.*

Spinach & Turkey Skillet

Makes 2 servings

6 ounces turkey breast
   tenderloin
1/8 teaspoon salt
2 teaspoons olive oil
1/4 cup chopped onion
2 cloves garlic, minced
1/3 cup uncooked rice
3/4 teaspoon dried Italian
   seasoning

1/4 teaspoon black pepper
1 cup fat-free reduced-sodium
   chicken broth, divided
2 cups torn fresh spinach
2/3 cup diced plum tomatoes
3 tablespoons freshly grated
   Parmesan cheese

1. Cut turkey tenderloin into bite-size pieces; sprinkle with salt. Heat oil in medium skillet over medium-high heat.

2. Add turkey pieces; cook and stir until lightly browned. Remove from skillet. Reduce heat to low. Add onion and garlic; cook and stir until tender. Return turkey to skillet. Stir in rice, Italian seasoning and pepper.

3. Reserve 2 tablespoons chicken broth. Stir remaining broth into mixture in skillet. Bring to a boil. Reduce heat. Simmer, covered, 14 minutes. Stir in spinach and reserved broth. Cover and cook 2 to 3 minutes more or until liquid is absorbed and spinach is wilted. Stir in tomatoes. Heat through. Serve with Parmesan cheese.

Note:

Do not wash spinach before storing it. Store loose spinach lightly packed in a plastic bag in the refrigerator. Leave prepackaged spinach in its original plastic bag. It will keep for three or four days.

Simmered Tuscan Chicken

Makes 6 servings

2 tablespoons BERTOLLI® Olive Oil

1 pound boneless, skinless chicken breasts, cut into 1-inch cubes

2 cloves garlic, finely chopped

4 medium potatoes, cut into ½-inch cubes (about 4 cups)

1 medium red bell pepper, cut into large pieces

1 jar (1 pound 10 ounces) RAGÚ® Old World Style® Pasta Sauce

1 pound fresh or frozen cut green beans

1 teaspoon dried basil leaves, crushed

Salt and ground black pepper to taste

In 12-inch skillet, heat oil over medium-high heat and cook chicken with garlic until chicken is thoroughly cooked. Remove chicken and set aside.

In same skillet, add potatoes and bell pepper. Cook over medium heat, stirring occasionally, 5 minutes. Stir in remaining ingredients. Bring to a boil over high heat. Reduce heat to low and simmer covered, stirring occasionally, 35 minutes or until potatoes are tender. Return chicken to skillet and heat through.

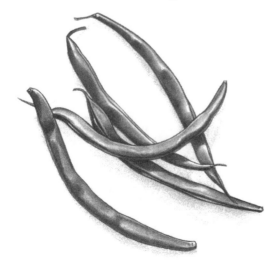

Hearty Kielbasa Dinner

Makes 4 servings

1 cup chopped onion
3 cloves garlic, minced
3 tablespoons dried oregano
   leaves
2 teaspoons chili powder
2 teaspoons black pepper
1 teaspoon cayenne pepper
2 teaspoons vegetable oil
28 ounces tomatoes
28 ounces canned cannellini or
   navy beans, rinsed and
   drained *or* 4 cups cooked
   beans

½ pound turkey kielbasa, thinly
   sliced
4 teaspoons sugar
10 ounces chopped frozen
   broccoli
2 cups hot cooked macaroni or
   rice, if desired

In large skillet, sauté onion, garlic, oregano, chili powder, black pepper and cayenne pepper in oil 5 minutes. Add tomatoes, beans, kielbasa and sugar. Simmer 15 minutes. Add broccoli and simmer 5 minutes. Serve over macaroni, if desired.

Tip: *This is a very spicy dish. If less spice is desired, reduce or eliminate the cayenne pepper.*

Favorite recipe from **The Sugar Association, Inc.**

One Skillet Spicy Chicken 'n Rice

Makes 4 to 6 servings

¼ cup all-purpose flour
1 teaspoon LAWRY'S®
  Seasoned Salt
6 to 8 chicken pieces, skinned
2 tablespoons vegetable oil
2 cans (14½ ounces each)
  whole peeled tomatoes,
  undrained and cut up

1 package (1.0 ounces)
  LAWRY'S® Taco Spices &
  Seasonings
1 cup thinly sliced celery
1 cup long-grain rice
½ cup chopped onion

Note:

Always use tongs to turn chicken pieces during cooking. This prevents the skin from being pierced, keeping the natural juices sealed inside.

In large resealable plastic food storage bag, combine flour and Seasoned Salt. Add chicken; shake to coat well. In large skillet, heat oil. Add chicken and cook over medium-high heat until browned. Continue cooking, uncovered, over low heat 15 minutes. Add remaining ingredients; mix well. Bring to a boil over medium-high heat; reduce heat to low, cover and simmer 20 minutes or until liquid is absorbed and chicken is cooked through.

Vegetable Pork Skillet

1 tablespoon CRISCO® Oil*
4 (4 ounces each) lean,
    boneless, center-cut pork
    loin chops, ½ inch thick
2 medium onions, thinly sliced
    and separated into rings
1 can (14½ ounces) whole
    tomatoes, undrained
¾ cup water
2 teaspoons paprika

1 teaspoon salt
½ teaspoon celery seed
¼ teaspoon pepper
¼ teaspoon garlic powder
3 medium unpeeled potatoes,
    chopped
1 package (9 ounces) frozen cut
    green beans

*Use your favorite Crisco Oil product.

1. Heat oil in large skillet on medium heat. Add meat. Cook until browned on both sides. Remove from skillet.

2. Add onions to skillet. Cook and stir until tender. Add tomatoes, water, paprika, salt, celery seed, pepper and garlic powder. Bring to a boil.

3. Return meat to skillet. Reduce heat to low. Cover; simmer 15 minutes.

4. Add potatoes. Cover; simmer 15 minutes.

5. Add beans. Cover; simmer 5 to 7 minutes or until potatoes and beans are tender.

Skillet Spaghetti Pizza

Makes 8 servings

Prep Time:
10 minutes

Cook Time:
23 minutes

1 pound bulk Italian sausage
1 tablespoon minced garlic
½ pound uncooked thin
   spaghetti, broken into
   2-inch lengths
1 jar (26 ounces) spaghetti
   sauce

1½ cups water
1 cup (4 ounces) shredded
   mozzarella cheese
½ cup diced green bell pepper
1⅓ cups *French's®* French Fried
   Onions

1. Cook sausage and garlic in large nonstick skillet over medium heat until browned, stirring frequently; drain.

2. Stir in uncooked spaghetti, spaghetti sauce and water. Bring to a boil; reduce heat to medium-low. Cover and simmer 15 minutes or until spaghetti is cooked, stirring occasionally.

3. Top spaghetti mixture with cheese, bell pepper and French Fried Onions; remove from heat. Cover and let stand 3 minutes until cheese is melted. Serve immediately.

Tip: *You can substitute link sausage; remove from casing before cooking.*

Variation: *Substitute other pizza toppings such as mushrooms, eggplant, olives or pepperoni for green peppers.*

Rice Pilaf with Fish Fillets

1 cup UNCLE BEN'S® ORIGINAL
   CONVERTED® Brand Rice
1 can (14½ ounces) fat-free
   reduced-sodium chicken
   broth
1 cup sliced green onions
2 cups sugar snap peas or
   snow peas

12 ounces Dover sole fillets
¼ cup reduced-fat Caesar salad
   dressing
2 tomatoes, cut into wedges
¼ cup chopped fresh parsley

1. In large skillet, combine rice, chicken broth and ½ cup water. Bring to a boil. Cover; reduce heat and simmer 12 minutes.

2. Add green onions and peas to rice pilaf. Season to taste with salt and pepper. Place fish fillets on pilaf. Spoon salad dressing onto fillets. Cover and cook over low heat 8 minutes or until fish flakes when tested with a fork and rice is tender.

3. Garnish with tomatoes and parsley.

<u>Variation:</u> *Orange roughy fillets or swordfish steaks can be substituted for sole fillets.*

Creole Shrimp and Rice

Makes 4 servings

Prep and Cook Time:
20 minutes

2 tablespoons olive oil
1 cup uncooked white rice
1 can (15 ounces) diced
   tomatoes with garlic,
   undrained
1½ cups water
1 teaspoon Creole or Cajun
   seasoning blend

1 pound peeled cooked
   medium shrimp
1 package (10 ounces) frozen
   okra *or* 1½ cups frozen
   sugar snap peas, thawed

Note:

**Olive oil is produced
when tree-ripened
olives are pressed. The
best olive oils are
extracted using a
chemical-free process.
They are classified as
extra-virgin or virgin.**

1. Heat oil in large skillet over medium heat until hot. Add rice;
cook and stir 2 to 3 minutes or until lightly browned.

2. Add tomatoes with juice, water and seasoning blend; bring
to a boil over high heat. Reduce heat to low. Cover; simmer
15 minutes.

3. Add shrimp and okra. Cook, covered, 3 minutes or until
heated through.

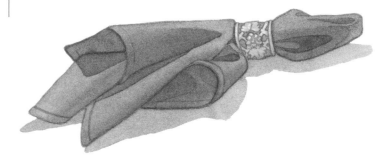

Coq au Vin & Pasta

4 large *or* 8 small chicken thighs (2 to 2½ pounds), trimmed of excess fat
2 teaspoons rotisserie or herb chicken seasoning*
1 tablespoon margarine
3 cups (8 ounces) halved or quartered mushrooms
1 medium onion, coarsely chopped
½ cup dry white wine or vermouth
1 (4.9-ounce) package PASTA RONI® Homestyle Chicken Flavor
½ cup sliced green onions

1 teaspoon paprika and 1 teaspoon garlic salt can be substituted.

Prep Time:
10 minutes

Cook Time:
30 minutes

1. Sprinkle meaty side of chicken with rotisserie seasoning. In large skillet over medium-high heat, melt margarine. Add chicken, seasoned side down; cook 3 minutes. Reduce heat to medium-low; turn chicken over.

2. Add mushrooms, onion and wine. Cover; simmer 15 to 18 minutes or until chicken is no longer pink inside. Remove chicken from skillet; set aside.

3. In same skillet, bring 1 cup water to a boil. Stir in pasta, green onions and Special Seasonings. Place chicken over pasta. Reduce heat to medium-low. Cover; gently boil 6 to 8 minutes or until pasta is tender. Let stand 3 to 5 minutes before serving.

Curried Chicken, Vegetables and Couscous Skillet

Makes 4 servings

Prep and Cook Time:
20 minutes

1 package (16 ounces) frozen vegetable medley, such as broccoli, carrots and cauliflower or bell pepper and onion strips
1 pound chicken tenders
2 teaspoons curry powder, divided

¾ teaspoon garlic salt
⅛ teaspoon ground red pepper
4½ teaspoons vegetable oil
1 can (about 14 ounces) chicken broth
1 cup uncooked couscous

1. Thaw vegetables according to package directions.

2. While vegetables are thawing, place chicken in medium bowl. Sprinkle with 1 teaspoon curry powder, garlic salt and ground red pepper; toss to coat.

3. Heat oil in large deep skillet over medium-high heat until hot. Add chicken mixture, spreading in one layer. Cook 5 to 6 minutes or until chicken is no longer pink in center, turning occasionally.

4. Transfer chicken to plate; set aside. Add broth and remaining 1 teaspoon curry powder to skillet; bring to a boil over high heat, scraping up browned bits on bottom of skillet.

5. Stir thawed vegetables into skillet; return to a boil. Stir in couscous; top with chicken. Cover and remove from heat. Let stand 5 minutes or until liquid is absorbed.

<u>Hint:</u> *For a special touch, add a dollop of plain yogurt to each serving.*

Wild Rice Meatball Primavera

1 pound ground turkey
½ cup seasoned bread crumbs
1 egg, beaten
2 tablespoons oil
1 can (10¾ ounces) condensed
   cream of mushroom soup

2 cups water
1 package (16 ounces) frozen
   broccoli medley, thawed
1 box UNCLE BEN'S® Long
   Grain & Wild Rice Fast
   Cook Recipe

1. Combine turkey, bread crumbs and egg; mix well. Shape into 1¼- to 1½-inch meatballs (about 20 to 22 meatballs).

2. Heat oil in large skillet over medium-high heat until hot. Cook meatballs 6 to 7 minutes or until brown on all sides. Drain on paper towels.

3. Combine soup and water in skillet; bring to a boil. Add meatballs, vegetables and contents of seasoning packet, reserving rice. Cover; reduce heat and simmer 5 minutes, stirring occasionally.

4. Add reserved rice to skillet; mix well. Cover; cook 5 minutes more or until hot. Remove from heat; stir well. Cover and let stand 5 minutes before serving.

Sweet Chicken Risotto

Makes 4 servings

Note:

To seed and slice a bell pepper, first remove the stem by cutting around the top with a paring knife. Pull out the stem—most of the seeds will come with it. Slice off the bottom of the pepper, then divide the pepper into two or three sections. Lay the sections flat, remove the remaining seeds and ribs, then slice it into strips.

¾ pound chicken breast, thinly sliced
¾ cup chopped onion
1 tablespoon vegetable oil
4 cups *or* 2 (14-ounce) cans chicken broth
2 cups uncooked instant brown rice
4 teaspoons sugar
1 tablespoon prepared horseradish

1 medium green bell pepper, sliced
1 medium red bell pepper, sliced
14 ounces canned black beans, rinsed and drained *or* 2 cups cooked black beans
¼ cup grated Parmesan cheese

In large skillet, sauté chicken and onion in oil 5 minutes. Add chicken broth, rice, sugar and horseradish. Simmer covered 15 minutes or until rice is tender (there should be extra liquid). Add peppers and black beans. Simmer 5 minutes. Sprinkle with cheese before serving.

Favorite recipe from **The Sugar Association, Inc.**

Pork Asado

Makes 6 to 8 servings

2 pounds lean, boneless pork
 shoulder, trimmed and
 cubed
1 clove garlic, minced
2 tablespoons salad oil
1 package (1.31 ounces)
 LAWRY'S® Spice &
 Seasonings for Taco Salad
1 cup water
1 can (1 pound 12 ounces)
 whole tomatoes

2 stalks celery, cut into 1-inch
 pieces
2 medium onions, quartered
1 can (18 ounces) sweet
 potatoes OR yams, drained
LAWRY'S® Seasoned Salt to
 taste
LAWRY'S® Seasoned Pepper
 to taste

In Dutch oven, brown pork and garlic in oil; add Spice &
Seasonings for Taco Salad, water, tomatoes, celery and onions.
Bring to a boil over medium-high heat; reduce heat to low, cover
and simmer 1 hour or until meat is tender. Add sweet potatoes
and season with Seasoned Salt and Seasoned Pepper to taste
during last 10 minutes of cooking.

Serving Suggestion: *Serve with warmed corn tortillas and a
green salad.*

One-Pot Chicken Couscous

Makes 8 servings

2 pounds boneless, skinless chicken breasts, cut into 1-inch chunks
¼ cup olive oil
4 large carrots, peeled and sliced
2 medium onions, diced
2 large cloves garlic, minced
2 cans (13¾ ounces each) chicken broth

2 cups uncooked couscous
2 teaspoons TABASCO® brand Pepper Sauce
½ teaspoon salt
1 cup raisins or currants
1 cup slivered almonds, toasted
¼ cup chopped fresh parsley or mint

Cook chicken in hot oil in 12-inch skillet over medium-high heat until well browned on all sides. With slotted spoon, remove chicken to plate. Reduce heat to medium. In remaining drippings cook carrots and onions 5 minutes. Add garlic; cook 2 minutes longer, stirring frequently.

Add chicken broth, couscous, TABASCO® Sauce, salt and chicken chunks. Heat to boiling, then reduce heat to low. Cover and simmer 5 minutes. Stir in raisins, almonds and parsley.

Hawaiian-Roni

1 pound boneless pork loin
    chops, cut into 1-inch
    pieces
¼ cup teriyaki sauce
1 (6.2-ounce) package RICE-A-
    RONI® Fried Rice
¼ cup chopped onion

2 tablespoons margarine or
    butter
1 (8-ounce) can pineapple
    chunks in juice, drained,
    reserving ¼ cup juice
1 cup sliced carrots
¼ cup slivered almonds, toasted

Makes 4 servings

Prep Time:
10 minutes

Cook Time:
30 minutes

1. In small bowl, combine pork and teriyaki sauce; set aside.

2. In large skillet over medium heat, sauté rice-vermicelli mix and onion with margarine until vermicelli is golden brown.

3. Slowly stir in 1 cup water, reserved ¼ cup pineapple juice, carrots, pork mixture and Special Seasonings; bring to a boil. Reduce heat to medium-low. Cover; simmer 15 to 20 minutes or until rice is tender and pork is no longer pink inside.

4. Stir in pineapple chunks. Cover; let stand 5 minutes before serving. Sprinkle with almonds.

<u>Tip:</u> *For variety, try sliced chicken or steak instead of pork.*

Tex-Mex Beef & Black Bean Skillet

Makes 6 servings

Prep Time:
10 minutes

Cook Time:
25 minutes

1 pound lean ground beef or ground turkey
1 medium onion, chopped
2 cloves garlic, minced
1 tablespoon Mexican seasoning*
1 (6.8-ounce) package RICE-A-RONI® Spanish Rice
2 tablespoons margarine or butter
1 (16-ounce) jar salsa *or*
   1 (14½-ounce) can diced tomatoes and green chiles, undrained

1 (16-ounce) can black beans, rinsed and drained
1 cup shredded Monterey Jack cheese or jalapeño pepper

*1 teaspoon chili powder, 1 teaspoon ground cumin, 1 teaspoon garlic salt and ¼ teaspoon cayenne pepper can be substituted.

1. In large skillet over medium-high heat, cook ground beef, onion and garlic until meat is no longer pink, stirring frequently. Drain; transfer to bowl. Toss with Mexican seasoning; set aside.

2. In same skillet over medium heat, sauté rice-vermicelli mix with margarine until vermicelli is golden brown.

3. Slowly stir in 2 cups water, salsa and Special Seasonings; bring to a boil. Cover; reduce heat to low. Simmer 10 minutes.

4. Stir in beef mixture and beans. Cover; simmer 8 to 10 minutes or until rice is tender. Top with cheese.

SPAM™ Skillet Casserole

Makes 6 servings

2 baking potatoes, cut into
⅛-inch slices
1 (12-ounce) can SPAM® Lite,
cubed
1 cup thinly sliced carrots
1 cup thinly sliced onion
½ cup thinly sliced celery
2 cloves garlic, minced
2 tablespoons all-purpose flour
1 teaspoon coarsely ground
black pepper

¾ teaspoon dried thyme leaves
1 (16-ounce) can no-salt-added
green beans, drained
1 (16-ounce) can no-salt-added
whole tomatoes, drained
and chopped
1 (5½-ounce) can no-salt-added
vegetable juice cocktail
Butter-flavored nonstick
cooking spray

Cook potatoes in boiling water 3 minutes or until crisp-tender. Drain. In large skillet, cook SPAM® until browned; remove from skillet. Add carrots to skillet; sauté 4 to 5 minutes. Add onion, celery and garlic; sauté until tender. Combine flour, pepper and thyme. Stir flour mixture into vegetable mixture; cook 1 minute, stirring constantly. Add SPAM®, green beans, tomatoes and vegetable juice cocktail. Bring to a boil. Reduce heat; simmer 5 minutes, stirring occasionally. Remove skillet from heat; arrange potato slices over top. Spray potato slices with cooking spray. Broil 6 inches from heat source 10 minutes or until golden.

Garlic Herb Chicken and Rice Skillet

Makes 4 servings

Prep Time:
none

Cook Time:
25 to 30 minutes

Note:

Cheese spreads (or pasteurized process cheese spreads) are similar to process cheese and cheese food, except they are softer, more spreadable and often have added flavorings or ingredients, such as olives or garlic.

4 TYSON® Individually Fresh Frozen® Boneless, Skinless Chicken Breasts
1 box UNCLE BEN'S® COUNTRY INN® Chicken Flavored Rice

1¾ cups water
2 cups frozen broccoli, carrots and cauliflower mixture
¼ cup garlic and herb soft spreadable cheese

COOK: CLEAN: Wash hands. In large skillet, combine chicken, water and contents of seasoning packet. Bring to a boil. Cover, reduce heat; simmer 10 minutes. Add rice, vegetables and cheese. Cook, covered, 10 to 15 minutes or until internal juices of chicken run clear. (Or insert instant-read meat thermometer in thickest part of chicken. Temperature should read 170°F.) Remove from heat; let stand 5 minutes or until liquid is absorbed.

SERVE: Dish out chicken to individual plates and serve while hot.

CHILL: Refrigerate leftovers immediately.

Tangy Shrimp with Angel Hair Pasta

2 tablespoons olive oil
2 teaspoons minced garlic
1 pound large shrimp, peeled and deveined
1⅓ cups *French's®* French Fried Onions, divided
1 cup chicken broth
¼ cup chopped fresh parsley

3 tablespoons lemon juice
½ teaspoon salt
¼ teaspoon ground black pepper
1 package (9 ounces) uncooked fresh angel hair or capellini pasta (or 1 pound dry pasta)

Makes 4 servings

Prep Time:
10 minutes

Cook Time:
about 5 minutes

1. Heat oil in 12-inch nonstick skillet over high heat. Add garlic and sauté about 30 seconds or until golden.

2. Add shrimp and cook 2 minutes. Stir in ⅔ *cup* French Fried Onions, broth, parsley, lemon juice, salt and pepper. Cook 2 minutes or until shrimp turn pink.

3. Meanwhile, cook pasta according to package directions using shortest cooking time; drain. Toss with shrimp mixture. Transfer to serving platter and sprinkle with remaining onions.

Turkey Orzo Italiano

Makes 4 servings

¼ pound mushrooms, sliced
½ cup green onions, sliced
2 tablespoons margarine
2 cups turkey broth or reduced-
   sodium chicken bouillon

1 cup uncooked orzo pasta
½ teaspoon Italian seasoning
½ teaspoon salt
⅛ teaspoon white pepper
2 cups cooked turkey, cubed

1. In large skillet, over medium-high heat, sauté mushrooms and onions in margarine for 1 minute. Add turkey broth and bring to a boil.

2. Stir in orzo, Italian seasoning, salt and pepper; bring to a boil. Reduce heat and simmer, covered, 15 minutes or until orzo is tender and liquid has been absorbed. Stir in turkey and heat throughout.

Favorite recipe from **National Turkey Federation**

Western Wagon Wheels

Makes 4 servings

Prep Time:
5 minutes

Cook Time:
25 minutes

1 pound lean ground beef
2 cups wagon wheel pasta,
   uncooked
1 can (14½ ounces) stewed
   tomatoes

1½ cups water
1 box (10 ounces) BIRDS EYE®
   frozen Sweet Corn
½ cup barbecue sauce
Salt and pepper to taste

• In large skillet, cook beef over medium heat 5 minutes or until well browned.

• Stir in pasta, tomatoes, water, corn and barbecue sauce; bring to a boil.

• Reduce heat to low; cover and simmer 15 to 20 minutes or until pasta is tender, stirring occasionally. Season with salt and pepper.

Skillet Turkey Tetrazzini

2 tablespoons margarine or
   butter
¾ pound boneless, skinless
   turkey breast or chicken
   breasts, cut into thin strips
1 cup sliced fresh mushrooms

½ cup chopped red or green bell
   pepper
⅔ cup milk
1 (5.1-ounce) package PASTA
   RONI® Angel Hair Pasta
   with Parmesan Cheese

Makes 4 servings

Prep Time:
10 minutes

Cook Time:
15 minutes

1. In large skillet over medium-high heat, melt margarine. Add turkey, mushrooms and bell pepper. Sauté 5 minutes or until turkey is no longer pink inside. Remove from skillet; set aside.

2. In same skillet, bring 1⅓ cups water and milk to a boil.

3. Stir in pasta and Special Seasonings. Reduce heat to medium. Gently boil uncovered, 4 to 5 minutes or until pasta is tender. Stir in turkey mixture. Let stand 3 minutes before serving.

Tip: *To make slicing easier, place turkey or chicken in the freezer for 10 minutes.*

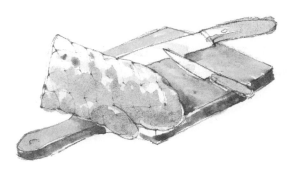

Chicken Vegetable Skillet

Makes 4 servings

8 chicken thighs, skinned, fat trimmed
¾ teaspoon salt, divided
1 tablespoon vegetable oil
3 medium red-skinned potatoes, scrubbed, cut in ¼-inch slices
1 medium onion, sliced
½ pound mushrooms, quartered

1 large tomato, coarsely chopped
¼ cup chicken broth
¼ cup dry white wine
½ teaspoon dried oregano leaves
¼ teaspoon black pepper
1 tablespoon chopped fresh parsley

Note:

Wine should be stored in a cool place with a consistent temperature between 45° and 65°F (55°F is ideal). Store it away from light and vibration. Do not turn or move stored wine. To prevent corks from drying out and air from entering bottles, store wine on its side.

Sprinkle chicken with ¼ teaspoon salt. In large nonstick skillet, heat oil to medium-high temperature. Add chicken and cook, turning, about 8 minutes or until brown on both sides. Remove chicken; set aside. In same pan, layer potatoes, onion, chicken, mushrooms and tomato. In 1-cup measure, mix broth and wine. Pour over chicken and vegetables. Sprinkle with oregano, remaining ½ teaspoon salt and pepper. Heat to boiling; cover and reduce heat to medium-low. Cook about 20 minutes or until chicken and vegetables are fork-tender. Sprinkle with parsley before serving.

Favorite recipe from **Delmarva Poultry Industry, Inc.**

No-Fuss Slow Cooker Meals

CHAPTER FOURTEEN

Beef with Apples and Sweet Potatoes

Makes 6 servings

Prep Time:
20 minutes

Cook Time:
8 to 9 hours

2 pounds boneless beef chuck
    shoulder roast
1 can (40 ounces) sweet
    potatoes, drained
2 small onions, sliced
2 apples, cored and sliced
½ cup beef broth
2 cloves garlic, minced

1 teaspoon salt
1 teaspoon dried thyme leaves,
    divided
¾ teaspoon black pepper,
    divided
1 tablespoon cornstarch
¼ teaspoon ground cinnamon
2 tablespoons cold water

Slow Cooker Directions

1. Trim fat from beef; cut beef into 2-inch pieces. Place beef, sweet potatoes, onions, apples, beef broth, garlic, salt, ½ teaspoon thyme and ½ teaspoon pepper in slow cooker. Cover; cook on LOW 8 to 9 hours.

2. Transfer beef, sweet potatoes and apples to platter; keep warm. Let liquid stand 5 minutes to allow fat to rise. Skim off fat.

3. Combine cornstarch, remaining ½ teaspoon thyme, ¼ teaspoon pepper, cinnamon and water; stir into cooking liquid. Cook 15 minutes or until juices are thickened. Serve sauce with beef, sweet potatoes and apples.

San Marino Chicken

1 chicken (3 pounds), skinned
   and cut up
¼ cup all-purpose flour
1 can (8 ounces) tomato sauce
⅓ cup chopped sun-dried
   tomatoes packed in oil
¼ cup red wine

1 tablespoon grated lemon peel
2 cups sliced mushrooms
2 cups *French's*® French Fried
   Onions, divided
   Hot cooked rice or pasta
   (optional)

Makes 4 servings

Prep Time:
5 minutes

Cook Time:
6 hours

Slow Cooker Directions

1. Lightly coat chicken pieces with flour. Place chicken in slow cooker. Add tomato sauce, sun-dried tomatoes, wine and lemon peel. Cover and cook on LOW setting for 4 hours (or on HIGH for 2 hours).

2. Add mushrooms and *1 cup* French Fried Onions. Cover and cook on LOW setting for 2 hours (or on HIGH for 1 hour) until chicken is no longer pink near bone. Remove chicken to heated platter. Skim fat from sauce.

3. Serve chicken with hot cooked rice or pasta, if desired. Spoon sauce on top and sprinkle with remaining onions.

Note:

Skinless chicken is best for the slow cooker because the skin tends to shrivel and curl during cooking.

Vegetable-Stuffed Pork Chops

Makes 4 servings

4 double pork loin chops, well trimmed
Salt and black pepper
1 can (15¼ ounces) kernel corn, drained
1 green bell pepper, chopped
1 cup Italian-style seasoned dry bread crumbs
1 small onion, chopped
½ cup uncooked long-grain converted rice
1 can (8 ounces) tomato sauce

Slow Cooker Directions

Cut pocket in each pork chop, cutting from edge nearest bone. Lightly season pockets with salt and pepper to taste. Combine corn, bell pepper, bread crumbs, onion and rice in large bowl. Stuff pork chops with rice mixture. Secure along fat side with wooden toothpicks.

Place any remaining rice mixture into slow cooker. Add stuffed pork chops to slow cooker. Moisten top of each pork chop with tomato sauce. Pour any remaining tomato sauce over top. Cover and cook on LOW 8 to 10 hours or until done.

Remove pork chops to serving platter. Remove and discard toothpicks. Serve pork chops with rice mixture.

Italian-Style Pot Roast

2 teaspoons minced garlic
1 teaspoon salt
1 teaspoon dried basil leaves
1 teaspoon dried oregano
    leaves
¼ teaspoon red pepper flakes
2½ to 3 pounds beef bottom
    round rump or chuck
    shoulder roast

1 large onion, quartered and
    thinly sliced
1½ cups prepared tomato-basil or
    marinara spaghetti sauce
2 cans (16 ounces each)
    cannellini or Great Northern
    beans, drained
¼ cup shredded fresh basil or
    chopped Italian parsley

Makes 6 to 8 servings

Prep Time:
15 minutes

Cook Time:
8 to 9 hours

Slow Cooker Directions

1. Combine garlic, salt, basil, oregano and pepper flakes in small bowl; rub over roast.

2. Place half of onion slices into slow cooker. Cut roast in half to fit into slow cooker. Place one half of roast over onion slices; top with remaining onion slices and other half of roast. Pour spaghetti sauce over roast. Cover; cook on LOW 8 to 9 hours or until roast is fork tender.

3. Remove roast from cooking liquid; tent with foil.

4. Let liquid in slow cooker stand 5 minutes to allow fat to rise. Skim off fat.

5. Stir beans into liquid. Cover; cook on HIGH 10 to 15 minutes or until beans are hot. Carve roast across the grain into thin slices. Serve with bean mixture and garnish with basil.

Thai Turkey & Noodles

Makes 6 servings

Note:

All parts of the coriander plant, including the seeds, the leaves and the root, are used in cooking and each has its own distinct flavor. Coriander leaves are more commonly known as cilantro.

1 package (about 1½ pounds) turkey tenderloins, cut into ¾-inch pieces
1 red bell pepper, cut into short, thin strips
1¼ cups reduced-sodium chicken broth, divided
¼ cup reduced-sodium soy sauce
3 cloves garlic, minced
¾ teaspoon red pepper flakes
¼ teaspoon salt
2 tablespoons cornstarch
3 green onions, cut into ½-inch pieces
⅓ cup creamy or chunky peanut butter (not natural-style)
12 ounces hot cooked vermicelli pasta
¾ cup peanuts or cashews, chopped
¾ cup cilantro, chopped

Slow Cooker Directions

Place turkey, bell pepper, 1 cup broth, soy sauce, garlic, red pepper flakes and salt in slow cooker. Cover and cook on LOW 3 hours.

Mix cornstarch with remaining ¼ cup broth in small bowl until smooth. Turn slow cooker to HIGH. Stir in green onions, peanut butter and cornstarch mixture. Cover and cook 30 minutes or until sauce is thickened and turkey is no longer pink in center. Stir well. Serve over vermicelli. Sprinkle with peanuts and cilantro.

Tip: *If you don't have vermicelli on hand, try substituting ramen noodles. Discard the flavor packet from ramen soup mix and drop the noodles into boiling water. Cook the noodles 2 to 3 minutes or until just tender. Drain and serve hot.*

Golden Harvest Pork Stew

1 pound boneless pork cutlets,
    cut into 1-inch pieces
2 tablespoons all-purpose flour,
    divided
1 tablespoon vegetable oil
2 medium Yukon gold potatoes,
    unpeeled and cut into
    1-inch cubes
1 large sweet potato, peeled
    and cut into 1-inch cubes
1 cup chopped carrots
1 ear corn, broken into 4 pieces
    or ½ cup corn

½ cup chicken broth
1 jalapeño pepper,* seeded and
    finely chopped
1 clove garlic, minced
1 teaspoon salt
¼ teaspoon black pepper
¼ teaspoon dried thyme leaves

Jalapeño peppers can sting and irritate the skin; wear rubber gloves when handling peppers and do not touch eyes. Wash hands after handling.

Makes 4 (2½-cup) servings

Slow Cooker Directions

1. Toss pork pieces with 1 tablespoon flour; set aside. Heat oil in large nonstick skillet over medium-high heat until hot. Brown pork 2 to 3 minutes per side; transfer to 5-quart slow cooker.

2. Add remaining ingredients except remaining flour to slow cooker. Cover; cook on LOW 5 to 6 hours.

3. Combine remaining 1 tablespoon flour and ¼ cup broth from stew in small bowl; stir until smooth. Stir flour mixture into stew. Cook on HIGH 10 minutes or until thickened. Adjust seasonings, if desired.

Autumn Harvest Sausage and Cabbage

Makes 6 to 8 servings

Prep Time:
30 minutes

Cook Time:
8 to 10 hours

1 package (12 ounces) reduced-
   fat pork sausage
8 cups chopped red cabbage
   (1 small head)
3 potatoes, diced
3 apples, diced
1 onion, sliced

½ cup sugar
½ cup white vinegar
 1 teaspoon salt
½ teaspoon black pepper
½ teaspoon ground allspice
¼ teaspoon ground cloves

Slow Cooker Directions

1. Cook sausage in large nonstick skillet over medium-high heat until no longer pink, stirring to separate; drain fat.

2. Combine sausage and remaining ingredients in large bowl; mix well. Spoon mixture into slow cooker. Cover; cook on LOW 8 to 10 hours or until potatoes are tender.

Hint: *It is easier to mix all the ingredients in a large bowl instead of the slow cooker because the slow cooker will be filled to the top until the cabbage cooks down.*

Cornbread and Bean Casserole

Makes 6 to 8 servings

Filling
- 1 medium onion, chopped
- 1 medium green bell pepper, diced
- 2 cloves garlic, minced
- 1 can (16 ounces) red kidney beans, rinsed and drained
- 1 can (16 ounces) pinto beans, rinsed and drained
- 1 can (16 ounces) diced tomatoes with jalapeño peppers, undrained
- 1 can (8 ounces) tomato sauce
- 1 teaspoon chili powder
- ½ teaspoon ground cumin
- ½ teaspoon black pepper
- ¼ teaspoon hot pepper sauce

Topping
- 1 cup yellow cornmeal
- 1 cup all-purpose flour
- 2½ teaspoons baking powder
- 1 tablespoon sugar
- ½ teaspoon salt
- 1¼ cups milk
- 2 eggs
- 3 tablespoons vegetable oil
- 1 can (8½ ounces) cream-style corn, undrained

Slow Cooker Directions

1. Lightly grease slow cooker. Cook onion, bell pepper and garlic in large skillet over medium heat until tender. Transfer to slow cooker. Stir in kidney beans, pinto beans, tomatoes with juice, tomato sauce, chili powder, cumin, black pepper and hot pepper sauce. Cover; cook on HIGH 1 hour.

2. Combine cornmeal, flour, baking powder, sugar and salt in large bowl. Stir in milk, eggs and oil; mix well. Stir in corn. Spoon evenly over bean mixture. Cover; cook on HIGH 1½ to 2 hours or until cornbread topping is done.

Tip: *Spoon any remaining cornbread into greased muffin cups; bake at 375°F 30 minutes or until golden brown.*

Cajun-Style Country Ribs

Makes 6 servings

Prep Time:
15 minutes

Cook Time:
6 to 8 hours

2 cups baby carrots
1 large onion, coarsely chopped
1 large green bell pepper, cut into 1-inch pieces
1 large red bell pepper, cut into 1-inch pieces
2 teaspoons minced fresh garlic
2 tablespoons Cajun or Creole seasoning mix, divided

3½ to 4 pounds country-style pork spareribs
1 can (14½ ounces) stewed tomatoes, undrained
2 tablespoons water
1 tablespoon cornstarch
Hot cooked rice

Slow Cooker Directions

1. Place carrots, onion, bell peppers, garlic and 2 teaspoons seasoning mix in slow cooker; mix well.

Note:

Cornstarch-thickened sauces can be savory or sweet. Using cornstarch instead of flour gives sauces a clear, glossy appearance. Cornstarch must be dissolved in a cold liquid before cooking.

2. Trim excess fat from ribs. Cut into individual riblets. Sprinkle 1 tablespoon seasoning mix over ribs; place in slow cooker over vegetables. Pour tomatoes with juice over ribs (slow cooker will be full). Cover; cook on LOW 6 to 8 hours or until ribs are fork tender.

3. Remove ribs and vegetables from cooking liquid to serving platter. Let liquid stand 5 minutes to allow fat to rise. Skim off fat.

4. Blend water, cornstarch and remaining 1 teaspoon Cajun seasoning. Stir into liquid in slow cooker. Cook on HIGH until sauce is thickened. Return ribs and vegetables to sauce; carefully stirring to coat. Serve with rice.

My Favorite Chicken

Makes 4 servings

1 chicken (about 3 pounds), cut
   into pieces
1 cup chopped onion
1 cup sliced celery
1 cup sliced carrots
½ teaspoon seasoning salt
½ teaspoon black pepper
¼ teaspoon garlic powder
¼ teaspoon poultry seasoning
3 to 4 medium potatoes, sliced
1 can (14 ounces) chicken broth

Slow Cooker Directions

Place chicken pieces, onion, celery, carrots, seasoning salt, black
pepper, garlic powder and poultry seasoning in slow cooker. Top
with potatoes. Pour broth over top. Cover; cook on HIGH
30 minutes. Turn to LOW; cook 6 to 8 hours.

Hungarian Lamb Goulash

Makes 6 servings

1 package (16 ounces) frozen
   cut green beans
1 cup chopped onion
1¼ pounds lean lamb stew meat,
   cut into 1-inch pieces
1 can (15 ounces) chunky
   tomato sauce
1¾ cups reduced-sodium chicken
   broth
1 can (6 ounces) tomato paste
4 teaspoons paprika
3 cups hot cooked noodles

Slow Cooker Directions

Place green beans and onion in slow cooker. Top with lamb.
Combine remaining ingredients, except noodles in large bowl;
mix well. Pour over lamb mixture. Cover and cook on LOW 6 to
8 hours. Stir. Serve over noodles.

Saucy Tropical Turkey

Makes 6 servings

Prep Time:
15 minutes

Cook Time:
6½ to 7½ hours

3 to 4 turkey thighs, skin
   removed (about
   2½ pounds)
2 tablespoons vegetable oil
1 small onion, halved and sliced
1 can (20 ounces) pineapple
   chunks, drained
1 red bell pepper, cubed

⅔ cup apricot preserves
3 tablespoons soy sauce
1 teaspoon grated lemon peel
1 teaspoon ground ginger
¼ cup cold water
2 tablespoons cornstarch
   Hot cooked rice or noodles

Slow Cooker Directions

1. Rinse turkey and pat dry. Heat oil in large skillet; brown turkey on all sides. Place onion in slow cooker. Transfer turkey to slow cooker; top with pineapple and bell pepper.

2. Combine preserves, soy sauce, lemon peel and ginger in small bowl; mix well. Spoon over turkey. Cover; cook on LOW 6 to 7 hours.

3. Remove turkey from slow cooker; keep warm. Blend water and cornstarch until smooth; stir into slow cooker. Cook on HIGH 15 minutes or until sauce is slightly thickened. Adjust seasonings, if desired. Return turkey to slow cooker; cook until hot. Serve with rice.

Slow-Cooked Pot Roast

1 tablespoon vegetable oil
1 beef brisket (3 to 4 pounds)
1 tablespoon garlic powder,
    divided
1 tablespoon salt, divided
1 tablespoon black pepper,
    divided

1 teaspoon paprika, divided
5 to 6 new potatoes, cut into
    quarters
4 to 5 medium onions, sliced
1 pound baby carrots
1 can (14½ ounces) beef broth

Makes 6 to 8 servings

Slow Cooker Directions

1. Heat 1 tablespoon oil on HIGH in slow cooker. Brown brisket on all sides. Remove brisket to plate. Season with 1½ teaspoons garlic powder, 1½ teaspoons salt, 1½ teaspoons pepper and ½ teaspoon paprika; set aside.

2. Season potatoes with remaining 1½ teaspoons garlic powder, 1½ teaspoons salt, 1½ teaspoons pepper and ½ teaspoon paprika. Add potatoes and onions to slow cooker. Cook on HIGH, stirring occasionally, until browned.

3. Return brisket to slow cooker. Add carrots and broth. Cover; cook on HIGH 4 to 5 hours or on LOW 8 to 10 hours or until meat is tender.

Mushroom Barley Stew

Makes 4 to 6 servings

Prep Time:
10 minutes

Cook Time:
6 to 7 hours

1 tablespoon olive oil
1 medium onion, finely
    chopped
1 cup chopped carrots (about
    2 carrots)
1 clove garlic, minced
1 cup pearl barley

1 cup dried wild mushrooms,
    broken into pieces
1 teaspoon salt
½ teaspoon black pepper
½ teaspoon dried thyme leaves
5 cups vegetable broth

Slow Cooker Directions

1. Heat oil in medium skillet over medium-high heat. Add onion, carrots and garlic; cook and stir 5 minutes or until tender. Place in slow cooker.

2. Add barley, mushrooms, salt, pepper and thyme. Stir in broth. Cover; cook on LOW 6 to 7 hours. Adjust seasonings, if desired.

Variation: *To turn this thick robust stew into a soup, add 2 to 3 additional cups of broth. Cook the same length of time.*

Shrimp Jambalaya

Makes 6 servings

1 can (28 ounces) diced tomatoes, undrained
1 medium onion, chopped
1 medium red bell pepper, chopped
1 rib celery, chopped (about ½ cup)
2 tablespoons minced garlic
2 teaspoons dried parsley flakes
2 teaspoons dried oregano leaves
1 teaspoon hot pepper sauce
½ teaspoon thyme leaves
2 pounds large shrimp, cooked, peeled and deveined
2 cups uncooked rice
2 cups fat-free reduced-sodium chicken broth

Slow Cooker Directions

Combine tomatoes with juice, onion, bell pepper, celery, garlic, parsley, oregano, hot pepper sauce and thyme in slow cooker. Cover and cook on LOW 8 hours or on HIGH 4 hours. Stir in shrimp. Cover and cook on LOW 20 minutes.

Meanwhile, prepare rice according to package directions, substituting broth for water. Serve jambalaya over hot cooked rice.

Note:

Always taste your finished slow cooker dish before serving and adjust the seasoning to your preference. Salt, pepper, seasoned salt, seasoned herb blends, lemon juice, soy sauce, hot pepper sauce or minced fresh herbs can perk up the flavor of any dish.

Mediterranean Meatball Ratatouille

Makes 6 (1⅔ cups) servings

2 tablespoons olive oil, divided
1 pound bulk mild Italian
   sausage
1 package (8 ounces) sliced
   mushrooms
1 small eggplant, diced
1 zucchini, diced
½ cup chopped onion
1 clove garlic, minced

1 teaspoon dried oregano
   leaves
1 teaspoon salt
½ teaspoon black pepper
2 tomatoes, diced
1 tablespoon tomato paste
2 tablespoons chopped fresh
   basil
1 teaspoon fresh lemon juice

Slow Cooker Directions

1. Pour 1 tablespoon olive oil into 5-quart slow cooker. Shape sausage into 1-inch meatballs. Place half the meatballs in slow cooker. Add half each of mushrooms, eggplant and zucchini. Top with onion, garlic. Sprinkle with half each of oregano, salt and black pepper.

2. Add remaining meatballs, mushrooms, eggplant and zucchini; sprinkle with remaining oregano, salt and black pepper. Top with remaining 1 tablespoon olive oil. Cover; cook on LOW 6 to 7 hours.

3. Stir in diced tomatoes and tomato paste. Cover; cook on LOW 15 minutes. Stir in basil and lemon juice; serve.

90's-Style Slow Cooker Coq au Vin

Makes 8 servings

2 packages BUTTERBALL®
   Boneless Skinless Chicken
   Breast Fillets
1 pound fresh mushrooms,
   sliced thick
1 jar (15 ounces) pearl onions,
   drained

½ cup dry white wine
1 teaspoon thyme leaves
1 bay leaf
1 cup chicken broth
⅓ cup flour
½ cup chopped fresh parsley

Slow Cooker Directions

Place chicken, mushrooms, onions, wine, thyme and bay leaf in slow cooker. Combine chicken broth and flour; pour into slow cooker. Cover and cook 5 hours on low setting. Add parsley. Serve over wild rice pilaf, if desired.

Cantonese Pork

Makes 8 servings

1 tablespoon vegetable oil
2 pounds pork tenderloin, cut
   into strips
1 can (8 ounces) pineapple
   chunks, undrained
1 can (8 ounces) tomato sauce
2 cans (4 ounces each) sliced
   mushrooms, drained

1 medium onion, thinly sliced
3 tablespoons brown sugar
2 tablespoons Worcestershire
   sauce
1½ teaspoons salt
1½ teaspoons white vinegar
   Hot cooked rice

Slow Cooker Directions

1. Heat oil in large nonstick skillet over medium-low heat. Brown pork on all sides. Drain excess fat.

2. Place all ingredients except rice in slow cooker. Cover; cook on HIGH 4 hours or on LOW 6 to 8 hours. Serve over rice.

Chicken Curry

Makes 2 servings

2 boneless skinless chicken
breast halves, cut into
¾-inch pieces
1 small onion, sliced
1 cup coarsely chopped apple,
divided
3 tablespoons raisins
1 clove garlic, minced
1 teaspoon curry powder

¼ teaspoon ground ginger
⅓ cup water
1½ teaspoons chicken bouillon
granules
1½ teaspoons all-purpose flour
¼ cup sour cream
½ teaspoon cornstarch
½ cup uncooked white rice

Note:

After opening, wrap raisins securely in plastic wrap or store them in an airtight container at room temperature. They will keep for several months. If refrigerated in a tightly covered container, raisins will keep for up to 1 year.

Slow Cooker Directions

Combine chicken, onion, ¾ cup apple, raisins, garlic, curry powder and ginger in slow cooker. Combine water and bouillon granules in small bowl until dissolved. Stir in flour until smooth. Add to slow cooker. Cover and cook on LOW 3½ to 4 hours or until onions are tender and chicken is no longer pink.

Combine sour cream and cornstarch in large bowl. Turn off slow cooker. Transfer all cooking liquid from chicken mixture to sour cream mixture; stir until combined. Stir mixture back into slow cooker. Cover and let stand 5 to 10 minutes or until sauce is heated through.

Meanwhile, cook rice according to package directions. Serve chicken curry over rice; garnish with remaining ¼ cup apple.

Hint: *For a special touch, sprinkle chicken with green onion slivers just before serving.*

Corned Beef and Cabbage

1 head cabbage (1½ pounds),
    cut into 6 wedges
4 ounces baby carrots
1 corned beef (3 pounds) with
    seasoning packet*
1 quart (4 cups) water

⅓ cup prepared mustard
    (optional)
⅓ cup honey (optional)

*If seasoning packet is not perforated, poke
several small holes with tip of paring knife.

Makes 6 servings

Slow Cooker Directions

1. Place cabbage in slow cooker; top with carrots.

2. Place seasoning packet on top of vegetables. Place corned beef, fat side up, over seasoning packet and vegetables. Add water. Cover; cook on LOW 10 hours.

3. Discard seasoning packet. Just before serving, combine mustard and honey in small bowl. Use as dipping sauce, if desired.

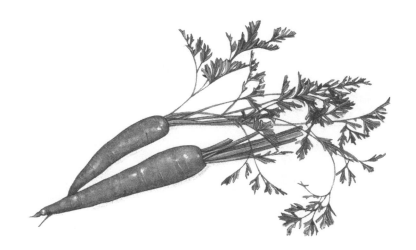

Lamb in Dill Sauce

Makes 6 servings

2 large boiling potatoes, peeled
and cut into 1-inch cubes
½ cup chopped onion
1½ teaspoons salt
½ teaspoon black pepper
½ teaspoon dried dill weed *or*
4 sprigs fresh dill
1 bay leaf

2 pounds lean lamb stew meat,
cut into 1-inch cubes
1 cup plus 3 tablespoons water,
divided
2 tablespoons all-purpose flour
1 teaspoon sugar
2 tablespoons lemon juice
Fresh dill (optional)

Slow Cooker Directions

Layer ingredients in slow cooker in the following order: potatoes, onion, salt, pepper, dill, bay leaf, lamb and 1 cup water. Cover and cook on LOW 6 to 8 hours.

Remove lamb and potatoes with slotted spoon; cover and keep warm. Remove and discard bay leaf. Turn heat to HIGH. Stir flour and remaining 3 tablespoons water in small bowl until smooth. Add half of cooking juices and sugar. Mix well and return to slow cooker. Cover and cook 15 minutes. Stir in lemon juice. Return lamb and potatoes to slow cooker. Cover and cook on HIGH 10 minutes or until heated through. Garnish with fresh dill, if desired.

Caribbean Sweet Potato & Bean Stew

2 medium sweet potatoes (about 1 pound), peeled and cut into 1-inch cubes
2 cups frozen cut green beans
1 can (15 ounces) black beans, rinsed and drained
1 can (14½ ounces) vegetable broth
1 small onion, sliced
2 teaspoons Caribbean or Jamaican jerk seasoning

½ teaspoon dried thyme leaves
¼ teaspoon salt
¼ teaspoon ground cinnamon
⅓ cup slivered almonds, toasted*
Hot pepper sauce (optional)

*To toast almonds, spread in single layer on baking sheet. Bake in preheated 350°F oven 8 to 10 minutes or until golden brown, stirring frequently.

Makes 4 servings

Prep Time:
10 minutes

Cook Time:
5 to 6 hours

Slow Cooker Directions

1. Combine all ingredients except almonds and pepper sauce in slow cooker. Cover; cook on LOW 5 to 6 hours or until vegetables are tender.

2. Adjust seasonings. Serve with almonds and hot pepper sauce, if desired.

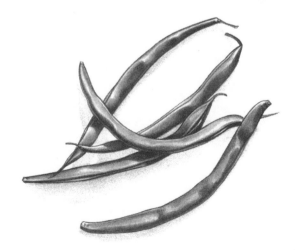

Chicken Stew with Dumplings

Makes 4 servings

2 cans (about 14 ounces each)
   chicken broth, divided
2 cups sliced carrots
1 cup chopped onion
1 large green bell pepper, sliced
½ cup sliced celery
⅔ cup all-purpose flour
1 pound boneless skinless
   chicken breasts, cut into
   1-inch pieces
1 large potato, unpeeled and
   cut into 1-inch pieces
6 ounces mushrooms, halved
¾ cup frozen peas

1 teaspoon dried basil
¾ teaspoon dried rosemary
¼ teaspoon dried tarragon
¾ to 1 teaspoon salt
¼ teaspoon black pepper
¼ cup heavy cream

Herb Dumplings
1 cup biscuit baking mix
¼ teaspoon dried basil
¼ teaspoon dried rosemary
⅛ teaspoon dried tarragon
⅓ cup reduced-fat (2%) milk

Slow Cooker Directions

Reserve 1 cup chicken broth. Combine carrots, onion, green bell pepper, celery and remaining chicken broth in slow cooker. Cover and cook on LOW 2 hours.

Stir flour into reserved 1 cup broth until smooth. Stir into slow cooker. Add chicken, potato, mushrooms, peas, 1 teaspoon basil, ¾ teaspoon rosemary and ¼ teaspoon tarragon to slow cooker. Cover and cook 4 hours or until vegetables are tender and chicken is no longer pink. Stir in salt, black pepper and heavy cream.

Combine baking mix, ¼ teaspoon basil, ¼ teaspoon rosemary and ¼ teaspoon tarragon in small bowl. Stir in milk to form soft dough. Spoon dumpling mixture on top of stew in 4 large spoonfuls. Cook, uncovered, 30 minutes. Cover and cook 30 to 45 minutes or until dumplings are firm and toothpick inserted in center comes out clean. Serve in shallow bowls.

Deviled Beef Short Rib Stew

4 pounds beef short ribs, trimmed
2 pounds small red potatoes, scrubbed and scored
8 carrots, peeled and cut into chunks
2 onions, cut into thick wedges
1 bottle (12 ounces) beer or non-alcoholic malt beverage

8 tablespoons *French's®* Bold n' Spicy Brown Mustard, divided
3 tablespoons *French's®* Worcestershire Sauce, divided
2 tablespoons cornstarch

Makes 6 servings (with 3 cups gravy)

Slow Cooker Directions

1. Broil ribs 6 inches from heat on rack in broiler pan 10 minutes or until well browned, turning once. Place vegetables in bottom of slow cooker. Place ribs on top of vegetables.

2. Combine beer, *6 tablespoons* mustard and *2 tablespoons* Worcestershire in medium bowl. Pour into slow cooker. Cover and cook on HIGH 5 hours* or until meat is tender.

3. Transfer meat and vegetables to large platter; keep warm. Strain fat from broth; pour broth into saucepan. Combine cornstarch with *2 tablespoons cold water* in small bowl. Stir into broth with remaining *2 tablespoons* mustard and *1 tablespoon* Worcestershire. Heat to boiling. Reduce heat to medium-low. Cook 1 to 2 minutes or until thickened, stirring often. Pass gravy with meat and vegetables. Serve meat with additional mustard.

*Or cook 10 hours on LOW.

Tip: *Prepare ingredients the night before for quick assembly in the morning. Keep refrigerated until ready to use.*

Note:

Deviled foods are foods that have been seasoned with a hot and spicy ingredient such as hot mustard, red pepper or hot pepper sauce.

Panama Pork Stew

Makes 6 servings

2 small sweet potatoes, peeled
   and cut into 2-inch pieces
   (about 12 ounces total)
1 package (10 ounces) frozen
   corn
1 package (9 ounces) frozen cut
   green beans
1 cup chopped onion

1¼ pounds lean pork stew meat,
   cut into 1-inch cubes
1 can (14½ ounces) diced
   tomatoes, undrained
¼ cup water
1 to 2 tablespoons chili powder
½ teaspoon salt
½ teaspoon ground coriander

Slow Cooker Directions

Place potatoes, corn, green beans and onion in slow cooker. Top
with pork. Combine tomatoes with juice, water, chili powder, salt
and coriander in large bowl. Pour over pork in slow cooker.
Cover; cook on LOW 7 to 9 hours.

Slow Cooker Hamburger Casserole

Makes 4 to 6 servings

4 medium potatoes, thinly
   sliced
3 carrots, thinly sliced
1 can (15 ounces) green peas,
   drained
1 can (15 ounces) corn, drained
3 medium onions, chopped

1½ pounds extra-lean ground
   beef, browned and drained
Salt
Black pepper
1 can (10¾ ounces) condensed
   tomato soup
1 soup can water

Slow Cooker Directions

Layer first 6 ingredients inside slow cooker in order listed,
occasionally seasoning with salt and pepper. Cover with tomato
soup and water. Cover; cook on LOW 6 to 8 hours or on HIGH 2 to
4 hours.

Layered Mexican-Style Casserole

2 cans (15½ ounces each) hominy, drained
1 can (15 ounces) black beans, rinsed and drained
1 can (14½ ounces) diced tomatoes with garlic, basil and oregano, undrained
1 cup thick and chunky salsa

1 can (6 ounces) tomato paste
½ teaspoon ground cumin
3 large (about 9-inch diameter) flour tortillas
2 cups (8 ounces) shredded Monterey Jack cheese
¼ cup sliced black olives

Makes 6 servings

Prep Time:
10 minutes

Cook Time:
6 to 8 hours

Stand Time:
5 minutes

Slow Cooker Directions

1. Prepare foil handles (see below). Spray slow cooker with nonstick cooking spray.

2. Stir together hominy, beans, tomatoes with juice, salsa, tomato paste and cumin in large bowl.

3. Press one tortilla in bottom of slow cooker. (Edges of tortilla may turn up slightly.) Top with one third of hominy mixture and one third of cheese. Repeat layers once. Press remaining tortilla on top. Top with remaining hominy mixture. Set aside remaining cheese.

4. Cover; cook on LOW 6 to 8 hours. Sprinkle with remaining cheese and olives. Cover; let stand 5 minutes. Pull out tortilla stack with foil handles.

Foil Handles: *Tear off three 18×2-inch strips of heavy-duty foil or use regular foil folded to double thickness. Crisscross foil strips in spoke design and place into slow cooker to make lifting of tortilla stack easier.*

Turkey Breast with Barley-Cranberry Stuffing

Makes 6 servings

2 cups fat-free reduced-sodium chicken broth
1 cup quick-cooking barley
½ cup chopped onion
½ cup dried cranberries
2 tablespoons slivered almonds, toasted
½ teaspoon rubbed sage

½ teaspoon garlic-pepper seasoning
1 fresh or frozen bone-in turkey breast half (about 2 pounds), thawed and skinned
⅓ cup finely chopped fresh parsley

Slow Cooker Directions

1. Combine broth, barley, onion, cranberries, almonds, sage and garlic-pepper seasoning in slow cooker.

2. Spray large nonstick skillet with nonstick cooking spray. Heat over medium heat until hot. Brown turkey breast on all sides; add to slow cooker. Cover; cook on LOW 3 to 4 hours or until internal temperature reaches 170°F when tested with meat thermometer inserted into the thickest part of breast, not touching bone.

3. Transfer turkey to cutting board; cover with foil and let stand 10 to 15 minutes before carving. Internal temperature will rise 5° to 10°F during stand time. Stir parsley into sauce mixture in slow cooker. Serve sauce with sliced turkey.

Easy Pork Chop Dinner

1 large onion, thinly sliced
3 to 4 medium baking potatoes, sliced
6 pork chops

1 can (10¾ ounces) reduced-fat condensed cream of celery soup
½ cup water or milk

Slow Cooker Directions

1. Place onion then potatoes in slow cooker. Top with pork chops.

2. Combine soup and water in small bowl; pour over chops. Cover; cook on LOW 6 to 8 hours.

Quick Tips for the Slow Cooker

1. Manufacturers recommend that slow cookers should be one-half to three-quarters full for the best results.

2. To make cleanup easier, spray the inside of the slow cooker with nonstick cooking spray before adding any food.

3. Cooking times are guidelines. Slow cookers, just like ovens, cook differently depending on heating units. The cooking times may need to be adjusted slightly.

4. Keep a lid on it! Slow cookers can take as long as 30 minutes to regain heat lost when the cover is removed. Only remove the cover when instructed to do so in the recipe.

5. Spinning the cover until the condensation falls off will allow you to see inside the slow cooker without removing the lid, which delays the cooking time.

6. Slow cooker recipes with raw meats should cook a minimum of 3 hours on LOW for food safety reasons.

7. Do not cook whole chickens in the slow cooker because the temperature of the chicken cannot reach the desired level quickly enough for food safety. Cut a whole chicken into quarters or parts.

8. Dairy products should be added at the end of the cooking time because they will curdle if cooked in the slow cooker for a long time.

9. For vegetables to cook properly, they need to be cut into uniform pieces in the size suggested in the recipe.

Sauerbraten

Makes 5 servings

1 boneless beef sirloin tip roast
   (1¼ pounds)
3 cups baby carrots
1½ cups fresh or frozen pearl
   onions
¼ cup raisins
½ cup water
½ cup red wine vinegar

1 tablespoon honey
½ teaspoon salt
½ teaspoon dry mustard
½ teaspoon garlic-pepper
   seasoning
¼ teaspoon ground cloves
¼ cup crushed crisp gingersnap
   cookies (5 cookies)

Slow Cooker Directions

1. Heat large nonstick skillet over medium heat until hot. Brown roast on all sides. Place roast, carrots, onions and raisins in slow cooker.

2. Combine water, vinegar, honey, salt, mustard, garlic-pepper seasoning and cloves in large bowl; mix well. Pour mixture over meat and vegetables. Cover; cook on LOW 4 to 6 hours or until internal temperature reaches 145°F when tested with meat thermometer inserted into thickest part of roast.

3. Transfer roast to cutting board; cover with foil. Let stand 10 to 15 minutes before slicing. Internal temperature will continue to rise 5° to 10°F during stand time.

4. Remove vegetables with slotted spoon to bowl; cover to keep warm. Stir crushed cookies into sauce mixture in slow cooker. Cover; cook on HIGH 10 to 15 minutes or until sauce thickens. Serve meat and vegetables with sauce.

Arroz con Pollo

6 chicken thighs, skin removed
1 can (14½ ounces) chicken
   broth
1 can (14½ ounces) stewed
   tomatoes
1 package (10 ounces) frozen
   peas

1 package (8 ounces) Spanish-
   style yellow rice mix
1½ cups *French's®* French Fried
   Onions, divided

Makes 6 servings

Prep Time:
10 minutes

Cook Time:
8 hours

Slow Cooker Directions

1. Coat slow cooker with vegetable cooking spray. Combine chicken, broth and tomatoes in slow cooker. Cover and cook on LOW setting for 4 to 5 hours (or on HIGH for 2 to 2½ hours) until chicken is fork-tender.

2. Stir in peas and rice mix. Cover and cook on LOW setting for 2 to 3 hours (or on HIGH for 1 to 1½ hours) until rice is cooked and all liquid is absorbed. Stir in *¾ cup* French Fried Onions. Spoon soup into serving bowls; top with remaining onions.

Tip: *Cook times vary depending on type of slow cooker used. Check manufacturer's recommendations for cooking chicken and rice.*

Italian Sausage and Vegetable Stew

Makes 6 (1-cup) servings

1 pound hot or mild Italian sausage, cut into 1-inch pieces

1 package (16 ounces) frozen mixed vegetables (onions and green, red and yellow bell peppers)

1 can (14½ ounces) diced Italian-style tomatoes, undrained

2 medium zucchini, sliced

1 jar (4½ ounces) sliced mushrooms, drained

4 cloves garlic, minced

2 tablespoons Italian-style tomato paste

Slow Cooker Directions

Heat large skillet over high heat until hot. Add sausage and cook about 5 minutes or until browned. Pour off any drippings.

Combine sausage, frozen vegetables, tomatoes with juice, zucchini, mushrooms and garlic in slow cooker. Cover and cook on LOW 4 to 4½ hours or until zucchini is tender. Stir in tomato paste. Cover and cook 30 minutes or until juices have thickened.

Serving Suggestion: *Serve with fresh hot garlic bread.*

Caribbean Shrimp with Rice

1 package (12 ounces) frozen
   shrimp, thawed
½ cup fat-free reduced-sodium
   chicken broth
1 clove garlic, minced
1 teaspoon chili powder
½ teaspoon salt

½ teaspoon dried oregano
   leaves
1 cup frozen peas
½ cup diced tomatoes
2 cups cooked long-grain white
   rice

Makes 4 servings

Slow Cooker Directions
Combine shrimp, broth, garlic, chili powder, salt and oregano in slow cooker. Cover and cook on LOW 2 hours. Add peas and tomatoes. Cover and cook on LOW 5 minutes. Stir in rice. Cover and cook on LOW an additional 5 minutes.

Stew Provençal

2 cans (about 14 ounces each)
   beef broth, divided
⅓ cup all-purpose flour
1½ pounds pork tenderloin,
   trimmed and diced
4 red potatoes, unpeeled, cut
   into cubes

2 cups frozen cut green beans
1 onion, chopped
2 cloves garlic, minced
1 teaspoon salt
1 teaspoon dried thyme leaves
½ teaspoon black pepper

Makes 8 servings

Slow Cooker Directions
Combine ¾ cup beef broth and flour in small bowl. Set aside.

Add remaining broth, pork, potatoes, beans, onion, garlic, salt, thyme and pepper to slow cooker; stir. Cover and cook on LOW 8 to 10 hours or on HIGH 4 to 5 hours. If cooking on LOW, turn to HIGH last 30 minutes. Stir in flour mixture. Cook 30 minutes to thicken.

Ham and Potato Casserole

Makes 6 to 7 servings

1½ pounds red potatoes, peeled and sliced
8 ounces thinly sliced ham
2 poblano chili peppers, cut into thin strips
2 tablespoons olive oil
1 tablespoon dried oregano leaves

¼ teaspoon salt
1 cup (4 ounces) shredded Monterey Jack or Pepper-Jack cheese
2 tablespoons finely chopped fresh cilantro

Note:

Vegetables such as potatoes and carrots can sometimes take longer to cook in a slow cooker than meat. Place evenly cut vegetables on the bottom or along the sides of the slow cooker when possible.

Slow Cooker Directions

1. Combine all ingredients except cheese and cilantro in slow cooker; mix well. Cover; cook on LOW 7 hours or on HIGH 4 hours.

2. Transfer potato mixture to serving dish; sprinkle with cheese and cilantro. Let stand 3 minutes or until cheese melts.

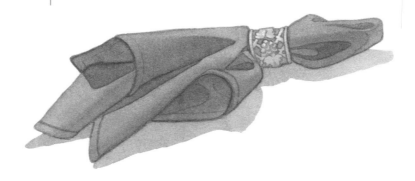

Lentil Stew over Couscous

Makes 12 servings

1 large onion, chopped
1 green bell pepper, chopped
4 ribs celery, chopped
1 medium carrot, cut
    lengthwise into halves,
    then cut into 1-inch pieces
2 cloves garlic, chopped
3 cups lentils (1 pound), rinsed
1 can (14½ ounces) diced
    tomatoes, undrained
1 can (14½ ounces) reduced-
    sodium chicken broth

3 cups water
¼ teaspoon black pepper
1 teaspoon dried marjoram
    leaves
1 tablespoon cider vinegar
1 tablespoon olive oil
4½ to 5 cups hot cooked
    couscous
    Carrot curls (optional)
    Celery leaves (optional)

Slow Cooker Directions

Combine onion, green bell pepper, celery, carrot, garlic, lentils, tomatoes with juice, broth, water, black pepper and marjoram in slow cooker. Stir; cover and cook on LOW 8 to 9 hours.

Stir in vinegar and olive oil. Serve stew over couscous. Garnish with carrot curls and celery leaves, if desired.

Nice 'n' Easy Italian Chicken

Makes 4 servings

1 pound boneless skinless
    chicken breasts
1 medium onion, chopped
8 ounces mushrooms, sliced
1 medium green bell pepper,
    chopped (optional)

1 medium zucchini, diced
1 jar (26 ounces) favorite
    spaghetti sauce

Slow Cooker Directions

Combine all ingredients in slow cooker. Cover; cook on LOW 6 to 8 hours.

Serving Suggestion: *Serve over the pasta of your choice.*

Irish Stew

Makes 6 servings

1 cup fat-free reduced-sodium
    chicken broth
1 teaspoon dried marjoram
    leaves
1 teaspoon dried parsley leaves
¾ teaspoon salt
½ teaspoon garlic powder
¼ teaspoon black pepper
1¼ pounds white potatoes,
    peeled and cut into 1-inch
    pieces

1 pound lean lamb stew meat,
    cut into 1-inch cubes
8 ounces frozen cut green
    beans
2 small leeks, cut lengthwise
    into halves then crosswise
    into slices
1½ cups coarsely chopped
    carrots

Slow Cooker Directions

Combine broth, marjoram, parsley, salt, garlic powder and pepper in large bowl; mix well. Pour mixture into slow cooker. Add potatoes, lamb, green beans, leeks and carrots. Cover and cook on LOW 7 to 9 hours.

Middle Eastern Vegetable Stew

Makes 4 to 6 servings

1 tablespoon olive oil
3 cups (12 ounces) sliced
   zucchini
2 cups (6 ounces) cubed peeled
   eggplant
2 cups (8 ounces) sliced
   quartered sweet potatoes
1½ cups cubed peeled butternut
   squash
1 can (28 ounces) crushed
   tomatoes in puree
1 cup drained chick-peas
   (garbanzo beans)

½ cup raisins or currants
1½ teaspoons ground cinnamon
1 teaspoon grated orange peel
¾ to 1 teaspoon ground cumin
½ teaspoon salt
½ teaspoon paprika
¼ to ½ teaspoon ground red
   pepper
⅛ teaspoon ground cardamom
   Hot cooked rice or couscous
   (optional)

Slow Cooker Directions

Combine all ingredients except rice in slow cooker. Cover and cook on LOW 5 to 5½ hours or until vegetables are tender. Serve over rice, if desired.

Note:

Butternut squash,
which weighs from
two to five pounds, is
cylindrical with a slight
bulbous base. The skin
is creamy tan and the
flesh is a yellowish-
orange. The flavor is
sweet and slightly
nutty.

Pineapple Chicken and Sweet Potatoes

Make 6 servings

⅔ cup plus 3 tablespoons
    all-purpose flour, divided
1 teaspoon salt
1 teaspoon ground nutmeg
½ teaspoon ground cinnamon
⅛ teaspoon onion powder
⅛ teaspoon black pepper
6 chicken breasts
3 sweet potatoes, peeled and
    sliced

1 can (10¾ ounces) condensed
    cream of chicken soup,
    undiluted
½ cup pineapple juice
¼ pound mushrooms, sliced
2 teaspoons packed light
    brown sugar
½ teaspoon grated orange peel
Hot cooked rice

Slow Cooker Directions

Combine ⅔ cup flour, salt, nutmeg, cinnamon, onion powder and black pepper in large bowl. Thoroughly coat chicken in flour mixture. Place sweet potatoes on bottom of slow cooker. Top with chicken.

Combine soup, pineapple juice, mushrooms, remaining 3 tablespoons flour, brown sugar and orange peel in medium bowl; stir well. Pour soup mixture into slow cooker. Cover and cook on LOW 8 to 10 hours or on HIGH 3 to 4 hours. Serve chicken and sauce over rice.

Slow Cooker Stuffed Peppers

1 package (7 ounces) Spanish
  rice mix
1 pound ground beef
½ cup diced celery
1 small onion, chopped
1 egg
4 medium green bell peppers,
  halved lengthwise, cored
  and seeded

1 can (28 ounces) whole peeled
  tomatoes, undrained
1 can (10¾ ounces) condensed
  tomato soup
1 cup water

Makes 4 servings

Slow Cooker Directions

1. Set aside seasoning packet from rice. Combine beef, rice mix, celery, onion and egg in large bowl. Divide meat mixture evenly among pepper halves.

2. Pour tomatoes with juice into slow cooker. Arrange filled pepper halves on top of tomatoes. Combine tomato soup, water and reserved rice mix seasoning packet in large bowl. Pour over peppers. Cover; cook on LOW 8 to 10 hours.

Roast Beef with Mushrooms and Vegetables

Makes 8 servings

1 tablespoon vegetable oil
1 boneless beef chuck shoulder
    roast (3 to 5 pounds)
6 medium potatoes, peeled and
    halved
1 bag (1 pound) baby carrots
1 medium onion, quartered

1 can (10¾ ounces) condensed
    cream of mushroom soup
1 can (4 ounces) sliced
    mushrooms, drained
1 cup water

Slow Cooker Directions

1. Heat oil in large skillet over medium-low heat. Brown roast on all sides. Drain excess fat. Place roast in slow cooker. (If necessary, cut roast in half to fit in slow cooker.) Add potatoes, carrots and onion around roast.

2. Combine soup, mushrooms and water together in medium bowl. Pour over roast. Cover; cook on LOW 6 to 8 hours.

Note:

Browning meat and poultry before cooking it in the slow cooker is not necessary but can enhance the flavor and appearance of the finished dish.

Chicken and Chile Pepper Stew

1 pound boneless skinless chicken thighs, cut into ½-inch pieces

1 pound small potatoes, cut lengthwise into halves and then cut crosswise into slices

1 cup chopped onion

2 poblano chile peppers,* seeded and cut into ½-inch pieces

1 jalapeño pepper,* seeded and finely chopped

3 cloves garlic, minced

3 cups fat-free reduced-sodium chicken broth

1 can (14½ ounces) no-salt-added diced tomatoes, undrained

2 tablespoons chili powder

1 teaspoon dried oregano leaves

Makes 6 servings

*Poblano chile peppers and jalapeño peppers can sting and irritate the skin; wear rubber gloves when handling peppers and do not touch eyes. Wash hands after handling.

Slow Cooker Directions

1. Place chicken, potatoes, onion, poblano peppers, jalapeño pepper and garlic in slow cooker.

2. Stir together broth, tomatoes with juice, chili powder and oregano in large bowl. Pour broth mixture over chicken mixture in slow cooker; mix well. Cover; cook on LOW 8 to 9 hours.

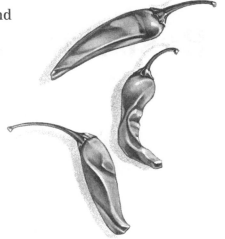

New World Pork Stew

Makes 4 servings

1½ pounds boneless pork sirloin,
    cut into ¾-inch cubes
3 small sweet potatoes, peeled
    and cut into 2-inch pieces
1 green bell pepper, seeded and
    sliced into strips
1 cup frozen corn kernels
1 onion, sliced
3 cloves garlic, minced

1 teaspoon chili powder
1 teaspoon ground coriander
½ teaspoon salt
2 cups water
1 (10-ounce) can diced
    tomatoes with green chiles,
    undrained
1 (9-ounce) package frozen cut
    green beans

Slow Cooker Directions

In 3½- to 4-quart slow cooker, combine pork, sweet potatoes, bell pepper, corn, onion, garlic and seasonings; mix well. Pour water and tomatoes with juice over pork mixture. Cover and cook on LOW 7 to 8 hours (or HIGH 3½ to 4 hours), adding frozen green beans during last 15 minutes of cooking time.

Best Ever Roast

Makes 6 to 8 servings

1 beef chuck shoulder roast
    (3 to 5 pounds)
1 can (10¾ ounces) condensed
    cream of mushroom soup
1 envelope (1 ounce) dry onion
    soup mix

4 to 5 medium potatoes,
    quartered
4 cups baby carrots

Slow Cooker Directions

1. Place roast in slow cooker. (If necessary, cut roast in half to fit in slow cooker.) Add soup and soup mix. Cover; cook on LOW 4 hours.

2. Add potatoes and carrots. Cover; cook on LOW 2 hours.

Chicken Azteca

2 cups frozen corn
1 can (15 ounces) black beans, rinsed and drained
1 cup chunky salsa, divided
1 clove garlic, minced
½ teaspoon ground cumin

4 boneless skinless chicken breasts
1 package (8 ounces) cream cheese, cubed
Hot cooked rice
Shredded Cheddar cheese

Makes 4 servings

Slow Cooker Directions

1. Combine corn, beans, ½ cup salsa, garlic and cumin in slow cooker. Arrange chicken breasts over top; pour remaining ½ cup salsa over chicken. Cover; cook on HIGH 2 to 3 hours or on LOW 4 to 6 hours or until chicken is tender.

2. Remove chicken; cut into bite-size pieces. Return chicken to slow cooker; add cream cheese. Cook on HIGH until cream cheese melts and blends into sauce.

3. Serve chicken and sauce over rice. Top with Cheddar cheese.

Note:

Do not use the slow cooker to reheat leftover foods. Transfer cooled leftover food to a plastic food storage container with a tight-fitting lid and refrigerate. Use a microwave oven, the range-top or oven for reheating.

The Best Beef Stew

Makes 8 servings

½ cup plus 2 tablespoons
all-purpose flour, divided
2 teaspoons salt
1 teaspoon black pepper
3 pounds beef stew meat,
trimmed and cut into cubes
1 can (16 ounces) diced
tomatoes in juice,
undrained
3 potatoes, peeled and diced

½ pound smoked sausage,
sliced
1 cup chopped leek
1 cup chopped onion
4 ribs celery, sliced
½ cup chicken broth
3 cloves garlic, minced
1 teaspoon dried thyme leaves
3 tablespoons water

Slow Cooker Directions

Combine ½ cup flour, salt and pepper in resealable plastic food
storage bag. Add beef; shake bag to coat beef. Place beef in
slow cooker. Add remaining ingredients except remaining
2 tablespoons flour and water; stir well. Cover and cook on
LOW 8 to 12 hours or on HIGH 4 to 6 hours.

One hour before serving, turn slow cooker to HIGH. Combine
remaining 2 tablespoons flour and water in small bowl; stir until
mixture becomes paste. Stir mixture into slow cooker; mix well.
Cover and cook until thickened. Garnish as desired.

Simple Slow Cooker Pork Roast

4 to 5 red potatoes, cut into
   bite-size pieces
4 carrots, cut into bite-size
   pieces
1 marinated pork roast (3 to
   4 pounds)

½ cup water
1 package (10 ounces) frozen
   baby peas

Makes 6 servings

Slow Cooker Directions

1. Place potatoes, carrots and pork roast in slow cooker. (If necessary, cut roast in half to fit in slow cooker.) Add ½ cup water. Cover; cook on LOW 6 to 8 hours or until vegetables are done.

2. Add peas during last hour of cooking. Adjust seasonings as desired.

Slow Cooker Veggie Stew

Makes 4 to 6 servings

1 tablespoon vegetable oil
⅔ cup sliced carrots
½ cup diced onion
2 cloves garlic, chopped
2 cans (14 ounces each) fat-free
   vegetable broth
1½ cups chopped green cabbage

½ cup cut green beans
½ cup diced zucchini
1 tablespoon tomato paste
½ teaspoon dried basil leaves
½ teaspoon dried oregano
   leaves
¼ teaspoon salt

Slow Cooker Directions

1. Heat oil in medium skillet over medium-high heat. Add carrots, onion and garlic. Cook and stir until tender.

2. Place carrot mixture and remaining ingredients in slow cooker. Cover; cook on LOW 8 to 10 hours or on HIGH 3 hours.

Slow-Cooked Beef Brisket Dinner

Makes 8 to 10 servings

1 beef brisket (4 pounds), cut in half
4 to 6 medium potatoes, cut into large chunks
6 carrots, cut into 1-inch pieces
8 ounces sliced mushrooms
½ large onion, sliced

1 rib celery, cut into 1-inch pieces
3 cubes beef bouillon
5 cloves garlic, crushed
1 teaspoon black peppercorns
2 bay leaves
Water

Note:

For easier preparation, cut up ingredients for the slow cooker the night before. Wrap and store meats and vegetables separately in the refrigerator.

Slow Cooker Directions

1. Place all ingredients in slow cooker, adding enough water to cover ingredients. Cover; cook on LOW 6 to 8 hours. Remove and discard bay leaves.

2. Remove brisket to cutting board. Slice across the grain and serve with vegetables.

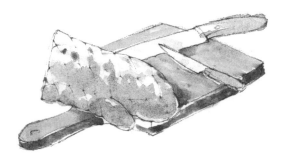

Tempting Stir-Fries

CHAPTER FIFTEEN

Peanut Chicken Stir-Fry

Makes 4 servings

1 package (6.1 ounces) RICE-A-RONI® With ⅓ Less Salt Fried Rice
½ cup reduced-sodium or regular chicken broth
2 tablespoons creamy peanut butter
1 tablespoon reduced-sodium or regular soy sauce
1 tablespoon vegetable oil

¾ pound skinless, boneless chicken breasts, cut into ½-inch pieces
2 cloves garlic, minced
2 cups frozen mixed carrots, broccoli and red pepper vegetable medley, thawed, drained
2 tablespoons chopped peanuts (optional)

Note:

Commercial peanut butter is a blend of ground roasted peanuts, vegetable oil and salt. Some brands contain sugar or a stabilizer that prevents the oil from separating. By law it must contain at least 90 percent peanuts.

1. Prepare Rice-A-Roni® mix as package directs.

2. While Rice-A-Roni® is simmering, combine chicken broth, peanut butter and soy sauce; mix with fork. Set aside.

3. In second large skillet or wok, heat oil over medium-high heat. Stir-fry chicken and garlic 2 minutes.

4. Add vegetables and broth mixture; stir-fry 5 to 7 minutes or until sauce has thickened. Serve over rice. Sprinkle with peanuts, if desired.

Veggie and Scallop Stir-Fry

1 tablespoon vegetable oil
1 bag (16 ounces) BIRDS EYE®
    frozen Farm Fresh Mixtures
    Pepper Stir Fry vegetables
½ pound small sea scallops
1 small onion, chopped *or*
    3 green onions, sliced

1 tablespoon light soy sauce
1 tablespoon Oriental salad
    dressing
⅛ teaspoon ground ginger
    Garlic powder
    Salt and black pepper
    Hot cooked rice (optional)

Makes 4 servings

Prep Time:
3 minutes

Cook Time:
10 to 12 minutes

• In wok or large skillet, heat oil over medium heat.

• Add vegetables; cover and cook 3 to 5 minutes or until crisp-tender.

• Uncover; add scallops and onion. Stir-fry 2 minutes.

• Stir in soy sauce and Oriental salad dressing.

• Reduce heat to low; simmer 3 to 5 minutes or until some liquid is absorbed.

• Stir in ginger, garlic powder and salt and pepper to taste; increase heat to medium-high. Stir-fry until all liquid is absorbed and scallops turn opaque and begin to brown.

• Serve over rice, if desired.

Sesame Pork with Broccoli

Makes 6 servings

1 can (14½ ounces) chicken broth
2 tablespoons cornstarch
1 tablespoon soy sauce
4 green onions with tops, finely diced
1 pound pork tenderloin, trimmed
1 tablespoon vegetable oil
1 clove garlic, minced
1½ pounds fresh broccoli, cut into bite-size pieces (about 7 cups)
2 tablespoons sliced pimiento, drained
Hot cooked rice (optional)
2 tablespoons sesame seed, lightly toasted

Combine chicken broth, cornstarch and soy sauce in small bowl; blend well. Stir in green onions; set aside. Cut pork tenderloin lengthwise into quarters; cut each quarter into bite-size pieces. Heat oil in wok or heavy skillet over medium-high heat. Add pork and garlic; stir-fry 3 to 4 minutes or until pork is tender. Remove pork; keep warm. Stir broth mixture; add to wok with broccoli. Cover and simmer over low heat 8 minutes. Add cooked pork and pimiento to wok; cook just until mixture is hot, stirring frequently. Serve over rice, if desired. Sprinkle with sesame seed. Garnish as desired.

Favorite recipe from **National Pork Board**

Beef with Cashews

1 pound beef rump steak, trimmed
4 tablespoons vegetable oil, divided
4 teaspoons cornstarch
½ cup water
4 teaspoons soy sauce
1 teaspoon sesame oil
1 teaspoon oyster sauce
1 teaspoon Chinese chili sauce

8 green onions with tops, cut into 1-inch pieces
1 piece fresh ginger (about 1-inch square), peeled and minced
2 cloves garlic, minced
⅔ cup unsalted roasted cashews (about 3 ounces)
Fresh carrot slices and thyme leaves for garnish

Makes 4 servings

1. Cut meat across grain into thin slices about 2 inches long.

2. Heat 1 tablespoon vegetable oil in wok or large skillet over high heat. Add half of meat; stir-fry until browned, 3 to 5 minutes. Remove from wok; set aside. Repeat with 1 tablespoon oil and remaining meat.

3. Combine cornstarch, water, soy sauce, sesame oil, oyster sauce and chili sauce in small bowl; mix well.

4. Heat remaining 2 tablespoons vegetable oil in wok or large skillet over high heat. Add green onions, ginger, garlic and cashews; stir-fry 1 minute. Stir cornstarch mixture; add to wok with meat. Cook and stir until liquid boils and thickens. Garnish, if desired.

Lemon Chicken Herb Stir-Fry

Makes 6 servings

1 tablespoon plus
 1½ teaspoons peanut oil
2 green onions, cut into 1-inch
 pieces
1 large carrot, julienne cut
4 boneless, skinless chicken
 breast halves (about
 1 pound), cut into strips
2 cups broccoli flowerettes
1 can (8 ounces) bamboo
 shoots, drained

1 cup LAWRY'S® Herb & Garlic
 Marinade with Lemon Juice
1 tablespoon soy sauce
½ teaspoon arrowroot
1 can (11 ounces) mandarin
 orange segments, drained
 (optional)
1 tablespoon sesame seeds
3 cups hot cooked rice

In large wok or skillet, heat oil. Add onions and carrot and cook over medium-high heat 5 minutes. Add chicken, broccoli and bamboo shoots; stir-fry 7 to 9 minutes until chicken is no longer pink in center and juices run clear when cut. In small bowl, combine Herb & Garlic Marinade with Lemon Juice, soy sauce and arrowroot; mix well. Add to skillet; continue cooking, stirring constantly, until sauce forms glaze. Stir in orange segments. Sprinkle with sesame seeds. Serve over hot rice.

Stir-Fry Tomato Beef

1 cup uncooked long-grain
   white rice
1 pound flank steak
1 tablespoon cornstarch
1 tablespoon soy sauce
2 cloves garlic, minced
1 teaspoon minced gingerroot
   or ¼ teaspoon ground
   ginger

1 tablespoon vegetable oil
1 can (14½ ounces)
   DEL MONTE® Stewed
   Tomatoes - Original Recipe

Makes 4 to 6 servings

Prep Time:
10 minutes

Cook Time:
20 minutes

1. Cook rice according to package directions.

2. Meanwhile, cut meat in half lengthwise, and then cut crosswise into thin slices.

3. Combine cornstarch, soy sauce, garlic and ginger in medium bowl. Add meat; toss to coat.

4. Heat oil in large skillet over high heat. Add meat; cook, stirring constantly, until browned. Add undrained tomatoes; cook until thickened, about 5 minutes, stirring frequently.

5. Serve meat mixture over hot cooked rice. Garnish, if desired.

Note:

Soy sauce is a dark, salty liquid made by fermenting boiled soy beans and wheat or barley. Although there are different varieties available, such as dark and light, the major commercial brands sold in the United States are all-purpose.

Shrimp with Snow Peas

Makes 4 servings

1 pound raw Florida shrimp
½ cup chicken broth
¼ cup soy sauce
3 tablespoons dry sherry or white wine
2 tablespoons cornstarch
2 teaspoons minced fresh ginger
¼ cup vegetable oil

1 (6-ounce) package frozen snow peas, thawed and patted dry, *or* ½ pound fresh snow peas
3 green onions, cut into 1-inch pieces
½ can (8 ounces) sliced water chestnuts
Hot cooked rice

Peel shrimp and, if large, cut into halves lengthwise. Combine chicken broth, soy sauce, sherry, cornstarch and ginger in small bowl; set aside. In wok or large skillet, heat oil until hot. Add shrimp. Cook, stirring rapidly, 3 to 4 minutes or until pink; remove. Add snow peas; stir-fry 3 to 4 minutes or until soft. Remove from wok; set aside. Repeat procedure with onions and water chestnuts. Add shrimp, snow peas, onions and water chestnuts to wok. Add chicken broth mixture and cook until sauce thickens slightly, about 2 to 3 minutes. Serve over rice.

Favorite recipe from **Florida Department of Agriculture and Consumer Services, Bureau of Seafood and Aquaculture**

Spicy Cherry Pork Stir-Fry

2 tablespoons sherry
1 teaspoon cornstarch
¼ teaspoon salt
½ pound boneless lean pork, cut into thin strips
1 to 3 tablespoons vegetable oil, divided
⅛ teaspoon crushed dried red chilies

1½ cups snow peas
1½ cups pitted Northwest fresh sweet cherries
1 can (8 ounces) pineapple chunks, drained
Thickening Sauce (recipe follows)

Combine sherry, cornstarch and salt in medium bowl; add pork and mix well. Let stand about 15 minutes. Heat 1 to 2 tablespoons oil in wok or skillet; add chilies and cook 30 seconds. Add pork mixture; stir-fry until pork is no longer pink. Remove pork from wok. Add 1 tablespoon oil to wok if needed; heat. Add snow peas; stir-fry about 1 minute or until crisp-tender. Add cherries, pineapple and cooked pork to wok; cook and stir 1 minute to heat fruit. Add Thickening Sauce; cook and stir until sauce thickens and coats mixture.

Thickening Sauce: *Combine ¼ cup chicken broth, 1 teaspoon sesame oil, 1 teaspoon cornstarch, ¼ teaspoon sugar and ¼ teaspoon ground black pepper.*

Tip: *Serve over cooked thin egg noodles or rice.*

Favorite recipe from **Northwest Cherry Growers**

Turkey Shanghai

Makes 4 servings

1 package (1¼ pounds)
PERDUE® FIT 'N EASY®
Fresh Skinless and
Boneless Turkey Breast
Tenderloins
½ cup white wine, divided
3 tablespoons reduced-sodium
soy sauce, divided
1 tablespoon cornstarch
Ground pepper to taste
1 tablespoon sugar
2 teaspoons rice vinegar or
white vinegar

1½ tablespoons vegetable oil
1 clove garlic, minced
1 teaspoon minced fresh ginger
2 carrots, shredded
⅓ pound green beans, split
lengthwise and lightly
steamed
½ cup thinly sliced scallions
2 cups hot cooked Chinese
noodles
Carrots and scallions cut in
flower shapes (optional)
Cilantro sprigs (optional)

Slice turkey in thin strips; place in medium bowl. Sprinkle with ¼ cup wine, 1 tablespoon soy sauce, cornstarch and pepper; toss to coat with mixture and marinate at room temperature 15 minutes. In small bowl, combine remaining ¼ cup wine, 2 tablespoons soy sauce, sugar and vinegar; set aside.

Over medium-high heat, heat wok or large, heavy nonstick skillet. Slowly add oil; stir in garlic, ginger and turkey. Stir-fry 3 to 4 minutes until turkey is cooked through. Add carrots, beans, scallions and reserved wine mixture; cook 1 to 2 minutes longer. Serve over Chinese noodles, garnished with carrot and scallion flowers and cilantro sprigs.

Creole Fried Rice and Beans

8 ounces kielbasa
3 tablespoons vegetable oil
1 large onion, chopped
1 rib celery, sliced
4 ounces green beans, cut into
    1-inch pieces
2 cloves garlic, chopped
½ cup water
4 cups cooked long grain white
    rice, cooled

¼ cup tomato sauce
½ teaspoon salt
½ teaspoon dried thyme leaves,
    crushed
¼ teaspoon hot pepper sauce
1 cup canned red kidney beans,
    drained and rinsed

Makes 4 to 6 servings

Cut kielbasa into ½-inch-thick slices; set aside.

Heat wok over medium-low heat 2 minutes or until hot. Drizzle oil into wok and heat 30 seconds. Add onion and celery; stir-fry 3 minutes. Add kielbasa, green beans and garlic; stir-fry 5 minutes. Add water; cover and cook until beans are crisp-tender.

Add rice, tomato sauce, salt, thyme and hot pepper sauce; stir-fry until rice is well mixed and heated through. Add kidney beans; stir-fry until heated through. Transfer to serving dish.

Note:

Woks range in size
from 12 to 24 inches in
diameter. A 14-inch
wok is a good choice
because it can be used
without interfering
with other burners
on the range.

Almond Chicken

Makes 4 servings

⅓ cup blanched whole almonds
1 pound boneless skinless
    chicken breasts or thighs
2 cloves garlic, minced
1 teaspoon minced fresh ginger
¼ teaspoon red pepper flakes
¾ cup chicken broth
¼ cup soy sauce

4 teaspoons cornstarch
4 large ribs bok choy (about
    ¾ pound)
2 tablespoons peanut or
    vegetable oil, divided
2 medium carrots, thinly sliced
    Chow mein noodles or hot
    cooked rice

1. Preheat oven to 350°F. Spread almonds on baking sheet. Toast 6 to 7 minutes until golden brown, stirring once. Set aside.

2. Cut chicken into 1-inch pieces. Toss chicken with garlic, ginger and red pepper flakes in medium bowl. Marinate chicken at room temperature 15 minutes.

3. Blend chicken broth and soy sauce into cornstarch in small bowl until smooth.

4. Cut bok choy stems into ½-inch pieces. Cut leaves crosswise into halves.

5. Heat wok or large skillet over medium-high heat. Add 1 tablespoon oil; heat until hot. Add chicken mixture; stir-fry 3 minutes or until chicken is no longer pink. Remove and set aside.

6. Heat remaining 1 tablespoon oil in wok; add bok choy stems and carrots. Stir-fry 5 minutes or until vegetables are crisp-tender. Stir broth mixture and add to wok along with bok choy leaves. Stir-fry 1 minute or until sauce boils and thickens.

7. Return chicken along with any accumulated juices to wok; heat through. Stir in almonds. Serve over chow mein noodles.

Grape and Lamb Stir-Fry

1¼ pounds lamb or beef, cut into
　　thin strips
2 tablespoons cornstarch,
　　divided
2 tablespoons soy sauce,
　　divided
1 clove garlic, minced
1 teaspoon grated fresh ginger
1 cup sliced celery
1 cup sliced onion
½ cup chopped green bell
　　pepper

2 tablespoons vegetable oil,
　　divided
2 cups California seedless
　　grapes
¼ cup water
2 tablespoons ketchup
½ teaspoon sugar
¼ teaspoon Worcestershire
　　sauce
　　Pan-fried noodles or rice

Combine lamb, 1 tablespoon cornstarch, 1 tablespoon soy sauce, garlic and ginger in large bowl; set aside. In large skillet, stir-fry celery, onion and pepper in 1 tablespoon oil 1 minute. Add grapes and stir-fry 1 minute longer; remove from pan. Heat remaining 1 tablespoon oil over high heat. Cook and stir lamb about 2 minutes or until browned and cooked to desired degree of doneness. Combine water, ketchup, remaining 1 tablespoon cornstarch, 1 tablespoon soy sauce, sugar and Worcestershire sauce. Stir into lamb in skillet. Cook until mixture bubbles. Add grape mixture; toss lightly to coat. Heat thoroughly. Serve over pan-fried noodles.

Favorite recipe from **California Table Grape Commission**

Zesty Stir-Fry Shrimp and Vegetables

Makes 4 servings (about 3¼ cups)

¾ cup reduced-sodium chicken broth
1 tablespoon cornstarch
  Grated peel and juice of ½ SUNKIST® lemon
1 teaspoon light soy sauce
2 teaspoons vegetable oil, divided
1 teaspoon sesame oil
¾ pound raw medium shrimp, peeled and deveined

1 medium clove garlic, minced
16 small button mushrooms
¾ cup ½-inch red bell pepper pieces
1 small onion, sliced
½ cup frozen peas, thawed
  Cooked Chinese-style noodles or linguine

Note:

Asian sesame oil is a strong-tasting oil made from sesame seeds. It is used in small amounts for flavoring Asian foods. Do not substitute it for other oils, such as olive oil. You can buy it in the imported (Asian) section of the supermarket or in specialty food shops.

Combine chicken broth, cornstarch, lemon juice and soy sauce; reserve. In large non-stick skillet, sprayed with non-stick cooking spray, heat 1 teaspoon vegetable oil and sesame oil. Stir-fry shrimp with garlic until shrimp just turns pink, about 2½ to 3 minutes. Remove shrimp with slotted spoon. Add remaining 1 teaspoon vegetable oil to skillet and stir-fry mushrooms, bell pepper and onion with lemon peel until vegetables are just tender, about 2½ to 3 minutes. Stir in cornstarch mixture. Cook over medium heat, stirring, until sauce thickens. Add shrimp and peas; heat. Serve over noodles.

Orzo with Chicken and Cabbage

8 ounces uncooked orzo pasta
¼ cup rice vinegar
¼ cup chicken broth
2 tablespoons packed brown
    sugar
2 tablespoons soy sauce
1 teaspoon cornstarch
1 tablespoon sesame chili oil
2 cups thinly sliced red cabbage
1 tablespoon seasoned stir-fry
    or hot oil

1 pound boneless skinless
    chicken breasts or tenders,
    cut into bite-size pieces
4 ounces snow peas
4 green onions with tops
    (separating white and
    green parts), sliced into
    ½-inch pieces
1 tablespoon sesame seeds,
    toasted

Makes 4 servings

1. Place 6 cups water in wok or large saucepan; bring to a boil over high heat. Add orzo; cook according to package directions until *al dente,* stirring occasionally. Drain; set aside.

2. Whisk together vinegar, chicken broth, brown sugar, soy sauce and cornstarch in small bowl; set aside.

3. Heat sesame chili oil in wok or large skillet over high heat. Add cabbage; stir-fry 2 to 3 minutes or until crisp-tender. Remove. Set aside on serving platter; keep warm.

4. Heat stir-fry oil in same wok over high heat. Add chicken; stir-fry 3 minutes. Add snow peas and white parts of green onions; stir-fry 1 to 2 minutes or until vegetables are crisp-tender. Add vinegar mixture, stirring until hot and slightly thickened. Add orzo and toss. Serve over cabbage. Sprinkle with green onion tops and sesame seeds.

Black Bean Garlic Fish

Makes 4 servings

1 tablespoon LEE KUM KEE®
   Black Bean Garlic Sauce
1 teaspoon water
½ teaspoon sugar
1 pound fish fillet
1 tablespoon cornstarch
1½ teaspoons LEE KUM KEE®
   Panda Brand Oyster
   Flavored Sauce

2 tablespoons vegetable oil
2 green onions, cut into pieces
2 stalks celery, cut into strips
1 medium carrot, cut into strips

1. In bowl, combine garlic sauce, water and sugar; set aside.

2. Rinse fish and pat dry with paper towel. Cut fish into 1-inch pieces; place in medium bowl.

3. Combine cornstarch and oyster flavored sauce. Add to fish; stir until coated. Marinate 10 minutes.

4. Heat oil in wok or skillet over medium-high heat. Add green onions; stir-fry until fragrant. Add fish to wok and stir-fry until half cooked, about 1 minute.

5. Add celery, carrot and garlic sauce mixture to wok. Stir-fry until all ingredients are cooked.

Pineapple Pork Stir-Fry

1 can (20 ounces) DOLE®
    Pineapple Chunks
½ pound lean pork loin
2 cloves garlic, pressed
1 yellow onion, cut into
    wedges
2 tablespoons minced
    gingerroot *or* 1 teaspoon
    ground ginger

1 tablespoon vegetable oil
2 tablespoons soy sauce
2 teaspoons cornstarch
1 bunch DOLE® Broccoli, cut
    into florets
½ cup chopped walnuts, toasted

• Drain pineapple chunks, reserving ½ cup juice.

• Cut pork into strips.

• In skillet or wok, stir-fry pork with garlic, onion and ginger in hot oil until pork is just pink.

• Mix reserved juice, soy sauce and cornstarch. Stir into pork mixture. Top with pineapple chunks, broccoli and nuts. Cover, cook 3 to 5 minutes longer until vegetables are tender-crisp. Stir before serving.

Broccoli Beef Stir-Fry

Makes 4 servings

½ cup beef broth
4 tablespoons HOLLAND
    HOUSE® Sherry Cooking
    Wine, divided
2 tablespoons soy sauce
1 tablespoon cornstarch
1 teaspoon sugar
2 tablespoons vegetable oil,
    divided

2 cups fresh broccoli florets
1 cup fresh snow peas
1 red bell pepper, cut into strips
1 pound boneless top round or
    sirloin steak, slightly frozen,
    cut into thin strips
1 clove garlic, minced
4 cups hot cooked rice

1. To make sauce, in small bowl, combine broth, 2 tablespoons cooking wine, soy sauce, cornstarch and sugar. Mix well and set aside. In large skillet or wok, heat 1 tablespoon oil. Stir-fry broccoli, snow peas and bell pepper 1 minute. Add remaining 2 tablespoons cooking wine.

2. Cover; cook 1 to 2 minutes. Remove from pan. Heat remaining 1 tablespoon oil; add meat and garlic. Stir-fry 5 minutes or until meat is browned. Add sauce to meat; cook 2 to 3 minutes or until thickened, stirring frequently. Add vegetables and heat through. Serve over cooked rice.

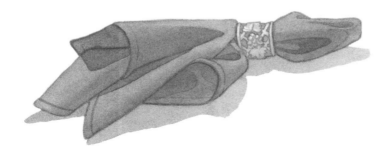

Oriental Chicken & Asparagus

6 TYSON® Fresh Boneless, Skinless Chicken Thighs
2 tablespoons cornstarch, divided
½ teaspoon salt
¼ pound fresh asparagus spears, trimmed and chopped
1 small red bell pepper, cut into thin strips

1 medium onion, sliced
2 tablespoons oyster sauce
1 clove garlic, minced
½ teaspoon sesame oil
1 can (14½ ounces) chicken broth
1 can (8 ounces) sliced water chestnuts, drained

Makes 4 servings

Prep Time:
10 minutes

Cook Time:
20 minutes

PREP: CLEAN: Wash hands. Cut chicken into strips. CLEAN: Wash hands. Combine 1 tablespoon cornstarch and salt in medium bowl. Add chicken and stir to coat. Refrigerate.

COOK: Spray large nonstick skillet with nonstick cooking spray. Heat over medium-high heat. Cook and stir asparagus, bell pepper, onion, oyster sauce, garlic and oil about 3 minutes. Remove from pan. Cook and stir chicken about 5 minutes or until internal juices of chicken run clear. (Or insert instant-read meat thermometer in thickest part of chicken. Temperature should read 180°F.) Add broth and water chestnuts to skillet. Combine remaining 1 tablespoon cornstarch and ¼ cup water; add to skillet. Cook and stir until sauce is thickened. Return vegetables to skillet and heat through.

SERVE: Serve with hot cooked rice, if desired.

CHILL: Refrigerate leftovers immediately.

Normandy Pork and Cabbage

Makes 4 servings

1 pound boneless pork loin or
   tenderloin
2 medium red baking apples,
   halved and cored
1 tablespoon vegetable oil
2 tablespoons butter or
   margarine, divided
1 package (8 ounces) shredded
   green cabbage for coleslaw
   or 2 cups shredded red
   cabbage

1 tablespoon all-purpose flour
1 teaspoon ground sage
½ teaspoon salt
¼ teaspoon black pepper
½ cup beef broth
½ cup apple juice or sweet
   apple cider
¼ cup heavy cream
   Hot cooked egg noodles
   Green onion curls for garnish

Trim fat from pork; discard. Cut pork crosswise into ¼-inch-thick slices. Cut each apple half into 6 wedges. Set aside.

Heat wok over high heat about 1 minute or until hot. Drizzle oil into wok and heat 30 seconds. Add 1 tablespoon butter and swirl to coat bottom. Add half the pork; stir-fry until well browned on both sides. Remove pork to large bowl. Repeat with remaining pork. Reduce heat to medium.

Add remaining 1 tablespoon butter to wok and swirl to coat bottom. Add apples; stir-fry about 2 minutes or just until apples soften. Remove apples to bowl with pork.

Add cabbage to wok; stir-fry just until wilted. Sprinkle with flour, sage, salt and black pepper; stir-fry until well mixed. Add broth and juice; cook and stir until sauce boils and thickens. Stir in cream; cook until heated through. Return pork and apples to wok. Stir in additional water if needed. Serve with noodles. Garnish, if desired.

<u>Hint:</u> *For best results in this recipe, use Cortland, Rome Beauty, Winesap or Arkansas Black apples. They will remain flavorful and firm during cooking.*

Stir-Fried Pasta with Chicken 'n' Vegetables

6 ounces angel hair pasta,
broken into thirds (about
3 cups)
¼ cup *Frank's® RedHot®* Cayenne
Pepper Sauce
3 tablespoons soy sauce
2 teaspoons cornstarch

1 tablespoon sugar
½ teaspoon garlic powder
1 pound boneless skinless
chicken, cut into ¾-inch
cubes
1 package (16 ounces) frozen
stir-fry vegetables

Makes 4 servings

Prep Time:
5 minutes

Cook Time:
15 minutes

1. Cook pasta in boiling water until just tender. Drain. Combine *Frank's RedHot* Sauce, *¼ cup water,* soy sauce, cornstarch, sugar and garlic powder in small bowl; set aside.

2. Heat *1 tablespoon oil* in large nonstick skillet over high heat. Stir-fry chicken 3 minutes. Add vegetables; stir-fry 3 minutes or until crisp-tender. Add *Frank's RedHot* Sauce mixture. Heat to boiling. Reduce heat to medium-low. Cook, stirring, 1 to 2 minutes or until sauce is thickened.

3. Stir pasta into skillet; toss to coat evenly. Serve hot.

Note:

The exact origin of
pasta is unknown. It
is mentioned in the
ancient histories of
many countries. The
Chinese have recorded
eating macaroni as
early as 5,000 B.C.

Rainbow Stir-Fried Fish

Makes 4 servings

Sauce
- ½ cup chicken broth
- 2 tablespoons LA CHOY® Soy Sauce
- 1 tablespoon cornstarch
- 1 teaspoon sugar
- ¼ teaspoon crushed red pepper (optional)

Fish and Vegetables
- 1 pound orange roughy filets,* cut into 1-inch chunks
- 1 tablespoon LA CHOY® Soy Sauce
- 3 tablespoons WESSON® Oil
- ½ cup julienne-cut carrots
- 1 teaspoon minced garlic
- 1 teaspoon minced fresh gingerroot
- 2 cups fresh broccoli flowerettes
- 1 can (8 ounces) LA CHOY® Sliced Water Chestnuts, drained
- 1 package (6 ounces) frozen pea pods, thawed and drained
- ½ cup diagonally sliced green onions

*Any firm-fleshed white fish can be substituted.

In small bowl, combine sauce ingredients; set aside. In medium bowl, combine fish and soy sauce; toss lightly to coat. In large nonstick skillet or wok, heat oil. Add fish mixture; stir-fry 2 to 3 minutes or until fish flakes easily with fork. Remove fish from skillet; drain. Set aside. Add carrots, garlic and ginger to same skillet; stir-fry 30 seconds. Add broccoli; stir-fry 1 minute. Add water chestnuts and pea pods; heat thoroughly, stirring occasionally. Return fish to skillet. Stir sauce; add to skillet. Heat, stirring gently, until sauce is thick and bubbly. Sprinkle with green onions. Garnish, if desired.

Honey Dijon Beef and Vegetable Stir-Fry

⅔ cup HEINZ® Tomato Ketchup
2 tablespoons honey Dijon mustard
1 tablespoon soy sauce
1 pound boneless beef sirloin steak, cut into thin strips

1 red bell pepper, cut into thin strips
1 onion, cut into thin wedges
2 cups broccoli florets
Hot cooked rice

Makes 4 servings

In small bowl, combine ketchup, ⅓ cup water, mustard and soy sauce; set aside. In large preheated nonstick skillet, quickly brown beef; remove. Cook pepper, onion and broccoli, stirring, until crisp-tender, about 4 minutes. Return beef to skillet and stir in reserved ketchup mixture; heat. Serve with rice.

Sweet 'n Sour Stir-Fry

2 tablespoons oil
1 cup thinly sliced carrots
1 cup snow peas
1 small green bell pepper, cut into chunks
1 medium tomato, cut into wedges
1 cup sliced water chestnuts
½ cup sliced cucumber, cut into halves

¾ cup WISH-BONE® Sweet 'n Spicy French Dressing*
2 tablespoons packed brown sugar
2 teaspoons soy sauce
Sesame seeds (optional)

Also terrific with WISH-BONE® Russian Dressing.

Makes about 6 servings

In 10-inch skillet, heat oil over medium heat and cook carrots, snow peas and green pepper, stirring frequently, 5 minutes or until crisp-tender. Add tomato, water chestnuts, cucumber and Sweet 'n Spicy French Dressing blended with brown sugar and soy sauce. Simmer 5 minutes or until vegetables are tender. Top, if desired, with sesame seeds.

Orange Chicken Stir-Fry

Makes 6 servings

½ cup orange juice
2 tablespoons sesame oil,
    divided
2 tablespoons soy sauce
1 tablespoon dry sherry
2 teaspoons grated fresh ginger
1 teaspoon grated orange peel
1 clove garlic, minced
1½ pounds boneless skinless
    chicken breasts, cut into
    strips

3 cups mixed fresh vegetables,
    such as green bell pepper,
    red bell pepper, snow peas,
    carrots, green onions,
    mushrooms and/or onions
1 tablespoon cornstarch
½ cup unsalted cashew bits or
    halves
3 cups hot cooked rice

Combine orange juice, 1 tablespoon oil, soy sauce, sherry, ginger, orange peel and garlic in large glass bowl. Add chicken; marinate in refrigerator 1 hour. Drain chicken, reserving marinade. Heat remaining 1 tablespoon oil in large skillet or wok over medium-high heat. Add chicken; stir-fry 3 minutes or until chicken is light brown. Add vegetables; stir-fry 3 to 5 minutes or until vegetables are crisp-tender. Combine cornstarch and marinade; add to skillet and stir until sauce boils and thickens. Stir in cashews; cook 1 minute more. Serve over hot rice.

Favorite recipe from **USA Rice Federation**

Moussaka-Style Beef and Zucchini

3 medium zucchini
1 tablespoon vegetable oil
1 pound lean ground beef
1 medium onion, chopped
2 cloves garlic, minced
1 teaspoon dried basil leaves

½ teaspoon ground cinnamon
2 cans (8 ounces each) tomato sauce
½ cup low-fat sour cream
1 egg yolk
¼ cup feta cheese

• Scrub zucchini; cut off ends. Cut each zucchini crosswise into thirds. Cut pieces lengthwise into slices.

• Heat wok over high heat. Drizzle oil into wok; heat 30 seconds. Add zucchini; cook 8 minutes, stirring often. Remove to medium bowl.

• Add beef to wok; stir-fry until well browned. Add onion and garlic; stir-fry 1 minute. Reduce heat to medium. Add basil and cinnamon; mix well. Stir in tomato sauce; cover and simmer 5 minutes. Mix sour cream and egg yolk in small bowl until well blended.

• Skim fat from beef mixture. Spread beef mixture evenly in wok. Arrange zucchini on top. Spoon sour cream mixture in center of zucchini. Cover; cook 5 minutes or until top is set. Sprinkle with cheese. Remove from heat; let stand 1 minute. Serve hot.

Note:

The wok, the primary cooking vessel of Asia, was developed centuries ago as a result of fuel shortages. Its rounded shape and long sloping side provide an extended cooking surface, which may be heated to very high temperatures with little fuel.

Tandoori Pork Sauté

Makes 4 servings

Nutty Rice (recipe follows)
8 ounces lean pork, cut into
   2×½-inch strips
½ cup sliced onion
1 clove garlic, minced
4 fresh California plums,
   halved, pitted and cut into
   thick wedges
1 cup plain low-fat yogurt

1 tablespoon all-purpose flour
1½ teaspoons grated fresh ginger
½ teaspoon ground turmeric
⅛ teaspoon ground black
   pepper
Additional plum wedges,
   orange sections and sliced
   green onions

Prepare Nutty Rice. Cook pork in nonstick skillet 2 minutes or until browned, turning occasionally. Transfer to platter. Add onion and garlic to skillet; cook 1 minute. Add plums; cook and stir 1 minute. Remove from heat and return pork to pan. Combine yogurt and flour; add to skillet. Stir in ginger, turmeric and pepper. Bring to a boil; reduce heat and simmer 10 minutes, stirring occasionally. Serve over Nutty Rice and surround with plum wedges, orange sections and green onions.

Nutty Rice: *Bring 2 cups water to a boil in medium saucepan. Add ¾ cup brown rice and ¼ cup wheat berries. (Or, omit wheat berries and use 1 cup brown rice.) Return to a boil. Reduce heat to low; cover and simmer 40 to 45 minutes or until rice is tender and liquid is absorbed.*

Favorite recipe from **California Tree Fruit Agreement**

Simply Sensational Stir-Fry

¼ cup orange juice or apple
   cider vinegar
2 tablespoons soy sauce
¼ cup oil
1 envelope GOOD SEASONS®
   Zesty Italian, Oriental
   Sesame or Honey French
   Salad Dressing Mix

1 pound lean boneless beef
   sirloin, chicken or pork loin,
   cut into strips
1 package (16 ounces) frozen
   mixed vegetables, thawed
2½ cups hot cooked MINUTE®
   Brown Rice

Makes 4 servings

Prep Time:
15 minutes

Cook Time:
10 minutes

MIX juice, soy sauce, oil and salad dressing mix in cruet or small bowl as directed on envelope.

HEAT large skillet on medium-high heat. Cook meat in 1 tablespoon of the dressing mixture 4 to 5 minutes or until cooked through.

ADD vegetables and remaining dressing mixture; cook and stir until vegetables are tender-crisp. Serve over rice.

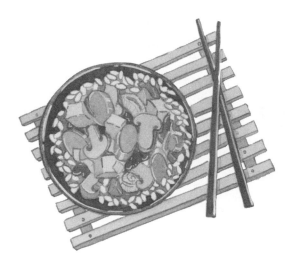

Green Dragon Stir-Fry

Makes 4 servings

2 tablespoons vegetable oil, divided
1 pound beef flank steak, very thinly sliced
1 bunch asparagus *or* 8 ounces green beans, cut into 2-inch pieces
1 green bell pepper, cut into strips
1 cup julienned carrots
3 large green onions, sliced
1 tablespoon minced fresh ginger
1 clove garlic, minced
¼ cup water
1 tablespoon soy sauce
1 tablespoon TABASCO® brand Green Pepper Sauce
½ teaspoon salt
2 cups hot cooked rice (optional)

Heat 1 tablespoon oil in 12-inch skillet over medium-high heat. Add flank steak; cook until well browned on all sides, stirring frequently. Remove steak to plate with slotted spoon.

Heat remaining 1 tablespoon oil in skillet over medium heat. Add asparagus, green bell pepper, carrots, green onions, ginger and garlic; cook about 3 minutes, stirring frequently. Add water, soy sauce, TABASCO® Green Pepper Sauce, salt and steak; heat to boiling over high heat.

Reduce heat to low; simmer, uncovered, 3 minutes, stirring occasionally. Serve with rice, if desired.

Tip: *This stir-fry is also delicious served over ramen or soba noodles.*

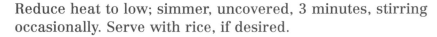

Spicy Honey Garlic Shrimp

3 tablespoons vegetable oil
1 pound shrimp, peeled and
    deveined
½ teaspoon salt
5 tablespoons LEE KUM KEE®
    Honey Garlic Sauce

2 green onions, sliced
2 tablespoons LEE KUM KEE®
    Chili Garlic Sauce

Makes 4 servings

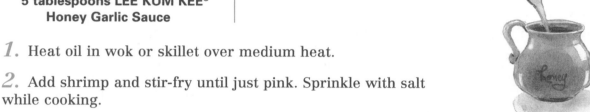

1. Heat oil in wok or skillet over medium heat.

2. Add shrimp and stir-fry until just pink. Sprinkle with salt while cooking.

3. Add honey garlic sauce, green onions and chili garlic sauce.

4. Stir-fry until green onions are tender and sauce is hot.

Stir-Fry Magic

Stir-frying—a rapid-cooking method invented by the Chinese—is the brisk cooking of small pieces of ingredients in hot oil over intense heat for a short time. The ingredients are kept in constant motion by stirring or tossing vigorously. Follow these simple steps for successful stir-frying:

• Prepare all the ingredients in advance, including cleaning, cutting, measuring and combining.

• Cut the meat and vegetables into uniform sizes and shapes to ensure even cooking. Matchstick pieces and strips will take less time to cook than large chunks of food.

• The best oil to use for stir-frying is peanut oil, corn oil or soybean oil. Olive oil, sesame oil and butter should not be used because they burn easily.

• Heat the wok or skillet first, and then add the oil.

• Make sure the oil is hot before adding any food. The oil is hot enough if a piece of vegetable sizzles when tossed into the pan.

• Keep the food in constant motion, tossing and stirring it with a flat metal or wooden spatula. This prevents it from burning and also seals in the flavor.

Italian-Style Chicken Stir-Fry

Makes 3 to 4 servings

Prep Time:
10 minutes

Cook Time:
8 minutes

Marinate Time:
1 hour

1 can (14.5 ounces) CONTADINA® Stewed Tomatoes, drained, ¼ cup juice reserved
3 tablespoons olive oil, divided
2 tablespoons chopped fresh basil *or* 1 teaspoon dried basil leaves, crushed
2 large cloves garlic, finely chopped
½ teaspoon salt
¼ teaspoon ground black pepper

¼ teaspoon crushed red pepper flakes (optional)
1 pound boneless, skinless chicken breast halves, cut into 3-inch strips
1 small green bell pepper, thinly sliced
1 small onion, thinly sliced
1 can (2¼ ounces) sliced ripe olives, drained
3 to 4 pita breads, warmed

1. Drain tomatoes reserving ¼ cup juice. Combine reserved tomato juice, 2 tablespoons oil, basil, garlic, salt, black pepper and red pepper flakes in medium bowl.

2. Add chicken; stir to coat. Cover; chill for at least 1 hour.

3. Heat remaining 1 tablespoon oil in large skillet over high heat. Add chicken mixture, bell pepper and onion; cook, stirring constantly, for 5 to 6 minutes or until chicken is no longer pink in center. Add tomatoes and olives; heat through.

4. Cut pitas in half; stuff mixture into pockets.

Chinese Pork & Vegetable Stir-Fry

2 tablespoons BERTOLLI® Olive Oil, divided	1 envelope LIPTON® Recipe Secrets® Onion Soup Mix
1 pound pork tenderloin or boneless beef sirloin, cut into ¼-inch slices	¾ cup water
6 cups assorted fresh vegetables*	½ cup orange juice
1 can (8 ounces) sliced water chestnuts, drained	1 tablespoon soy sauce
	¼ teaspoon garlic powder

Use any of the following to equal 6 cups: broccoli florets, snow peas, thinly sliced red or green bell peppers or thinly sliced carrots.

Makes about 4 servings

In 12-inch skillet, heat 1 tablespoon oil over medium-high heat; brown pork. Remove and set aside.

In same skillet, heat remaining 1 tablespoon oil and cook assorted fresh vegetables, stirring occasionally, 5 minutes. Stir in water chestnuts and onion soup mix blended with water, orange juice, soy sauce and garlic powder. Bring to a boil over high heat. Reduce heat to low and simmer, uncovered, 3 minutes. Return pork to skillet and cook 1 minute or until heated through.

Tip: *Pick up pre-sliced vegetables from your local salad bar.*

Gingered Fish with Bok Choy

Makes 4 servings

1¼ pounds skinless mahi mahi fillets, cut 1 inch thick
2 tablespoons sake or dry sherry
½ teaspoon salt, divided
¼ teaspoon black pepper
1 piece fresh ginger (1 inch long), peeled

1 pound bok choy
4 green onions with tops
¼ cup teriyaki sauce
¼ cup water
1 tablespoon cornstarch
¼ cup vegetable oil, divided
2 cloves garlic, minced
Hot cooked rice

Note:

Bok choy, a vegetable popular in Asian cuisines, is a member of the crucifer family, which includes cabbage. Bok choy has 8- to 10-inch-long white or greenish-white stalks and large dark green leaves. The stalks are generally wider than those of celery and are not ribbed.

Rinse mahi mahi and pat dry with paper towels. Cut fish into 1¼-inch-wide pieces. Combine sake, ¼ teaspoon salt and black pepper in large bowl. Add fish and gently toss to coat; set aside.

Thinly slice ginger. Stack ginger, a few slices at a time, and cut into fine strips. Separate bok choy leaves from stems. Rinse and pat dry. Stack leaves and cut into 1-inch slices. Cut stems diagonally into ½-inch slices. Keep leaves and stems separate.

Cut onions into 1-inch pieces. Stir teriyaki sauce and water into cornstarch in cup until smooth; set aside.

Heat wok over high heat about 1 minute or until hot. Drizzle 1 tablespoon oil into wok and heat 30 seconds. Add bok choy stems; stir-fry about 2 minutes or until crisp-tender. Add bok choy leaves and garlic; stir-fry until tender. Sprinkle with remaining ¼ teaspoon salt. Transfer to serving plate; cover and keep warm.

Drizzle remaining 3 tablespoons oil into wok and heat 30 seconds. Add fish mixture; stir-fry 4 minutes or until fish is lightly browned and flakes easily when tested with fork. Place fish over bok choy.

Add onions and ginger to wok. Stir teriyaki mixture until smooth and add to wok. Stir-fry until sauce boils and thickens. Spoon sauce over fish. Serve with rice.

Sweet 'n' Sour Chicken Stir-Fry

3 tablespoons ketchup
1 tablespoon vinegar
1 tablespoon soy sauce
2 boneless skinless chicken breasts, cut into 1-inch cubes
1 tablespoon vegetable oil

½ package (16 ounces) frozen stir-fry vegetables or other frozen vegetable combination (such as broccoli, bell peppers, mushrooms and onions)
1 can (20 ounces) DOLE® Pineapple Chunks, drained

Makes 6 servings

• Combine ketchup, vinegar and soy sauce in small bowl; set aside.

• Cook and stir chicken in large skillet or wok in hot oil over medium-high heat until chicken is browned.

• Stir in vegetables; cover. Reduce heat to low; cook 2 to 3 minutes or until vegetables are tender-crisp, stirring occasionally. Stir in pineapple chunks and sauce; cook and stir until pineapple is heated through.

Tip: *Fresh vegetable combinations can be used in place of frozen vegetables. When using fresh vegetables, add 2 tablespoons of juice from canned pineapple and increase cooking time to 4 minutes or until vegetables are tender-crisp.*

Stir-Fry of Wild Rice, Snow Peas and Pork

Makes 4 servings

3 tablespoons vegetable oil
½ pound pork tenderloin, sliced
    ¼ inch thick
1 cup sliced celery
1 cup sliced green onions
1 cup sliced fresh mushrooms
1 can (8 ounces) sliced water
    chestnuts, drained
½ pound fresh or thawed frozen
    snow peas

1 tablespoon grated fresh
    gingerroot
2 cups cooked wild rice
3 tablespoons soy sauce
1 tablespoon dry sherry
½ teaspoon salt
1 tablespoon cornstarch
½ cup cashews, sunflower
    seeds or shredded or
    cut-out carrots for garnish

Heat oil in heavy skillet or wok; add pork and stir-fry over high heat for 2 minutes until meat is no longer pink. Add celery, green onions, mushrooms, water chestnuts, snow peas and ginger. Stir-fry for 5 minutes over high heat until vegetables are crisp-tender. Add wild rice, stirring until evenly blended. Combine soy sauce, sherry and salt; mix into cornstarch. Add to skillet, cooking and stirring about 1 minute until thickened and rice mixture is coated with glaze. Garnish, if desired.

Favorite recipe from **Minnesota Cultivated Wild Rice Council**

Szechwan Beef

1 pound ground beef
1 tablespoon vegetable oil
1 cup sliced carrots
1 cup frozen peas
⅓ cup water
3 tablespoons soy sauce
2 tablespoons cornstarch

¼ teaspoon ground ginger
1 jar (7 ounces) baby corn
1 medium onion, thinly sliced
Sliced mushrooms and olives
  as desired
¼ cup shredded Cheddar cheese
1⅓ cups uncooked instant rice

1. In wok or large skillet, brown ground beef; remove from wok and set aside. Drain fat.

2. Add oil to wok or skillet and return to medium heat. Add carrots and peas and stir-fry about 3 minutes.

3. In small cup combine water and soy sauce with cornstarch and ginger. Add to vegetables in wok.

4. Return ground beef to wok along with baby corn, onion, mushrooms, olives and cheese. Cook over medium heat until all ingredients are heated through.

5. Prepare instant rice according to package directions. Serve beef and vegetables over rice.

Favorite recipe from **North Dakota Beef Commission**

Angel Hair Noodles with Peanut Sauce

Makes 6 servings

¼ cup Texas peanuts, puréed
2 tablespoons low-fat chicken broth or water
1 tablespoon soy sauce
1 tablespoon rice vinegar
10 ounces dried bean thread noodles

½ tablespoon vegetable oil
1 pound chicken breast, boned, skinned and thinly sliced
½ cucumber, peeled, seeded and cut into matchstick pieces
2 medium carrots, shredded
Additional Texas peanuts

To make sauce, combine peanut purée, chicken broth, soy sauce and vinegar in small bowl; set aside.

Bring 4 cups water to a boil in medium saucepan. Add noodles, stirring to separate strands. Cook, stirring, 30 seconds or until noodles are slightly soft. Drain in colander and rinse under cold running water. Drain well; cut noodles into halves and set aside.

Heat wok or wide skillet over high heat. Add oil, swirling to coat sides. Add chicken and stir-fry 1 minute or until opaque. Add cucumber, carrots and sauce; cook, stirring to mix well. Remove from heat. Add noodles and toss until evenly coated. Garnish with additional peanuts, if desired.

Favorite recipe from **Texas Peanut Producers Board**

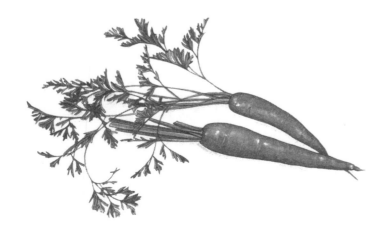

Beef, Peppers and Tomato Stir-Fry

1 package (6.8 ounces) RICE-A-RONI® Beef Flavor
1 pound well-trimmed top sirloin steak
¼ cup margarine or butter, divided
  Salt and pepper (optional)
½ red or green bell pepper, cut into strips
½ yellow bell pepper, cut into strips
1 medium onion, sliced
4 plum tomatoes, sliced into quarters
2 tablespoons dry red wine *or* 1 tablespoon Worcestershire sauce

Note:

Wine loses flavor quickly when exposed to oxygen. Leftover wine should be sealed tightly and stored in the refrigerator for a day or two.

1. Prepare Rice-A-Roni® Mix as package directs.

2. While Rice-A-Roni® is simmering, thinly slice meat across the grain.

3. In second large skillet, melt 2 tablespoons margarine over medium-high heat. Sauté meat 5 minutes or until no longer pink. Remove from skillet; sprinkle with salt and pepper, if desired. Set aside; keep warm.

4. In same skillet, sauté bell peppers and onion in remaining 2 tablespoons margarine 3 minutes or until crisp-tender. Stir in meat.

5. Meanwhile, add tomatoes and wine to rice during last 5 minutes of cooking. Serve rice topped with meat mixture.

Teriyaki Stir-Fry Chicken Dinner

Makes 4 to 6 servings

1 package (about 1¾ pounds) PERDUE® Fresh Chicken or OVEN STUFFER® Wingettes (12 to 16)
Salt and black pepper to taste
2 tablespoons vegetable oil
1 cup broccoli florets
1 can (8 ounces) sliced water chestnuts, drained
4 carrots, sliced
4 green onions, thinly sliced

½ cup water
¼ cup packed brown sugar
¼ cup soy sauce
3 tablespoons dry sherry or white vinegar
2 cloves garlic, finely chopped
2 teaspoons grated fresh ginger
2 cups warm cooked rice
Additional sliced green onions for garnish (optional)

Sprinkle wingettes with salt and pepper.

In large nonstick wok or skillet over medium-high heat, heat oil. Stir-fry broccoli 1 minute; add water chestnuts and carrots. Stir-fry 1 minute longer and add 4 sliced onions; stir-fry a few seconds. Remove vegetables and reserve.

Add wingettes to wok and cook until lightly browned on all sides, about 5 minutes. Reduce heat to low; cover and cook 10 minutes, turning occasionally. Remove wingettes to paper towel and pour off drippings. Return wingettes and vegetables to pan; add remaining ingredients except rice and additional onions. Stir until well mixed. Cook, turning frequently, until wingettes are glazed and sauce is thickened, about 3 to 5 minutes. Serve hot over rice, sprinkling with additional green onions, if desired.

Seafood Stir-Fry with Indonesian Rice

2 cups water
1 cup long-grain rice
2 tablespoons reduced-sodium
   soy sauce
½ teaspoon red pepper flakes
¼ cup olive oil
½ cup chopped green onions
½ cup chopped celery
½ cup chopped green or red bell
   pepper
½ cup sliced mushrooms
1 cup chopped broccoli
2 cups loosely packed spinach
   leaves or red cabbage

1 cup bean sprouts
2 cloves garlic, crushed
1 medium tomato, cut into
   wedges
12 ounces crab- or lobster-
   flavored surimi seafood,
   flake or chunk style
½ cup cucumber, sliced, for
   garnish
1 hard-boiled egg, chopped, for
   garnish
¼ cup dry-roasted peanuts, for
   garnish

Combine water, rice, soy sauce and red pepper flakes in 2-quart saucepan. Cover and bring to a boil; reduce heat to low and cook 15 minutes, or until rice is tender and water is absorbed, adding a little water if necessary. Meanwhile, heat oil in wok or 12-inch skillet. Add onions, celery, bell pepper and mushrooms and cook 3 minutes. Add broccoli and cook 2 minutes. Stir in spinach, bean sprouts and garlic; add cooked rice. Reduce heat to low; arrange tomato and surimi seafood over mixture. Cover and cook until heated through, about 3 minutes. Garnish with cucumber, egg and peanuts, if desired.

Favorite recipe from **National Fisheries Institute**

Ground Beef Chow Mein

Makes 4 to 6 servings

Note:

Green onions, or scallions, are onions that are harvested when immature. All other onions are classified as dry onions, meaning that they are harvested when mature and then allowed to dry until their skins are papery.

Sauce
- ⅓ cup beef broth
- 3 tablespoons LA CHOY® Soy Sauce
- 1 tablespoon cornstarch
- 1 teaspoon garlic powder
- 1 teaspoon dry mustard
- ½ teaspoon sugar
- ½ teaspoon black pepper

Meat and Vegetables
- 1 pound lean ground beef
- 2 tablespoons WESSON® Oil
- 2 cups sliced fresh mushrooms
- 1 can (14 ounces) LA CHOY® Bean Sprouts, drained
- 1 can (14 ounces) LA CHOY® Chop Suey Vegetables, drained
- ½ cup sliced green onions
- 1 can (5 ounces) LA CHOY® Chow Mein Noodles

In small bowl, combine sauce ingredients; set aside. In large nonstick skillet, brown ground beef; remove from skillet. Drain. Heat oil in same skillet. Add mushrooms; cook and stir 1 to 2 minutes or until tender. Stir in bean sprouts and chop suey vegetables; heat thoroughly, stirring occasionally. Return ground beef to skillet. Stir sauce; add to skillet with green onions. Cook, stirring constantly, until sauce is thick and bubbly. Serve over chow mein noodles.

Sesame Chicken

1 pound boneless skinless
    chicken breasts or thighs
⅓ cup teriyaki sauce
2 teaspoons cornstarch
1 tablespoon peanut or
    vegetable oil
2 cloves garlic, minced
2 large green onions, cut into
    ½-inch slices

1 tablespoon toasted sesame
    seeds*
1 teaspoon dark sesame oil

*To toast sesame seeds, spread seeds in
small skillet. Shake skillet over medium heat
2 minutes or until seeds begin to pop and turn
golden.*

Makes 4 servings

1. Cut chicken into 1-inch pieces; toss chicken with teriyaki
sauce in small bowl. Marinate at room temperature 15 minutes
or cover and refrigerate up to 2 hours.

2. Drain chicken reserving marinade. Blend reserved marinade
into cornstarch in cup until smooth.

3. Heat wok or large skillet over medium-high heat. Add peanut
oil; heat until hot. Add chicken and garlic; stir-fry 3 minutes or
until chicken is no longer pink. Stir marinade mixture and add to
wok along with onions and sesame seeds. Stir-fry 30 seconds or
until sauce boils and thickens. Stir in sesame oil.

BBQ Pork Stir Fry

Makes 4 servings

1 (2-cup) bag UNCLE BEN'S®
   Boil-in-Bag Rice
1 pound whole pork tenderloin
1 tablespoon oil
2 teaspoons minced garlic
2 teaspoons minced fresh
   ginger

1 package (16 ounces) frozen
   stir-fry vegetable medley
⅔ cup barbecue sauce
2 tablespoons chopped fresh
   cilantro (optional)

1. Cook rice according to package directions.

2. Trim tenderloin of any fat; cut in half lengthwise, then into ¼-inch slices.

3. Heat oil in large skillet over medium-high heat until hot. Add pork, garlic and ginger; cook about 3 minutes or until pork is no longer pink.

4. Add vegetables and ¼ cup water. Cover; cook 3 minutes, stirring occasionally.

5. Stir in barbecue sauce. Cover; reduce heat and simmer 5 to 7 minutes or just until vegetables are tender and pork is cooked through.

6. Serve pork and vegetables over rice. Garnish with chopped cilantro, if desired.

Tip: *Choose a stir-fry vegetable medley, such as sugar snap peas, carrots, onions and mushrooms for this recipe.*

Chicken Thai Stir-Fry

Makes 4 servings

2 tablespoons vegetable oil
4 boneless, skinless chicken
   breast halves, cut into
   ½-inch strips
2 teaspoons grated fresh ginger
2 cloves garlic, minced
2 cups broccoli flowerets
1 medium yellow squash, cut
   into ¼-inch slices
1 medium red bell pepper, cut
   into 2-inch strips
⅓ cup creamy peanut butter

¼ cup reduced-sodium soy
   sauce
2 tablespoons white vinegar
2 teaspoons brown sugar
½ teaspoon crushed red pepper
⅓ cup reduced-sodium chicken
   broth, fat skimmed
8 ounces linguine, cooked
   according to package
   directions
2 green onions, white and
   green parts, thinly sliced

In large skillet, heat oil over medium-high heat. Add chicken, ginger and garlic; cook and stir about 5 minutes or until chicken is lightly browned and fork-tender. Remove chicken mixture to bowl; set aside. To drippings in same skillet, add broccoli, squash and red bell pepper strips. Cook, stirring, about 5 minutes or until vegetables are crisp-tender. Remove vegetables to bowl with chicken; set aside. To same skillet, add peanut butter, soy sauce, vinegar, brown sugar and crushed red pepper; stir in chicken broth. Return chicken and vegetables to pan; heat through. Serve over linguine. Sprinkle with green onions.

Favorite recipe from **Delmarva Poultry Industry, Inc.**

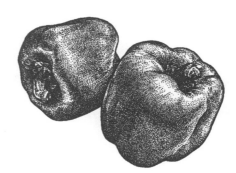

Stir-Fried Beef and Vegetables

Makes 4 servings

Prep Time:
25 minutes

Total Time:
35 minutes

Note:

It's easier to slice meat thinly if it's partially frozen. Wrap the steak in plastic wrap and freeze for 15 minutes. Always cut meat against the grain unless a recipe specifically says to slice it with the grain.

⅔ cup beef broth or stock
2 tablespoons soy sauce
  Pinch of ground cinnamon
¼ teaspoon freshly ground
  black pepper
2 teaspoons cornstarch
2 tablespoons cold water
3 tablespoons CRISCO® Oil*
1 tablespoon chopped fresh
  ginger
2 teaspoons jarred minced
  garlic *or* 1 large clove garlic,
  peeled and minced

1 pound lean beef, such as
  flank steak or boneless
  sirloin, trimmed and cut
  into ¼-inch-thick slices
1 carrot, peeled and thinly
  sliced
1 bunch scallions (or green
  onions), trimmed and cut
  into 1-inch pieces
¼ pound fresh snow peas,
  rinsed and stems removed

Use your favorite Crisco Oil product.

1. Combine broth, soy sauce, cinnamon and pepper in small bowl. Set aside. Combine cornstarch and water in small bowl. Stir to dissolve.

2. Heat oil in wok or large skillet on medium-high heat. Add ginger and garlic. Stir-fry 30 seconds. Add beef, carrot and scallions. Stir-fry 3 minutes or until beef is no longer red. Add broth mixture. Cook 2 minutes. Add snow peas. Cook 2 minutes, or until snow peas are bright green. Stir in cornstarch mixture. Cook 1 minute or until thickened. Serve immediately.

Tip: *If using canned broth, pour the remainder of the can into an ice cube tray and freeze. Once frozen, store the cubes in an air-tight plastic bag. That way you'll always have the few tablespoons of broth needed for many recipes.*

Seafood Teriyaki Stir-Fry

Makes 4 servings

¾ cup LAWRY'S® Teriyaki
   Marinade with Pineapple
   Juice
¾ pound sole, flounder, haddock
   or perch fillets, cut into
   cubes
2 tablespoons peanut oil
1 teaspoon minced fresh ginger

½ teaspoon LAWRY'S® Garlic
   Powder with Parsley
2 cups broccoli flowerettes
2 green onions, cut into 1-inch
   pieces
1 large carrot, thinly sliced
1 tablespoon water

In large resealable plastic food storage bag, combine Teriyaki
Marinade and sole; seal bag. Marinate in refrigerator at least
30 minutes. Remove sole; discard used marinade. In wok or large
skillet, heat oil. Add sole, ginger and Garlic Powder with Parsley;
stir-fry over medium-high heat 2 to 4 minutes. Add remaining
ingredients; stir-fry until sole flakes easily when tested with fork
and vegetables are crisp-tender.

Serving Suggestion: *Serve over crisp chow mein noodles.*

Hot and Spicy Onion Beef

**Makes about
4 servings**

2 tablespoons soy sauce,
  divided
1 tablespoon cornstarch,
  divided
¾ pound flank steak, thinly
  sliced across the grain
2 tablespoons dry sherry
1 teaspoon Oriental sesame oil
1 teaspoon chili paste
  (optional)

2 tablespoons vegetable oil
1 large onion (12 to 14 ounces),
  sliced vertically
1 teaspoon minced garlic
  Dried whole red chili peppers
  to taste
1 tablespoon water

Combine 1 tablespoon soy sauce and 1 teaspoon cornstarch
in medium bowl. Add beef; stir to coat. Let stand 30 minutes.
Combine remaining tablespoon soy sauce, sherry, sesame oil and
chili paste in small bowl; set aside. Heat wok or large skillet over
medium heat. Add vegetable oil, swirling to coat sides. Add onion,
garlic and chili peppers; cook and stir until onion is tender. Add
beef; stir-fry 2 minutes or until lightly browned. Add soy sauce
mixture and mix well. Combine remaining 2 teaspoons cornstarch
and water; mix into onion mixture. Cook and stir until sauce boils
and thickens.

Favorite recipe from **National Onion Association**

Bangkok Chicken

1 pound boneless skinless
   chicken breasts
2 tablespoons chopped green
   onion
1 teaspoon anchovy paste *or*
   1 canned anchovy fillet
3 cloves garlic, halved
¼ teaspoon red pepper flakes
3 tablespoons vegetable oil
1 cup drained canned button
   mushrooms or straw
   mushrooms

1 cup drained canned baby corn
3 tablespoons reduced-sodium
   soy sauce
2 teaspoons sugar
¾ cup fresh basil leaves
   Boston or romaine lettuce
   leaves

Makes 4 servings

Rinse chicken and pat dry with paper towels. Cut chicken crosswise into ¼-inch-thick slices; set aside.

Place onion, anchovy paste, garlic and red pepper flakes in food processor or blender; process until smooth. Set aside.

Heat wok over high heat about 1 minute or until hot. Drizzle oil into wok and heat 30 seconds. Add chicken; stir-fry until chicken is no longer pink in center. Remove chicken to large bowl. Reduce heat to medium.

Add onion mixture to wok; stir-fry 1 minute. Add mushrooms and corn; mix well. Add soy sauce and sugar; stir until sugar dissolves. Return chicken to wok; stir-fry until heated through. Add basil; toss gently to combine.

Line serving platter with lettuce leaves. Spoon chicken onto lettuce. Garnish as desired.

Acknowledgments

The publisher would like to thank the companies and organizations listed below for the use of their recipes in this publication.

American Lamb Council
Barilla America, Inc.
BC-USA, Inc.
BelGioioso® Cheese, Inc.
Birds Eye®
Blue Diamond Growers®
Bob Evans®
Butterball® Turkey Company
California Olive Industry
California Poultry Federation
California Table Grape Commission
California Tree Fruit Agreement
California Wild Rice Advisory Board
Campbell Soup Company
Chef Paul Prudhomme's Magic Seasoning Blends®
Clamato® is a registered trademark of Mott's, Inc.
COLLEGE INN® Broth
Colorado Potato Administrative Committee
ConAgra Foods®
Delmarva Poultry Industry, Inc.
Del Monte Corporation
Dole Food Company, Inc.
Filippo Berio® Olive Oil
Florida Department of Agriculture and Consumer Services, Bureau of Seafood and Aquaculture
Florida Department of Citrus
The Fremont Company, Makers of Frank's & SnowFloss Kraut and Tomato Products
The Golden Grain Company®
Guiltless Gourmet®
Hebrew National®
Heinz North America
The Hidden Valley® Food Products Company
Hillshire Farm®
Holland House® is a registered trademark of Mott's, Inc.
Hormel Foods, LLC
Idaho Potato Commission

Kahlúa® Liqueur
Kraft Foods Holdings
Lawry's® Foods
Lee Kum Kee (USA) Inc.
McIlhenny Company (TABASCO® brand Pepper Sauce)
Michigan Apple Committee
Minnesota Cultivated Wild Rice Council
Mushroom Council
National Fisheries Institute
National Honey Board
National Onion Association
National Pork Board
National Turkey Federation
Nestlé USA
Newman's Own, Inc.®
Norseland, Inc. / Lucini Italia Co.
North Dakota Beef Commission
North Dakota Wheat Commission
Northwest Cherry Growers
Perdue Farms Incorporated
The Quaker® Oatmeal Kitchens
Reckitt Benckiser Inc.
RED STAR® Yeast, a product of Lasaffre Yeast Corporation
Riviana Foods Inc.
Sargento® Foods Inc.
The J.M. Smucker Company
Sonoma® Dried Tomatoes
Southeast United Dairy Industry Association, Inc.
StarKist® Seafood Company
The Sugar Association, Inc.
Property of © 2003 Sunkist Growers, Inc. All rights reserved
Texas Peanut Producers Board
Tyson Foods, Inc.
Uncle Ben's Inc.
Unilever Bestfoods North America
USA Dry Pea & Lentil Council
USA Rice Federation
Veg•All®
Washington Apple Commission
Wisconsin Milk Marketing Board

Index

Metric Conversion Chart

VOLUME MEASUREMENTS (dry)

1/8 teaspoon = 0.5 mL
1/4 teaspoon = 1 mL
1/2 teaspoon = 2 mL
3/4 teaspoon = 4 mL
1 teaspoon = 5 mL
1 tablespoon = 15 mL
2 tablespoons = 30 mL
1/4 cup = 60 mL
1/3 cup = 75 mL
1/2 cup = 125 mL
2/3 cup = 150 mL
3/4 cup = 175 mL
1 cup = 250 mL
2 cups = 1 pint = 500 mL
3 cups = 750 mL
4 cups = 1 quart = 1 L

VOLUME MEASUREMENTS (fluid)

1 fluid ounce (2 tablespoons) = 30 mL
4 fluid ounces (1/2 cup) = 125 mL
8 fluid ounces (1 cup) = 250 mL
12 fluid ounces (1 1/2 cups) = 375 mL
16 fluid ounces (2 cups) = 500 mL

WEIGHTS (mass)

1/2 ounce = 15 g
1 ounce = 30 g
3 ounces = 90 g
4 ounces = 120 g
8 ounces = 225 g
10 ounces = 285 g
12 ounces = 360 g
16 ounces = 1 pound = 450 g

DIMENSIONS

1/16 inch = 2 mm
1/8 inch = 3 mm
1/4 inch = 6 mm
1/2 inch = 1.5 cm
3/4 inch = 2 cm
1 inch = 2.5 cm

OVEN TEMPERATURES

250°F = 120°C
275°F = 140°C
300°F = 150°C
325°F = 160°C
350°F = 180°C
375°F = 190°C
400°F = 200°C
425°F = 220°C
450°F = 230°C

BAKING PAN SIZES

Utensil	Size in Inches/Quarts	Metric Volume	Size in Centimeters
Baking or Cake Pan (square or rectangular)	8×8×2	2 L	20×20×5
	9×9×2	2.5 L	23×23×5
	12×8×2	3 L	30×20×5
	13×9×2	3.5 L	33×23×5
Loaf Pan	8×4×3	1.5 L	20×10×7
	9×5×3	2 L	23×13×7
Round Layer Cake Pan	8×1½	1.2 L	20×4
	9×1½	1.5 L	23×4
Pie Plate	8×1¼	750 mL	20×3
	9×1¼	1 L	23×3
Baking Dish or Casserole	1 quart	1 L	—
	1½ quart	1.5 L	—
	2 quart	2 L	—